Pope's Creek, at Wakefield

THE WASHINGTONS
AND
THEIR HOMES

By

JOHN W. WAYLAND

CLEARFIELD

Reprinted
Virginia Book Company
Berryville, Virginia, 1973

Reprinted by
Genealogical Publishing Co., Inc.
with permission of
Virginia Book Company for
Clearfield Company, Inc.
Baltimore, Maryland
1998, 2004

International Standard Book Number: 0-8063-4775-9

Made in the United States of America

Note: In this reprint, chapter half titles have
been omitted, and hence, there are no pages numbered
15-16, 31-32, 51-52, 69-70, 85-86, 109-110, 127-128,
151-152, 169-170, 183-184, 199-200, 211-212, 221-222,
233-234, 243-244, 253-254, 269-270, 283-284, 297-298,
and 311-312.

OUTLINE OF CONTENTS

List of Illustrations

List of Maps and Plans

Preface

APPENDIX

OUTLINE OF CONTENTS

vii

LIST OF ILLUSTRATIONS

MAPS AND PLANS

PREFACE

Most of the materials for this work have been gathered from public records, family Bibles, and tombstone inscriptions, and from a first-hand acquaintance with the several homes of the Washingtons presented herein. Books relating to the Washingtons and pertinent articles in historical magazines have been freely consulted. References are made in proper connections. Various members of the Washington family now living have been most obliging, and I acknowledge special obligation to Miss Anne Madison Washington of Washington City, Mr. Julian H. Washingtn of Mount Vernon, and Rev. Richard B. Washington of Hot Springs, Va. The late Colonel Forrest Washington Brown of Charles Town gave generous and valuable assistance upon numerous occasions. The McClure Company, Inc., publishers, of Staunton, Va., have contributed materially by granting the use of a number of engravings from "Historic Homes of Northern Virginia and the Eastern Panhandle of West Virginia."

It is with pleasure that I make special acknowledgment to my friend, Mr. Richard E. Griffith Sr., of Winchester, Va., for his untiring and valuable co-operation. His intimate acquaintance with the records relating to old families and homes in Northern Virginia has enabled him to make a number of important contributions, and his unflagging interest has been most encouraging. Dr. A. D. Henkel of Winchester and others in that city have given assistance.

JOHN W. WAYLAND.

Harrisonburg, Va.
October 19, 1944.

PREFACE

...in the materials for this ... have ... printed in
... family Bibles, ... personal
... ... and acquaintance with the several lines of ...
... preserved herein. Several articles in the Washington and prominent articles in higher ... ... have been
freely quoted. References are made in proper connections.
I take no note of the Washington family but have
been most obliging, and I acknowledge special obligation to
... Stedman Washington, Washington City; Mr. Thomas Washington, Mount Vernon; ... ... Richard B. Washington of Hot Springs, Va. The late Colonel Bennet Washington Green of Charles Town have generous and valuable assistance.
... ... historic obligation. The Michie Company, Inc.,
publishers, of Charlottsville, Va. have contributed materially by
granting the use of a number of engravings in our "Historic
Homes of Southern Virginia and the Eastern Panhandle of
West Virginia."

It is with pleasure that I make special acknowledgment to
my friend, Mr. Richard E. Griffith Sr., of Winchester, Va., for
his untiring and valuable co-operation. His intimate acquaintance with the records relating to old families and homes in
Northern Virginia has enabled him to make a number of important ... to this work and his unflagging interest has been most
encouraging. Mr. A. D. Hankel of Winchester and ... ...
city have given assistance also.

                              JOHN W. WAYLAND

Harrisonburg, Va.,
October 1, 1944.

CHAPTER I

WAKEFIELD

Driving southeast a few miles from Oak Grove in Westmoreland County, Virginia, on Route 3, the old King's Highway, one passes Latanes and soon comes to Wakefield Corner. Here turning northeast into a straight road through the woods, a pointed white shaft of granite is seen ahead at a distance of nearly two miles. It is 51 feet high and bears a striking resemblance to the monument over the grave of Mary Washington at Fredericksburg. At this tall shaft one may turn to the left and drive a mile to the Washington grave-yard near Bridges Creek, or pass it and go directly ahead a short distance through an avenue of cedars to the restored mansion of Wakefield on Pope's Creek. This Wakefield house stands on the site and approximates the size and character of the one in which George Washington was born, February 22, 1732, the home of Augustine Washington and his second wife, Mary Ball.

During many years past there was much confusion in different printed statements concerning Washington's birthplace, and as the year 1932, the bi-centennial of his birth, approached and plans were made for celebrating the event and restoring the Wakefield mansion, there was sharp controversy as to the spot the house should occupy. While many persons were satisfied that it should be placed on the west bank of Pope's Creek, where it was placed, others declared that it belonged near the old family graveyard, on the east side of Bridges Creek.

In 1664 John Washington, great-grandfather to George, purchased from David Anderson 150 acres on the east side of Bridges Creek, later settling on it. His house was and the old graveyard is on this tract. After him, his son John Washington lived here, while another son, Lawrence, George's grand-father, lived west of Bridges Creek. In 1717 and 1718 Augustine Washington, George's father, purchased several tracts from the Abbington family. These tracts aggregated 150 acres and lay on the west side of Pope's Creek. On this purchase Augustine Washington in 1720 finished building a house, the one in which he lived until 1735, in which in 1732 his son George was born; which burned down on Christmas Day, 1780, and which has recently been restored on the same site.

In 1734 Augustine Washington added 25 acres to his Pope's Creek planta-tion by purchasing the islands and marshes at the mouth of the creek, and in 1742, while living on the Ferry Farm opposite Fredericksburg, he made an exchange of lands with his cousin John Washington and thus acquired the Bridges Creek place, the one on which the old family graveyard is located. By these successive purchases and trades Augustine Washington united the Bridges Creek place with that on Pope's Creek and thus owned all or practi-cally all the land between the two streams, which are not much more than a mile apart. He or others after him called his plantation Wakefield, but the

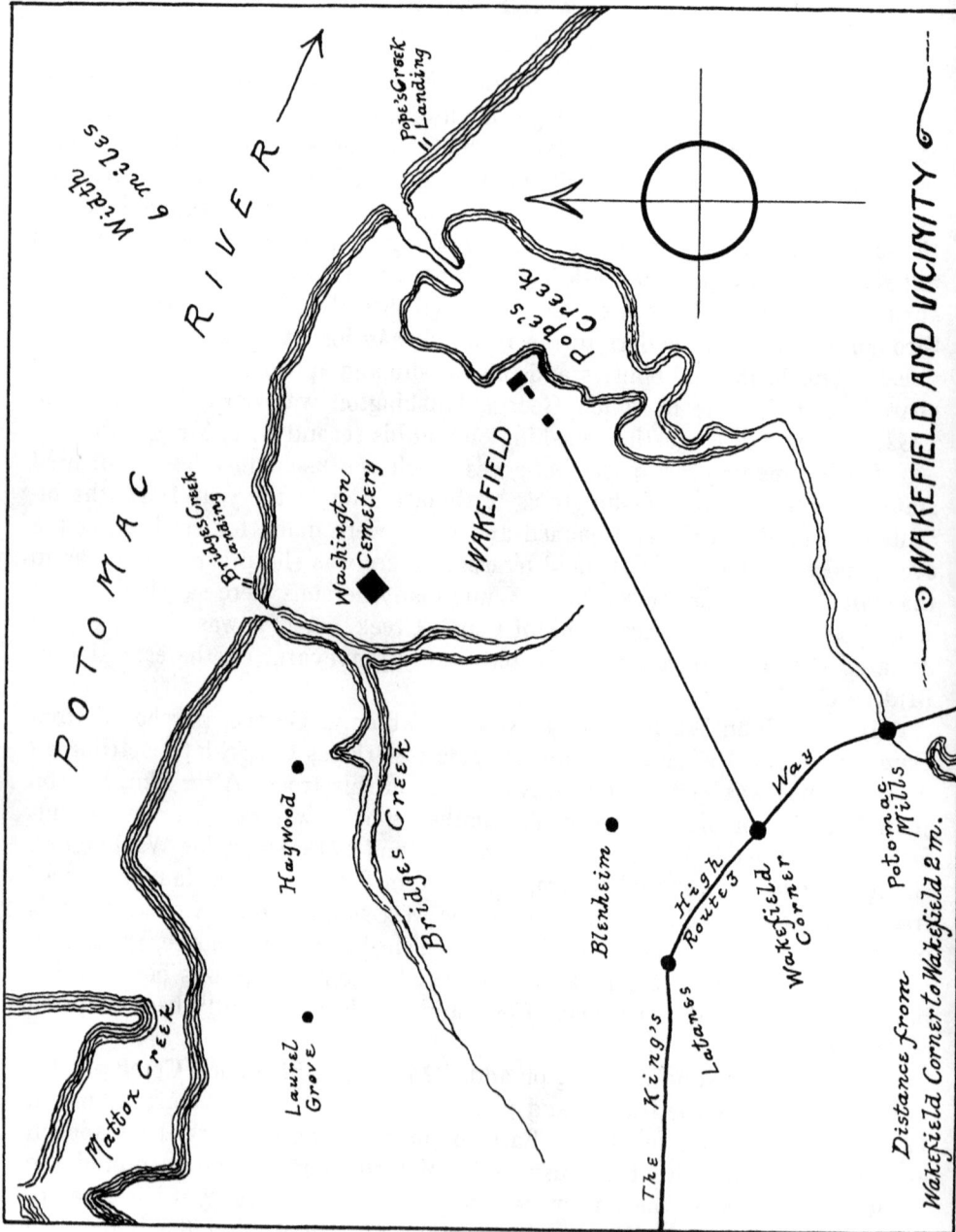

WAKEFIELD AND VICINITY

name of Bridges Creek naturally clung to the northwestern portion of it. Thus it is easy to see how confusions arose, some persons using one name, some the other.

It is possible that the name Wakefield was given to the plantation between the two creeks by Augustine Washington, father of George, though by William Lanier Washington (1865-1933) it was credited to William Augustine Washington, a grandson of George's father. This can hardly be accepted, however, if the name Wakefield was in current use as early as 1773, as is claimed; for William Augustine Washington, son of George's half-brother Augustine, was only sixteen years old in 1773. George's father died in 1743. He was succeeded in title at Wakefield by his son Augustine, who died in 1762. William Augustine was the next owner and he was residing at Wakefield in 1780 when the house burned. Thereafter the place was sometimes referred to as the "Burnt House Plantation."

The evidence that Wakefield, the Burnt House Plantation, on Pope's Creek, was the birthplace of George Washington is conclusive. In 1813 George Corbin Washington, a son of William Augustine, sold the Burnt House Plantation to John Gray, reserving the family graveyard and "sixty feet square of ground on which the House stood in which Genl. George Washington was born." George Corbin Washington, born in 1789, certainly had definite information from his father, William Augustine, as to where the latter was living in 1780 when his house burned, for William Augustine lived until 1810. In 1815 General Washington's adopted son, George Washington Parke Custis, born in 1781, journeyed to Wakefield and placed on the site of Burnt House a stone with this inscription: "Here, The 11th of February, 1732, (Old Style) George Washington was born." The title to the reservations made in 1813 by George Corbin Washington passed to his son Lewis Washington and from him in 1858 to the state of Virginia, thence in 1882 to the Federal Government. In 1883 the Government purchased eleven acres adjacent to the site upon which Mr. Custis had placed his marker in 1815. In 1896 a corps of army engineers uncovered and mapped the foundations of the old house and Congress erected a tall monument on the spot. In 1930, when steps were being taken to restore the Burnt House, the monument was moved to its present location, a short distance southwest of the house site.

In the foregoing citations concerning the location of Washington's birthplace the author has followed in the main the excellent work on the "Historic Northern Neck of Virginia," by H. Ragland Eubank, published in 1934, and an article by Charles O. Paullin, "The Birthplace of George Washington," issued in 1933 by the Division of Publications, Carnegie Institute of Washington, Washington, D. C.

It is a matter of interest, in view of the many gibes cast at Parson Weems, that he probably made the first correct statement in print as to the place where Washington was born. He doubtless was mistaken in saying that Augustine Washington, George's father, married first a Miss Dandridge, but the most

Wakefield Mansion, as being restored in 1931; From the Southwest. Hackberry tree in foreground. Photo by Holladay of Richmond.

painstaking and scholarly research tends to prove that he was correct in his statement that George "was born on Pope's creek, in Westmoreland county, the 22nd day of February, 1732." This declaration appeared in one of the early editions of Weems's "A History of the Life and Death, Virtues and Exploits of General George Washington, with Curious Anecdotes Equally Honourable to Himself and Exemplary to His Young Countrymen," only a few years after Washington's death, and certainly the 80 editions of Weems's book have done a great deal, in the hands and minds of its millions of readers, to make this particular fact a national possession. It does not stir the imagination as does the cherry tree story, but it may be taken with less pruning.

Augustine Washington I (1694-1743), son of Lawrence Washington and his wife Mildred Warner, married (1) in 1715 Jane Butler, daughter of Caleb Butler and his wife Mary Foxhall. He lived first, as it appears, at Haywood, on the west side of Bridges Creek, where his sons Lawrence and Augustine were born, moving into his new house on Pope's Creek in 1720 or 1721. In the new house were born Jane, in 1722, and Butler, about 1724. Butler died in infancy; his mother in the year 1728. In 1731 the father married (2) Mary Ball and brought her to his house on Pope's Creek where her first three children were born: George, on February 22, 1732; Elizabeth, familiarly known as Betty, on July 1, 1733; and Samuel, November 27, 1734. Mary Ball Washington named her oldest son for her guardian, Colonel George Eskridge, of Sandy Point.

It has been said that her son was the first Washington in this country to bear the name George, but this is untrue. Records in the land office in Richmond show that on September 28, 1730, King George II, through his Virginia governor, William Gooch, granted to George Washington of Isle of Wight County 235 acres, lying between Nottoway Swamp and the Flag Swamp, on the north side of Nottoway River; corner to the said Washington's other land and adjoining Richard Drake. Inasmuch as this George Washington was of legal age in 1730, we may assume that he was at least 23 years older than the son of Mary Ball Washington. Perhaps this George of Isle of Wight County in 1730 was a son of that audacious George Washington who was charged in 1650 in Bermuda with speaking disrespectfully of the King.

More about Mary Ball, her birthplace, and her early life will be given in the next chapter.

The "river barons" of the Northern Neck and other parts of Tidewater Virginia had beauty as well as ample space and fertility before them, and many of them selected spots of rare loveliness for their homes. Wakefield, like Bushfield, Mount Vernon, Chatham, and others, has charms of nature as an alluring background for its wealth of history. Although the mouth of Pope's Creek is constricted and choked, its shores opposite Wakefield are wide apart and the intervening waters are inviting. The shorelines are gracefully curved and profusely decorated with trees, among which the conical cedars seem to

Restored mansion at Wakefield—from the Northeast—the side facing Pope's Creek. Photo December 17, 1937.

Pope's Creek at Wakefield—From the northeast side of the mansion.
Photo December 17, 1937.

predominate. The ground level on which the mansion stands is well elevated above the level of the water, affording a view that reaches out to the mighty Potomac, whose width beyond the mouth of Pope's Creek is six or seven miles.

Around the restored mansion at Wakefield are gardens and verdant lawns. Some of the hedges of English box are believed to be over 125 years old. The big hackberry treee at the southwest side (rear) of the house may be quite as old as the hedges, but it has almost certainly grown up since the fire of 1780, which would have killed any growing thing so near. Farther away, round about, are productive fields and tracts of timber in which the evergreen holly, bearing its red berries in season, is conspicuous. In an effort to picture the past in the present, the fields have been fenced with split wooden rails laid up in zigzag pattern and bound down with stakes and riders.

The Washingtons loved good land and much of it. In 1726 Augustine Washington purchased from his sister Mildred and her husband, Roger Gregory, a large tract up in Stafford (now Fairfax) County, on Hunting Creek, part of which is familiar to us as Mount Vernon. To this tract in 1735, soon after the death of his young daughter Jane, he moved, going up the Potomac by boat. In his family at that time were his sons Lawrence and Augustine, aged respectively nineteen and eighteen, and three childrn by his second wife, George, Betty, and Samuel, all under four years of age. At Hunting Creek he remained until the latter part of 1738, then moved to the Ferry Farm opposite Fredericksburg, with John Augustine and Charles added to his family. More of this later.

At the death of Augustine Washington in 1743 Wakefield passed to his son Augustine II; from him in 1762 to his son William Augustine, who was the proprietor in 1780 when the house burned. William Augustine then enlarged the house at Blenheim and later built at Haywood, using at both places, it is said, bricks from the old house at Wakefield. He also built a brick barn at Haywood which was standing in 1934. (See the "Historic Northern Neck of Virginia," by H. Ragland Eubank, 1934, page 41.) William Augustine Washington died at Georgetown, D. C., in 1810 and Wakefield descended to his son, George Corbin Washington (1789-1854), who in 1813 sold to John Gray, making certain reservations, as already shown. In 1856 Wakefield was restored to the Washington family when William Augustine's granddaughter, Elizabeth Washington, married John E. Wilson, whose father had purchased it ten years earlier. Her grandsons later conveyed to the Wakefield Association the greater part of the 400 acres now composing the Wakefield memorial tract. The public is indebted to Mr. Eubank, named above, for tabulating and publishing many specific details of these transactions.

In 1857 was first published Bishop William Meade's monumental work, "Old Churches, Ministers, and Families of Virginia," in which appears the following interesting items:

Restored mansion, well, and kitchen at Wakefield, from the South. Pope's Creek is beyond to the right. Photo June, 1933.

THE WASHINGTON FAMILY SEAT AND VAULT

I recently paid a visit to the old family seat of the Washingtons, which is sometimes said to be on Pope's Creek, and sometimes on Bridge's Creek, near the Potomac. The farm lay between the two, which are about a mile apart, near their junction with the Potomac. The family mansion lies near Pope's Creek, and the vault where the dead were deposited near Bridge's Creek. The latter appears to have been favourable to a rich growth of cedars, and may have been chosen for this reason. Or it may be that one of the two brothers first settled there. The estate is still in the family, or in the possession of one intermarried with the family. Some years since it was owned by Mr. John Gray of Traveller's Rest, near Fredericksburg, who either repaired one of the outhouses or a wing of the old one, or built a small house for his overseer out of the old materials. The brick chimney is all that remains of the Washington mansion,—the birthplace of General Washington,—except the broken bricks which are scattered about over the spot where it was built. The grandson of Mrs. General Washington, Mr. Custis, of Arlington, some years since placed a slab with a brief inscription on the spot, but it is now in fragments. I was happy to hear that a bill had passed one branch of our Legislature, appropriating a sum of money for enclosing this spot, as well as the vault in a neighboring field nearly a mile off. I also visited that spot, which no one can look upon without distress and even disgust. The condition of all such vaults as were once common in some parts of Virginia, especially in the Northern Neck, must after the lapse of time be necessarily thus distressing and disgusting, like the sepulchres of old when filled "with rottenness and dead men's bones." The vault where so many of the Washington family are interred is in an open field and unenclosed. A small space around it is covered with grass, briers, shrubs, and a few small trees. Itself can only be distinguished by the top of the brick arch which rises a little above the surface. The cavity underneath has been very properly filled up with earth by Mr. Laurence Washington, one of its late proprietors, to prevent the bones of the dead being taken away by visitors, who had thus begun to pillage it. Not far from the vault there was a large slab lying on the ground, with the name of one of the family and two of his children. There were also fragments of another. It is to be hoped that the Legislature will resolve on putting a permanent enclosure around this also.

No doubt Bishop Meade's graphic description had a considerable influence in bringing about the subsequent measures for appropriate care and restoration.

In October, 1878, when the acquisition of Wakefield by the Federal Government was in contemplation, Secretary of State William M. Evarts, with a party which included General William T. Sherman and Charles C. Perkins, made a trip down the Potomac from Washington City on the U.S.S. *Tallapoosa*, and inspected the Pope's Creek home-site. General Sherman made a rough map of the place and Mr. Perkins sketched the remains of the old brick chimney, supposed to have belonged to the kitchen of the Wakefield mansion house. These ruins were found a short distance in the rear (southwest) of the mansion house site, at the spot where the restored kitchen may be seen today.

Box-bordered walk in the garden at Wakefield, with cedars in the background. Photo August 15, 1938, looking southeast from the mansion.

In 1882, as already noted, the state of Virginia transferred to the Federal Government the reservations it had acquired from Lewis William Washington (son of George Corbin) in 1858, to-wit, the old graveyard at Bridges Creek and the Burnt House plat at Pope's Creek; and the next year the Government purchased eleven or twelve acres around the Burnt House plat. In 1896 the latter was marked by the granite monument already mentioned.

The recent improvements at Wakefield, as both Dr. Paullin and Mr. Eubank show, date from the organization of the Wakefield National Memorial Association at Washington City in 1923, with the object of restoring the old Washington graveyard at Bridges Creek and the Augustine Washington house at Pope's Creek, and putting the surrounding grounds as much as possible in the appearance they had in colonial times. The most active leader in originating and perfecting this organization was Josephine Wheelwright Rust (Mrs. Harry L. Rust), a Washington descendant. With the aid of Mr. John D. Rockefeller, Jr., and many other patriotic donors, a large part of the Wakefield plantation, formerly owned by Augustine Washington I, was purchased and improved. In 1930 the Federal Government provided $80,000 for removing the granite shaft of 1896 to its present site and for reconstructing the Burnt House on its original foundations.

The present house, in accordance with plans made by Mr. Edward W. Donn, Jr., architect, is typical of Virginia homes of the early 18th century, and is believed to be also a reproduction that is generally faithful to the original which stood on the same spot. The old foundations were a valuable guide, and another old house at another place in Tidewater Virginia was available as a model. Colonel Burgess Ball, a Revolutionary soldier who marrried Frances Washington, daughter of Charles and niece of George, declared that the house at Wakefield was like the Christian house near Providence Forge, in New Kent County. The Christian house was still standing in 1934. (See Eubank's "Historic Northern Neck of Virginia," page 43.) The adjacent gardens also follow styles of the same early period. The graveyard has been restored from a neglected and ruinous state by the construction of a new vault, the placing of new table tombs for certain members of the family, and the erection of a strong enclosing wall of brick. In 1932 the Wakefield Association officially conveyed its holdings to the Federal Government, and the Wakefield Plantation, comprising nearly 400 acres, is now a national memorial, under the care of the National Park Service. It is open perpetually, free of charge, to the public. A sundial in the restored garden bears an inscription which is true to history and instinct with poetry:

> "A place of rose and thyme and scented earth,
>   A place the world forgot,
> But here a matchless flower came to birth;
>   Time paused and blessed the spot."

Old Washington Cemetery at Bridges Creek. Photo December 17, 1937.

In almost every direction from Wakefield, and not far away, are other old homes and home-sites that time has blessed and the world will not forget: the birthplace of James Monroe, near Colonial Beach; Stratford of the Lees, north of Montross; Bushfield, the home of John Augustine Washington and the birthplace of his distinguished son, Judge Bushrod Washington; and Epping Forest, the birthplace of Mary Ball, between Farnham and Lancaster; to mention only a few.

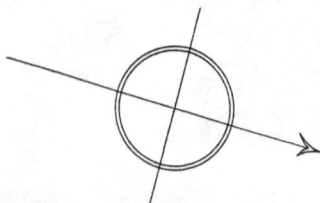

PLAN OF THE WASHINGTON CEMETERY
AT BRIDGES CREEK
SIZE 70 X 70 FEET INSIDE THE BRICK WALL

CHAPTER II

THE ROSE OF EPPING FOREST

Who gave this name to Mary Ball, the second wife of Augustine Washington and the mother of George Washington, no one knows at this time, but it is said to have been familiarly used. If so, it indicates that she, as a young woman, possessed attractive qualities and had endeared herself to a number of people. It suggests that she was admirable, perhaps beautiful, and drew others to her; and it refers to her birthplace and earliest home, Epping Forest.

Epping Forest, the historic homestead, is located in Lancaster County, Virginia, seven miles northwest from Lancaster Court House and two miles in the same direction from the village of Lively. The old mansion, a portion of which is the house in which Mary Ball was born, stands in a grove on the southwest side of the highway, back a distance of about 150 yards. Most of the trees on the spacious lawn are probably native, others were planted by successive owners of the home. Among these trees are a number of ancient cedars and one or two giant oaks. Some of them were doubtless growing in their places when Mary Ball was born, in 1708. Here in 1680 Mary's father, Colonel Joseph Ball, established himself on land inherited from his father, Colonel William Ball, whose wife was Hannah Atherold, married in London in 1638. The estate of Epping Forest, with the exception of a few years, has been held continuously by members of the Ball family. In 1933, when the photographs shown herewith were made, the owner was Mr. J. D. Jesse, whose wife was a Miss Ball.

The road which leads past Epping Forest is the main highway in this part of the Northern Neck, and may be followed from Fredericksburg southeastward through King George, Oak Grove, Montross, Warsaw, and Farnham, to Lancaster, Kilmarnock, Whitehouse, and Westland. The place last named is on the point of land on the north side of the Rappahannock River, where the latter enters Chesapeake Bay. This excellent road is Route 3 in the Virginia highway system and follows with slight deviations the old trail which has been known from early times as the King's Highway. The section which passes Epping Forest was formerly designated as Chinn's Lane.

Mary Ball, who became Augustine Washington's second wife in 1731, was the daughter of her father's second wife, Mary Montague, the widow Johnson, whom Joseph Ball married early in 1708. The date of this marriage is rather definitely indicated by an indenture which is on record in the county clerk's office of Lancaster County whereby Colonel Joseph Ball conveyed his home place (Epping Forest) to his son Joseph Ball, reserving dower rights therein for the wife he was about to marry. Colonel Joseph Ball is described as of St. Mary's White Chapel Parish, the county of Lancaster in the dominion of Virginia, Gentleman; the tract of land conveyed was the same whereon Colonel

Said to be a picture of Mary Ball Washington as a young woman. Its genuineness is questioned.

Ball was then dwelling and contained by estimation 720 acres. The conveyance was made in consideration of "ye filial obedience & respect which his said son Jos. Ball Junr has att all times yielded to his said father as alsoe out of fatherly love & affection . . . AND alsoe for divers other good causes & considerations him the said Col. Jos. Ball thereunto especially moveing, . . . & it is ye true intent & meaning of these presents that if ye said Col. Jos. Ball shall take a wife that then it should be lawful for him to assigne for her dower during her natural life soe much of ye said tract of land whereon ye said Col. Jos. Ball now dwells as shall be included within the following bounds . . . "

The foregoing instrument was drawn up on February 7, 1707. This date in the New Style is February 18, 1708. A memorandum was added declaring that livery and seisin and possession was made by delivery of turf and twig taken from the land conveyed. Four days later, that is on February 22, 1708, by our calendar, the deed was recorded.

About the same date Colonel Joseph Ball executed a deed of gift to his son and his three daughters of his personal and household property. Evidently he was securing them in their rights and conciliating them in their tempers in the face of his approaching marriage, which no doubt took place shortly thereafter, that is to say, in the latter part of February or early in March, 1708; and we may assume that his daughter Mary was born in November or December of the same year.

Mary Ball was the only child of her parents. Her father, Colonel Joseph Ball, died in 1711. Her mother then married her third husband, Captain Richard Hewes, who lived at Cherry Point, near Lewisetta, on the Potomac, in Northumberland County, about fifteen miles north of Epping Forest. Cherry Point, now Cowart's Point, was accordingly the home of Mary Ball from the time she was three or four years old until she was thirteen, her mother dying in 1721. Captain Hewes had died several years earlier.

The will of Mrs. Hewes, Mary Ball's mother, is an interesting document and throws a flood of light on her daughter and the cordial relations that evidently existed between them. It is presented in full herewith.

In the name of God Amen, the seventeenth Day December in the year of our Lord one thousand seven hundred and twenty.

I Mary Hewes of St. Stephen's Parish, Northumberland County, widow, being sick and weak in body but of sound and perfect memory, thanks be to Almighty God for the same, and calling to mind the uncertain state of this transitory life, and that the flesh must yield unto Death, when it shall please God to call, do make and ordain this my last will and Testament.

First, I give and bequeath my soul (to God) that gave it to me, and my body to the Earth to be buried in Decent Christian burial at the discretion of my executors in these presents nominated. And as touching such Worldly estate which it hath pleased God to bestow upon me, I give, devise and dispose of in the following manner and form. *Imprimis,* I give and devise unto my Daughter Mary Ball one young likely negro woman to be purchased for her out of my Estate by my Execu-

The old mansion at Epping Forest, from the northeast. Photo June, 1933.

tors and to be delivered unto her the said Mary Ball at the age of Eighteen years, but, my will is that if the said Mary Ball shall dye without Issue lawfully begotten of her body that the said negro woman with her increase shall return to my loving son John Johnson to him, his heirs and assigns forever.

Item. I give and bequeath unto my said Daughter Mary Ball two gold rings, the one being a large hoop and the other a stoned ring.

Item. I give unto my said Daughter Mary Ball one young mare and her increase which said mare I formerly gave her by word of mouth.

Item. I give and bequeath unto my said Daughter Mary Ball sufficient furniture for the bed her father Joseph Ball left her, vizt: One suit of good curtains and fallens, one Rugg, one Quilt, one pair of Blankets.

Item. I give and bequeath unto my said Daughter Mary Ball two Diaper Table clothes marked M. B. with inck, and one Dozen of Diaper napkins, two towels, six plates, two pewter dishes, two basins, one large iron pott, one Frying pan, one old trunk.

Item. I give and bequeath unto my said Daughter Mary Ball, one good young Paceing horse together with a good silk plush side saddle to be purchased by my Executors out of my Estate.

Item. I give and bequeath unto my Daughter Elizabeth Bonum one suit of white and black callico, being part of my own wearing apparel.

Item. All the rest of my wearing apparel I give and bequeath unto my said Daughter Mary Ball, and I do hereby appoint her (to) be under Tutiledge and government of Capt. George Eskridge during her minority.

Item. My will is I do hereby oblige my Executors to pay to the proprietor or his agent for the securing of my said Daughter Mary Ball her land, Twelve pounds if so much (be) due.

Item. All the rest of my Estate real and personal whatsoever and wheresoever I give and devise unto my son John Johnson, and to his heirs lawfully to be begotten of his body, and for default of such Issue I give and devise the said Estate unto my Daughter Elizabeth Bonum, her heirs and assigns forever.

Item. I do hereby appoint my son John Johnson and my trusty and well beloved friend George Eskridge Executors of this my last will and Testament and also revoke and Disannul all other former wills or Testaments by me heretofore made or caused to be made either by word or writing, ratifying and confirming this to be my last Will and Testament and no other.

In witness whereof I have hereunto sett my hand and seal the Day and Date at first above written.

The mark and seal of Mary Hewes were appended; also the marks of Robert Bradley and Ralph Smithwest and the signature of David Straughan as witnesses. The death of the testator soon followed, in 1721. John Johnson died soon after his mother; his will and hers were recorded the same day. The first bequest or devise in his will was the following:

Imprimis. I give and bequeath unto my sister Mary Ball all my land in Stafford which my father-in-law Richard Hewes gave me, to the said Mary Ball and her heirs lawfully to be begotten of her body forever.

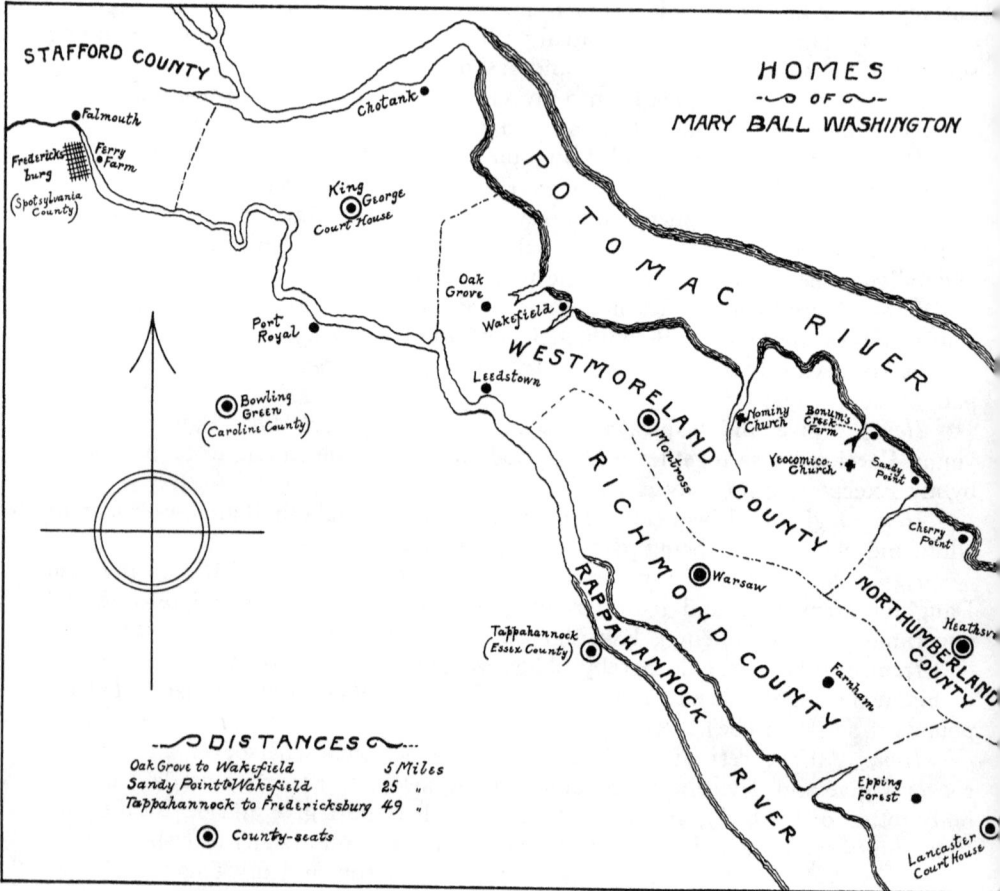

The land herein devised to Mary Ball was probably the same which she in her will, made at Fredericksburg in 1788, gave to her son, General George Washington, and described by her as "all my Lands on Accokeek Run in the County of Stafford."

It will be observed that young Mary Ball, by the provisions of her mother's will, was provided with two riding horses and a silk plush side-saddle; and the fact that her mother by "word of mouth" had previously given her the young mare indicates that the girl of twelve was already riding horse-back. Her love of horses soon became well known, for Samuel Bonum, who died early in 1726/7, willed her his young dapple-gray riding horse. Bonum had married her half-sister, Elizabeth Johnson, and lived at Bonum's Creek

Farm, which was located three and a half miles up the Potomac from Sandy Point, the home of Colonel George Eskridge, Mary Ball's guardian. The ten years from the death of her mother in 1721 till her marriage in 1731 she spent with her sister at Bonum's Creek and with her guardian at Sandy Point, and doubtless it was within this period that she became known as the "Rose of Epping Forest." Some particulars of her active life during these years may be accepted with a fair degree of certainty, though no portrait of her prior to her marriage seems to be in existence. One that has been widely circulated and long accepted as of her is now believed to represent a young woman of England, name unknown, and to have been painted a number of years before Mary Ball was born. Two other portraits, one dating about 1759, the other about 1782, are believed to be genuine. (See a note by Charles A. Hoppin, in *Tyler's Quarterly Magazine*, January 1931, page 153.)

That Mary Ball, the Rose of Epping Forest, while resident at Bonum's Creek and Sandy Point, did much horseback riding may safely be assumed, and her love for horses was no doubt later kept up and transmitted to her sons, and perhaps her daughter too. General Washington, as is well known, was fond of horses and a splendid rider. If she had not been well provided with horses of her own, her guardian, Colonel George Eskridge, and her half-sister, Mrs. Bonum, could have supplied her. Historic Wilton and Matholic, the latter the original home of the Lees in Westmoreland County, are named as among the places she visited. These are at short distances northwest from Sandy Point and Bonum's Creek farm. To the south, through Richmond County and down into old Lancaster, she covered longer distances, going of course to Epping Forest, her birthplace and the burial place of her mother; to St. Mary's White Chapel, beyond Epping Forest; and to "Rare Old Bewdley," the home of Ball kinsfolk. To Pecatone, home of the Corbins, and Yeocomico Church, both within a radius of two miles from Bonum's Creek, her rides were frequent.

Yeocomico and Nominy were the two old churches of Cople Parish, the former at the head of Yeocomico Creek, the latter about ten miles farther northwest on Nominy River. Nominy Church was built in 1704 on land donated by Youell Watkins. Yeocomico was fifty years older, the original frame building having been replaced by one of native brick in 1706. Of Yeocomico, Bishop William Meade, writing in 1838, gives the following interesting story:

Yeocomico Church, so called after the river of that name, is one of the old churches, being built in the year 1706. The architecture is rough, but very strong, and the materials must have been of the best kind. Its figure is that of a cross, and situated as it is, in a little recess from the main road, in the midst of some ancient trees, and surrounded by an old brick wall which is fast mouldering away, it cannot fail to be an object of interest to one whose soul has any sympathy for such scenes. It has undergone but little repair since its first erection, and indeed has needed little. It is not known or believed that a single new shingle has ever been put upon the roof, and the pews and whole interior are the same. During the late war [1812] it was shamefully abused by the soldiers who were quartered in it while watching the movements of the British on the Potomac. The Communion table was removed into the yard, where it served as a butcher's block, and was entirely defaced. Being of substantial materials, however, it admitted of a new face and polish, and is now restored to its former place, where it will answer, we trust, for a long time to come, the holy purposes for which it was originally designed.

It would have been gratifying to the good bishop, as it is to others who have a proper respect for things sacred, to know that Yeocomico Church and the brick wall around it have been well taken care of, and that the building is still being used regularly for worship.

At Yeocomico Church, then a comparatively new brick structure, Mary Ball met and learned to know the McCartys, the Fitzhughs, the Steptoes of Hominy Hall, the Jacksons of Wilton, several families of the Lees, and various others. Meeting early on the church yard, the parishioners exchanged greetings and neighborhood news before the hours of worship, and afterward lingered for additional cordial exchanges interspersing the good-byes. Nominy Church, too, was within easy riding distance, and there she saw the Thompsons, the Ashtons, the Ayletts, the Bushrods, and the Carters of Nominy Hall.

And not all of her horseback riding was to church and to the homes of neighbors. Fox-hunting was a favorite sport of the early Virginians, and we may be right certain that young Mary Ball had some share in it personally as well as by proxy later, when her sons rode hard and frequently in the chase. Seated firmly in her side-saddle of silk plush, she listened excitedly to the baying of the hounds and guided her mount with a skilful hand. Samuel Bonum's dapple-gray, the young mare or one of her increase, if not the "good young Paceing horse," may have been an excellent hunter.

On her frequent rides to church, to neighboring homes, and on fox-hunts she did not lack for company. Colonel Eskridge had seven children, we are told, the fifth one a girl named Sarah, who was just a little older than Mary Ball. And if girl companions were lacking at any time, can we doubt that there were well-grown boys and gallant young men by no means averse to riding with the Rose of Epping Forest? On the hunts, especially, we can assume that the young squires of the Northern Neck were on hand in plenty. It must be evident, however, that the Rose was not easily plucked. Sixteen, seventeen, and eighteen were favorite ages for girls to marry in those days; nineteen and twenty were years of maturity; she did not marry until twenty-two or twenty-three. But she may have had many suitors. It sometimes happens that the belle of a neighborhood waits longest to choose a husband.

We are not to suppose that Mary Ball spent all of her time riding, visit-

Epping Forest, from the King's Highway (Route 3). Photo June, 1933.

ing, fox-hunting, and flirting, or even going to church. She had her proper tasks in the household and no doubt discharged them acceptably. Outdoor duties must have pleased her. If she did not have her own small garden, she certainly had a corner in the big garden in which she might carry out her own plans. In her later years she spent much of her time in her garden, behind the small house in Fredericksburg, and doubtless her love of herbs, shrubs, and flowers, no less than her habit of working among them, had its beginnings in early life. She profited by moral and religious instruction received at home and in the churches, and she also enjoyed some teaching in reading, writing, good speech, and other subjects of apppropriate nature. Her illustrious son is credited with the following statement concerning one of her teachers:

Thomas Baker was a man of refined character, and devoted much of his leisure, of which he had a good deal, in guiding my mother in religious knowledge, which her mind was naturally inclined to receive, also in directing her studies in such other branches of instruction as he deemed most fitting and likely to serve in the education of her children. He was in the habit of reading translations of the portions of the best classic authors, and which he was very apt in making interesting by contrasts with modern writers.

This most excellent man derived very real pleasure in these labors of love, as he was pleased to speak of my mother as "the most amiable yet the most impressionable character I have ever known, a girl of great personal attractions, and yet utterly unconscious of their possession."

(See "The Mother of Washington," by Nancy Byrd Turner, 1930, pages 59, 62.)

A French lady, whose name has not been preserved, is also spoken of as a teacher of Mary Ball. Evidently the cultural training of the girl was not neglected. Her half-brother, Joseph Ball, was sent to England for his later education, and he became a man of affairs on both sides of the Atlantic. Her relations with him were cordial, and her associations with him broadened her outlook, contributing refining influences and increasing her capacity for understanding business and enjoying life.

Inasmuch as Sandy Point is some twenty-five miles from Wakefield, and Bonum's Creek Farm almost as far, the question may arise, How did Augustine Washington make the acquaintance of Mary Ball? Several possibilities should be recognized. Neighborhoods were large in those days—we are repeatedly surprised at the extent of the areas over which the people, occasionally at least, kept up their goings and comings. If Mary Ball and her young associates rode twenty-five miles down to Epping Forest, Bewdley, and St. Mary's White Chapel, Augustine Washington may have ridden even farther in various directions. Wakefield, Bonum's Creek, and Sandy Point are all in the same county, Westmoreland. Colonel Eskridge, we are told, was a lawyer —he and Augustine Washington probably met at the county-seat on court days. Eskridge, it is said, looked after legal business for Captain Washington, and good evidence of this is found in a deed of uses which was drawn up in

George Eskridge, Mary Ball's guardian. Miss Nellie Henson of Berryville, a descendant, supplied a photograph of the original portrait.

1726 between Augustine Washington and his wife Jane Butler, of the one part, and Lawrence Butler and George Eskridge of the other part, and recorded in the archives of Westmoreland County. Captain Washington may have paid occasional visits to Sandy Point on business, and the families may have met occasionally on Sundays at the churches, Yeocomico and Nominy. Now and then, indeed, the Eskridges, Mrs. Bonum, and Mary Ball may have ridden or driven up to the church in Washington Parish, close to Wakefield.

Augustine Washington and Mary Ball were married at Sandy Point on March 17, 1731 (N. S.), the Rev. Walter Jones of Cople Parish officiating. The house in which the vows were pledged burned many years later, says Mr. Eubank, but the present dwelling was erected at some time after 1800 on th old foundations. Parson Weems, in his inimitable blending of fact and fiction, might lead us to believe that it was a wedding of December and May. He says:

Fully persuaded still, that "it is not good for man to be alone," he [Augustine Washington] renewed, for the second time, the chaste delights of matrimonial love. His consort was Miss Mary Ball, a young lady of fortune, and descended from one of the best families in Virginia.

From his intermarriage with this charming girl, it would appear that our hero's father must have possessed either a very pleasing person, or highly polished manners, or perhaps both; for, from what I can learn, he was at that time at least forty years old! while she, on the other hand, was universally toasted as the belle of the Northern Neck, and in the full bloom and freshness of love-inspiring sixteen. This I have from one who tells me that he has carried down many a sett dance with her; I mean that amiable and pleasant old gentleman, John Fitzhugh, Esq., of Stafford, who was, all his life, a neighbour and intimate of the Washington family.

In sober fact, there was a considerable difference in the ages of the bride and groom—he was 37, not far from forty; but she was much over sixteen, though still, no doubt, the belle of the Northern Neck and still, at twenty-two or more, possessing most if not all the charms of sweet sixteen. We assume that she had courage and a degree of confidence in herself, and in the man she married, as well, for she faced responsibilities and problems that might have held back one who was inclined to be timid. She went to Wakefield and took charge of her husband's home in which were three children of a former marriage: two sons, one of fifteen, the other of fourteen, and a daughter of nine. The boys about this time, or soon thereafter, were sent to England to school.

Remarkable as it may seem, Parson Weems does not give us any except the barest statements about the birth of his hero, George Washington, and nothing about his baptism. Bishop Meade ("Old Churches, Ministers, and Families of Virginia," Vol. II, reprint of 1900, pages 162, 163) does better. Writing in 1838 of Pope's Creek Church he says:

It was near to this church that General Washington was born. It was in this that he was baptized. Here it was that he received those early impressions of religion which, instead of being effaced by age, seemed to grow with his growth and strengthen with his strength. The proofs of this have been abundantly furnished in the "Religious Opinions and Character of Washington," by the Rev. Mr. McGuire, a work recently published, and for which the writer deserves the thanks of every friend of Washington, of religion, and of our country.

I have said that this church is now in ruins, and I would add, that about twenty-six years ago [1812], when I was in Deacon's Orders, I remember to have been in it, with the Rev. Mr. Norris, an early and beloved associate in the ministry, at which time it was beginning to decay in the roof; but there was a large congregation, and twenty-eight children were brought forward for baptism. It was the first service which had been performed in it for a long time, and from that period it continued to decay, until a few years ago it was set on fire in order to prevent the injury, from the falling of the roof, to the cattle which were accustomed to shelter there.

Thus far the bishop quotes from his report to the convention of 1838. Shortly before his book was published in 1857 he added the following:

It ought to be added that so attached were the citizens of the county to this old building, that the excuse for its destruction by fire was not readily admitted. Indeed, so indignant were they, that it was brought before the grand jury and the court. The result, however, was the acquittal of the party. It has now been twenty years since the above-mentioned visit, and I have often within that time passed the same spot, at each time perceiving the disappearance of all that was old, and the rise and growth of what was new. Trees and shrubs have been growing up over and around the old site, rendering it more difficult each year to the passing traveller to find out where old Pope's Creek Church once stood.

Parson Weems takes the Washingtons directly from Wakefield to Fredericksburg, as follows:

Little George had scarcely attained his fifth year, when his father left Pope's Creek, and came up to a plantation which he had in Stafford, opposite to Fredericksburg. The house in which he lived is still to be seen [about 1806?]. It lifts its low and modest front of faded red over the turbid waters of Rappahannock; whither, to this day, numbers of people repair, and, with emotions unutterable, looking at the weather-beaten mansion, exclaim, "Here's the house where the great Washington was born!"
But it is all a mistake; for he was born, as I said, at Pope's creek, in Westmoreland county, near the margin of his own roaring Potomac.
(See Weems's "Washington," Mount Vernon Edition, page 17.)

The eloquent parson was right in declaring that the "great Washington" was born on Pope's Creek; but when the family left Pope's Creek in 1735, after "the ice cleared in the river," they went up the "roaring Potomac," and not across the country to the Rappahannock. Three years or so they lived on the banks of the Potomac, at or near Hunting Creek, where Mount Vernon is now a shrine. Here Mary Ball Washington's two younger sons were born: John Augustine, on January 24, 1736, and Charles, on May 13, 1738 (both dates N. S.). Then, or soon thereafter, the house at Hunting Creek burned. This may have been a reason for leaving that place. At any rate, the family towards the end of 1738 moved to the Ferry Farm, recently purchased, opposite Fredericksburg. Charles Moore, who has made extensive researches in Washington family history over a long period of years, is of the opinion that Augustine Washington located at Fredericksburg to be more convenient to the work he had to do in getting out iron ore and in hauling pig-iron to the shipping points on the rivers. (See "The Family Life of George Washington," by Charles Moore, 1926, pages 21, 24.)

As reflecting the character and disposition of Mary Ball Washington, one of the most significant incidents of her life is still to be noted, and it should not be overlooked. Among the books which she found at Wakefield when she went there as a bride was a copy of Sir Matthew Hale's "Contemplations" on moral and religious qualities. On the fly-leaf was written the name of the preceding wife, "Jane Washington." Underneath it the new wife wrote "And Mary Washington." The book, thus inscribed, became one of Mary's most cherished possessions. She read it to her stepsons and later to her own sons and daughter. It passed to her illustrious son, General Washington, who prized it highly.

CHAPTER III

AT FERRY FARM

Augustine Washington, his wife Mary Ball, and their children, after three and a half years on or near Hunting Creek in Prince William County, Va., moved to a newly-purchased home on the Rappahannock River, in King George County. The homestead they left on Hunting Creek is now in Fairfax County, and is famous as Mount Vernon; the one to which they went is now in Stafford County and is becoming familiar to the American people as the Ferry Farm. The move was made in the late autumn of 1738. The Ferry Farm lies on the northeast side of the river, opposite the lower and newer portion of the city of Fredericksburg, the city being in Spotsylvania County. In early days the town was half a mile above the Ferry Farm and the ferry which belonged to it, which was operated across the river from the farm.

The time when Captain Washington moved to the Ferry Farm and the exact location of the place are definitely indicated by a number of circumstantial facts. On April 21, 1738, an advertisement in the *Virginia Gazette* offered for sale a tract of 100 acres of land belonging to the estate of William Strother, Gentleman, deceased, late of King George County; the said tract lying about two miles below the falls of the Rappahannock, close to the river, and improved with a "very handsome Dwelling house, three store houses, several other convenient out houses, and a Ferry belonging to it, being the Place where Mr. Strother lived." Several other tracts belonging to the Strother estate were also offered in the same advertisement, among them one of 160 acres, with houses, etc., adjoining the home place.

On November 2, 1738, as shown in Deed Book No. 2 of King George records, John Grant and wife Margaret, the latter executrix of her late husband William Strother, conveyed to Augustine Washington, Gentleman, of Prince William County, "All that Messuage Tenement and Mansion House where the said William Strother lately Dwelt and all those several pieces or parcells of Land thereunto adjoining and upon which the said Mansion stands containing together by Estimation Two Hundred and Eighty Acres be the same more or less scituate Lying and being in the Parish of Brunswick in the county of King George aforesaid."

The Ferry Farm, sometimes in earlier days referred to also as the Pine Grove Farm, lies on the river about two miles below the old town of Falmouth and the falls of the Rappahannock, thus answering the description in the advertisement of April 1738. George Washington inherited the Ferry Farm by his father's will, but his mother continued to live on it until 1772 or thereabouts. He on September 13, 1771, surveyed the "Fields where my Mother lives." A plat of this survey fits the Ferry Farm in its bearing of the compass, its location on the river, the course of the "Great Road," the slope northeast of the road, and the "Gully leading to the Ferry Landing." A map of this survey

Ferry Farm from the hills just northeast of the highway (Route 3), with Fredericksburg across the river in the background. In the left foreground are the barns of Ferry Farm; the old home-site is in the trees at the right. Photo 1933.

and a picture of the gully leading down to the ferry landing may be seen in the *William and Mary College Quarterly Historical Magazine* for April 1937. Moreover, the unbroken tradition at Fredericksburg identifies the Ferry Farm as the homestead of Augustine Washington and his family.

The 280 acres, more or less by estimation, which Margaret Grant, late widow and executrix of William Strother, conveyed to Augustine Washington, may readily be accepted as the 100-acre tract, containing the mansion house of William Strother, plus the 160-acre tract "adjoining thereto," described in the advertisement of April 21, 1738.

On December 1, 1738, Captain Washington added to his acreage near Fredericksburg, purchasing from Rosewell Neale 300 acres, "by estimation," lying "near the Falls of Rappahannock River adjoining to the Land of the said Augustin Washington and Henry Fitzhugh Esquire formerly in the Occupation of Margaret Strother widdo. of William Strother." These several purchases gave Captain Washington a plantation including and adjoining the Ferry Farm altogether of between 560 and 580 acres. In the deed made to him on November 2, 1738, he is spoken of as of Prince William County; in the one made to him on December 1 he is of King George County. Evidently, therefore, he moved from Hunting Creek to the Ferry Farm at some time between November 2 and December 1, 1738. Here he lived during the remaining four years and five months of his life.

The most complete and circumstantial account of Augustine Washington's purchase and occupation of the Ferry Farm that the author has seen has been compiled by Mr. George H. S. King and was published in the *William and Mary Quarterly,* referred to above, pages 265-281.

On the Ferry Farm today, beside the "Great Road," the ancient "King's Highway," now Virginia State Route No. 3, is a tablet erected by the State Conservation and Development Commission bearing this inscription:

WASHINGTON'S BOYHOOD HOME

At this place George Washington lived most of
the time from 1739 to 1747. Here, according to
tradition, he cut down the cherry tree.
Washington's father died here in 1743; the farm
was his share of the paternal estate. His
mother lived here until 1771.

Augustine Washington dealt extensively in lands. In 1725 he had sold certain tracts in King George County, not far from Fredericksburg, to the Principio Iron Company of Virginia and Maryland. He himself, like Alexander Spotswood, Charles Chiswell and his son John, William Byrd of Westover, and Colonel Henry Willis of Fredericksburg, was interested and perhaps actively engaged in the iron business. Charles Moore is of the opinion that he moved

Old shop or office, under extra roof, at Ferry Farm, dating from the time of the Washingtons. Photo about 1925.

to the Ferry Farm to be more conveniently situated for mining and hauling iron ores and for transporting pig-iron to shipping points on the Potomac. (See "The Family Life of George Washington," by Charles Moore, 1926, pages 21, 24.) We may obtain enlightening glimpses of Fredericksburg and the iron industry thereabouts from the sprightly narrative of William Byrd who paid the young town a visit in 1732, following his sojourn at Germanna with Spotswood, the "Tubal Cain of Virginia." Quoting from Byrd's "Progress to the Mines":

Col. Willis walked me about his town of Fredericksburg. It is pleasantly situated on the south shore of Rappahannock river, about a mile below the falls. Sloops may come up and lie close to the wharf, within thirty yards of the public warehouses, which are built in the figure of a cross. Just by the wharf is a quarry of white stone that is very soft in the grounnd, and hardens in the air, appearing to be as fair and fine grained as that of Portland. Besides that, there are several other quarries in the river bank, within the limits of the town, sufficient to build a large city. The only edifice of stone yet built is the prison; the walls of which are strong enough to hold Jack Sheppard, if he had been transported thither.

Though this be a commodious and beautiful situation for a town, with the advantages of a navigable river, and wholesome air, yet the inhabitants are very few. Besides Col. Willis, who is the top man of the place, there are only one merchant, a tailor, a smith, and an ordinary keeper; though I must not forget Mrs. Levistone, who acts here in the double capacity of doctress and coffee woman. And were this a populous city, she is qualified to exercise two other callings. It is said the court-house and the church are going to be built here, and then both religion and justice will help to enlarge the place.

Two miles from this place is a spring strongly impregnated with alum, and so is the earth all about it. This water does wonders for those that are afflicted with dropsy. And on the other side of the river, in King George county, twelve miles from hence, is another spring of strong steel water, as good as that at Tunbridge Wells. Not far from this last spring are England's iron mines, called so from the chief manager of them, though the land belongs to Mr. Washington. These mines are two miles from the furnace, and Mr. Washington raises the ore, and carts it thither for twenty shillings the ton of iron that it yields. The furnace is built on a run, which discharges its waters into Potomac. And when the iron is cast, they cart it about six miles to a landing on that river. Besides Mr. Washington and Mr. England, there are several other persons, in England, concerned in these works. Mr. England can neither write nor read; but without those helps, is so well skilled in iron works, that he does not only carry on his furnace, but has likewise the chief management of the works at Principia, at the head of the bay, where they have also erected a forge and make very good bar iron.

Col. Willis had built a flue to try all sorts of ore in, which was contrived after the following manner. It was built of stone four feet square with an iron grate fixed in the middle of it for the fire to lie upon. It was open at the bottom, to give a free passage to the air up to the grate. Above the grate was another opening that carried the smoke into a chimney. This makes a draught upward, and the fire rarefying the air below, makes another draught underneath, which causes the

—*From Historic Homes*

Ferry Farm as seen across the Rappahannock from a position near the "Sentry Box." Photo by Morrison, 1933.

fire to burn very fiercely, and melt any ore in the crucibles that are set upon the fire. This was erected by a mason called Taylor. . . .

The sun rising very bright, invited me to leave this infant city; accordingly, about ten, I took leave of my hospitable landlord, and persuaded parson Kenner to be my guide to Massaponux, lying five miles off, where I had agreed to meet Col. Spotswood. We arrived there about twelve, and found it a very pleasant and commodious plantation. The colonel received us with open arms, and carried us directly to his air furnace, which is a very ingenious and profitable contrivance. The use of it is to melt his sow iron, in order to cast it into sundry utensils, such as backs for chimneys, andirons, fenders, plates for hearths, pots, mortars, rollers for gardeners, skillets, boxes for cart wheels; and many other things, which, one with another, can be afforded at twenty shillings a ton, and delivered at people's own homes. And, being cast from the sow iron, are much better than those which come from England, which are cast immediately from the ore for the most part.

The Mr. Washington to whom Colonel Byrd refers may have been Augustine Washington, then operating at long range, for Byrd's visit to Fredericksburg was six years before Captain Washington located there; but there were other Washingtons in King George County.

By 1738, when Augustine Washington moved to the Ferry Farm, the town of Fredericksburg had no doubt grown considerably and the business in iron and other industries centering there had expanded correspondingly. Courts were being held at Fredericksburg already in 1732 when Byrd was there, and no doubt the court house which he says was then in prospect was soon erected. Fredericksburg, succeeding Germanna, was the county-seat of Spotsylvania County until 1782 or thereabouts. A church was built soon after Colonel Byrd's visit. The first rector was Rev. Patrick Henry, uncle to the famous orator. Rev. James Marye succeeded him in 1734, having charge of the church in Fredericksburg and also another on the Po River, his salary for the two being 16,000 pounds of tobacco. In 1738 the colonial assembly authorized the holding of fairs in Fredericksburg twice a year for the sale of cattle, provisions, and all kinds of merchandise. The next year a new survey revealed that the town had outgrown its original fifty acres, and measures were taken to keep up with the healthy expansion. In 1742 builders were forbidden to construct any more chimneys of wood and mud, and all such then in use were to be replaced with others of stone or brick within three years. On April 6 of the same year (1742) Augustine Washington was chosen one of the trustees of the town of Fredericksburg. He did not live in the town, but had evidently purchased property therein.

Fredericksburg was not the only center of trade in the vicinity. At the falls Falmouth, on Washington's side of the river, and only two miles above his home, was a vigorous rival of Fredericksburg. It was nearer to the settlements in Stafford and Prince William, and on their side of the river. The ferry that was established on the Rappahannock in 1742, from the land of William Thornton in King George County across the river to the wharf at the public lot in Fredericksburg, must have been some distance above the Ferry Farm, and therefore nearer Falmouth.

We may accept the story of the cherry tree in its main features, even if we do question the fine language of Parson Weems. If George had a hatchet and was a normal boy the hacking of things was inevitable; and it is conceivable and believable that he told the truth about the little tree and various other things. Both Falmouth and Fredericksburg claim a share in the boy's education. "Hobby," one of his early teachers, is said to have been William Grove. It may be said that he had teachers in both towns, but not much is known of them and it seeems pretty certain that he did not spend many years in school. This does not mean that his education was neglected. Parson Weems makes it appear that his father took pains in teaching and training him, and we may also give some credit to his mother, who was so careful to preserve the copy of Sir Matthew Hale's "Contemplations" that had belonged to her husband's first wife. George probably got his first lessons in surveying from his father. Parents in those days had a chance to get acquainted with their children and to impart to them something from their own experience and judgment. Home associations were not so immediately challenged and overshadowed. Furthermore, young George took himself in hand rather seriously. He wrote out repeatedly 110 "Rules of Civility." This had some value, we believe, in steadying his penmanship and perhaps his character too. "By their fruits ye shall know them." "The fact that young Washington wrote out these rules before he was sixteen years old," says Charles Moore, "and that he practiced them all his life, has caused them to be regarded as one of the most important parts of his education. Undoubtedly they were; they expressed in concrete form the ambition which he always displayed, namely, by diligence to stand before the best of the earth and not before mean men." Nicholas Cresswell, who was strongly prejudiced against him, declared, "His person is tall and genteel, . . . his behaviour and deportment easy, genteel, and obliging, with a certain something about him which pleases everyone who has anything to do with him."

George was only eleven years old when his father died and was at Chotank, about twenty miles from home, visiting some of his cousins, when his father's illness became serious. It evidently befel rather suddenly and terminated quickly, for Augustine Washington made his will one day and died the next. But George reached home, we are told, before his father died. The record in the family Bible gives the day of his death as April 12, 1743. By our calendar it would be April 23. The body was carried back to Westmoreland and placed in the family vault or graveyard at Bridges Creek.

At that time, so fateful for the mother and children at Ferry Farm, Elizabeth (Betty, as she was familiarly known) was a girl of ten; Samuel was between eight and nine; John Augustine was a few months over seven; and Charles not quite five. Mildred, born at Ferry Farm on July 2, 1739, had died on November 3 (N. S.) the following year. Accordingly, all the children who

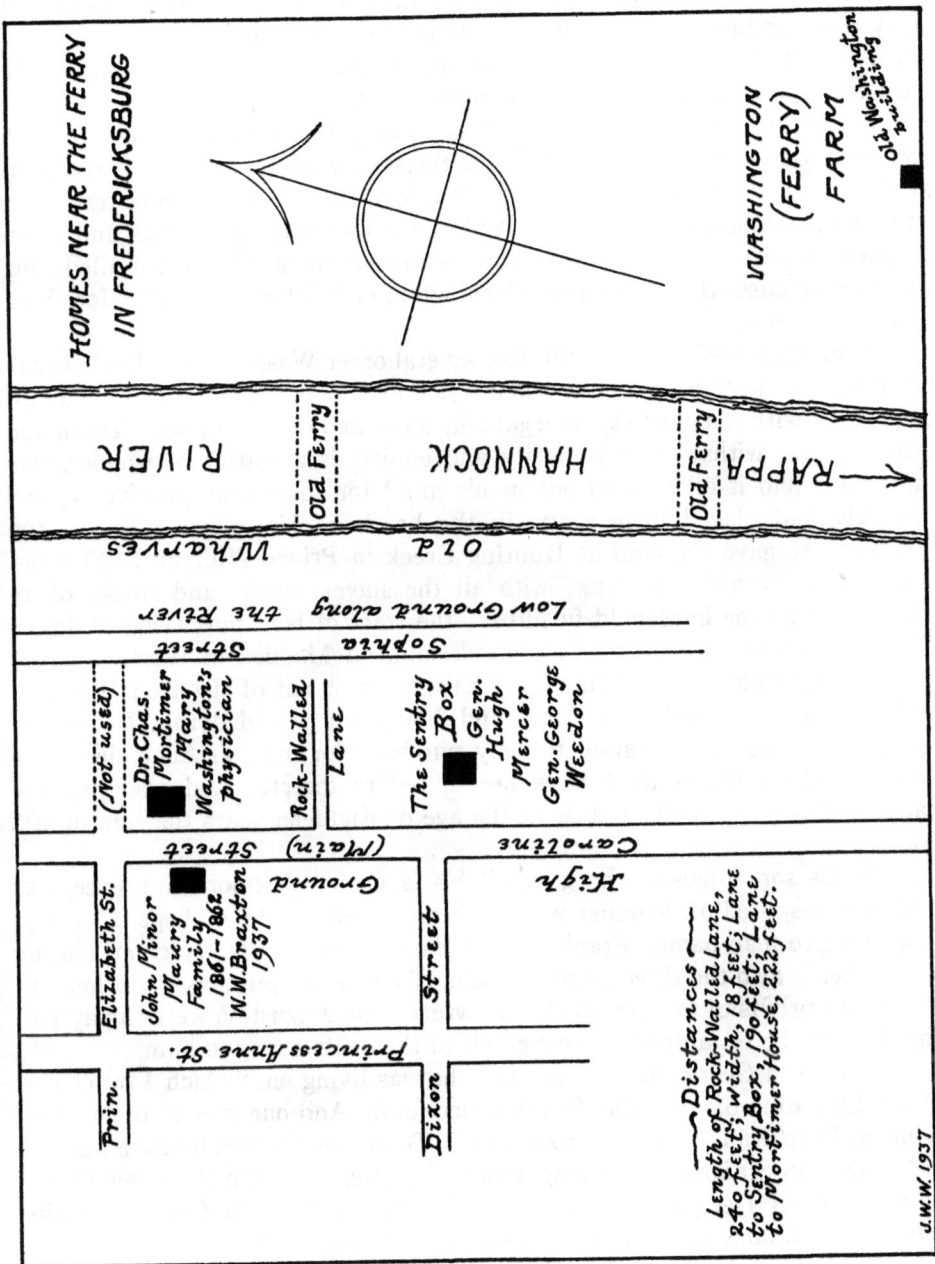

HOMES NEAR THE FERRY
IN FREDERICKSBURG

WASHINGTON (FERRY) FARM

Old Washington building

RAPPA—→ HANNOCK RIVER

Old Ferry   Old Ferry   Old Ferry

Old Wharves

Low Ground along the River

Sophia Street

(Not used)

Dr. Chas. Mortimer
Mary Washington's physician

Rock-Walled Lane

The Sentry Box

Gen. Hugh Mercer

Gen. George Weedon

Elizabeth St.

John Minor
Mary Family
1861-1862
W.W.Braxton 1937

Ground Street (Main)

Caroline

High

Prin.

Princess Anne St.

Dixon Street

—Distances—
Length of Rock-Walled Lane,
240 feet; width, 18 feet; Lane
to Sentry Box, 190 feet; Lane
to Mortimer House, 222 feet.

J.W.W. 1937

were living in April 1743 were old enough to go to school and if they attended school in Fredericksburg we may picture them in the early mornings on the ferry crossing the river, and then climbing the steep bank to Caroline Street, which is still the main street of the town. At that time, we may believe, the narrow sheltered lane, a miniature canyon, led straight up the bank, as it does today. Starting 200 feet from the water's edge, it goes up 240 feet. It is 18 feet wide, paved with cobblestones, and the rock walls on either side reach up at some places to a height of 15 feet. Trees overshadow it and vines festoon it. In spring, summer, and autumn it is almost a tunnel of cool banks and green or golden leaves. No one seems to know who constructed this rock-walled lane, but we may guess that Augustine Washington, or William Strother before him, had a hand in it.

Augustine Washington's will, like several other Washington wills that may be cited, is a masterpiece. How a man "sick and weak," as he declares himself to be, even with the most expert legal aid, could make a will of such length and intricacy, yet withal of such clarity and equity, is a matter of wonder. He must have had it all worked out in his mind for some time previously, and probably had placed memoranda in the hands of his lawyer. To his son Lawrence he gave the land at Hunting Creek in Prince William, 2500 acres, with the water mill adjoining; with all the slaves, cattle, and stocks of all kinds; and all the household furniture; the tract of land purchased of James Hooe and adjoining the said Lawrence's land on Maddox in Westmoreland; also "all the right title and interest I have to in or out of the Iron Works in which I am concerned in Virginia and Maryland provided that he do and shall, out of the profits raised thereby purchase for my son Augustine three young working slaves as I have herein before directed and also pay my daughter Betty when she arrives at the age of Eighteen years the sum of 400 pounds."

To his son Augustine he gave all his lands in Westmoreland, except as otherwise disposed of, together with 25 head of neat cattle, 40 hogs, 20 sheep, "and a negro man named Frank besides those negroes formerly given him by his mother"; also the three young working slaves to be purchased for him out of the first profits of the iron works. Lawrence and Augustine were to pay half the debts of the testator and to have half of the debts owing to him.

To his son George he gave the land he was living on, "which I purchased of the Executors of Mr. Wm. Strother deceased. And one moiety of my land lying on Deep Run and ten negro Slaves." To his son Samuel he gave his land at Chotank in Stafford, containing about 600 acres, and also the other moiety of his land on Deep Run. This stream is in Spotsylvania County, flowing into the Rapahannock a short distance below Fredericksburg.

To his son John Augustine he gave his land "at the head of Maddox in the County of Westmoreland," about 700 acres. To Charles he devised "the land I purchased of my son Lawrence Washington whereon Thomas Lewis now lives, adioining to my said son Lawrence's land above devised. I also give unto my said son Charles and his heirs the land I purchased of Gabriel Adams in the County of Prince William containing about 700 acres."

All the rest of the slaves not particularly devised were to be divided equally among his wife and his three sons, Samuel, John, and Charles, the wife to have among others Ned, Jack, Bob, Sue, and Lucy; her share to go after her death to the four sons, George, Samuel, John, and Charles; and her share thus devised was intended to be in lieu and satisfaction of her dower in the slaves. The wife and her four sons were to have in equal shares all the rest of the personal estate, not particularly bequeathed, and she was to have also the crops made at Bridges Creek, Chotank, and Rappahannock quarters at the time of the testator's death for the support of herself and children; "and the liberty of working my land at Bridge Creek Quarter for the time of Five years next after my decease, during which time she may fix a quarter on Deep Run."

In a long paragraph of over 500 words minute directions are given for adjustments that might be necessary because of possible deaths without heirs or because one or the other of his sons Augustine and George might prefer this or that. "Lastly," his son Lawrence and his good friends Daniel McCarty and Nathaniel Chapman, Gentlemen, were appointed executors.

The will was signed April 11 (O. S.), 1743, and witnessed by Robert Jackson, Anthony Strother, and James Thompson.

On the same day and before the same witnesses Augustine Washington added several codicils to his will, one providing that "if my lands at Chotank devised to my son Samuel should by course of law be taken away then I give to the said Samuel in lieu thereof a tract of Land in Westmoreland County where Benjamin Wicks and Thomas Finch now live by estimation 700 acres." To George were given three lots in Fredericksburg, one purchased of Colonel John Walton, the other two of the executors of Colonel Henry Willis, "with all the Houses and appurtenances thereunto belonging." His executors were empowered to sell a certain piece of land, probably of the home place, to Anthony Strother if they believed it to be for George's benefit.

Augustine Washington's will was proved before the court of King George County on May 6 (O. S.), 1743.

A very interesting and significant item in Captain Washington's will is yet to be mentioned. It reads as follows:

And it is my will and desire that my said four sons [George, Samuel, John, and Charles] Estates may be kept in my wife's hands until they respectively attain the age of twenty one years, in case my said wife continues so long unmarried but in case she should happen to marry before that time I desire it may be in the power of my Executors to oblige her husband from time to time as they shall think proper to give security for the performance of this my last will in paying and delivering my said four sons their Estates respectively as they come of age, or on failure to give such security to take my said sons and their estates out of the custody and tuition of my said wife and her husband.

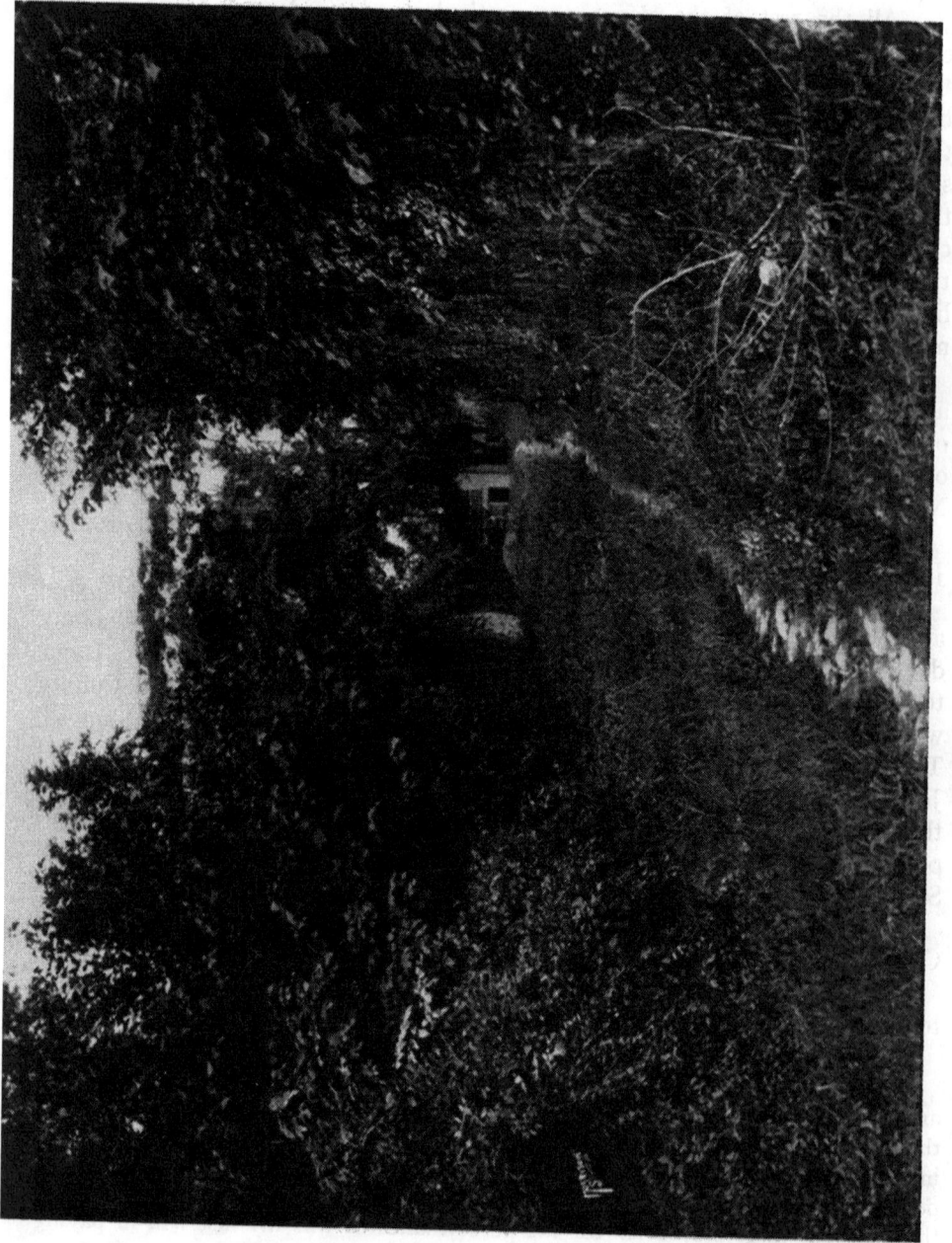

The old rock-walled lane shown on the opposite page, from a photograph made by Morrison in 1933, leads up from one of the old ferries of Ferry Farm to Caroline Street in Fredericksburg. The Washington children, in all probability, climbed this lane of mornings on their way to school in the town. It is paved with well-worn cobblestones and is overhung by trees and vines that cluster the sides.

The "Rose of Epping Forest" did not marry again, though she was only thirty-five when Augustine Washington died. If one should search for possible reasons he could easily find them in the provisions just quoted from Captain Washington's will. An even remote contingency of losing custody of her children and their estates was naturally a serious consideration to Mrs. Washington, and the obligation to give bonds to the executors on demand "or else" probably dampened the ardor of the most desirable suitors. By the time her son Charles was of legal age she was a matron of fifty-one. Neither before nor after that time did she "happen to marry."

Will Book No. 1 of King George County, in which Augustine Washington's will was recorded, was carried off at some time during the Civil War, 1861-65, but the Washington family had a copy. From this other copies were secured, and from one of these the will was printed in *Tyler's Quarterly Historical and Genealogical Magazine*, issue of July 1927, pages 34-38.

After his father's death George Washington spent much of his time for several years with his half-brother Augustine at Wakefield, where it is said he went to school to a Mr. Williams. He later sojourned with Lawrence at Mount Vernon, where he met Lord Fairfax; but Ferry Farm continued to be his mother's home and his home. There it was, no doubt, that his trunk was put on a ship for him to go to sea, and taken off again because his mother did not want him to go. There, as well as elsewhere, he rode horses, vaulted with long poles, heaved heavy weights, threw across the river, and did various other things that might be expected of him, his brothers, and other young fellows. I quote from Parson Weems:

"Egad! he ran wonderfully," said my amiable friend, John Fitzhugh, Esq., who knew him well. "We had nobody here-abouts that could come near him. There was a young Langhorne Dade, of Westmoreland, a confounded clean made, tight young fellow, and a mighty swift runner too. But then he was no match for George. Langy, indeed, did not like to give it up; and would brag that he had sometimes brought George to a tie. But I believe he was mistaken; for I have seen them run together many a time; and George always beat him easy enough."

Col. Lewis Willis, his play-mate and kinsman, has been heard to say, that he has often seen him throw a stone across Rappahannock, at the lower ferry of Fredericksburg. It would be no easy matter to find a man, now-a-days, who could do it.

Indeed his father before him was a man of extraordinary strength. His gun, which to this day is called Washington's fowling-piece, and is now the property of Mr. Harry Fitzhugh, of Chotank, is of such enormous weight, that not one man in fifty can fire it without a rest. And yet throughout that country it is said, that he made nothing of holding it off at arms length, and blazing away at the swans on Potomac; of which he has been known to kill, rank and file, seven or eight at a shot.

By careful measurements, the Rappahannock at the lower ferry, the Washington ferry, has been ascertained to be about 115 yards in width.

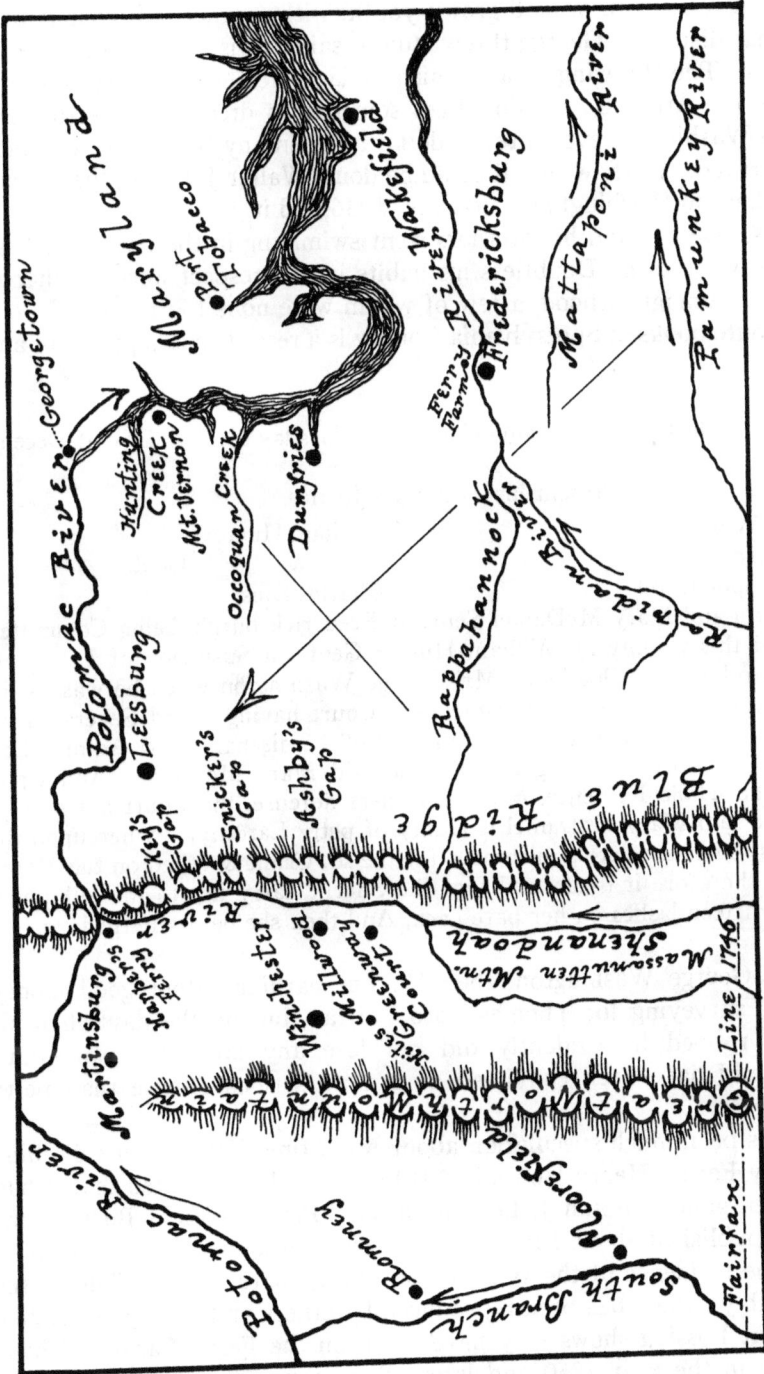

Map showing Wakefield, Hunting Creek, Ferry Farm, Fredericksburg, Mount Vernon, Greenway Court, Winchester, and the South Branch Valley, all familiar in the boyhood experiences of George Washington

Almost any vigorous man or well-grown youth, with a practiced hurling arm, can throw that distance. George threw stones, said Lewis Willis, and we may well believe it. The throwing of a Spanish dollar, like the throwing of a sovereign across the Atlantic, was doubtless somebody's dream or afterthought. That George Washington ever threw a dollar away in any such useless fashion is yet to be proved. To show that it could be done, Walter Johnson, the famous baseball pitcher, on Washington's birthday, 1936, did it.

Of course, George and his brothers went swimming in the river. He kept it up until he was grown. Doubtless his habits in this respect were familiar to the people of the neighborhood, a few of whom were none too honest. In one of the old minute books of Spotsylvania County is a record that is pertinent and interesting:

At a Court held for Spotsylvania County on Tuesday the 3rd. Day of December, Anno Domini, 1751

Present his Majesty's Justices

John Waller	William Hunter	
Richard Tutt	&	Gent.
John Spotswood	Charles Dick	

Ann Carrol and Mary McDaniel Senr. of Fredericksburgh, being Committed to the Gaol of this County by William Hunter Gent, on Suspicion of Felony, & Charged with robing the Cloaths of Mr. George Washington when he was washing in the River some time last Summer, the Court having heard Severall Evidences Are of Oppinion that the said Ann Carroll be discharged, & Admitted an Evidence for our Lord the King Against the said Mary McDaniel. And Upon Considering the whole Evidence, & the prisoners defense, the Court are of Oppinion that the said Mary McDaniel is Guilty of petty Larceny,— whereupon the said Mary desired Immediate punishment for the sd. Crime & relied on the Mercy of the Court, therefore it is ordered that the Sheriff carry her to the Whipping post, & inflict fifteen lashes on her bare back, And then she be discharged &c.

In 1751 George Washington, then 19, was earning rather good money exploring and surveying for Thomas Lord Fairfax, but on the day when his clothes were robbed he evidently did not lose any large sum, or Mary McDaniel would have been convicted of a more serious offense than petty larceny.

There has been much speculation about Augustine Washington's dwelling house at Ferry Farm. Henry Howe, in 1844 or thereabouts, stated that it had long since been gone. Benson J. Lossing, in his "Pictorial Field Book of the Revolution," published about 1850, gives a picture of a small house which he asserts was the residence of the Washington family at this place. This is the picture, probably, which has been reproduced by others and widely circulated. The house that Lossing shows may have stood on the Ferry Farm and have been standing in the year 1850 and later; there were several houses on the farm in Augustine Washington's day; but it was hardly the one in which the

Washingtons had lived. The house of William Strother, in which Augustine Washington lived from 1738 to 1743, was described in the advertisement reprinted above as a "Mansion," "a very handsome Dwelling house." It must have been a commodious house to hold the abundant furniture that is catalogued and to contain the various rooms that are named in the appraisement lists of Augustine Washington's personal effects. Furniture is designated as belonging to the hall, the hall back room, the parlour, the back room, the passage, the hall chamber, and the parlour chamber; also the dairy, the closet, the store house, the kitchen, the quarter, etc. Captain Washington evidently belonged to the class of well-to-do planters. This might be guessed from his large and widely-distributed tracts of land.

Among his personal and household belongings he had spoons, a watch, and a sword, valued altogether at 23 pounds and 10 shillings. Among the pieces of china were 9 gilt saucers, 6 gilt cups, a large blue and white bowl, and 9 custard cups. There were 11 beds, 6 tables, large and small, 15 chairs, 11 of them with leather bottoms; 13 table cloths, 33 napkins, 1 suit of silk and cotton curtains, 1 suit of silk curtains. He had a set of cooper's tools and a set of surveyor's instruments. In the store room he had many yards of different kinds of cloth: "Fustin," Shalloon Revans, Irish linen, plaid, "Oznabrigs," etc. On the home farm were 9 cows and heifers, 9 other cattle, 19 hogs, 11 sheep, and 2 horses. At the same place were 20 Negro slaves, and at the quarter 7, all of whom were named. Among those at the "Home House" were Jack, Bob, Toney, Lucy, Sue, Phillis, and Hannah; among those at the quarter were Tim, Ralph, Balinda, and Winnie.

Besides the "very handsome Dwelling house," which stood on the Ferry Farm in 1738, there were three store houses and several other convenient outhouses. One of these, not the mansion, was evidently the one seen and pictured by Lossing in or about 1850. At present there is only one building, a small structure that may have been an office, remaining on the Ferry Farm that was probably there in the time of the Washingtons. For better protection, an extra roof has been put over it.

Inventories of Captain Augustine Washington's personal estate are on record at King William Court House, and printed copies may be found in the *William and Mary College Quarterly*, April 1937, pages 269-273, and in *Tyler's Quarterly*, April 1938, pages 216-218.

On September 13, 1771, as already noted, George Washington made a survey of the "fields" where his mother lived. On September 18, 1772, he purchased of Michael Robinson and wife Esther the home in Fredericksburg to which his mother shortly thereafter moved and where she spent the remainder of her life. In October 1772 he advertised the Ferry Farm for sale in the *Virginia Gazette*, "A Tract of 600 acres, including about 200 of cleared land, lying on the north side of Rappahannock river, opposite to the lower end of Fredericksburg." He states in this advertisement that on this tract, "a little above the road," is one of the most agreeable situations for a house that is to be found on the whole river. This implies that the mansion house of his father was not then standing. Possibly the burning of that house was one reason for his mother moving across the river to Fredericksburg about this time. At some time prior to 1776 the Ferry Farm was sold to General Hugh Mercer, but neither he nor his family, we are told, ever resided thereon. General Mercer was killed at the battle of Princeton early in 1777.

We are indebted to Judge Francis T. Brooke (1763-1851) for a graphic picture of George Washington in the period now before us. Brooke's boyhood home was at Smithfield, on the Rappahannock, four miles below Fredericksburg. In 1849 he had printed in Richmond "A Narrative of My Life for My Family," from which the following paragraphs are quoted.

I knew Washington in my boyhood. He came to Smithfield with General Spotswood, in 1773, I think it was. He was then a Colonel in the British Army. I remember his dress; he wore a deep blue coat, a scarlet waistcoat, trimmed with a gold chain, and buckskin small clothes, boots, spurs, and sword. He had with him a beautiful greyhound, was fond of the sports of the field, and proposed to my father, who had a tame deer, to try if the greyhound could catch him; to which my father assented, and after leaping over the yard palings, they went through the garden where they leaped the palings again; when the deer turned towards the river, he got a start of the greyhound, and got into the river before he could catch him. General Washington was afterwards at Smithfield two or three times; he was fond of horses, my father had some excellent ones, so had Gen. Spotswood; they took the horses to the road, and mounted the boys upon them, to try their speed.

General Washington, in the year 1774, came to Fredericksburg to review the independent companies. After the review, they gave him a collation in the old market-house, where he had all the boys of a large grammar school, of which I was one, brought to him; gave them a drink of punch, patted them upon their heads, and asked them if they could fight for their country. After the war he frequently came to Fredericksburg, where his mother resided, and his only sister, Mrs. Lewis.

CHAPTER IV

BETTY WASHINGTON LEWIS AND KENMORE

Jane Washington, George's half-sister and ten years his senior, died early in 1735, shortly before the family moved away from Wakefield. His sister Mildred, born at Ferry Farm on June 21 (O. S.), 1739, died there at the age of 16 months. Elizabeth, familiarly known as Betty, was the only girl of the family to grow up and the only sister that George knew with any sense of companionship. She was born at Wakefield, the birthplace of George and Samuel, on June 20 (O. S.), 1733. The date of her birth in the New Style, or Gregorian Calendar, would be July 1, 1733. Inasmuch as we habitually give George's birthday in the New Style, as February 22, it will be consistent to follow the same practice with reference to other members of the family.

Betty's portrait represents her as a vigorous and full-blooded woman, with some features that are in rather striking resemblance to those of her elder brother. She was his junior by only 16 months or a little more. George Washington Parke Custis, who remembered her very well, said that it was a matter of frolic with her to don a cloak and put on a military cap; and then such was the "perfect resemblance" that had she appeared on her brother's steed, battalions would have presented arms, and senates risen to do her homage. It has been recorded also that George and Betty closely resembled their mother in form, carriage, and contour of their faces. They also inherited her health, mental vigor, and sterling virtues, but not her seriousness, which grew in later life to be a depressing sadness.

Betty Washington on May 7, 1750, married Colonel Fielding Lewis of Fredericksburg. She was then nearly seventeen; he was a widower of twenty-five or thereabouts. He was, says Bishop Meade, a son of the second Robert Lewis of Gloucester County, Va. (See "Old Churches, Ministers, and Families of Virginia," reprint of 1900, Vol. II, page 232.) According to Dr. Lyon G. Tyler, he was born July 7, 1725, the son of Colonel John Lewis of Warner Hall, Gloucester County, and his wife Frances Fielding. (See "Encyclopedia of Virginia Biography," 1915, Vol. 1, page 277.) He removed to Fredericksburg early in life, was a merchant of high standing and wealth, a vestryman, and a magistrate. In 1758 he took oath as county lieutenant of Spotsylvania County, and from 1760 to 1768 he was a member of the Virginia House of Burgesses. His first wife was Catherine Washington, a daughter of John Washington and his wife Catherine Whiting. This John was a brother to Augustine Washington, George's father. Accordingly, both wives of Colonel Lewis were near relatives of General Washington, the first being his cousin, the second his sister. Catherine had three children, only one of whom lived to any considerable age. This one was John Lewis, who married five times, and is mentioned occasionally in Washington's diaries. In 1785 he was at Abingdon, above Alexandria. In April of that year he was brought down on

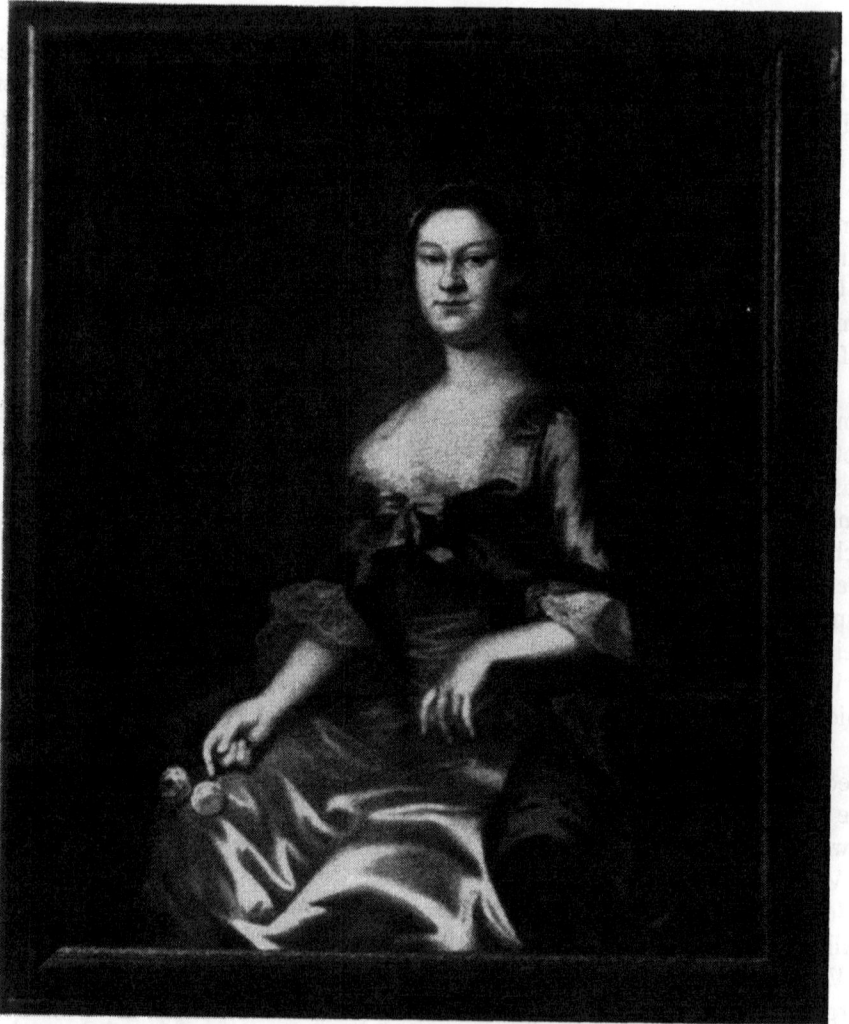

Betty Washington Lewis, the only sister of General George Washington to grow to womanhood.

Washington's barge to Mount Vernon, where he spent nearly eight weeks recovering from illness. In April 1791 he, in Fredericksburg, recently returned from Richmond, gave Washington information as to Patrick Henry's interest in the Yazoo Company and his plans for promoting it. He moved to Kentucky, where he left descendants.

Betty Washington Lewis had a number of children, some of whom died in childhood. Following is a list of her children, with dates of their births, as given by Louise Pecquet du Bellet in "Some Prominent Virginia Families," Vol. IV (1907), pages 25, 26:

Fielding, February 14, 1751; Augustine, January 22, 1752; Thomas, June 24, 1755; George, March 14, 1757; Mary, April 22, 1759; Charles, October 3, 1760; Samuel, May 14, 1763; Elizabeth, February 23, 1765; Lawrence, April 4, 1767; Robert, June 25, 1769; Howell, December 12, 1771. These names and dates agree substantially with those given by Mrs. Roger A. Pryor in her "The Mother of Washington and Her Times," 1903, pages 112, 113, and by Mrs. John Gray Goldsmith, a descendant, in 1938. Among those who died in childhood or without issue were Thomas, Mary, and Samuel. Charles was living on April 26, 1775, aged nearly fifteen, when his uncle, George Washington, gave him a guinea and recorded the gift along with others in an expense account. But evidently Charles was not living on October 19, 1781, when his father, Colonel Fielding Lewis, made his will. Therein the testator names only John (of his first marriage), Fielding, George, Lawrence, Robert, Howell, and his son-in-law Charles Carter, Esq., husband of Betty.

General Washington making his will 18 years later, that is in July 1799, names Fielding, George, Robert, Lawrence, Howell, and Betty Carter.

Concerning some of Betty Washington Lewis's children a good deal is known; regarding others the information is meager. Fielding, the eldest, was remembered rather liberally by his grandmother, Mary Washington, in her will. To him, then thirty-seven, she left her Negro man Frederick; also eight silver tablespoons, half her cooking ware, her blue and white tea china, a bookcase, an oval table, one bed and bedstead, a pair of sheets, a pair of blankets, a white cotton counterpane, two tablecloths, six red leather chairs, half of her pewter, and half of her iron kitchen furniture. This Fielding Lewis, it is said, died in Fairfax County, Virginia. Concerning him, Mr. Richard E. Griffith, Sr., of Winchester, supplies the following items: He married a Miss Alexander and settled in what is now Clarke County, Va., on land willed him by his father, just north of "Old Chapel," which later was owned by Captain Thomas Taylor Byrd, son of William Byrd III of Westover. Some of this land is still in the Byrd family. Most of it is owned by Colonel "Wild Bill" Donovan, whose family now (1941) reside there.

Elizabeth Lewis, born in 1765, was the Betty Carter named in her grandmother Washington's will of May 20, 1788. She had married Charles Carter in probably 1784. Fitzpatrick, in his "The Diaries of George Washington," 1925 edition, Vol. II, page 356, note, says that Charles Carter of Culpeper

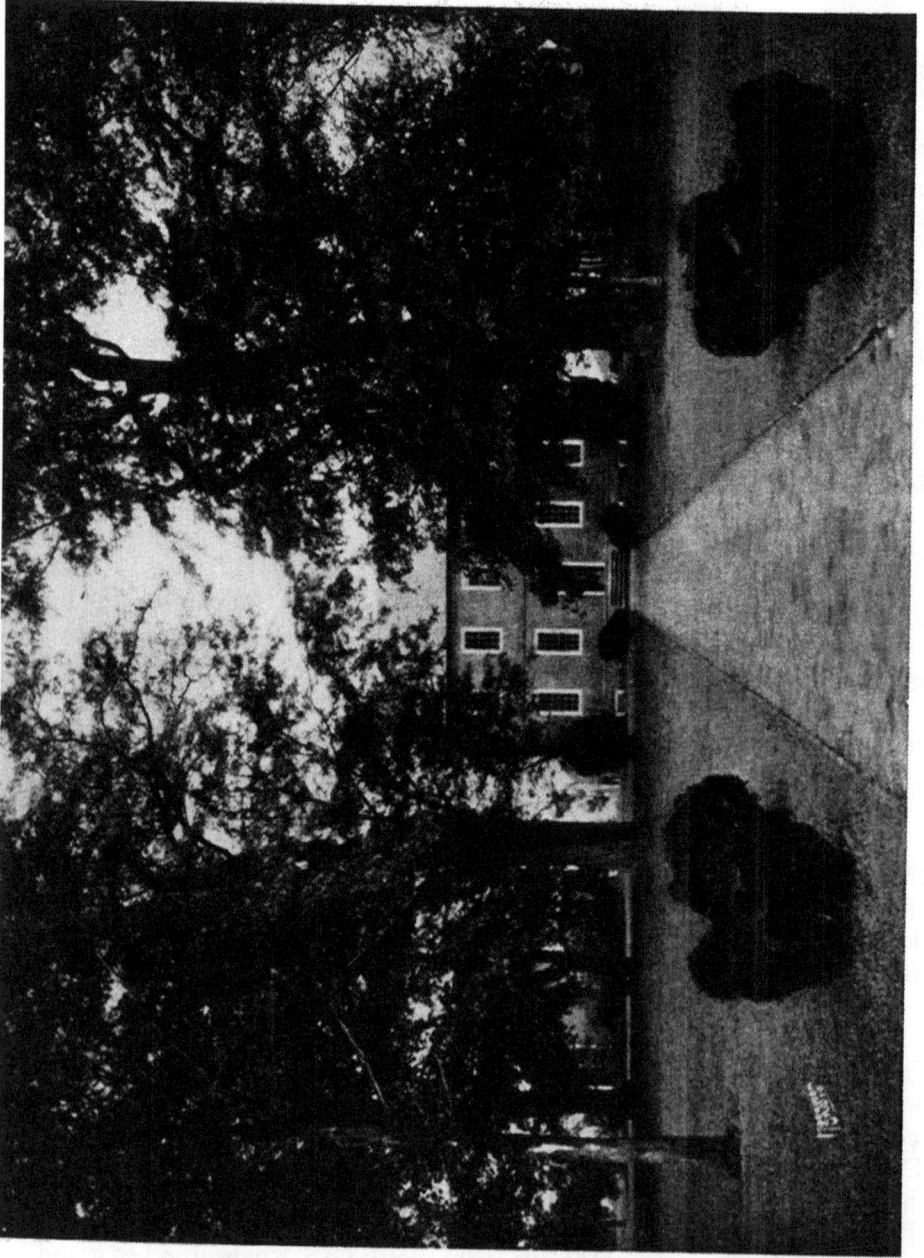

—*From Historic Homes*

Kenmore, home of Betty Washington Lewis. Photo by Morrison, 1933.

married Betty Lewis, Washington's niece, in 1787. On the same page and the following one he prints Washington's diary for April 4 and 5, 1785, in which it is recorded that George Lewis and his wife and "Mr. Chas. Carter and his wife and Child" were at Mount Vernon. George Lewis and Mrs. Charles Carter were almost certainly the nephew and niece of General Washington, and if so Betty Lewis and Charles Carter had been married in 1784 or earlier.

Mary Washington by her will left to her granddaughter Betty Lewis Carter her Negro woman Little Bet and her future increase; also her largest looking glass, her walnut writing desk with drawers, a square dining table, one bed and bedstead, a white Virginia cloth counterpane, purple curtains, her red and white tea china, tea spoons, "the other half of my pewter, Crokery ware, & the remainder of my Iron kitchen Furniture"; with other articles specified; and the said Betty Carter was to have also one-third of Mrs. Washington's wearing apparel.

Bishop Meade states that Elizabeth Lewis married Mr. Charles Carter and was one of the most interesting and exemplary of Christians.

George Lewis, born in 1757, served with distinction in the Revolution. In his arms General Hugh Mercer expired after having been mortally wounded in the battle of Princeton. He was a captain in Baylor's regiment and commanded Washington's life guard. Near the close of the war he married and settled at "Springbury ," on the Shenandoah River, four miles south of Berryville, now in Clarke County, Va., where he was active in affairs of church and state. In the Whisky Insurrection of 1794 he was major in command of a body of cavalry. After residing some years near Berryville he removed to Fredericksburg, and thence to King George County, dying there at his home Marmion in 1821. He enjoyed to the fullest extent the esteem and confidence of his uncle, General Washington, who bequeathed him a sum of money and one of his swords. Following is the paragraph in the General's will which relates to this sword and four others:

To each of my nephews, William Augustine Washington, George Lewis, George Steptoe Washington, Bushrod Washington, and Samuel Washington, I give one of the swords or cutteaux of which I may die possessed; and they are to chuse in the order they are named.—These swords are accompanied with an injunction not to unsheath them for the purpose of shedding blood, except it be for self defence, or in defence of their country and its rights; and in the latter case, to keep them unsheathed, and prefer falling with them in their hands to the relinquishment thereof.

Robert, one of the younger sons of Colonel Fielding Lewis and his wife Betty Washington, was the private secretary of General Washington during a part of the time he was President. In 1791 he located in Fredericksburg where, as a private citizen, as mayor of the town, and as a member of the Episcopal Church, he was generally esteemed and beloved. He was elected

A Kenmore interior, about 1925.

mayor in 1820 and served until his death, February 10, 1829. In 1824, as mayor, he delivered the address of welcome to Lafayette. "The presence of the friend of Washington," he declared, "excites the tenderest emotions and associations among a people whose town enjoys the distinguished honor of having been the residence of the Father of His Country during the days of his childhood and youth."

Replying, General Lafayette said in part: "At this place, sir, which calls to our recollection several among the most honored names of the Revolutionary war, I did, many years ago, salute the first residence of our paternal chief, received the blessing of his venerated mother, and of his dear sister, your own respected parent."

Howell Lewis visited his uncle, General Washington, at Mount Vernon in February, 1798, remaining from the 23d of the month to the 28th. He was then between 26 and 27 years of age. On November 29 of the next year he and his wife came to Mount Vernon where they remained about ten days, leaving for home, which was probably in Fredericksburg or its vicinity, on December 9. This was just four days before Washington's fatal illness developed. Later (in 1812) Howell Lewis moved to Kanawha County, now in West Virginia, where he inherited 1300 acres of land and where he lived until his death in 1822, leaving descendants. (See "The Family Life of George Washington," by Charles Moore, 1926, page 233; and "Old Churches, Ministers, and Families of Virginia," by William Meade, printing of 1900, Vol. II, pages 232, 233.) Howell Lewis owned 1000 acres in now Clarke County, Va., the place called "Llewellyn," which passed to his brother Lawrence, who sold it to Warner Washington, Jr.

Lawrence Lewis, son of Colonel Fielding and Betty Washington Lewis, is said to have been General Washington's favorite nephew. He, after the General's retirement from public life, spent much of his time at Mount Vernon. In 1794 he served as an aide to General Daniel Morgan in the expedition to quell the Whisky Insurrection. On February 22, 1799, at Mount Vernon, he married Nelly Custis, Washington's adopted daughter—Martha Washington's granddaughter. The morning had been rainy, as Washington records, with the mercury at 30. "Wind a little more to the Northward. Afterwards very strong from the No. Wt. and turning clear and cold." The Rev. Thomas Davis and Mr. George Calvert came to dinner—the mid-day meal; "and Miss Custis was married abt. Candle light to Mr. Lawe. Lewis." The bride lacked a month of being twenty years old; the groom, 41 days later, was thirty-two.

Lawrence Lewis and his wife were remembered handsomely in Washington's will, which was written on July 9, 1799, the anniversary of the disastrous rout of Braddock's army 44 years before. They received about 2000 acres of land, including the mill on Dogue Run. Near the mill they built in 1805 the handsome brick house which still remains and which is familiar among the historic homes of that region. (See "Historic Homes of Northern Vir-

Restored tomb of Betty Washington Lewis at "Western View." Photo 1938.

ginia and the Eastern Panhandle of West Virginia," by John W. Wayland, 1937, pages 560, 561.)

Lawrence Lewis was the last active executor of Washington's will, of the seven named by the testator, though he did not live to close up all business of the estate. He continued to reside at Mount Vernon until the death of Mrs. Washington, May 22, 1802. He died at Arlington, the home of his brother-in-law, George W. P. Custis, on November 30, 1839. Mr. Custis, also an executor named by Washington, evidently deferred to Mr. Lewis, and after the latter's death seems to have delegated the business of the executors to John A. Washington III. (See "The Family Life of George Washington," by Charles Moore, 1926, page 217.) After the death of Lawrence Lewis his widow, Nelly Custis Lewis, moved from Woodlawn to Audley, near Berryville, where her son, Lorenzo Lewis, had been living, and where she resided until her death, July 15, 1852.

In or about 1752 Colonel Fielding Lewis erected his brick mansion at the west side of the town of Fredericksburg. Here he and his second wife, Betty Washington, lived and reared their family and entertained their large circle of kinsfolk and friends. The place at first was called Millbank, but for many years it has been known as Kenmore. The main building is 52 by 42 feet, outside measurement, the longer dimension parallel with Washington Avenue, which is at a distance of about 50 yards on the west. At an equal distance on the south runs Lewis Street. The mansion is flanked at each end by a smaller building, also of brick. These end buildings have recently been restored to their original forms and locations. Tradition has it that the Kenmore bricks were brought from England, but they were probably made in the vicinity, on Colonel Lewis's land. Captain S. J. Quinn, writing in 1908, says that excellent clay for the making of bricks is to be found near at hand and that the signs of an old brickyard were still to be seen.

The interior stucco work of Kenmore is elegant, equal in artistic design and workmanship to the best in this country. It stood for nearly a century and a half without repair, so far as is known, till about 1893, when Mr. William Key Howard "gave it some slight touches." The beautiful old stairway was climbed by some of the daintiest feet in Virginia. The Lewises, in their days of prosperity, dispensed a lavish hospitality. General Washington, as his diaries show, was frequently their guest. Fredericksburg was his old home; it was the home of his mother and his sister. His brother Samuel lived in the vicinity until 1769, and his brother Charles until 1780, or thereabouts. Besides, Fredericksburg was on his direct course journeying to Richmond and returning thence to Mount Vernon, and was also a convenient resting-place on the land route to Williamsburg. Occasionally Mrs. Washington and other members of the family accompanied him to Fredericksburg, as, for example, in August 1770, when he, Mrs. Washington, and Patsy Custis spent eight or nine days there. On the first day of the month they dined at his mother's on

"Western View," Charles Carter Homestead, 1938. The car, the boy, and the man are standing on the foundations of the old mansion.

the Ferry Farm. He then spent part of the afternoon in town, returning to his mother's in the evening. The next day he met the officers of the first regiment of Virginia troops at Captain Weedon's to determine upon procedure regarding the lands granted them for services in the French and Indian War. Mrs. Washington and Patsy dined at Colonel Lewis's (Kenmore), where they all lodged. On the 3d they dined at his brother Charles's where they spent the evening, but they lodged again at Colonel Lewis's. After church on Sunday, the 5th, and also on the 7th and 8th, they dined at Kenmore, probably lodging the night of the 8th on the Ferry Farm, since they breakfasted with his mother the morning of the 9th, just before they set out for home.

It would be tedious to recount all the visits of Washingon to Kenmore, but certainly one that he made in the summer of 1788 should not be overlooked. His record of it in his diary, under dates of June 10 to 16, is as follows:

Between 9 and 10 o'clock [Tuesday, June 10, 1788] set out for Fredericksburgh accompanied by Mrs. Washington, on a visit to my Mother. Made a visit to Mr. and Mrs. Thompson in Colchester, and reached Colo. Blackburn's to dinner, where we lodged. He was from home. The next Morning, about Sun rise we continued our journey, breakfasted at Stafford's Court House, and intended to have dined at Mr. Fitzhugh's of Chatham, but he and lady being from home we proceeded to Fredericksburgh, alighted at my Mother's and sent the Carriage and horses to my Sister Lewis's, where we dined and lodged. As we also did the next day, the first in company with Mr. Fitzhugh, Colo. Carter and Colo. Willis and their Ladies, and Genl. Weedon. The day following (Friday), we dined in a large Company at Mansfield (Mr. Man Page's).

On Saturday we visited Genl. Spotswood's, dined there and returned in the Evening to my Sister's. On Sunday we went to Church, the Congregation being alarmed (without cause) and supposing the Gallery at the No. End was about to fall, were thrown into the utmost confusion; and in the precipitate retreat to the doors many got hurt.

Dined in a large Company at Colo. Willis's, where, taking leave of my friends, we recrossed the River, and spent the evening at Chatham. The next Morning before five Oclock we left it, travelled to Dumfries to breakfast, and reached home to a late dinner, . . .

At this time, 1788, Washington's mother was living in Fredericksburg, near her daughter, Mrs. Lewis. Colonel Lewis had died seven years before and wealth had departed from Kenmore, but hospitality was still maintained, at least upon occasions such as we have set before us in the foregoing narrative.

At the outbreak of the Revolution 600 men gathered at the Rising Sun Tavern in Fredericksburg and adopted a series of fiery resolutions, endorsing Patrick Henry's resistance to Lord Dunmore, the royal governor, who had aroused much fear and alarm by removing a store of powder at Williamsburg. These Fredericksburg resolutions, we are told, were penned by Colonel Fielding Lewis in the main room of Kenmore mansion. Shortly afterwards, when

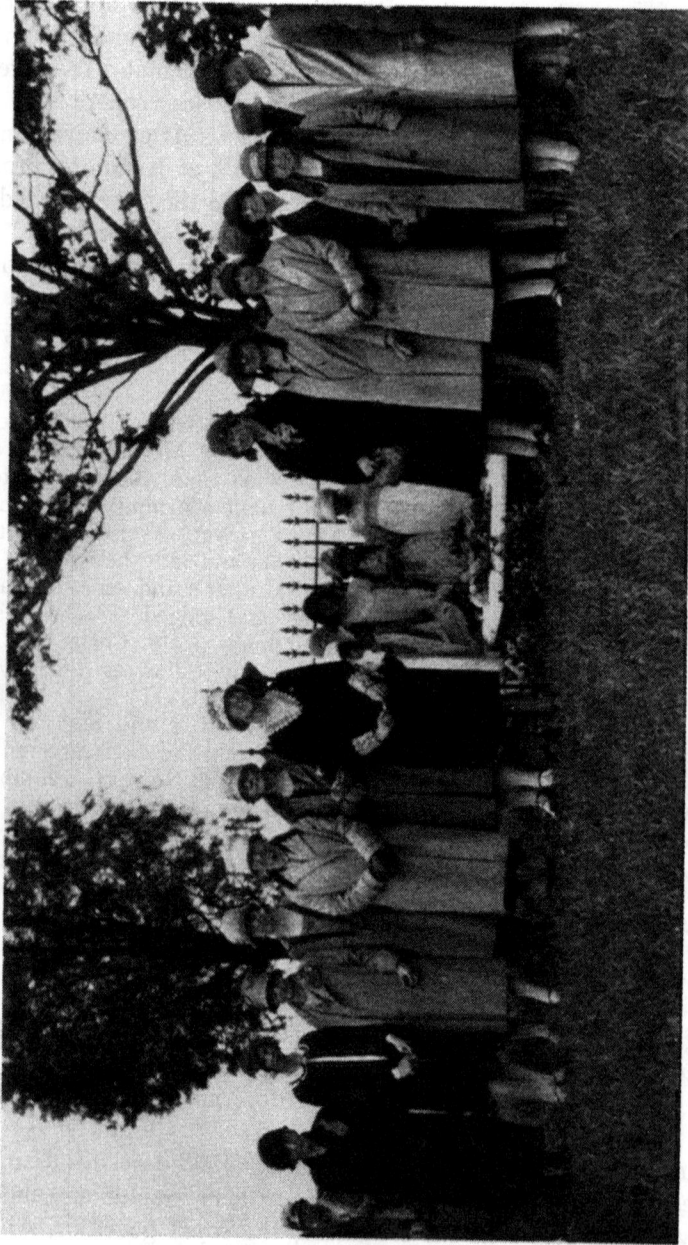

Dedication, 1927, of the restored tomb of Betty Washington Lewis at "Western View," two miles east of Culpeper, Va., by the Culpeper Minute Men Chapter, D. A. R.

the Virginia Assembly provided for a manufactory of arms and ammunition at Fredericksburg, Fielding Lewis, then a man of fifty, was one of five commissioners appointed to direct the work. He and Charles Dick carried on the operations. The factory, or one of the factories, was located on the north side of the Rappahannock, just above Falmouth. Only a few years ago ruins of the old forge could still be seen there.

The small appropriations that the revolting colony was able to make were soon exhausted. Then Colonel Lewis used 7000 pounds of his own money and borrowed more, to continue the factories, mortgaging Kenmore and his other properties heavily. Before the treaty of peace was concluded he died, in December 1781 or January 1782. His will had been drawn up on October 19, 1781, the very day that his brother-in-law received the surrender of Cornwallis at Yorktown. He was buried, it is said, under the front steps of St. George's Episcopal Church in Fredericksburg.

Poverty faced his widow, Betty Washington Lewis, and her children. In a brave struggle for competence she opened at Kenmore a boarding school for girls, but in 1796 she sold the cherished home and went to live with her daughter Betty, the wife of Charles Carter, at Western View, in Culpeper County. There she died and was buried.

Western View, two miles east of Culpeper Court House, was in the days of its prosperity a handsome and well-appointed country place. The mansion house was burned or otherwise removed many years ago, but the outlines of the foundation may still be traced by trenches where the walls ran and small mounds that indicate the positions of the chimneys. The spacious grounds are shaded by many ancient trees, which give the old homestead an air of dignity and historic charm. The driveway that led up to the front of the dwelling is still deeply furrowed from the wheels and hoofs of years long gone—following its gentle curves one may easily fall into dreams. A few hundred yards to the west of the home site a small grove shelters the family graveyard. There until a few years ago the grave of Betty Washington Lewis was marked only with small rough stones. Now it is covered with a substantial table tomb and enclosed with a strong iron fence. The slab bears the following inscription:

SACRED
TO THE MEMORY OF
MRS. BETTY WASHINGTON LEWIS
WHO WAS THE WIFE OF
COL. FIELDING LEWIS
AND THE SISTER OF
GENERAL GEORGE WASHINGTON
BORN AT WAKEFIELD
JUNE 20, 1733
DIED AT WESTERN VIEW
CULPEPER CO.
MARCH 31, 1797

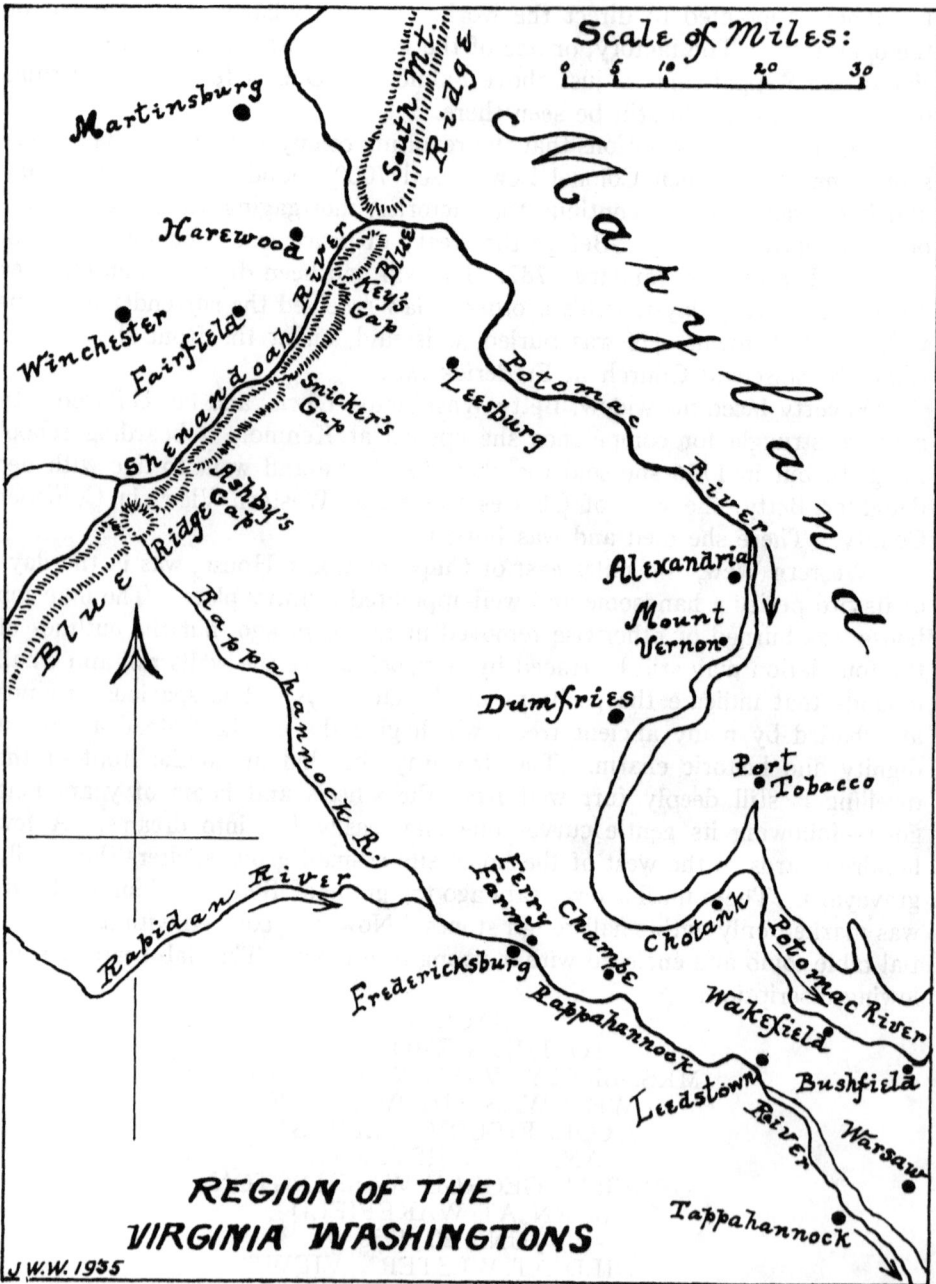

REGION OF THE
VIRGINIA WASHINGTONS

J.W.W. 1935

Erected in 1927 by
The Culpeper Minute Men
Chapter, D. A. R.

Mrs. Lewis's daughter, Betty Lewis Carter, is buried at "North Hill," in Clarke County, Va., near "Springbury," where her brother, Major George Lewis, had lived for some years. North Hill is just southwest of the highway near the northwest end of the bridge over the Shenandoah River at Castleman's Ferry. The old graveyard is half-way up the hill in a small grove of ash and walnut trees. Small rough stones show the locations of some of the graves. Mrs. Carter's is the only one with an inscribed marker, a large slab of marble broken through the middle. Some years ago it was fixed on a brick base by the Fort Loudoun Chapter, D. A. R. On the slab her virtues are commemorated and the following items of information are given concerning herself and her family:

IN MEMORY OF
Mrs. Betty Carter
relict of the late Charles Carter, Esqr.
She was born in the town of Fredericksburg
on the 22nd day of February, 1765,
and departed this life on Good Friday,
the 9th of April, 1830,
aged 65 years.
She was the daughter of Mrs. Betty Lewis,
only sister of Genl. George Washington.
* * * * *
Also in memory of
Mrs. Sarah C. Peyton,
Elizabeth W., and Edward Carter,
Children of Charles & Betty Carter,
interred in this place.

In 1908 Kenmore was the residence of Mr. Clarence Randolph Howard. In 1922 the Kenmore Association was formed. This organization of patriotic women, with branches in many states, has acquired the property, restored it as much as possible to its original condition, and collected therein furniture and portraits of rare beauty and value. The grounds, with their deftly placed trees and shrubs, present a scene of unpretentious but unsurpassed charm. The distance from the Mary Washington house, up the gentle incline of Lewis Street, is only 300 yards. Almost in front of the mansion, in a spacious parkway of Washington Avenue, stands an imposing monument to General Hugh Mercer, who died in the arms of young George Lewis on the battlefield of Princeton. A short distance farther to the west rises the tall white shaft over the grave of Mary Washington, in the spot chosen by herself, beneath the stately trees that overhang Meditation Rocks, and in plain sight of Kenmore, her daughter's home.

CHAPTER V

MARY WASHINGTON IN FREDERICKSBURG

May 7, 1833, was notable in the historical calendar of Fredericksburg, a calendar which is liberally spangled with red-letter days. In a distinguished assemblage President Andrew Jackson was the guest of honor and the chief speaker. The occasion was the laying of a cornerstone for a monument to Mary, the mother of Washington, who had died here forty-four years earlier. A great throng had assembled. Colonel John Bankhead as chief marshal led the imposing parade which preceded the addresses by the President and other eminent men; the speeches were followed by feasting and drinking in which wines, liquors, and barbecued beef were served to some 5000 people under a big tent.

Judge John T. Goolrick, in his interesting volume, "Historic Fredericksburg," pages 153, 154, states that President Jackson came down by boat from Washington to Quantico, and thence by land conveyance; and relates how the President was rudely accosted on the way by a Major Randolph whose appeal from a court martial to the President had not met with the favor which the Major had hoped for.

The laudable steps taken in 1833 to erect a monument to Mary Washington were not thoroughly successful, though a handsome and elaborate design was fashioned and the lower sections put in place. Work was arrested, probably for lack of money, and the unfinished structure stood on the ground for many years. Finally a new movement, to which our attention shall be directed later, was more successful.

At some time between 1770 and 1776 Mary Washington, urged and aided by her son George and her daughter Betty, Mrs. Fielding Lewis, left the Ferry Farm, moved across the river, and took up her abode in a small frame house which, enlarged on two sides, is still well preserved at the corner of Charles Street and Lewis Street. On September 18, 1772, George Washington, for 225 pounds, purchased this site, with whatever improvements were then on it, of Michael Robinson and his wife Esther. The land area consisted of two half-acres, described on the plat of the town as the lots numbered 107 and 108, the same that Michael Robinson had purchased of Fielding Lewis and his wife Betty on October 13, 1761; with all houses, edifices, buildings, orchards, gardens, etc., thereunto belonging. Lot No. 107 is in the corner of the streets, Charles and Lewis, and contains the dwelling house; lot No. 108 lies alongside Lewis Street and extends up towards Kenmore, the home of Fielding and Betty Lewis.

Perhaps Mrs. Washington moved over the same autumn (1772). If the house was enlarged beforehand, her moving was later. In March 1775, as General Washington's diary shows, he spent three or four days in Fredericksburg, and that may have been the time when he and his sister, Mrs. Lewis,

Mary Washington House, on Lot 107, Fredericksburg. See map. Photo about 1925.

assisted their mother in moving and getting settled in her new home. Whenever it was, Charles Washington, Mary's youngest son, who was still living in Fredericksburg, probably rendered assistance also. The new location, as already indicated, placed Mrs. Washington within a few rods of Kenmore, her daughter's home, and probably within two or three blocks of her son Charles's residence.

Her house stood flush on the street corner, fronting 26 feet on Charles Street, with the gable of 18 feet on Lewis—it is of the original house that we are now speaking. The main floor may have been divided by partitions, but if so they have all been removed and visitors now see the main floor all in one. Above is a half-story with dormer windows. The bedroom in the half-story was occasionally occupied, we are told, by General Washington, General Lafayette, and other distinguished guests of Mrs. Washington.

Whatever the dates were, the original house, just described, has been enlarged by two additions, one of frame, 21 by 32 feet, two stories high, alongside Charles Street; the other, of brick, 18 by 26 feet, one story, abutting on Lewis Street. This brick annex was probably used as a dining room. The kitchen, with its wide fireplace, iron crane, and collection of pots, pans, and kettles, is only a few feet away. Around the kitchen and beyond, towards Kenmore, is the old garden in which Mrs. Washington was so often found at work among her shrubs and flowers. It may be that some still growing here were planted by her. Old-time flowers, medicinal herbs, dwarf box, tree box, and trees of several varieties remain. One of the trees is an ailanthus, another is a species of paper tree.

In this garden are now preserved two interesting relics—carved pieces of marble that were parts of the monument to Mrs. Washington that was projected in 1833, but never finished. These marbles and other assembled materials stood or lay on the ground at her grave for many years—were there during the years of the Civil War—and were between the firing lines in the fierce battles of December 1862, when some of them were broken by shot and shell.

The distance from the Mary Washington house to Kenmore mansion is only 300 yards up a slight incline, along Lewis Street. One of the box-bordered paths in the garden leads towards Kenmore, and along this fragrant walk the aging woman frequently passed, to and fro, on her familiar visits to Kenmore and the rocky ledge on the hillside just beyond, where, under the sheltering oaks on balmy days, she spent many a quiet hour reading and meditating. The ledge has come to be known as "Meditation Rocks." There she selected the spot for her grave.

It appears certain that Lewis Street was named for Mrs. Washington's distinguished son-in-law, Colonel Fielding Lewis, of Kenmore, and it is probable that Charles Street derived its name from her son, Charles Washington, though this conclusion has not been verified. Nearly all the old streets of Fredericksburg were named for members of the royal family in England. Says Captain S. J. Quinn:

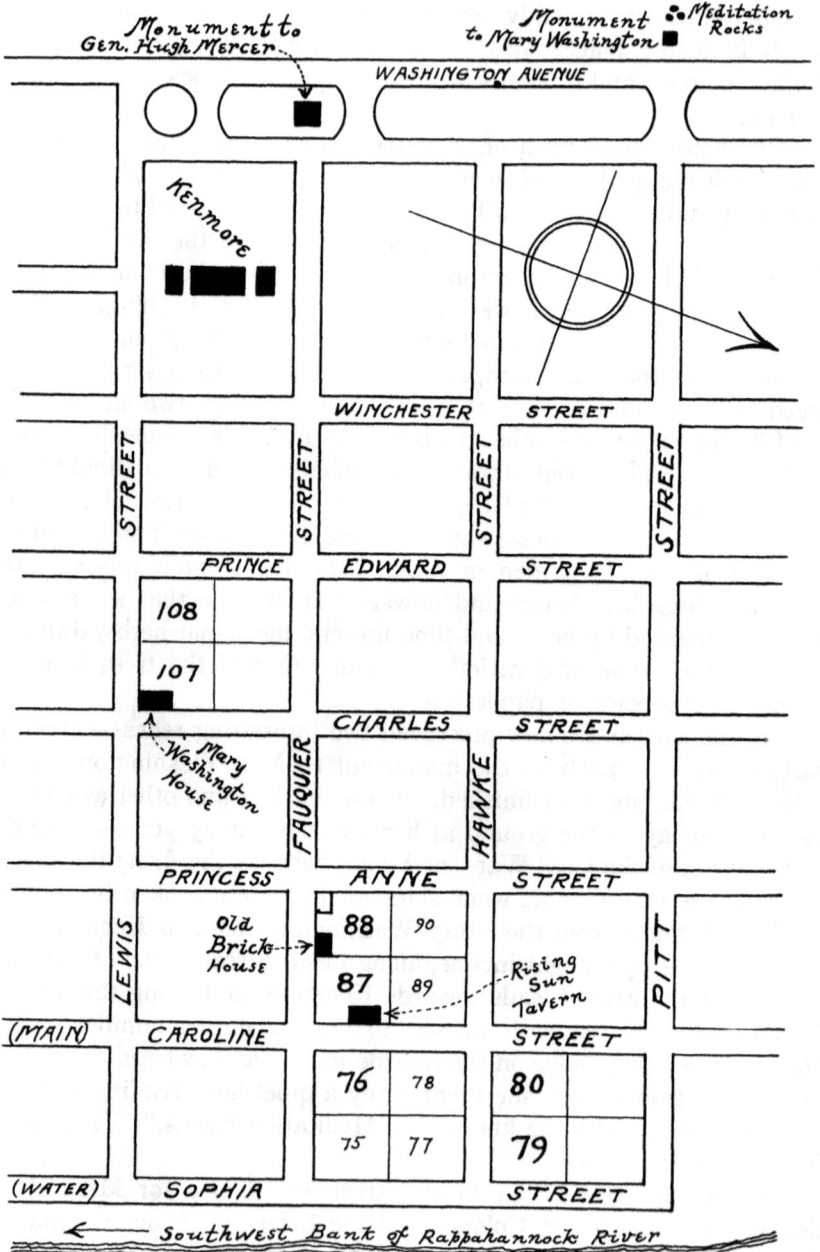

Some of the Houses and Lots in Fredericksburg Owned by the Washingtons

Sophia Street was named for the sister of George II; Caroline for his wife; Princess Anne for one of his daughters, and Prince Edward for his grandson. The cross streets were named, Princess Elizabeth for a daughter of George II; Frederick for his eldest son; William for his second son, and Amelia for a daughter. George was named for the King himself; Charlotte for the wife of George III; Hanover for the House of Hanover, and Prussia for the country of Prussia. This includes every street in the original survey except Charles and Wolfe. We do not know for whom these two streets were named, and we think the evidence is very clear that they were not laid out as streets at the time of the original survey.

(See "The History of the City of Fredericksburg, Virginia," by S. J. Quinn; 1908; pages 37, 38.)

Charles Washington was a property-owner and otherwise a man of consequence in Fredericksburg until or almost until 1780. A few years later a town was laid out on his land in what is now Jefferson County, West Virginia, and named in his honor Charles Town. In this town the streets were named for members of the Washington family, much as the streets of Fredericksburg were named for members of the royal family.

Among the distinguished guests whom Mrs. Washington received from time to time in her unpretentious home in Fredericksburg were George Mason, Thomas Jefferson, John Marshall, several of the Lees, and General Lafayette. The last, it is said, found her at work in the garden, and when he departed remarked, "I have seen the only Roman matron of my day." It was in the garden, too, as tradition has it, that Mrs. Washington one day declared to some friends concerning her illustrious son, then in the thick of the Revolutionary War, "I am sure I shall hear some day that they have hung George."

This was a possible tragedy feared, certainly not hoped for, though Mrs. Washington remained loyal to the King—was an avowed Tory. She, like Lord Fairfax, Washington's first employer and his continuing friend, could love George and get along cordially with her neighbors, even though she could not approve of the Revolution. We can imagine her mingled or conflicting emotions when she read her son's personal message to her after his hazardous and eventful crossing of the Delaware, as she stated the news to a group of neighbors: "Well, George has crossed the Delaware and defeated the King's troops at Trenton." Five years later, when word came that he had received the surrender of Cornwallis at Yorktown, she had perhaps become reconciled to the new order that seemed inevitable. Her wishes had kept her son from being a sailor—the boy had been obedient as well as respectful. As a man he continued to be respectful, though he could not always be obedient. She no doubt gave due consideration to the responsibilities that manhood had thrust upon him.

Mary Washington reached and slightly passed the mark of four-score years, in spite of the fact that a cancer, painful and incurable, hastened the

Garden in rear of Mary Washington House, Fredericksburg. Photo by Holladay, 1931.

end. Two neighbors, Dr. Charles Mortimer and Dr. Elisha Hall, were her physicians. The skill of the eminent Dr. Benjamin Rush of Philadelphia was also enlisted in her behalf, but evidently without avail. Dr. Hall was a cousin to Dr. Rush and consulted him with regard to Mrs. Washington. On July 6, 1789, Dr. Rush wrote to Dr. Hall as follows:

The respectable age and character of your venerable patient lead me to regret that it is not in my power to suggest a remedy for the cure of the disorder you have described in her breast. I know nothing of the root you mention, found in Carolina and Georgia, but, from a variety of inquiries and experiments, I am disposed to believe that there does not exist in the vegetable kingdom an antidote to cancers. All the *supposed vegetable* remedies I have heard of are compounds of some mineral caustics. The arsenic is the most powerful of any of them. It is the basis of Dr. Martin's powder. I have used it in many cases with success, but have failed in some. From your account of Mrs. Washington's breast I am afraid no great good can be expected from the use of it. Perhaps it may cleanse it, and thereby retard its spreading. You may try it diluted in water. Continue the application of opium and camphor, and wash it frequently with a decoction of red clover. Give anodynes, when necessary, and support the system with bark and wine. Under this treatment she may live comfortably many years, and finally die of old age.

But the sanguine possibility expressed by Dr. Rush was not justified by the event—Mrs. Washington died seven weeks after his letter was written.

According to Captain Quinn, whose valuable history of Fredericksburg was published in 1908, Dr. Hall lived on the lot which was later occupied by the residence of Dr. J. E. Tompkin. The home of Dr. Mortimer, Mrs. Washington's other doctor, was far down on Main (Caroline) Street, not far from the historic "Sentry Box," which was the residence in succession of two soldiers of the Revolution, General Hugh Mercer and General George Weedon. Midway between the "Sentry Box" and the Mortimer house, which is a two-story brick structure well preserved, is the narrow rock-walled lane which leads up from the old ferry on the river to Main Street. This is the lane by which Mary Washington's children and other members of her household, crossing from Ferry Farm, came up into the lower part of the town. The Mortimer house, says Captain Quinn, was built by Roger Dixon, a gentleman of means, who owned most of the land at the lower part of the town, in or about the year 1764. Shortly after that date the property was purchased by Dr. Charles Mortimer, who was the first mayor of Fredericksburg, and the friend and physician of Mary Washington.

Pleasing stories are told of an elaborate dinner which was given in the Mortimer home, following a grand ball in the old market house, in celebration of victory and peace at the end of the Revolution. Maria Mortimer, sixteen years old, the Doctor's only daughter, with her hair done up in lady-like style for the first time, presided, and her ready wit, no less than her grace and beauty, won the plaudits of the distinguished company, among whom were

CHARLES STREET

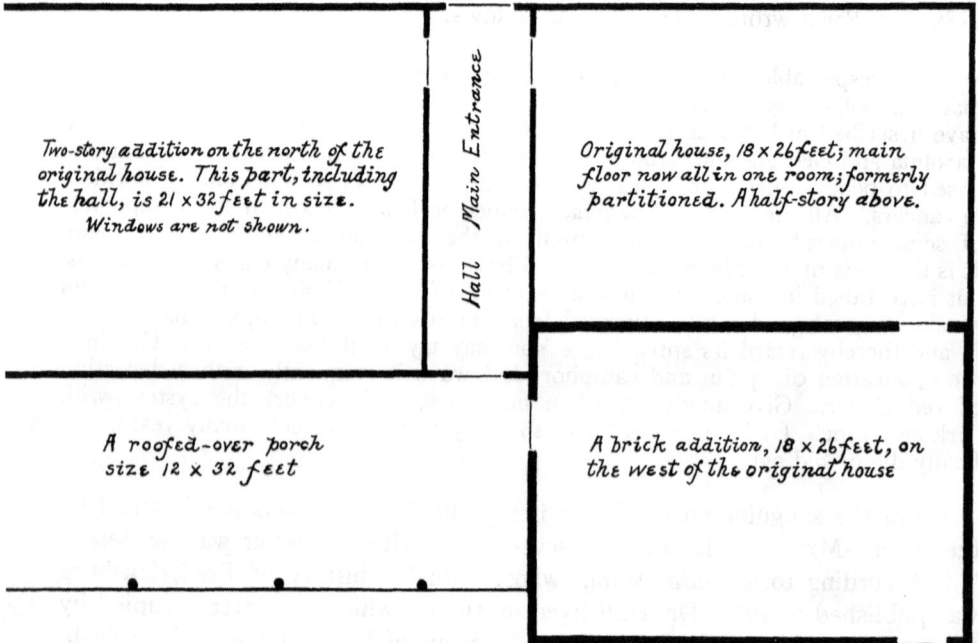

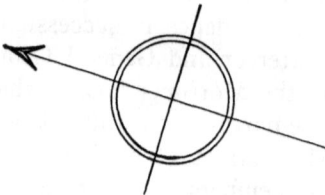

Two-story addition on the north of the original house. This part, including the hall, is 21 x 32 feet in size. Windows are not shown.

Hall Main Entrance

Original house, 18 x 26 feet; main floor now all in one room; formerly partitioned. A half-story above.

A roofed-over porch size 12 x 32 feet

A brick addition, 18 x 26 feet, on the west of the original house

Fence

PLAN OF MARY WASHINGTON HOUSE

CORNER OF CHARLES AND LEWIS STREET, FREDERICKSBURG

Kitchen, with wide fireplace, crane, &c.

GROUNDS IN REAR OF THE HOUSE

THE GARDEN EXTENDS FARTHER WESTWARD

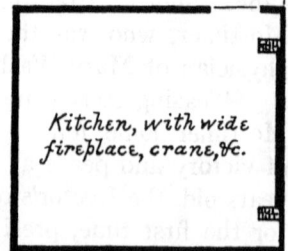

Lafayette, Count d' Estaing, Rochambeau, and General Washington. But little Maria was most elated, if reports may be credited, at having danced with Washington himself.

Critical historians have a habit of dissecting good stories. From recent disclosures it appears that the ball referred to above was not held until February 1784, two or three years later than was generally supposed, and that the distinguished French officers named were probably not present. See the *Virginia Magazine of History and Biography*, April, 1941, pages 152-156.

No doubt General Washington, his brothers, and their sister, Mrs. Fielding Lewis, as well as their mother, were frequent visitors at the genial doctor's house. From its rear windows one looks across the river to the Ferry Farm on the opposite bank, with the Stafford hills rising in the background. To the river wharves long ago sailing ships came up to discharge their cargoes from across the Atlantic, having gone out laden with tobacco, iron, and other products of the new country. Here George Washington, as a vigorous boy and youth, threw stones across the river, and here on Washington's birthday in 1936 Walter Johnson threw a silver dollar across just to prove that it could be done.

The distance from Mary Washington's house down to Dr. Mortimer's is about three-quarters of a mile—perhaps a little more. She may have walked down occasionally, but it is probable that in her later years she drove, riding in her phaeton, drawn by the bay horse, or perhaps in her chaise ("chair"), drawn by one of the blacks. The driver in any case was almost certainly one of her Negro men, Tom or Frederick. In her will she devised Tom to her son Charles, Frederick to her grandson, Fielding Lewis. The phaeton and the bay horse went to her daughter, Betty Lewis, the "chair" and the two blacks to her grandson, Corbin Washington.

The original of Mrs. Washington's will may be seen in the office of the city clerk in Fredericksburg. It was drawn on May 20, 1788; written for her by James Mercer, one of the subscribing witnesses; and signed by her in a good plain hand. Following is an accurate copy, with the paragraphs arranged as in the original, though the distribution of words in the lines has not been preserved. The spelling of words, use of capitals, and punctuation (or lack of it) have been carefully followed.

WILL OF MARY WASHINGTON

In the Name of God! Amen—I Mary Washington of Fredericksburg in the County of Spotsylvania, being in good health, but calling to mind the uncertainty of this Life and willing to dispose of what remains of my worldly Estate, do make & publish this my last will, recommending my Soul into the Hands of my Creator, hoping for a remission of all my Sins through the merits & mediation of Jesus Christ, the Saviour of Mankind; I dispose of all my worldly Estate as follows—

Monument to Mary Washington at Fredericksburg begun in 1833. Some of these materials were still on the ground during the battles of December, 1862, and were partly shattered by shot and shell. In 1894 the new (present) monument was dedicated on the same spot.

Imprimis I give to my Son General George Washington all my Lands on Accokeek Run in the County of Stafford & also my Negroe Boy George to him & his Heirs for ever. also my best bed, bedstead & Virginia Cloth Curtains (the same that stands in my best Room) my quilted blue & white Quilt & my best dressing Glass—

Item I give and devise to my Son Charles Washington my Negroe Man Tom to him & his assigns for ever—

Item I give and devise to my Daughter Betty Lewis, my Phaeton & my bey Horse.

Item I give & devise to my Daughter in Law Hannah Washington my purple Cloath cloak lined with Shag—

Item I give & devise to my grand Son Corbin Washington my Negroe wench Old Bet my riding Chair & two blk Horses, to him & his Assigns for ever—

Item I give & devise to grand Son Fielding Lewis my Negroe man Frederick to him & his Assigns for ever, also eight Silver table Spoons, half my Cooking ware, & the blue & white Tea China, with the book Case, Oval Table, one Bed bedstead, one pr. Sheets, one pr. blankets & white Cotton Counterpaine—two table Cloaths, Six red leather Chairs, half my pewter & one half my Iron kitchen Furniture—

Item I give & devise to my grandson Lawrence Lewis my Negroe wench Lydia to him & his assigns for ever—

Item I give & devise to my grand daughter Betty Carter, my negroe woman little Bet & her future increase to her & her Assigns for ever—Also my largest looking glass, my walnut writing Desk with Drawers, a square dining Table, one Bed Bedstead, bolster, one pillow one blanket, & pr. Sheets, white Virginia Cloth Counterpaine & purple Curtains, my red & white tea China, tea Spoons, & the other half of my pewter, Crokery ware, & the remainder of my Iron kitchen Furniture—

Item I give to my grand Son George Washington my next best dressing Glass, one Bed, Bedstead bolster, 1 pillow 1 pr Sheets 1 blanket & Counterpaine—

Item I devise all my wearing apparel to be equally divided between my grand Daughters, Betty Carter, Fanny Ball, & Milly Washington—but shou'd my Daughter Betty Lewis fancy any one two or three Articles, she is to have them before a division thereof—

Lastly I nominate & appoint my said Son General George Washington Executor of this my will, and as I owe few or no debts I direct my Executor to give no Security—nor to appraise my Estate, but desire the same may be allotted to my Devisees with as little trouble & delay as may be—desiring their acceptance thereof as all the Token I now have to give them of my Love for them—In witness whereof I have hereunto set my Hand & Seal this 20th day of May 1788—

Mary Washington (SEAL)

Witness
John Ferneyhough

Signed Sealed and published
in our presence & signed by Us   Js. Mercer
in the presence of the sd. Mary   Joseph Walker
Washington & at her desire

The daughter-in-law, Hannah Washington, to whom went the "purple Cloath cloak lined with Shag," was the widow of John Augustine Washington, who had died just the year before. Hannah was the daughter of Colonel John Bushrod of Bushfield, Westmoreland County, Va., and the mother of Judge Bushrod Washington, a later owner of Mount Vernon, and of Corbin Washington. To her General George Washington left a "mourning ring of the value of one hundred dollars" in his will made July 9, 1799.

Corbin Washington, younger brother of Judge Bushrod Washington, born in 1765, married Hannah Lee, daughter of Richard Henry Lee. He died in Fairfax County, Va., in 1799 or 1800.

Fielding Lewis and Lawrence Lewis were sons of Colonel Fielding Lewis

Monument at the grave of Mary Washington, dedicated in 1894. It occupies the site of a monument that was begun in 1833. Photo 1931.

and his second wife, Betty Washington. Lawrence married Nelly Custis, General Washington's adopted daughter, on February 22, 1799.

Mary Washington had two Washington grandsons named George: George Augustine (1763-1793), son of Charles Washington, and George Steptoe (1774-1809), son of Samuel Washington. The former was probably her legatee. Betty Carter was the daughter of Colonel Fielding Lewis and his wife Betty Washington. Fanny Ball was the daughter of Charles Washington and the wife of Colonel Burgess Ball. "Milly Washington" was the daughter of either John Augustine Washington or his brother Charles—each had a daughter Mildred.

Three weeks after Mary Washington had made her will her son, General Washington, and his wife paid her a visit, as recorded in the General's diary. They stopped on the way down at Colchester, Rippon Lodge, Stafford Court House, and Chatham. They intended to dine at Chatham the second day, but inasmuch as the Fitzhughs were not at home they crossed the river to Fredericksburg, alighted at Mrs. Washington's, and sent the horses and carriage to Kenmore, where they dined and lodged. This was on Wednesday, June 11, 1788. The General's mother was probably declining rapidly at this time. She died on August 25, the next year, aged eighty-one. Her will was proved on October 23, 1789, in the hustings court for the town of Fredericksburg by the oath of James Mercer, Esq., and ordered to be certified. It was further proved on October 22, 1804, by the oath of Joseph Walker.

In 1889, a hundred years after the death of Mary Washington, patriotic women in Fredericksburg and Boston revived the movement for erecting a monument over her grave, Mrs. James P. Smith, Mrs. John T. Goolrick, and Mrs. Margaret Hetzel being active leaders in the enterprise. Through the influence of an organization in Fredericksburg, a national association was formed in Washington City with Mrs. Chief Justice Waite as president. On May 10, 1894, President Cleveland was the chief figure at the dedication of a tall white shaft where President Jackson had made his address 61 years before. A special train from Washington brought the President, Chief Justice Fuller, members of the Cabinet, ladies of the National Mary Washington Association, Daughters of the American Revolution, and the U. S. Marine Band. Governor Charles T. O'Ferrall came from Richmond. Among Mary Washington's descendants present were members of the Ball family and Mr. Lawrence Washington, a descendant of her son, John Augustine Washington. The main address was delivered by the distinguished orator, Hon. John Warwick Daniel. The monument is composed of a solid granite shaft 50 feet high, resting on a square base with the inscription, "Mary, the Mother of Washington," in raised letters. The total height is nearly 60 feet.

In the Masonic lodge room in Fredericksburg, in which are preserved many historic treasures, is a small painting of the original unfinished monument to Mary Washington which was removed in 1893 to give place to the present one.

"Meditation Rocks," near Kenmore, favorite resort in old age of Mary Washington. Her grave and monument are near by. Photo 1933.

CHAPTER VI

EARLIER YEARS AT MOUNT VERNON

The first Washington to own land at Hunting Creek, now Mount Vernon, was John, George's great-grandfather. He was born in 1632, just a hundred years before his eminent descendant, and died in 1676, the year of Bacon's Rebellion. In 1669 John Washington and Nicholas Spencer had 5000 acres surveyed on Hunting Creek and applied for a patent to it. The patent was issued early in 1674. Washington willed his 2500 acres to his son Lawrence, who left it to his daughter Mildred. She sold it to her brother Augustine, George's father. The latter, as we have seen in a preceding chapter, lived there from 1735 to 1738 and in his will, made at Ferry Farm in 1743, left it to his son Lawrence, George's older half-brother.

Lawrence Washington, soon after his father's death in April 1743 married Ann, eldest daughter of William Fairfax of Belvoir, and lived at Mount Vernon. The first house there, it is said, had burned in or about 1739. A new one, the nucleus of the present mansion, was built when Lawrence Washington and Ann Fairfax were married, or shortly before, and in it they made their home. Lawrence named the place Mount Vernon in honor of Admiral Vernon, under whom he had served in the West Indies. By 1747 and thereabouts George Washington, a lad of fifteen, was occasionally at Mount Vernon, where he became acquainted with Thomas Lord Fairfax, who soon employed him as an explorer and surveyor. In 1751, when Lawrence went to Barbadoes in a vain search for health, George went with him, recording his observations and experiences in a most interesting diary. One of his experiences in Barbadoes was small pox. George, coming home ahead of Lawrence, reached Mount Vernon on March 6, 1752, with messages from Lawrence to his wife Ann and young daughter Sarah. Lawrence went from Barbadoes to Bermuda, but soon returned to Virginia. He made his will on June 20 (O. S.), 1752, and died on July 26 (August 6).

Lawrence Washington, though only 35 or thereabouts when he died, was a man of means, influence, and wide experience. He had been educated in England; had served as a member of the House of Burgesses from the new county of Fairfax from 1742 to 1749; in 1749 had been one of the organizers of the Ohio Company, which received from King George II a grant for 500,000 acres of land in the Ohio Valley. He, like his father, was interested in the manufacture of iron on both sides of the Potomac; was a captain in the British army, and had served under Admiral Vernon in the expedition against Carthagena on the coast of South America. Later he was commissioned a major in the Virginia service. His will, which is recorded at Fairfax, Va., provided for the payment of his debts and the construction at Mount Vernon of a "proper vault" for the interment of himself and family.

His wife Ann was to have the use, benefit, and profits of all his lands

Major Lawrence Washington, owner of Mount Vernon from 1743 to 1752; from a portrait now in the possession of the Mount Vernon Ladies' Association. Mr. Julian H. Washington supplied this photograph which was made while the portrait was owned by his family.

on Little Hunting Creek and Doeg Run, with all houses and edifices thereon, during her natural life, with the use, labor, and profit from half of his Negroes. She was to have also the use of his lands surveyed on the South Fork of Bullskin in Frederick County, during her natural life, and if Sarah should die without issue before her mother the Bullskin tract was to go to Ann and her heirs forever. And she was to have a part of the household goods, liquors, etc.

His daughter Sarah and her heirs were to have all his real and personal estate in Virginia and Maryland after his debts were paid and special bequests taken off; but if Sarah should die without issue his real and personal estate was to be disposed of as follows:

His stock, interest, and estate in the Principio, Accokeek, Kingsbury, Lancashire, and North East Iron Works in Virginia and Maryland, reserving one-third of the profits for his wife, and the two tracts of land in Frederick County which he had purchased of Colonel Cresap and Gerrard Pendergrass were to go to his brother Augustine;

All his lands in Fairfax County, with improvements thereon, after the decease of his wife, were to go to his brother George; and during her life George was to have use of an equal share of the lands given to his brothers Samuel, John, and Charles;

All those several tracts of land in Frederick County of which he was possessed, except the tract on the South Fork of Bullskin and the two purchased of Cresap and Pendergrass, were devised to Samuel, John (John Augustine), and Charles; and the devisees to pay Betty Lewis 150 pounds.

Other dispositions were made of his lands near Salisbury Plain, those on a branch of Goose Creek, and his two lots in Alexandria. His share and interest in the Ohio Company were to be sold and the proceeds applied to his debts. He appointed as executors Hon. William Fairfax, George Fairfax, his brothers Augustine and George, and his friends Nathal. Chapman and Major John Carlyle. William Fairfax was his father-in-law, George Fairfax was his brother-in-law; Nathaniel Chapman was one of the executors of his father, Augustine Washington; John Carlyle was a merchant of Alexandria.

John Carlyle that same year (1752) built a house in Alexandria which still remains, one of the most celebrated in that historic old town. Carlyle, too, was a brother-in-law of Lawrence Washington, having married Sarah Fairfax, a daughter of William.

Lawrence Washington died in the late summer of 1752. His will was proved on September 26 (October 7). Sarah, his young daughter, died soon afterwards. Ann, the widow, married George Lee of Westmoreland County, December 17, 1752; died in 1761.

George Washington in 1754 bought out the right, title, and interest of his sister-in-law and thus became the full owner of Mount Vernon. There he and his brother John Augustine kept "bachelor's hall" until 1756, when

Lawn and northwest front of Mount Vernon Mansion. This was originally the main front. Photo by Holladay, 1921.

John married Hannah Bushrod of Westmoreland and brought her to his
brother's home. John and Hannah managed the estate while George was away
in the French and Indian War. George on January 6, 1759, married Mrs.
Martha Custis and about that time repaired and enlarged the dwelling house,
raising it from a story and a half to two stories and a half. In it, as thus
enlarged, he, his wife, and her children lived for many years.

Life at Mount Vernon even in those days did not altogether lack refinements. On May 1, 1761, Washington sent a letter to Robert Cary & Co.,
London merchants, informing them of his marriage to Mrs. Custis and directing them to address him thereafter in regard to any business they had with
the estate of Mrs. Washington's late husband, Daniel Parke Custis; and at
the same time he gave them an order for a quantity of furniture, clothing,
seeds, and books on agriculture. In September of the same year he forwarded
another order for various articles: three pounds of Scotch snuff, an hogshead
of the best porter, three gallons of Rhenish wine in bottles; busts of Alexander
the Great, Julius Cæsar, Charles XII of Sweden, Prince Eugene, the Duke
of Marlborough; "two Wild Beasts, not to exceed twelve inches in height nor
eighteen in length"; and for Mrs. Washington "a salmon-colored Tabby of
the enclosed pattern, with satin flowers, to be made in a sack and coat; a
Cap, Handkerchief, Tucker and Ruffles to be made of Brussels lace, or point,
. . . to cost £20"; satin shoes, both black and white, of the smallest 5's.
(See "The Family Life of George Washington," by Charles Moore, 1926,
pages 75, 76.)

Lace for luxury, wines for good fellowship, snuff for a custom of the
times; seeds for the farmer, books for the student; wild beasts for the hunts-
man and the lover of the chase; effigies of great commanders for the soldier.
In not many years the soldier was again called forth, not to brilliance, but
to fortitude; not to great armies with abundant resources, but finally to great
victories.

Early in the Revolution, in the summer of 1775, Lord Dunmore ascended
the Potomac as far as Occoquan, with the intention, as it appeared, of making
Mrs. Washington a prisoner and desolating the estates of Mount Vernon and
Gunston Hall; but the Prince William militia, aided by a severe storm, check-
ed his advance. He then retired down the river after destroying some mills
and other property. In 1781 British armed vessels came up the river, plun-
dering and destroying. One approached Mount Vernon, but Lund Washington, the General's cousin who was manager there during the war, purchased
immunity by giving the commander of the vessel refreshments and supplies.
For this the General reproved Lund severely. In a letter to him he wrote
as follows:

It would have been a less painful circumstance to me to have heard that,
in consequence of your non-compliance with their request, they had burned my
house and laid the plantation in ruins. You ought to have considered yourself

Mount Vernon Mansion, from the south—the usual view. This front faces the Potomac River.

as my representative, and should have reflected on the bad example of communi-
cating with the enemy and making a voluntary offer of refreshment to them with
a view to prevent a conflagration. . . . I am fully persuaded that you acted from
your best judgment, and believe that your desire to preserve my property and
rescue the buildings from impending danger was your governing motive; but to
go on board their vessels, carry them refreshments, commune with a parcel of
scoundrels, and request a favor by asking a surrender of my negroes was ex-
ceedingly ill-judged, and, it is to be feared, will be unhappy in its consequences,
as it will be a precedent for others and may become a subject of animadversion.

From time to time during the Revolution Mrs. Washington spent considerable periods with the General in camp, where she gave much attention
to the sick and needy soldiers, as, for example, in the terrible winter at Valley
Forge. She remarked in later years that it had been her fortune to be at
the opening and the close of all the campaigns of the war. In the summer
months, when hostilities were active, she retired to Mount Vernon and there
gave a fine example to her country-women of thrift and economy. Her dress
during the time of the war is said to have been remarkable for its simplicity,
being composed almost entirely of home-made materials, as were the clothes
of her numerous servants. Among the various domestic industries that she
is reported to have kept going on, was the constant operation of sixteen spin-
ning wheels. On one occasion when two dresses of cotton striped with silk
were admired, she explained that the stripes were woven from the ravelings of
brown silk stockings and old crimson damask chair covers.

The visits of General Washington himself to his home at Mount Vernon
during the Revolution are said to have been infrequent. Early in September
1781 he arrived unexpectedly, late at night, and paused there a day or two
while his army, with that of Rochambeau, was moving southward to join
Lafayette against Cornwallis at Yorktown.

Early in 1784, when Washington heard that Lafayette was planning to
visit America, he sent a message to Madame Lafayette inviting her to accom-
pany the General. "Come, then," he wrote, "let me entreat you, and call my
cottage your home; . . . you will see the plain manner in which we live, and
meet with rustic civility; and you shall taste the simplicity of rural life." The
"cottage," built by his half-brother Lawrence in or about 1743 and enlarged
by himself in 1759, was then of the old gable-roof style, with only four rooms
on each floor. It was soon to be further enlarged and improved.

Much of his time in the earlier half of the year 1785 and occasional
periods in 1786 Washington spent in laying off the gardens and grounds of
Mount Vernon, in planting trees, shrubs, and flowers, and in tending, trim-
ming, and grafting. Evidently he had this work in prospect in the autumn
of 1784 during his trip to the Ohio Valley, for he records in his diary that
he planted six buckeye nuts that he had brought from the mouth of Cheat
River, six acorns from the South Branch of the Potomac, and eight nuts of
the Kentucky coffee tree. His relatives and friends learned of his plans and

Martha Dandridge Custis Washington in early life.

sent him various offerings: his sister Betty, Mrs. Fielding Lewis, of Fredericksburg, provided some filbert sprouts; Mrs. Grayson, whose husband William Grayson had been one of his aides in the Revolution, made him a present of four aspen trees and eight yew trees; Colonel George Mason of Gunston Hall sent him some cherry grafts and rose shoots; Colonel Josiah Parker of Norfolk supplied wild honeysuckle and a number of live oaks; General Henry Lee of Westmoreland donated a dozen horse chestnuts and an equal number of cuttings of tree box; Mr. William Blake of South Carolina presented a royal palmetto; Governor George Clinton of New York, four linden trees; his nephew, George Augustine Washington, 48 seeds of the mahogany tree, which he had brought from the West Indies; and his brother, John Augustine, two barrels of holly berries, from Westmoreland County.

In 1786 were completed, also, certain additions to the mansion house, for which he had made plans shortly before the outbreak of the Revolution. His life was a busy one, his interests were many and varied, and his efficient versatility was amply demonstrated. He operated fisheries on the Potomac; grew tobacco, much of which was shipped to London; he was a successful producer of and dealer in live stock; he was a land surveyor and a skilful engineer of river navigation; he was a merchant miller, supplying not only a local trade, but also shipping flour, corn, and casks to Madeira and the West Indies. His operations as a manufacturer of linen and woollen goods are less familiar, but they evidently were of considerable importance. Nicholas Cresswell, a young Englishman who had been detained in America by the Revolution and who regarded Washington as the leader of an unjustified rebellion, was constrained to speak of him as a "great and wonderful man." Says Cresswell in his journal, "He lived as a country gentleman, much noted for his hospitality, great knowledge in agriculture, and industry in carrying his various manufactories of Linen and Woollen to greater perfection than any man in the Colony."

Inasmuch as Washington's methodical operations in agriculture are now but little known, one may be justified in speaking of them somewhat at length. He was a scientific farmer, shaping his practice upon enlightened theory. He made systematic experiments, observed them carefully, recorded them accurately, and from the knowledge thus gained proceeded to further experiments. He read the best books then available on the subject and made abstracts of them. He kept in touch with the Agricultural Society of Philadelphia, perhaps with other similar bodies. He exchanged seeds and plants with his neighbors and carried on a correspondence with Thomas Jefferson, Arthur Young, and others regarding crops, planting, and cultivation. His diaries, which cover nearly every day of his life from the time he was sixteen years old until the day before his death, a period of 51 years, show clearly his methodical habits of work and study. Such habits, of course, were laborious, but also conducive to successful business and scientific progress.

As a practical farmer, proceeding logically, Washington was on the look-

General Washington's barn at Mount Vernon, erected 1782.

out for good land, wherever he might find it. Carefully he noted the various qualities of soil, and as opportunity was afforded he made tests of different crops here and there to determine the best soil for each particular crop. In May and again in October of the year 1763 he journeyed to the region of the Great Dismal Swamp, on the borders of Virginia and North Carolina, and wrote extended notes of his observations. As early as 1728 Colonel William Byrd had written of the "Great Dismal," as he called it:

It would require a great sum of money to drain it, but the public treasure could not be better bestowed, than to preserve the lives of his majesty's liege people, and at the same time render so great a tract of swamp very profitable, besides the advantage of making a channel to transport by water-carriage goods from Albemarle sound into Nansemond and Elizabeth river, in Virginia.

Some such reclamation and development project as Colonel Byrd suggested was actually undertaken by Washington and a number of associates in an improvement company which they organized and which was chartered in 1764. Only a few of Washington's notes concerning the "Great Dismal" can be given here, but these are typical of his style and method, of his careful observations and specific statements:

Between Cypress Swamp and the last mentioned one we went on horse-back not less than half a mile into the Great Swamp (Dismal) without any sort of difficulty, the horses not sinking over the fetlocks. The first quarter abounding in Pine and Galebury bushes, the Soil being much intermixed with Sand, but afterwards it grew blacker and richer with many young Reeds and few pines, and this, it may be observed here, is the nature of the Swamp in general.

Washington and his associates spent a good deal of money on their Dismal Swamp project. He visited the Swamp again in 1766, 1767, and 1768, possibly at other times. For a while he was manager for the Dismal Swamp Company, as he stated in a letter to Patrick Henry in 1785. It is doubtful, however, whether he or his partners ever realized any adequate returns on their investments in this enterprise. In 1799, when he made his will, he still owned several hundred acres in what he called the "rich Dismal swamp"; and in 1793 he had estimated his holdings in the Dismal Swamp as worth 5000 pounds.

In the Ohio Valley in the autumn of 1770 Washington and Dr. James Craik, with a half-dozen companions, made extended explorations, locating lands for themselves and others. Under date of November 1 he wrote:

A little before eight Oclock we set off with our Canoe up the River, to discover what kind of Lands lay upon the Kanhawa [Kanawha]. The Land on both sides this River just at the Mouth is very fine; but on the East side when you get towards the Hills (which I judge to be about 600 or 700 yards from the River) it appears to be wet, and better adapted for Meadow than tillage; this bottom continues up the East side for about 2 Miles, and by going up the Ohio, a good Tract might be got of bottom Land including the old Shawna Town, which is about 3 Miles up the Ohio just at the Mouth of a Creek, where the aforementioned bottom ends on the East side the Kanhawa.

At the mouth of the Kanawha (the Great Kanawha) Washington and his fellow explorers were upon the ground made bloody and famous four years later, October 10, 1774, in the battle fought there between the whites under Colonel Andrew Lewis and the Indians under Cornstalk and other celebrated chiefs; the site now occupied by the historic town of Point Pleasant.

Besides his land in the Dismal Swamp and some 30,000 acres in the valley of the Ohio River and its tributaries, Washington owned lands in Maryland, Pennsylvania, New York, the District of Columbia, and nine counties of Virginia, including Frederick, Berkeley, Fauquier, Loudoun, and Fairfax. The tracts containing and surrounding Mount Vernon, in Fairfax County, comprised 4000 acres or more. In a letter to Arthur Young, of England, written December 12, 1793, Washington gives interesting particulars about his five farms at and near Mount Vernon, to wit: the Mansion House Farm, Union Farm, Dogue Run Farm, Muddy Hole Farm, and the River Farm. River Farm, the largest, contained 1207 acres of arable land. On it were an overseer's house, a large barn and stables, and quarters for 50 or 60 Negro slaves. Muddy Hole Farm, 476 acres, was supplied with a barn and stables, an "overlooker's" house, and quarters for about 30 Negroes. Dogue Run Farm, 650 acres, had an overseer's house, quarters for 40 or more Negroes, and a new barn. This barn, on a new plan, was circular in shape, thus constructed for convenience in threshing wheat, barley, and similar grain. Union Farm, containing 928 acres of arable land and meadow, was provided with a house for the overseer, quarters for 50-odd Negroes, and a new brick barn. This barn, the owner thought, was equal perhaps to any in America, and for conveniences of all kinds, particularly for sheltering and feeding horses, cattle, and other live stock, scarcely to be exceeded anywhere.

Of the five farms named, that surrounding the mansion house was the smallest, approximating 300 acres. Surrounding and separating these several farms were extensive tracts of woodland.

Although Washington was sometimes termed a tobacco planter (and he was a large grower of tobacco), he did not limit his agricultural operations to tobacco-growing, by any means. He grew wheat, corn, oats, barley, flax, hemp, and other staples, together with various food crops such as potatoes, turnips, carrots, etc. He not only cultivated a wide diversity of crops, he was also continually making observations and tests with seeds, adaptability of soils, methods of planting and cultivation, best weather conditions, and the proper times for sowing and harvesting. Composts of stable manure and muck from the pocosons (swamps) were carefully and regularly prepared. Tables for rotation of crops in the several fields were made out for seven years in advance, and certain plants were put on the schedule for their fertilizing values. Beans, clover, buckwheat, and potatoes were highly regarded for

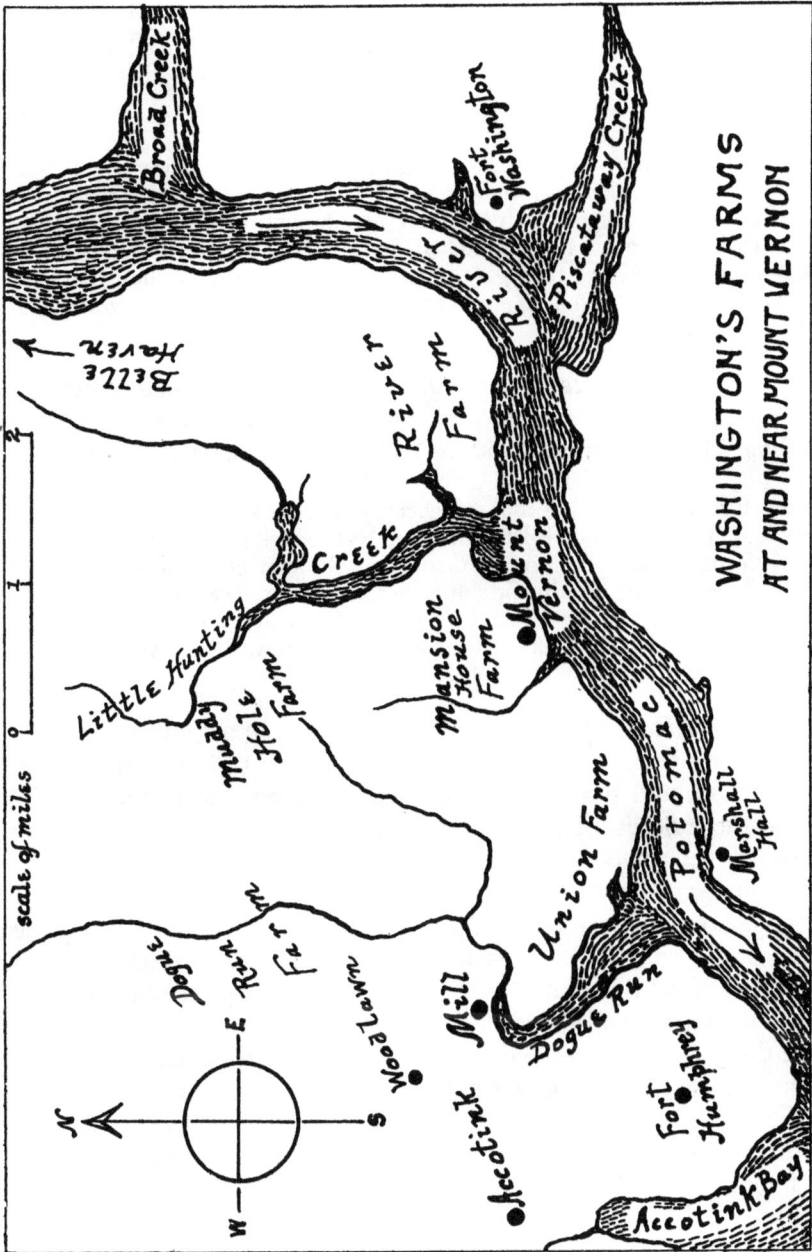

WASHINGTON'S FARMS
AT AND NEAR MOUNT VERNON

their virtues in renewing and mellowing the soil. In a letter to William Strick-
land, of England, he wrote: "The practice of plowing in buckwheat twice in
the season as a fertilizer is not new to me." To Thomas Jefferson, in 1795,
he voiced his enthusiasm for potatoes to improve land. After speaking of
various crops that might be plowed under to loosen and enrich the soil, he
added:

> But of all the improving and ameliorating crops, none in my opinion is equal
> to potatoes, on stiff and hard bound land, as mine is. I am satisfied, from a
> variety of instances, that on such land a crop of potatoes is equal to an ordinary
> dressing. In no instance have I failed of good wheat, oats, or clover, that follow-
> ed potatoes; and I conceive they give the soil a darker hue. I shall thank you for
> the result of your proposed experiments relative to the winter vetch and pea,
> when they are made.

To illustrate the care and minute accuracy with which Washington in
his early years at Mount Vernon carried on his plant laboratories, examples are
not wanting. On March 24, 1760, he entered the following memoranda:

> In the Evening, in a Bed that had been prepared with a mixture of Dung on
> Saturday last, I sowed Choice Lucerne and Rye Grass in the Garden, to try their
> Goodness, doing it in the following Order: at the end next the Corner were two
> Rows of Clover Seed; in the 3d, 4th, 5th, and 6th Rye Grass—the last Row
> thinnest Sowed; 7th and 8th Barley (to see if it would come up)—the last also
> thinnest Sown; 9, 10, 11, 12th Lucerne—first a few Seeds at every 4 Inches
> distance, the next thicker, and so on to the last which was very thick.

Early the next month (April 1760) he prepared a small piece of ground
in the lower corner of the garden for sowing a little trefoil seed given him by
Colonel Fairfax, and next to it he planted Lucerne, "both done with design
to see how these Seeds answer in that Ground." He sowed his fallow field in
oats; got several composts and laid them to dry in order to mix with earth
brought from a certain field, "to try their several Virtues"; sowed barley near
the tobacco house; harrowed and cross-harrowed another plat intended for
Lucerne. In the autumn of 1764 he sowed "a few Oats" at Doeg Run to see
if they would stand the winter. Oats were usually sown in the early spring.

Doeg Run, commonly written Dogue Run, or Dogue Creek, flows into the
Potomac through a considerable estuary about two and a half miles southwest
of Mount Vernon. Washington's famous grist mill stood at the edge of Dogue
Run Farm, near the head of the estuary. It was restored in 1932 in connection with the Washington Bi-Centennial. One day at the mill he made a test
of the buhrstone's grinding capacity, noting the results with his usual par-
ticularity:

> I tried what time the Mill required to grind a Bushel of Corn, and to my
> Surprize found she was within 5 minutes of an hour about it. This old Anthony
> [the miller] attributed to the low head of Water, but whether it was so or not

Washington's Mill, on Dogue Run, as restored in 1932. Photo 1934.

I can't say; her Works all decayed and out of Order, which I rather take to be the cause. This Bushel of Corn when Ground measured near a Peck more Meal.

Along with the several operations already indicated were also carried on the curing and stacking of hay, the gathering of apples for "Cyder," the repairing of the mill, and various other activities appropriate to the changing seasons on the different plantations. It would be difficult to enumerate all the products of skilled and unskilled labor that were brought forth in the course of a year by the large number of workers—slaves, hired freemen, and perhaps some indentured servants. The master was continually riding about from one field to another, to the mill, to the fish house by the river, and from plantation to plantation, keeping an eye on the various kinds of work and appraising the skill, industry, and dependableness of the several workers. One day, for example, he went into the woods where his carpenters were hewing timbers and sawing plank. He found that four of them, George, Tom, Mike, and Young Billy, all probably Negro slaves, had hewed only 120 feet in about three-quarters of a day. He "sat down therefore and observed." Under his eye Tom and Mike in less time than 30 minutes cleared away the bushes from around a poplar, felled it, and hewed each his side of the trunk twelve inches deep (probably a face 12 inches wide) on a 10-foot length. Then they consumed 25 minutes getting the cross-cut saw, sawing off the hewed log in two places, and putting it on the blocks for squaring it. But in 20 minutes more they had finished it. His conclusion was:

It appears very clear, that allowing they work only from Sun to Sun and require two hours at Breakfast, they ought to yield each his 125 feet while the days are at their present length.

The season was early in the month of February.

While Tom and Mike were working out their twenty feet of hewed timber, George and Young Billy sawed 30 feet of plank. So it was obvious, in the opinion of the master, "making the same allowance as before (but not for the time required in piling the stock, etc.) that they ought to saw 180 feet of plank," in a day.

The sawing was probably done over a saw-pit, with the squared timber on a scaffold over the pit, one sawyer standing on top of the timber, the other in the pit beneath, pulling the saw alternately down and up.

The next day a man arrived with fifteen hogs which he had driven over to Mount Vernon from one of Washington's farms in Frederick County, across the Blue Ridge Mountains, a total distance of 70 or 75 miles. The following day the hogs were butchered, yielding 1614 pounds of pork. The man was paid ten shillings for driving them over. Occasionally, if not usually, specific records were kept of the number of pounds of bacon secured from slaughtered hogs, each one evaluated separately, with notes showing the loss of weight from the shrinkage of the meat in drying.

The squaring and sawing of timber in the woods was being done with a definite purpose. A house for Petit, a brickmaker employed at Mount Vernon, was to be moved a considerable distance and renovated, perhaps enlarged and re-roofed. The following diary entries are pertinent:

Set my Waggons to draw in Stocks and Scantling, and wrote to Mr. Stuart of Norfolk for 20 or 30 or more thousand Shingles, 6 Barrles Tar, 6 of Turpentine, and 100 weight of Tallow or Myrtle wax, or half as much candles.

A day later he "Ordered all the Fellows from the different Quarters to assemble at Williamson's Quarter in the Morning to move Petit's House." In the morning: "Went out early myself and continued with my People till 1 o'clock, in which time we got the house about 250 yards. . . . The Ground being soft and Deep we found it no easy matter with 20 hands, 8 Horses, and 6 Oxen to get this House along."

But the next day conditions were more favorable. "A Small Frost happening last Night to Crust the Ground caused the House to move much lighter, and by 9 o'clock it was got to the spot on which it was intended to stand."

Building materials were needed also for improvements around the mansion house. A month and a half later was entered this record:

Agreed to give Mr. William Triplet £18 to build the two houses in the Front of my House (plastering them also), and running walls for Pallisades to them from the Great house and from the Great House to the Wash House and Kitchen also.

This was in the latter part of March, 1760, somewhat over a year after Washington's marriage. Adjuncts for convenience and service in the "Great House" were being provided. And we should observe in this connection that the front of the "Great House" at that time was the side towards the northwest, not the side towards the river, which is now generally supposed to be the front.

Washington, the expert and scientific farmer and astute man of business, was not devoid of mechanical genius. He was discriminating in his selection and equipment of plows and other farming implements. He went a step farther, as is proved by the following diary entries:

Spent the greatest part of the day in making a new plow of my own Invention.

The next day:

Sat my Plow to work and found she answered very well in the Field in the lower Pasture which I this day began plowing with the large Bay Mare and Rankin—Mulatto Jack continuing to Plow the Field below the Garden.

The new plow was made in the Mount Vernon blacksmith shop by Wash-

General George Washington.
From a portrait by Sharples.

ington and his Negro smith, Peter. They had been working at it at intervals for more than a week before they succeeded in perfecting it. The date was March 1760, thirty-five years before the celebrated invention of an improved plow by Thomas Jefferson. To get a thoroughly satisfactory plow was no easy matter, and more than a quarter of a century later, that is, in 1787, Washington was still making trial of plows, as well as of various seeds, some of the latter sent to him by Arthur Young from England. And as late as 1792 he was contemplating experiments with a plow fashioned after a description given by a Mr. Lambert of England.

Washington was quick to observe the effect of different kinds of work on his horses. One day in the spring plowing season he wrote:

Put the Pole-end Horses into the Plow in the Morning and the Postillion and hand Horses in in the afternoon, but the Ground being well swarded over and very heavy plowing I repented putting them in at all, for fear it should give them a Habit of Stopping in the Chariot.

The chariot was a heavy closed carriage, drawn by four horses. Two were hitched close up to the vehicle, one on either side of the pole, or tongue; the other two were hitched out in front, to the end of the pole. A chariot drawn by four was usually driven ahead at a rather swift gait, and it is easy to see that if the front horses stopped or slacked suddenly, without command, the result might be serious—not merely annoying. The postillion and hand horses were doubtless the two that were hitched on the sides of the pole and next to the chariot. One of these was sometimes mounted by a rider called a postillion. On more than one occasion, in stormy weather, Washington ordered out his chariot for the benefit of his guests from Belvoir, Alexandria, and other places in the neighborhood, who had come to Mount Vernon in open carriages or on horseback, to protect them on their return journeys against rain, snow, or cold winds.

During the war of the Revolution, as already noted, the Mount Vernon estate was left in the hands of Lund Washington, a distant cousin of the owner. During the first four years that Washington was President his nephew, George Augustine Washington, had charge as resident manager. George Augustine died in 1793, and was succeeded by others. For his managers Washington prepared carefully written instructions, and from them a weekly report in detail was required.

Reference has been made to the numerous trees and shrubs that Washington planted at Mount Vernon. He seems to have loved trees almost as much as horses. A particular account of his tree-planting at various times, especially in 1785, would be a long story in itself.

What a boon reliable weather forecasts would have been to this careful farmer and operator of many outdoor activities! But he made the best of the situation without them. He observed weather conditions very minutely and kept an almost daily record of his observations. The temperature, rain-

Martha Dandridge Custis Washington in old age. From a portrait by Sharples.

fall, snowfall, and directions of the wind were all tabulated. Judging from the character of many of his meteorological records, we may guess that he had an index of his weather-vane inside the house, where he could observe it at any hour, day or night. Consider such items as the following:

Very cloudy. Wind at South till 9 o'clock at Night, when it instantaneously shifted to No. West and blew a hurricane.

Many of the notes he made concerning the weather were not included in his ordinary diaries. That the keeping of weather records was habitual with him is evident from his diary entry following August 20, 1798:

No account kept of the weather, &c. from hence to the end of the Month, on account of my Sickness, which commenced with a fever on the 19th and lasted until the 24th, which left me debilitated.

Washington had no children of his own, but he was fond of young people and devoted much time and means to several of his nephews, especially George Steptoe and Lawrence Augustine Washington, sons of his brother Samuel, and Lawrence Lewis, son of his daughter Betty. His constant and devoted care was given to his step-children, John Parke and Martha Custis, and later to John Parke's children, George and Eleanor (Nelly) Custis.

Mrs. Washington's daughter, Martha (Patsy) Custis, was subject to fits. Persistent efforts were made to cure or relieve her. In February 1769 Washington paid Joshua Evans a pound and 10 shillings for a ring for Patsy—an iron ring, which, according to an old superstition, was believed to have curative properties. The following summer she was taken to Bath (Berkeley) medicinal springs; early in 1771 to Williamsburg, where she received treatment and medicine from "Mr. Jno. Carter," a well-known physician of the colonial capital. But she evidently made no real improvement, and on June 19, 1773, Washington wrote in his diary: "About five oclock poor Patsy Custis Died Suddenly."

Patsy was 17 years old, and in spite of her affliction had contributed much to the home life of Mount Vernon; her death was a great blow to her mother, and affected Washington profoundly. Though not "given to bursts of sensibility," he in this bereavement "evinced the deepest affliction." A tenderness and expressiveness that are almost unexpected in him are manifest in a letter which he wrote the next day to Burwell Bassett:

Yesterday . . . the Sweet Innocent Girl Entered into a more happy and peaceful abode than any she has met with in the afflicted Path she hitherto has trod. She rose from dinner about four o'clock in better health and spirits than she appeared to have been in for some time; soon after which she was seized with one of her usual Fits, and expired in it, in less than two minutes without uttering a word, a groan or scarce a sigh—This sudden and unexpected blow, I scarce need add has almost reduced my poor Wife to the lowest ebb of Misery.

In the spring and summer of 1791, while President, Washington made an extended tour of the country, going down through Virginia and the Carolinas into Georgia, and returning to Philadelphia, which was then the national capital, through Frederick and Taneytown, Maryland, and York and Lancaster, Pennsylvania. He and Mrs. Washington traveled in his old English coach, in which "not a nail or screw failed." His baggage wagon was drawn by two horses. Near the outset of this tour he spent a week at Mount Vernon making preparations and writing out directions to the members of his cabinet and giving them a list of the places where he might be reached at certain times in case of any unusual emergency. The first day out from Mount Vernon was marked with a notable adventure, in which disaster was happily averted. His own account of this incident is graphic and interesting:

Recommenced my journey with Horses apparently much refreshed and in good spirits.

In attempting to cross the ferry at Colchester with the four horses hitched to the Chariot, by the neglect of the person who stood before them, one of the leaders got overboard when the boat was in swimming water and 50 yards from the shore—with much difficulty he escaped drowning before he could be disengaged. His struggling frightened the others in such a manner that one after another and in quick succession they all got overboard harnessed and fastened as they were and with the utmost difficulty they were saved and the Carriage escaped being dragged after them, as the whole of it happened in swimming water and at a distance from the shore. Providentially—indeed miraculously—by the exertions of people who went off in Boats and jumped into the River as soon as the Batteau was forced into wading water—no damage was sustained by the horses, Carriage or harness.

Among the relics at Mount Vernon are pointed out a Jacob's Staff and a surveying compass, the latter bearing on its face the following legend: "G. Chandlee W/L. A. Washington." These instruments are believed to have been made on General Washington's order for his nephew, Lawrence Augustine Washington, who was of legal age a year or two before the General died. The compass, and probably the Jacob's Staff too, was obviously the work of Goldsmith Chandlee, a skilled maker of clocks and mechanical instruments, whose shop was in Winchester, and who came of a distinguished line of artificers. See *Antiques*, May 1941, pages 240, 241; also "Hopewell Friends History," pages 174, 175.

CHAPTER VII

BEAUTIFUL BUSHFIELD

Of all the children of Augustine and Mary Ball Washington, their third son, John Augustine, was most intimately identified with their first home, Westmoreland County, Virginia. Though he was born in Prince William County, in the part now Fairfax, where he spent several years of his early manhood and where he was later a frequent visitor, his landed patrimony, his wife's home, and his own home for nearly or quite thirty years were in Westmoreland. There he died and was buried. In Westmoreland too, he in the year 1766, with 114 other patriots, pledged life and fortune in a celebrated protest against the famous Stamp Act; and ten years later he aided materially in the Revolution.

The 700 acres at the "head of Maddox" that Augustine Washington in 1743 willed to his son John Augustine had come down to him from his ancestors—was the first land they had owned in Virginia. It lies north of Oak Grove, on both sides of the highway leading to Colonial Beach. "Maddox" is now known as Mattox Creek and is a navigable arm of the Potomac, entering into the river just a little more than a mile above Bridges Creek. The location of this land devised to him by his father may explain in a measure why John Augustine Washington married and lived in Westmoreland: Bushfield is only twenty miles or so from the "head of Maddox" by the old King's Highway and connecting roads. He was not more than twenty years old when he married Hannah Bushrod, for, according to the record in his father's Bible, he was born "ye 13th of Jany. about 2 in ye Morn 1735/6," which by our calendar would be January 24, 1736; and Charles Moore, in his Washington chronology, shows that he, then the manager at Mount Vernon for his brother George, brought his bride to that place on April 13, 1756. The marriage, we assume, had taken place at Bushfield only a short time before.

Hannah was the daughter of John Bushrod of Bushfield and his wife Mildred Corbin. John Bushrod made his will February 14, 1760, and it was proved before the court of Westmoreland County on December 30 of the same year. He left land, furniture, and 35 slaves to his daughter Hannah Washington; three slaves each to his granddaughters Mary and Jenny Washington; other devises and bequests to other members of his family. Hon. Richard Corbin and John Washington were made executors.

George Washington married and brought his wife to Mount Vernon early in 1759. Not long thereafter, probably the same year or the next, John Augustine and his wife Hannah left Mount Vernon and took up their residence at Bushfield. It may be that the declining health of her father, John Bushrod, had something to do with their going to Bushfield at this time. Inasmuch as they had two daughters, Mary and Jenny, when John Bushrod made his will on February 14, 1760, it seems probable that both of them were born at

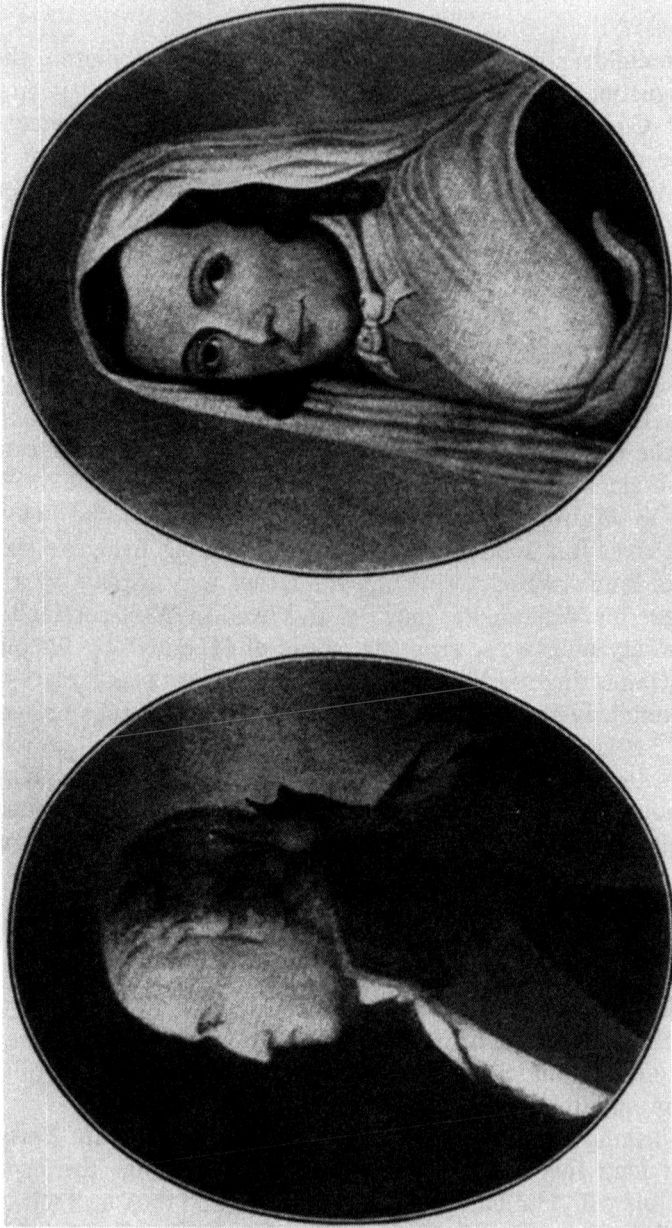

Colonel John Augustine Washington and wife, Hannah Bushrod.

Mount Vernon. It was a year or two, however, before John Augustine Washington closed up his business at Mount Vernon, for on September 21, 1761, he had a sale at which his brother George purchased several cows and calves, some yearlings, and other cattle, 16 in all.

At Bushfield, on June 5, 1762, was born John Augustine's son, Bushrod Washington, later the eminent jurist. He was given the family name of his maternal grandfather. His brother was born in 1765 and named Corbin after the family of his mother's mother.

The year 1765 was a notable one in Westmoreland and other parts of Virginia, a year of widespread alarm, by reason of the Stamp Act which the British Parliament had passed at the vernal equinox. At Leedstown, on the Rappahannock, in the southwestern corner of Westmoreland, in February 1766, to a meeting presided over by Richard Parker, later a judge, Richard Henry Lee presented a series of articles, or resolutions of protest, to which he and many other young men signed their names, binding themselves in a solemn compact in behalf of liberty and rights of property. In the court house at Montross, the county-seat of Westmoreland, one today may read these articles blazoned on a tablet, to wit:

Roused by danger, and alarmed at attempts, foreign and domestic, to reduce the people of this country to a state of abject and detestable slavery, by destroying that free and happy constitution of government, under which they have hitherto lived,—We, who subscribe this paper, have associated, and do bind ourselves to each other, to God, and to our country, by the firmest ties that religion and virtue can frame, most sacredly and punctually to stand by, and with our lives and fortunes to support, maintain, and defend each other in the observance and execution of these following articles:

First. We declare all due allegiance and obedience to our lawful Sovereign, George the third, King of Great Britain. And we determine to the utmost of our power to preserve the laws, the peace and good order of this Colony, as far as is consistent with the preservation of our Constitutional rights and liberty.

Secondly. As we know it to be the Birthright privilege of every British subject (and of the people of Virginia as being such), founded on Reason, Law, and Compact; that he cannot be legally tried, but by his peers; and that he cannot be taxed, but by consent of a Parliament, in which he is represented by persons chosen by the people, and who themselves pay a part of the tax they impose on others. If therefore, any person or persons shall attempt by any action or proceeding, to deprive this Colony of those fundamental rights, we will immediately regard him or them, as the most dangerous enemy of the community; and we will go to any extremity, not only to prevent the success of such attempts, but to stigmatize and punish the offender.

Thirdly. As the Stamp Act does absolutely direct the property of the people to be taken from them without their consent expressed by their representatives, and as in many cases it deprives the British American Subject of his right to trial by jury; we do determine, at every hazard, and, paying no regard to danger or to death, we will exert every faculty, to prevent the execution of the said Stamp Act in any instance whatsoever within this Colony. And every abandoned wretch, who shall be so lost to virtue and public good, as wickedly to contribute

Bushfield, home of John Augustine Washington, from the southeast. Photo December, 1937.

to the introduction or fixture of the Stamp Act in this Colony, by using stampt paper, or by any other means, we will, with the utmost expedition, convince all such profligates that immediate danger and disgrace shall attend their prostitute purposes.

Fourthly. That the last article may most surely and effectually be executed, we engage to each other, that whenever it shall be known to any of this association, that any person is so conducting himself as to favor the introduction of the Stamp Act, that immediate notice shall be given to as many of the association as possible; and that every individual so informed, shall, with expedition, repair to a place of meeting to be appointed as near the scene of action as may be.

Fifthly. Each associator shall do his true endeavor to obtain as many signers to this association, as he possibly can.

Sixthly. If any attempt shall be made on the liberty or property of any associator for any action or thing to be done in consequence of this agreement, we do most solemnly bind ourselves by the sacred engagements above entered into, at the risk of our lives and fortunes, to restore such associate to his liberty, and to protect him in the enjoyment of his property.

In testimony of the good faith with which we resolve to execute this association we have this 27th day of February, 1766, in Virginia, put our hands and seals hereto.

Richard Henry Lee
Will. Robinson
Lewis Willis
Thos. Lud. Lee
Samuel Washington
Charles Washington
Moore Fauntleroy
Francis Lightfoot Lee
Thomas Jones
Rodham Kenner
Spencer M. Ball
Richard Mitchell
Joseph Murdock
Richd. Parker
Spence Monroe
John Watts
Robt. Lovell
John Blagge
Charles Weeks
Willm. Boothe
Geo. Turberville
Alvin Moxley
Wm. Flood
John Ballatine, jr.
William Lee
Thos. Chilton
Richard Buckner
Jos. Pierce
Will. Chilton
John Williams

William Sydnor
John Monroe
William Cocke
Willm. Grayson
Wm. Brockenbrough
Saml. Selden
Richd. Lee
Daniel Tibbs
Francis Thornton, jr.
Peter Rust
John Lee, jr.
Francis Waring
John Upshaw
Meriwether Smith
Thos. Roane
Jas. Edmondson
Jas. Webb, jr.
John Edmondson
Jas. Banks
Smith Young
Laur. Washington
W. Roane
Rich. Hodges
Jas. Upshaw
Jas. Booker
A. Montague
Rich'd Jeffries
John Suggett
John S. Woodcock
Robt. Wormeley Carter

John Blackwell
Winder S. Kenner
Wm. Bronaugh
Wm. Pierce
John Berryman
John Dickson
John Broone
Edwd. Sanford
Charles Chilton
Edward Sanford
Daniel McCarty
Jer. Rush
Edwd. Ransdell
Townshend Dade
John Ashton
W. Brent
Francis Foushee
John Smith, jr.
Wm. Ball
Thos. Barnes
Jos. Blackwell
Reuben Meriwether
Edw. Mountjoy
Wm. J. Mountjoy
Thos. Mountjoy
John Mountjoy
Gilbt. Campbell
Jos. Lane
John Beale, jr.
John Newton

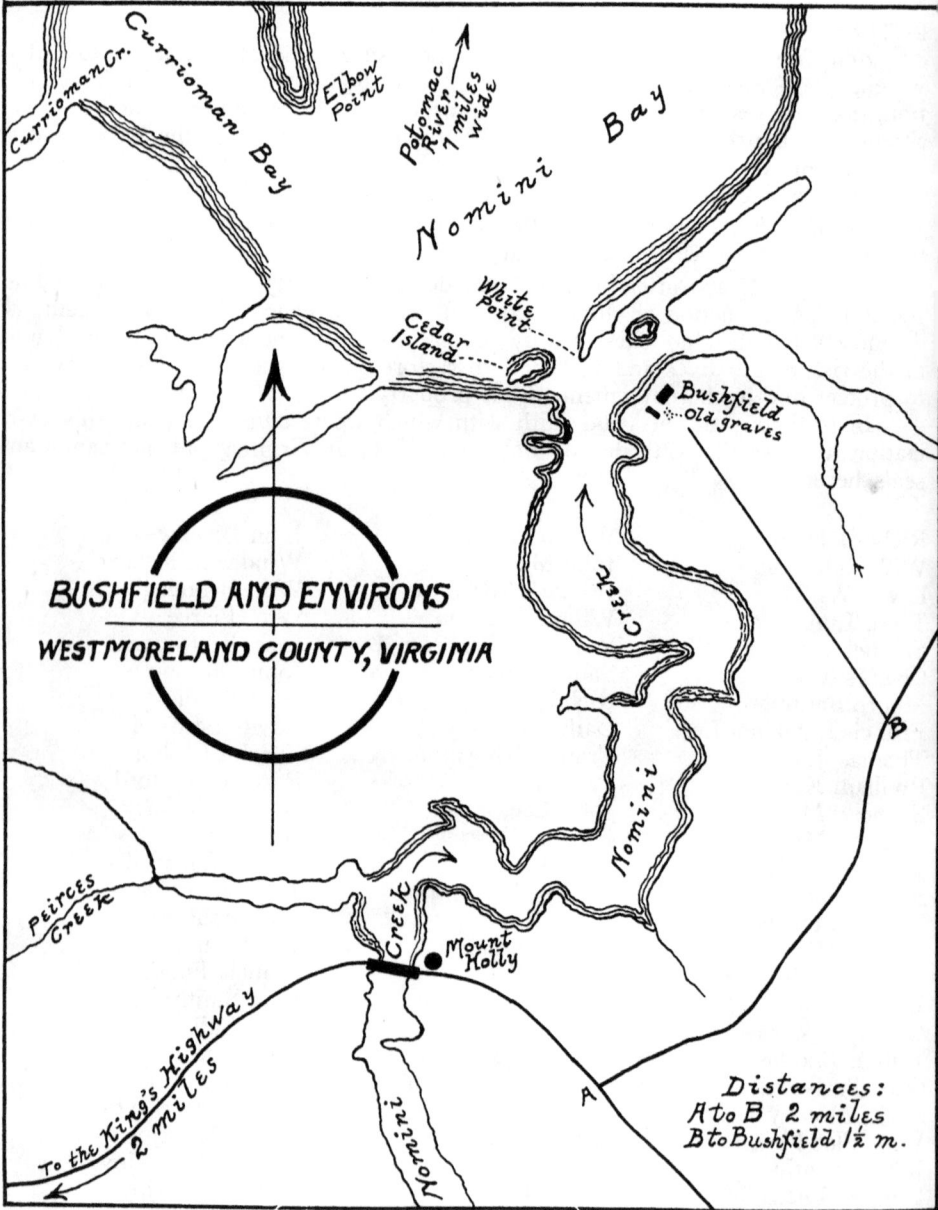

BUSHFIELD AND ENVIRONS

WESTMORELAND COUNTY, VIRGINIA

Distances:
A to B 2 miles
B to Bushfield 1½ m.

Will. Beale, jr.
Chs. Mortimer
John Edmondson, jr.
Charles Beale
Peter Grant
Thompson Mason
Jona. Beckwith
Jas. Sanford
John Belfield

W. Smith
John Augt. Washington
Thos. Belfield
Edgcomb Suggett
Henry Francks
John Bland, jr.
Jas. Emerson
Thos. Logan
Jo. Milliken

Ebenezer Fisher
Hancock Eustace
John Richards
Thos. Jett
Thos. Douglas
Max Robinson
John Orr

Two of the Lees here signing, Richard Henry and Francis Lightfoot, ten years later signed the Declaration of Independence. Spence Monroe was the father of a future President of the United States, who at this time was eight years old. Daniel McCarty was probably one of the "good friends" whom Augustine Washington twenty-three years before had chosen to be one of the executors of his will, though we may guess that most of the signers were younger than he. Nine are designated as "juniors." The prime mover, Richard Henry Lee, was only 34; his brothers, Thomas Ludwell and Francis Lightfoot, were 36 and 32 respectively. Richard Parker was 34; Samuel Washington and Charles Washington, both from the vicinity of Fredericksburg, were 32 and 28. John Augustine Washington, then living at Bushfield, was thirty.

It is probable that Charles Mortimer, like Samuel and Charles Washington, was from Fredericksburg or its neighborhood, and was the same Charles Mortimer who was later the first mayor of Fredericksburg and one of the physicians of Mary Washington.

George Bancroft, referring to the events leading up to the Revolution, spoke of Virginia ringing an alarm bell for the continent. The Westmoreland Association of 1766 no doubt should be recognized in the alarm that was sounded.

In 1774, when supplies for the people of Boston, distressed by the closing of their port, were being raised in different parts of the colonies, John Augustine Washington was chairman of the relief committee in Westmoreland County and forwarded 1092 bushels of grain. The next year he was a member of the county committee of safety, in which Richard Lee, Richard Henry Lee, Daniel McCarty, Richard Parker, George Steptoe, John Ashton, and Thomas Chilton were among his associates. He evidently was prominent in the religious life of his county, as well as in civic affairs, for at the close of the Revolution he was elected one of the vestry of Yeocomico Church, the other vestrymen chosen at the same time being Vincent Marmaduke, Jeremiah G. Bailey, Samuel Rust, John Crabb, Richard Lee, George Garner, George Turberville, Patrick Sanford, John Rochester, and Samuel Templeman. (See "Colonial Churches," Richmond, Va., 1908; sketch of Yeocomico Church, by Rev. J. Poyntz Tyler; pages 224-228.)

George Washington was an occasional visitor at Bushfield. In May 1768

Bushfield from the northwest—bay side. Photo December, 1937.

he, after spending several days at his plantation and other places in King William County, set out for Nomini. Bushfield is on Nomini River (Creek). He dined at Hobb's Hole, now Tappahannock, on the 20th, where he must have crossed the Rappahannock River the same day or the next, though he says nothing about it in his diary account. When he reached Bushfield on the 21st, which evidently was Saturday, his brother John and his wife were "up the Country." Because of their absence from home he crossed over to a neighbor's, Mr. Booth's, where he remained several days, going to church at Nomini on Sunday. On Tuesday he went up to Pope's Creek, his birthplace, where he stayed all day. On Wednesday he reached his brother Sam's in King George County, where he found his brother John's wife. John came the next day. After spending several days in Fredericksburg and vicinity he returned home on the 31st.

The last week in August of the same year, 1768, Washington spent partly with his brother John at Bushfield. This time he came down the Potomac from Chotank, in King George County, in his schooner, fishing with a seine in Machodoc Creek, Nomini Bay, and other places thereabout. He was at Bushfield two or three days, taking dinner there on Sunday, the 28th, after attending services at Nomini Church.

Washington's diary entries show that his brother John was at Mount Vernon a number of times in the years between 1760 and 1787. When Washington returned home from court at Alexandria the evening of February 22, 1770, he found his brothers Samuel and John, the latter's wife and daughter, Mr. Lawrence Washington and daughter, and the Rev. Mr. Smith. They were evidently giving him a birthday party. Not only so, but they remained for a week, going away on the first of March. In January 1771 John and Lawrence Washington spent two days at Mount Vernon, on their way to Frederick County, in the Shenandoah Valley. This Lawrence was probably the one to whom Washington in his will many years later left a spy-glass and a gold-headed cane; who lived at Chotank, and whom the testator describes as an acquaintance and friend of his juvenile years.

On Saturday, June 18, 1785, in the afternoon, John Augustine Washington came to Mount Vernon from Alexandria, having come up to that place by water. He was his brother's guest for the next five days, spending intervals in Alexandria, where he evidently had business or was visiting friends. Within this same month his son Bushrod, his brother Charles, Charles's son George Augustine, and George Steptoe, Samuel's son, were also at Mount Vernon for periods of varying lengths. Besides these Washingtons, there were many other guests coming and going. It is hard to see how General Washington had any time to look after his landscaping and planting of trees, shrubs, flowers, and grasses, in which he was so earnestly engaged all this spring and summer.

Washington's diary entries show that his brother John was at Mount Vernon on four subsequent occasions. On Wednesday, October 19, 1785, the

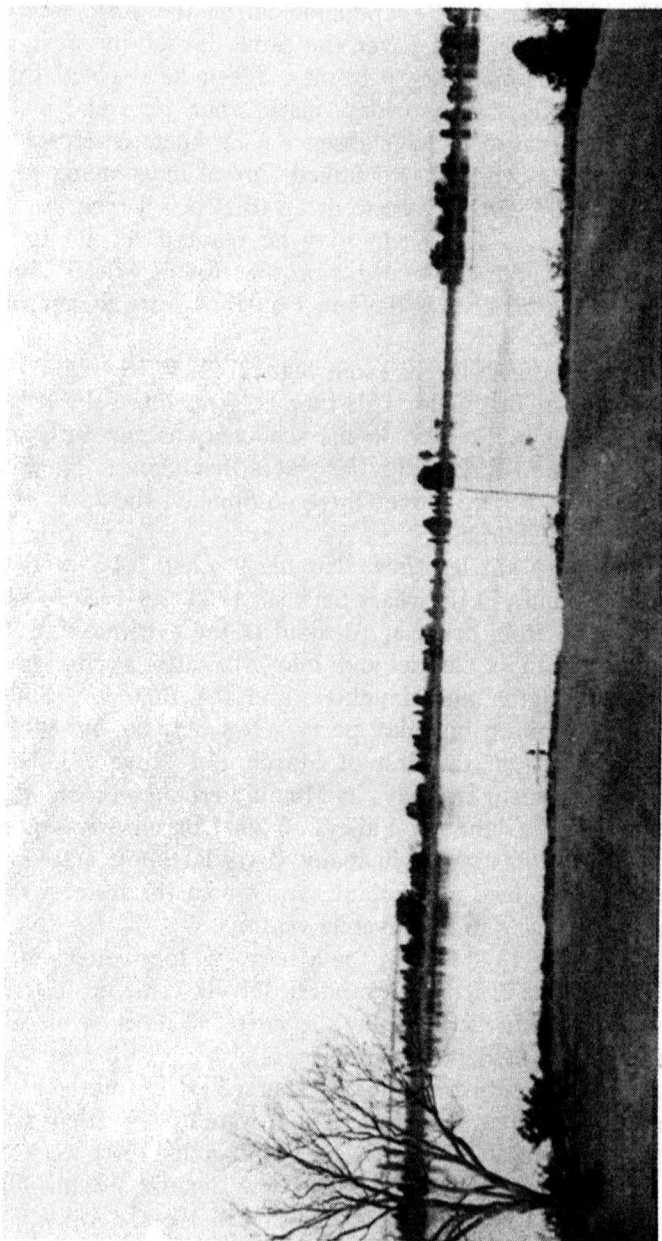

View northwest from Bushfield towards Nomini Bay. Photo October, 1933.

General reached home and found there his brother John, his wife, his daughter Milly, his sons Bushrod and Corbin, Bushrod's wife, Mr. William Washington, with his wife and four children, and Colonel Blackburn. Mr. William Craik came in the evening. This William Washington was the son of Augustine, the General's half-brother, and had married Jane (or Jenny) Washington, oldest child of John Augustine and his wife Hannah Bushrod. Colonel Blackburn was Bushrod's father-in-law. This group has very much the look of a wedding party—Bushrod Washington, aged 23, and Julia Ann Blackburn had been married only a short time before; and the date was an interesting anniversary—Cornwallis had surrendered at Yorktown just four years past. At this particular time General Washington was engaged in directing the construction of a canal around the Great Falls of the Potomac, and at the same time Houdon, the French sculptor, was at Mount Vernon making his celebrated bust of Washington.

John Augustine Washington's last visit to his brother at Mount Vernon, so far as we have record, was in October 1786, when he was there three days. He went away expecting, no doubt, to return, for he was then not quite fifty-one, but on January 10, 1787, almost his birthday, the General made the following entries:

> Just before Dinner Mr. Brindley, Manager of the Susquehanna works, and his Son in law came in on their way to South Carolina.

> About the same time I recd. by express the acct. of the sudden death (by a fit of Gout in the head) of my beloved Brother, Colo. Jno. Auge. Washington.

> At home all day.

The day of his death was evidently the 8th or 9th of the month. A messenger (express), by hard riding, could scarcely have made the distance between Bushfield and Mount Vernon in less than a day and a half.

These Washingtons were notably short-lived. None of them except the mother, Mary Ball, reached three score years and ten. The father, Augustine Washington, was only 49 when he made his will one day and died the next. His son Lawrence, who died in 1752, was not over 36; Augustine (II), who died just ten years later, was not over 44. George, eldest child of the second wife, died in 1799, lacking a few months of being 68; Charles, the youngest to grow up, died the same year, a few months over 61. Betty (Mrs. Fielding Lewis) died in 1797, aged nearly 64. Samuel, who died at Harewood in 1781, was almost exactly 47. John Augustine was 51, lacking only a few days.

Although John Augustine Washington died suddenly, as his brother states, he evidently had premonitions of early death or took time by the forelock as a wise precaution, for he made his will on June 22, 1784. Most of the Washington wills are classics, and this one is no exception. For the information it gives about the maker, his family, and the manner of life that was carried on at Bushfield, it is given below in full, excepting the preamble.

Imprimis I bequeath to my beloved Wife Hannah Washington during her natural life, the use of one third of all the Negroes I am possessed of among which are to be included my waiting man Jerry, his wife suck, my Semstres Jenny, Billy her Husband and her daughter Venus. Billy, Jenny & Venus I impower my Wife to devise to such of my Children by her as she please. I give to my said Wife one half of all my furniture both house and Kitchen, all my plate, my Chariott and the four horses that belong to it, all the plough horses and the stocks of Cattle, Sheep and Hogs on the Bushfield Estate and all the plantation utensils. I also give to my beloved Wife thirty pounds a Year during her widowhood to be raised out of the Estate hereafter devised to my sons Bushrod and Corbin and regularly paid to her, the above Legacys are to be free from any incumbrance of debts contracted by me, and are intended in lieu of her dower in my Estate with which Legacys I hope my said Wife will be satisfyed as she is entitled besides to all the lands her Father left her, but if she should never the less claim her right of dower in my Estate then the above Legacys to be void.

Item for the purpose of discharging my just debts and payment of the Legacys hereafter devised to my Daughters, it is my Will and desire that my Executors hereafter named make sale of and Lawfull Conveyances for my Lands in Loudoun County purchased of George Carters Estate and containing abt 2500 Acres one half my Stock of Cattle Horses Sheep & Hogs in Berkley and Loudoun Countys, the residue of my Furniture, my Crops on hand at the time of my death and debts due me to be applyed also to the same purpose, also so many Negroes to be sold out of those hereafter bequeathed to my sons Bushrod Washington and Corbin Washington as may be found necessary, the whole sails to be on reasonable Credit; if my Executors hereafter named should Judge it most for the interest of my sons to sell a larger proportion of Negroes for the purpose of paying my debts and Legacys & reserve the lands above directed to be sold, they are at liberty to do so, and in that case I give and bequeath my land in Loudoun to my two sons Bushrod and Corbin and their Heirs and assigns to be Equally divided between them.

Item I give and bequeath to my Daughter Jenny Washington and her heirs 600 pounds specie, and confirm to her the gift of the Negroes she has recd. from me, the sums of money advanced my son in law Will Augt. Washington and the presents in other things made since her Marriage.

Item I give to my Grandaughter Ann Aylett Washington a Negro Girl between the age of six and ten years old.

Item I give to my Daughter Mildred Washington 1000 pounds specie to be raised as soon as possible after my death by my Executors and put to interest on good landed security for the use of my said Daughter Mildred and untill this is done my said Daughter Mildred to be allowed Fifty pounds a Year out of ye Estate left my sons Bushrod and Corbin but provided my said daughter Mildred should die before she comes of age or Marrys then it is my Will and desire that the Legacys given her be Equally divided between her surviving Brothers and sister. I also give my daughter Mildred a Negro Girl.

Item I give and devise to my son Bushrod Washington his Heirs and Assigns the following Tracts of Land. the tract of Land in Berkley patented in
my own Name Joining the lands of Rutherford, Nourse, Blackbourn & containing
643 Acres. my Land in Stafford County conveyed to me by my mother Mrs.
Mary Washington adjoining the lands of Downmans Estate and Colo. Burgis Ball
on Rapehanock and containing 400 Acres, two surveys made for me on or near
the Waters of Redstone Creek each survey containing 320 Acres one of them in
my own name calld the forks, the other I had surveyed in the name of Lawrence
Washington and is called Bears Range the surveys are adjoining each other and
form a square. I also Give to my son Bushrod one half of my Negroes not
otherwise disposed of after my Debts and Legacys are paid and one half of my
stock not otherwise disposed of.

Item I give and devise to my son Corbin Washington his Heirs and Assigns
all the lands I hold and am possessed of in Berkley County not otherwise disposed
of and the remaining half of my Negroes and stock not otherwise disposed of,
reserving to my son Bushrod Washington the use of the tract of Land I purchased of Mr. James Russell of London and a field on the Land I purchased of
Robert Washington known by the name of Smoots field to assist in working his
Negroes on during his Mother's Natural life, and in Case my son Bushrod should
be defeated in his Just expectations of inheriting his Mothers land which she
possesses under her Fathers Will at her death then it is my will and desire that
one third of the Land given my son Corbin be laid off according to quality for
my son Bushrod which upon that contingency I give to him and his Heirs and
assigns for ever.

Item I give one third of my Negroes lent to my wife during her Natural
life; at her death it is my Will and desire they should be equally divided between
my sons Bushrod & Corbin and their Heirs.

Item it is my Will and desire that in Case either of my sons Bushrod or
Corbin should die without Lawfull issue that the lands devised to each son so
dying shall descend to the surviving son and his Heirs and assigns and the Negroes
left to such of my sons so dying shall be equally divided among all my surviving
children.

Item what ever Estate I may be possessed of, or have any right or claim to,
not disposed of by this my last Will, be equally divided between my two sons
Bushrod and Corbin and their Heirs &c. &c.

Lastly I constitute and appoint my Beloved Wife Hannah Washington dur-
ing her Widowhood and no longer Executrix and my much esteemed Brother
Genl. Washington and my sons Bushrod Washington and Corbin Washington
Executors of this my last will and testament in Witness where of I have here unto
set my hand & seale this 22d day of June 1784.
John Augustine Washington (L S)

On November 19, 1785, certain additions were made to this will: a deed
of gift had been made to Bushrod (following the latter's marriage) of 41
Negroes—they were to be deducted from the number that might fall to him
later. The testator had purchased land near Bath (now Berkley Springs)

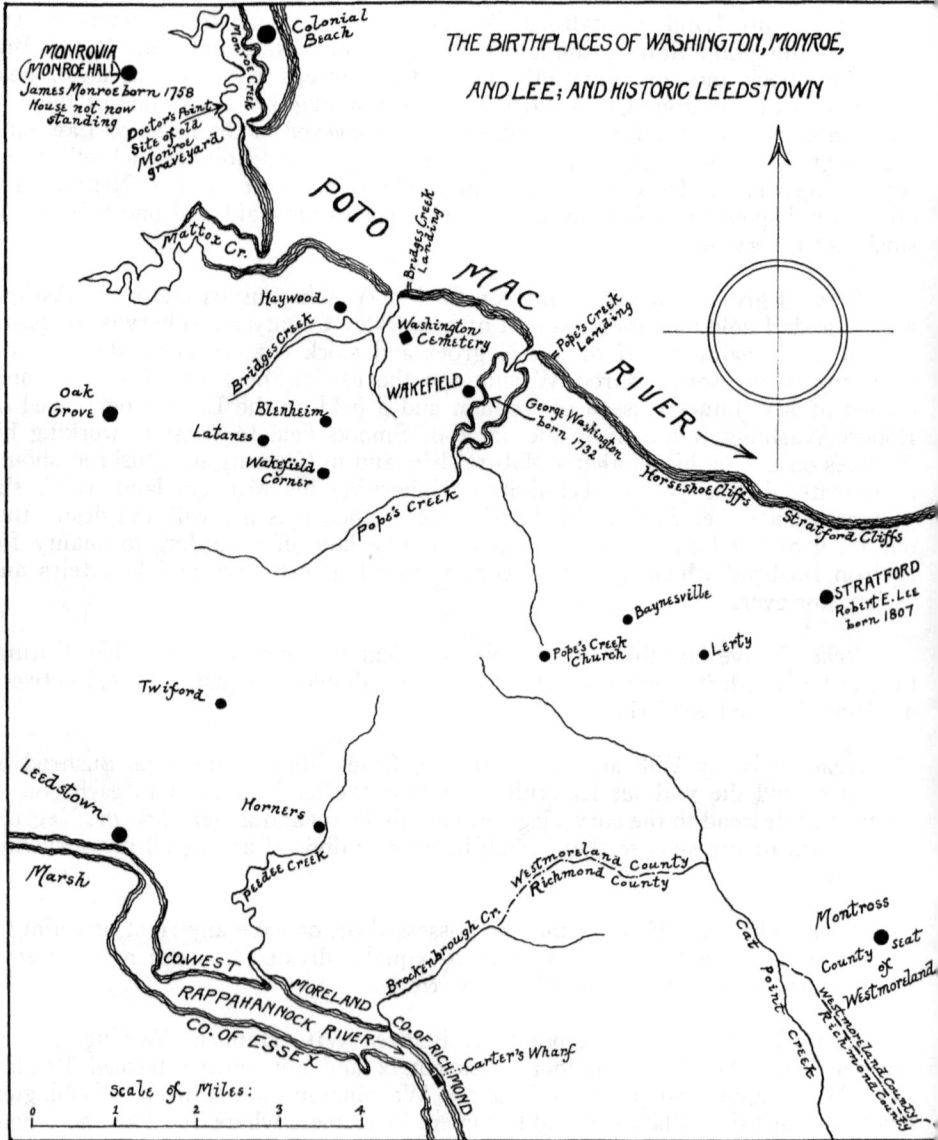

THE BIRTHPLACES OF WASHINGTON, MONROE, AND LEE; AND HISTORIC LEEDSTOWN

Colonial Beach

MONROVIA (MONROE HALL)
James Monroe born 1758
House not now standing

Doctor's Point
Site of old Monroe graveyard

Monroe Creek

POTO MAC RIVER

Mattox Cr.

Bridges Creek Landing

Haywood

Washington Cemetery

Bridges Creek

Pope's Creek Landing

WAKEFIELD

George Washington born 1732

Oak Grove

Blenheim

Latanes

Wakefield Corner

Pope's Creek

Horseshoe Cliffs

Stratford Cliffs

STRATFORD
Robert E. Lee born 1807

Baynesville

Pope's Creek Church

Lerty

Twiford

Leedstown

Horners

Pedee Creek

Marsh

Westmoreland County
Richmond County

Brockinbrough Cr.

Montross
County seat of Westmoreland

Cat Point Creek

CO. WEST MORELAND

RAPPAHANNOCK RIVER

CO. OF ESSEX

CO. OF RICHMOND

Carter's Wharf

Westmoreland County / Richmond County

Scale of Miles:
0   1   2   3   4

of Robert Throckmorton Jr., 213 acres; this tract and two lots in the town of Bath were to be applied to debts and legacies. He confirmed to his grandson Augustine Washington and his heirs a Negro boy Griffin and to his granddaughter Hannah Bushrod Washington a Negro girl Harriet.

The will was admitted to record on July 31, 1787, more than six and a half months after the testator's death. See Westmoreland Deeds and Wills, Book No 18, pages 6-10.

Bushfield, the home of John Augustine Washington and the birthplace of his illustrious son, Judge Bushrod Washington, occupies a splendid location on the east bank of Nomini River, just where the latter widens into Nomini Bay. It is two and a half miles north of the village of Mount Holly and seven miles northeast of Montross, the county-seat, measuring these distances on direct air lines. The estate was originally owned, says Mr. H. Ragland Eubank, by Rice Maddox, who conveyed it to John Bushrod, the grandfather of Hannah Bushrod Washington. The old mansion house of John Augustine Washington's time was shelled and burned by the British in the War of 1812; the present handsome edifice is of comparatively recent date. Its upper galleries command a magnificent view over the broad waters to the west and north.

Hannah Bushrod Washington, we are told, had a horror of being buried alive, and in a long will which she wrote with her own hand gave specific directions intended to protect herself against such a fate. Her grave is at Bushfield. Her son Corbin Washington and his wife, Hannah Lee, daughter of Richard Henry, were also buried at Bushfield. Corbin and his wife lived for many years at Walnut Farm, which lies near Bushfield and was originally a part of that estate, but they died in Fairfax County, where they were living on October 19, 1799, when Corbin made his will, and in November 1799 when they were visited by General Washington. Corbin and his wife both died soon thereafter. His will was probated April 21, 1800; hers was made on June 17, 1800, and probated January 18, 1802. She describes herself as of Fairfax County, states that the name of her home place is Selby, and expresses her desire to be buried at Bushfield, with her husband.

By accident or design, several of the Washington wills were made on historic anniversaries. General Washington wrote his on July 9, a day in the calendar made memorable by the defeat of Braddock in 1755, in which Washington, then a young Virginia colonial officer, did so much to retrieve disaster. Corbin and Colonel Fielding Lewis wrote theirs on October 19, the date of Cornwallis's surrender at Yorktown. June 17, the date of Hannah Lee Washington's will, was the day of the month that had been signalized early in the Revolution by the battle of Bunker Hill.

None of these good people was, we trust, buried alive, but all or nearly all of them lie in graves that are now unmarked and, in consequence, that cannot be exactly located. Neither John Augustine Washington nor his wife, Hannah

Bushrod, nor Corbin Washington nor his wife, Hannah Lee, has a tombstone, so far as any can now be found at Bushfield. Two or three old Bushrod stones remain, and these are carefully guarded by the present owners of this historic homestead, but all the Washington stones, if any were ever there, and probably such were there once, have long since disappeared. Some of them, it may be, were broken down when the old mansion was burned in 1814; others, perhaps, were carried off by vandals or relic-hunters. It is a rather pathetic fact that we are unable at this time to locate with certainty the grave of any one of General Washington's three brothers. John Augustine is buried at Bushfield, but the spot is unknown; Charles is believed to be buried somewhere on his farm as Charles Town, but nobody can say just where; Samuel lies somewhere in or near the little stone-walled cemetery at Harewood, but his grave has no definite marker. Not until 1927 was the grave of Betty Washington Lewis, the sister of these men, appropriately marked.

It is stated by T. R. B. Wright, in his history of Westmoreland County, published in 1912, that Robert B. Cason, Esq., was at that time the owner of Bushfield. The present (1938) owners and occupants are Messrs. Mark S. Willing and R. D. McFadon, who acquired the property in 1914. A small brick building, among other structures, was then on the place. Around it the present commodious and well-appointed dwelling was constructed in 1917.

CHAPTER VIII

HISTORIC HAREWOOD

Harewood, the home of Samuel Washington, George's oldest full brother, is situated three and a half miles northwest of Charles Town, home and town of Charles Washington, the General's youngest full brother. The Harewood house is a rather small building, simple in design, of plain exterior, standing on a slight elevation in a native grove on the southwest side of the highway that leads from Charles Town to Middleway. It is constructed of limestone, the native rock in which the surrounding hills and vales abound. At the foot of the Harewood hill, on the southeast side, numerous ledges rear their rugged gray masses above the surface of the ground.

Harewood is one of the few Washington homes that still remain substantially in their original form. It has been changed very little since it was built, the chief modifications being found in connection with the approaches and entrance. In the days of Samuel Washington and his immediate successors the main entrance was on the side towards Charles Town—the southeast side; now the main entrance is on the northwest. Some of the oaks and other native trees that formerly stood near the house have been replaced with maples and locusts that now are old. Hedges of box and other decorative shrubs on the southeast survive from the days when the approach to the mansion was from that side.

In the edge of the highway at the present entrance gate is a metal tablet bearing the following inscription:

HAREWOOD
ERECTED IN 1771. THE HOME OF COLONEL
SAMUEL WASHINGTON, COUNTY LIEUTENANT.
HIS BROTHER GENERAL GEORGE WASHINGTON
VISITED HERE AND GENERAL LAFAYETTE
AND LOUIS PHILLIPE OF FRANCE WERE
ENTERTAINED HERE. IN THIS HOUSE
JAMES MADISON AND DOLLY PAYNE TODD
WERE MARRIED. SAMUEL WASHINGTON
DIED IN 1781 AND IS BURIED IN THE
GRAVE YARD SOUTH OF THE HOUSE.

Erected by the
Jefferson County Historical Society
of West Virginia, 1932.

Harewood House was evidently built in 1769-70, inasmuch as Colonel Samuel Washington and his family moved into it from their earlier home in King George County in September 1770. Details in reference to their removal to Harewood will appear farther on.

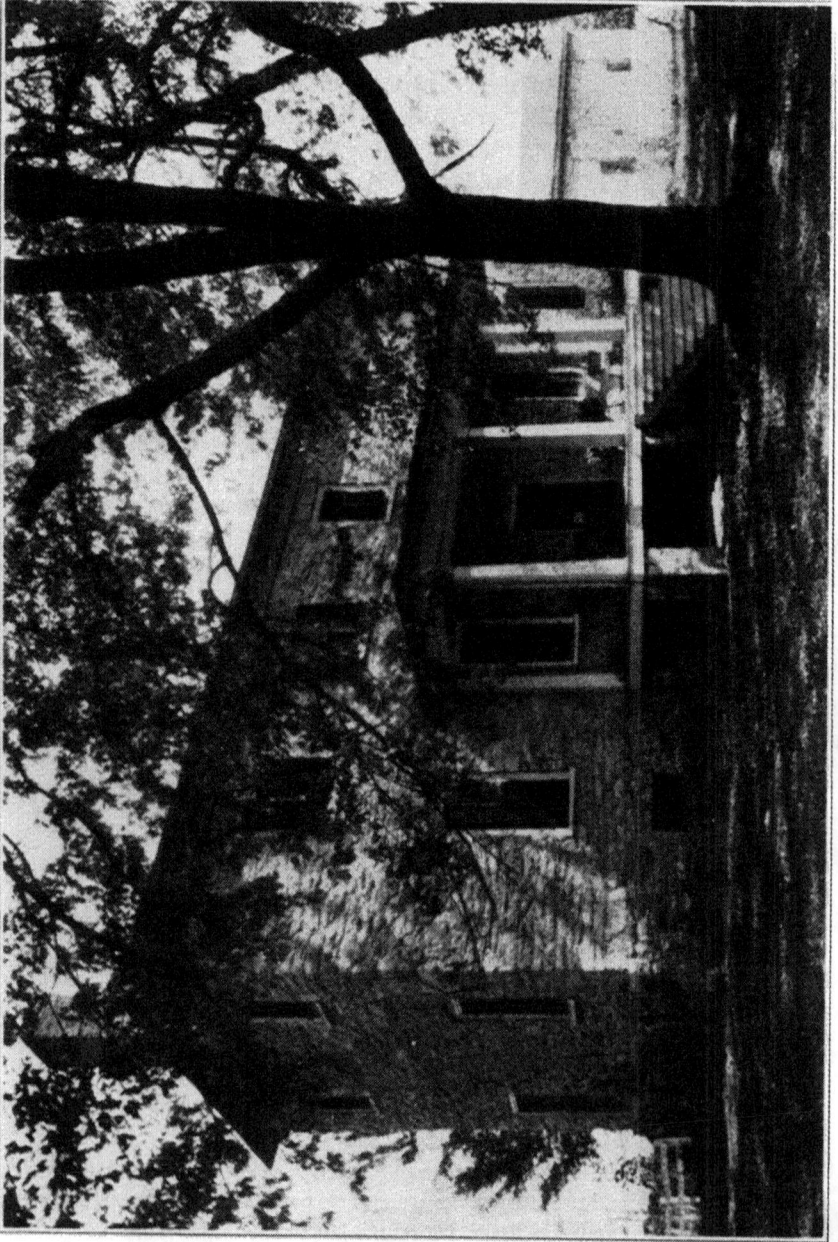

Harewood, home of Colonel Samuel Washington, oldest full brother of George Washington. Photo 1929, from the north.

Samuel Washington was born at Wakefield, on Pope's Creek, Westmoreland County, Va., the birthplace of his brother George and his sister Elizabeth (Betty), on November 27 (N. S.), 1734, "about 3 in ye Morning." The attention of the public has been so much centered upon George that his brothers and sisters have been neglected, and consequently very little is now generally known about them. We delight in being disciples of Parson Weems —in rehearsing the stories of George's youthful vigor, ambition, studious habits, and filial devotion. Very few stories, if any, have come down to us concerning Betty, Samuel, John Augustine, and Charles. Betty was a wholesome, vigorous woman, bearing a striking resemblance to her brother George. John Augustine, as we have seen, was an active member of his community and a fearless patriot, but is remembered best by his beautiful home, Bushfield, on the Nomini, and the fact that he was the father of the eminent jurist, Bushrod Washington. Charles attained wealth and public honors, and built for himself a fitting monument in the town that bears his name, though he lies in an unmarked and unknown grave. Samuel, next to George, rose highest in public service, civil and military, but we know very little of his boyhood and early habits. Whether he could throw across the Rappahannock River or subdue wild young horses, we are not told. Did his father buy him a hatchet? If he had one, either his own or the one that George laid aside, we can be certain that he too went about hacking things, though we imagine he was shrewd enough to give cherry trees a wide berth. As he grew up he developed a keen fancy for the girls—if he did not we are puzzled to explain why he married five of them, one after the other, from time to time. He lived as a boy in three different counties of Virginia, Westmoreland, Prince William, and Stafford; as a man he lived and held public office in three, Stafford, Frederick, and Berkeley, but he never was an old man: he died at the age of forty-seven. Harewood was his home for eleven years, 1770 to 1781.

In 1766, when Samuel Washington was 32 years old, he was a justice of the peace in Stafford County. He was then living in or near the Chotank community, wherein lay the 600 acres of land willed to him in 1743 by his father, Augustine Washington. Chotank was then in Stafford, but is now in the northern part of King George County. It was a Washington settlement, in which several families of that name lived for generations. Many interesting particulars concerning them may be found on pages 18-21 of that valuable work by H. Ragland Eubank, entitled "Historic Northern Neck of Virginia," and published in 1934. George Washington frequently, in traveling southward from Mount Vernon to Williamsburg and other places thereabout, would ferry across the Potomac at or near Mount Vernon into Maryland, go down to Port Tobacco and Cedar Point, and thence across the Potomac again into Virginia to Chotank, thus cutting off the great bend of the Potomac that sweeps over westward into the counties of Prince William and Stafford, in Virginia. He did this in April 1760, when his chaise broke down on the Maryland side of the river. He had to walk part of the way to Port Tobacco and was there detained the whole day getting the chaise mended, no smith being nearer than six miles. After lodging over night at Dr. Halkerson's, he set out early the next morning (Sunday), crossed the Potomac from Cedar Point—the river is here three miles wide—and reached his brother's house in time for dinner. Samuel already had his second wife, Mildred Thornton, daughter of Colonel John Thornton and his wife, Mildred Gregory. His first wife, Jane Champe, was a daughter of Colonel John Champe, who lived between Chotank and Fredericksburg.

The dates of Samuel's several marriages are not definitely known, but in September 1781, when he made his will, his son Thornton was evidently of age—21 years or more; hence we may infer that Samuel and his second wife, Mildred Thornton, were married as early as 1760 or 1759.

On September 1, 1768, George Washington came up the Potomac from Westmoreland County, where he had been fishing with a seine and visiting his brother John at Bushfield. He was on his own schooner—slept on it the night of the 1st while it lay at anchor between Swan Point and Cedar Point. The next day he came up as far as Hooe's Ferry, there quitted the vessel and walked to his brother Sam's house. Ten days before he had been here, on his way down—had embarked on his schooner near here. The vessel evidently was kept in the river opposite Chotank, probably in Samuel Washington's care. It was left here on September 5 when George Washington crossed the river to the lower point of Nanjemoy, on the Maryland side, where one of his men met him with the chariot and took him home.

Records show that Samuel Washington was a magistrate in Stafford County from 1766 to and including 1769, though following his name in the list of July 27, 1767, is written the word "Removed." No doubt he was already spending part of his time in Frederick County, where he owned land, and where he was preparing to build at Harewood. Among the magistrates who were contemporary with him in Stafford were four other Washingtons, John, Bailey, Robert, and Lawrence. The two last named were doubtless the "acquaintances and friends" of George Washington's "juvenile years" to whom he willed spy-glasses and gold-headed canes.

In 1766 Samuel Washington, with his younger brothers, John Augustine and Charles, signed the bold Articles of Westmoreland, drawn up and adopted at Leedstown, protesting against the British Stamp Act. These, with the names of all the signers, have already been presented in full in a preceding chapter.

In May 1769, and again in October of the same year, Samuel Washington was listed among the magistrates of Frederick County. Evidently he was by this time well identified with his new place of residence. Among his associates of the Frederick County court at this time were Taverner Beale, who in 1772 became the first sheriff of Dunmore (now Shenandoah) County; Angus McDonald, worthy sire of distinguished sons; Warner Washington, Samuel's first-cousin; Rev. Charles Mynn Thruston, later one of the fighting parsons of the Revolution; and Thomas Lord Fairfax, proprietor of the Northern Neck. Frederick County at this time (1769) included the present counties of Shenandoah, Page, Warren, and Clarke in Virginia, together with Berkeley, Jefferson, and a part of Morgan, in West Virginia.

It should be remembered that in colonial Virginia, and for many years after the Revolution, the magistrates, or justices of the peace, performed very important functions. They constituted the county court and also exercised the powers now vested in the county board of supervisors. They tried cases, civil and criminal, heard chancery suits, provided for the settlement of estates, laid out roads, gave permission for the construction of mill dams, authorized the erection of bridges, and had in hand the building of court houses, jails, and other public edifices. They sometimes appointed the clerks of the court, coroners, and constables; also captains of militia and subordinate officers. They recommended to the governor persons fit to be sheriff, county lieutenant, and colonel of militia; also such as were deemed suitable to be added to their own body as magistrates. The latter, as well as the sheriff and the higher officers of the militia, were approved or commissioned by the governor.

All four of the Washington brothers, George, Samuel, John Augustine, and Charles, sons of Augustine and Mary Ball Washington, had lands in the lower Shenandoah Valley, lying first in the county of Frederick, then (after 1772) in Berkeley, then (after 1801) in Jefferson. Their first holdings in that region apparently came to them by the will of their older half-brother Lawrence of Mount Vernon, in 1752. Lawrence at different times had acquired various tracts in Frederick. For example, on May 16, 1751, he had purchased from Robert Worthington 230 acres on "a Branch of Potowmack called Evatts Marsh being a Branch of the River Shenandoah." (See Frederick County Deed Book No. 2, page 278; and "Hopewell Friends History," 1936, pages 183, 184.)

Evatts Marsh (Evitt's Run) heads several miles northwest of Charles Town, at or near Harewood, runs southeastward near the ruins of St. George's Chapel, thence on through Charles Town, and enters the Shenandoah River just below the main highway bridge, at or near the site of William Vestal's old bloomery.

Lawrence Washington in his will made June 20, 1752, and probated September 26 of the same year, left to his half-brothers Samuel, John, and Charles all those several tracts of land in Frederick County of which he was possessed, except the tract on the South Fork of Bullskin and the two tracts purchased of Colonel Cresap and Gerrard Pendergrass, his brother (half-brother) George to have use of an equal share in the devises during the natural life of the devisor's wife; the devisees to pay Betty (Washington) Lewis 150 pounds. (See Fairfax County Will Book A, pages 539-542.)

Evidently in the division of the Frederick County lands among the Washington brothers, the tract of 230 acres on Evatts Marsh fell to Samuel.

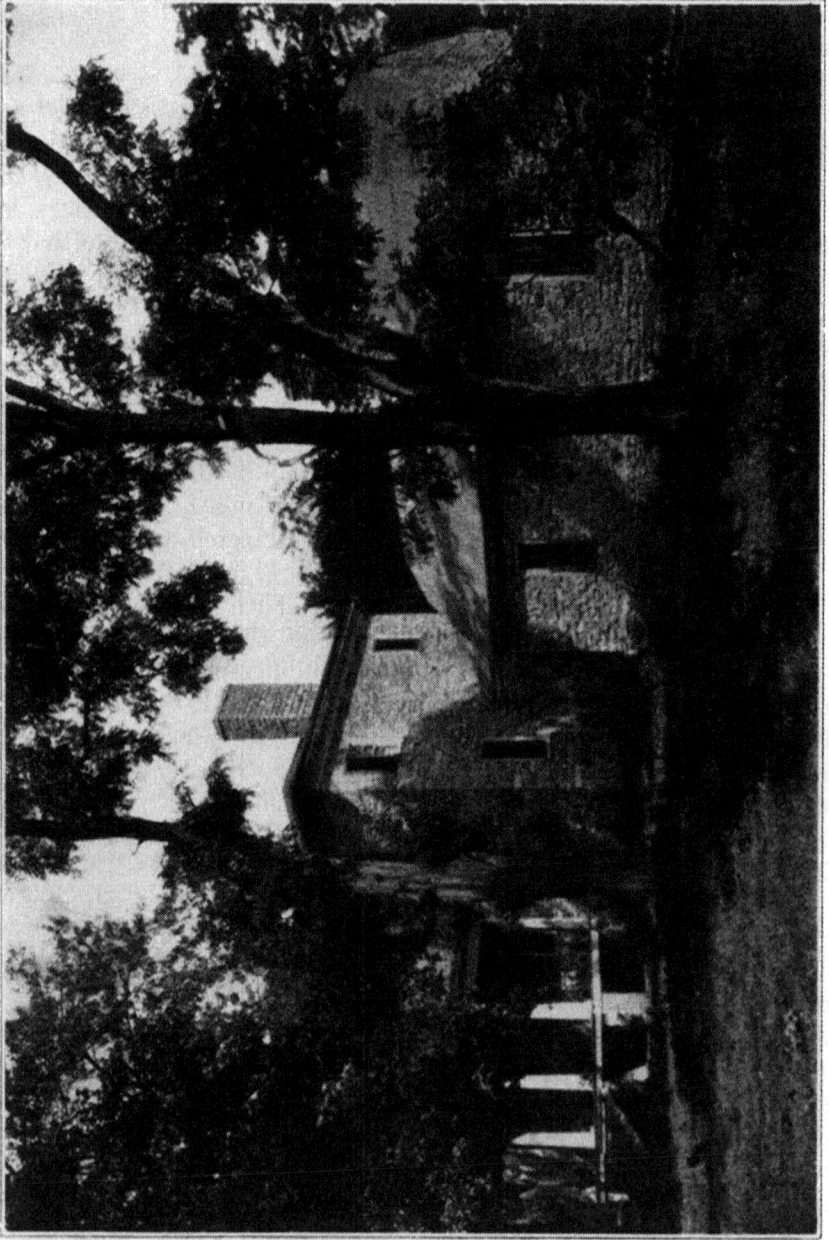

Harewood, from the west. Photo by Morrison, 1929.   *—From Historic Homes*

Thereon he built Harewood. This same tract, with temporary dwellings for the slaves and an overseer, may have been the "quarter" which was visited by George Washington in 1760, and mentioned in his diary. On Sunday, May 4, of that year he set out from Mount Vernon for Frederick County, to see certain of his Negroes who there lay ill of the smallpox. He reached Frederick late on Monday afternoon, in time to witness the burial of Richard Mounts, one of his overseers. At the same time he learned that Harry and Kit, two of his Negroes, were dead of the smallpox, and that Roger and Phillis were recovering from it. The next day, Tuesday, May 6, 1760, he recorded: "Visited my Brother's Quarter, and just call'd at my own in my way to Winchester." (See the "Diaries of George Washington," Fitzpatrick edition of 1925, Vol. I, page 159.)

In September 1770 Samuel Washington and his family moved to Frederick. On the way they sojourned two weeks at Mount Vernon. The following excerpts from George Washington's diary for certain days of September 1770 set the facts before us.

1st. Returned from the Arbitration of Colchester. In the evening my Brothr. Sam and his wife and children came hither from Fredericksburg in their way to Frederick.

2. At home all day with the Company before mentioned. Mr. Adam's Miller came here and went to see my Mill.

3. Went in the Evening a fishing with my Brothers Saml. and Charles.

*   *   *   *   *   *   *   *

9. Colo. Lewis, my Sister and Brother Charles went away. At Home all day.

10. My Brothr. Saml. and self rid to the Mill and Back to Dinner.

*   *   *   *   *   *   *   *

14. Rid to the Mill and Ditchers in the forenoon with my Brother; in the afternoon went a fishing.

15. Rid to Alexandria with my Brothr. and returned to Dinner.

16. At home all day. My Brothr. Sam and his Wife set of in my Chariot for his House in Frederick. . . .

(See Washington's Diaries, Fitzpatrick edition of 1925, Vol. I, pages 396, 397.)

Soon after Samuel Washington and his family were established in their new home in the Valley they were visited by George Washington. He on October 5, 1770, set out from Mount Vernon in company with Dr. James Craik for Redstone, in western Pennsylvania. They dined at Bryan Fairfax's and lodged over night in Leesburg. These particulars Washington records in his diary of that date. The next day, October 6, he writes:

"Bated at Old Codley's. Dind and lodgd at my Brother Sam's." In another entry of the same day he says: "Fed our Horses on the Top of the Ridge at one Codley's and arrived at my Brother Samls. on Worthington's Marsh a little after they had dind, the distance being about 30 Miles."

"Old Codley" it appears kept a wayside tavern at the summit of the pass of the Blue Ridge in Williams's Gap, later known as Snicker's Gap. The village of Bluemont, formerly Snickersville, lies on the eastern side of this pass, to which roads converge from different directions, coming up through the piedmont. The main highway, which follows the course of an old trail, comes up through Leesburg, Hamilton, Purcellville, and Round Hill. Washington and Dr. Craik evidently had started from Leesburg very early in the morning, as was the custom of horseback travelers in those days, and had baited (watered and fed) their horses at Codley's on top of the Ridge at ten or eleven o'clock. Here they were still fifteen miles or so from Samuel Washington's at Harewood and thus needed three hours or more to reach Harewood. They arrived there "a little after they had dind," but still in time to be served with a meal not later, probably, than one-thirty or two o'clock in the afternoon.

The total distance from Leesburg to Samuel Washington's was (and is) about thirty miles—by way of Snicker's Gap. It would have been four or five miles nearer, on a more direct course, to have come up from Leesburg to Hillsboro and Vestal's Gap, now Keys's Gap, and so on through the site of the present Charles Town, and thence three and a half miles farther on north-west to Harewood. The mountain is perhaps less steep at Keys's Gap, but it may be that the crossing of the river there was more difficult. It would seem that Washington on his trips to the Valley most frequently crossed the Blue Ridge at Snicker's, though he sometimes crossed at Vestal's (below Snicker's) and sometimes at Ashby's (above Snicker's). In March 1748, the first time he ever came over, he, George Fairfax, and James Genn, "ye surveyor," crossed at Ashby's; in April 1754, when, as a lieutenant-colonel, he led several companies of Virginia troops against the French on the Ohio, he crossed at Vestal's. (See "Historic Homes of Northern Virginia and the Eastern Pan-handle of West Virginia," by John W. Wayland, 1937, pages 40, 41.)

It was the habit of the early settlers in the lower Shenandoah Valley to speak of a small watercourse as a "marsh." Washington says that he and Dr. Craik "arrivd at my Brother Samls. on Worthington's Marsh." This was also called "Evatts Marsh," and is now familiar as Evitt's Run. Midway between Harewood and Charles Town it flows past an old homestead called Piedmont and the ruins of St. George's Chapel. As early as 1729 or 1730 Robert Worthington, a Quaker from New Jersey, had obtained a grant for 3,000 acres and settled at Piedmont, which he called "Quarry Banks New Stile," thus honoring his old home in Cheshire, England, which was named Quarry Banks. (See "Hopewell Friends History," 1936, pages 183, 184.)

After spending a month and a half in the Ohio Valley in October and November, 1770, Washington and Dr. Craik returned to the valley of the Shenandoah on their way home. On November 29 Washington was again at his brother Sam's, on Worthington's Marsh. In his diary he wrote: "Set out early and reachd my Brothers by one oclock. . . . Doctr. Craik having business

by Winchester went that way to meet at Snicker's to morrow by 10 Oclock."
The next day, Friday, November 30, he wrote: "According to Appointment the
Doctr. and I met, and after Breakfasting at Snickers proceeded on to Wests
where we arrivd at or before Sunset."

Again early the next spring Washington visited his brother Samuel at
Harewood, this time spending five or six days there. In company again with
Dr. Craik, he had crossed the Blue Ridge at Ashby's Gap, crossed the Shenandoah River at Berry's Ferry, and lodged over night (March 3, 1771) at
Greenway Court, where he had been a familiar figure twenty years before
while in the service of Lord Fairfax. The next day he dined in Winchester
with a number of the officers who had served in the French and Indian War,
and who were now seeking their shares in an allotment of 200,000 acres of
land that had been given them. The following day (March 5) he was in
Winchester all day, and there dined with Lord Fairfax. On the 6th he dined
at his lodging place, which was in the tavern of Philip Bush, and in the afternoon ("in ye Eveng." he says) he went home with his brother, Samuel Washington. The distance from Winchester to Harewood is about 25 miles. Accordingly, it must have been late, several hours after dark, by the time they
arrived at Harewood.

All the next day Washington was busily engaged at Harewood writing
instructions and dispatches for Captain William Crawford, the surveyor of the
200,000 acres of land. Crawford had been with Washington and Dr. Craik
in the Ohio Valley the preceding autumn spying out this land. Crawford had
long been a personal friend of Washington. He rose to the rank of colonel in
the Revolution, and in 1782, after having retired to his farm in western Pennsylvania, was persuaded to lead an expedition against the British and the
Indians in northern Ohio. Falling into the hands of the enemy, he was burned
to death by the Indians on June 11 (1782).

On the third day at Harewood Washington finished writing the instructions and dispatches for Captain Crawford and drew up also certain directions
for Marcus Stephenson, who was to bear the dispatches, etc., to Captain
Crawford. The same day a Mr. Dick and "the two Mr. Nurse's" dined with
him at Harewood. One of these was James Nourse, who, like Samuel
Washington, was prominent in the early history of Berkeley County. The
next day (March 10) Washington dined at Mr. Nourse's, but returned to his
brother's in the evening. On the 11th he left Harewood for Mount Vernon,
which he reached the evening of the 13th, having lodged the first night at
Warner Washington's, the second in Leesburg. This time he crossed the
Ridge at Snicker's. Goose Creek, below Leesburg, was so high that he was
obliged to go some distance upstream and ferry over at Hough's Mill; thence
he went around by Thomison Ellzey's.

Warner Washington, a first-cousin to George and Samuel, was at this
time (1771) living at or near Fairfield, where he and his family resided for

Harewood interior, with portrait of Col. Samuel Washington over the mantel. In this room James Madison and Dolly Payne Todd were married, 1794.

many years thereafter. Fairfield is located about nine miles south of Harewood, and on the direct course towards Snicker's Gap. It is now in the northeastern edge of Clarke County, Va., near the railroad station of Gaylord, which was at first called Fairfield Station. George Washington, on his trips to Harewood and other places in the Shenandoah Valley, stopped rather frequently at Fairfield with his cousin Warner. The latter was his elder by 17 years, but in spite of that the two were evidently devoted to each other.

In the early summer of 1772 George Washington was at Fairfield and Harewood again. After two days at Fairfield, he, with Warner Washington and a Mr. Willis, went down to Samuel Washington's, where they dined and stayed all night. In the Shenandoah Valley north and northeast are "down." The next day, June 2, Washington did some surveying in the neighborhood.

On February 28 and March 1, 1773, Warner Washington and Samuel Washington were visitors at Mount Vernon. Again in September of the same year Samuel Washington was at Mount Vernon, spending three or four days there. On this occasion he was accompanied by his wife and two children. This was his fourth wife, Anne Steptoe. The two children were probably Ferdinand and George Steptoe. Ferdinand, the oldest child of Anne, Samuel's fourth wife, was born July 16, 1767, as shown in the birth register of St. Paul's Church, Stafford County, Va. (See *Tyler's Quarterly Historical and Genealogical Magazine*, July 1934, page 46.) George Steptoe was probably born in or about 1770.

In March 1774 George Washington spent several days with his cousin Warner and his brother Samuel, as shown by his diary entries. This seems to be the first time that he applies the name Fairfield to the home of Warner Washington and Harewood to the home of his brother Samuel. It may be that the names were adopted about this time, but even so they have been in use for a period of at least 170 years.

No sooner was Samuel Washington well settled in the Shenandoah Valley than he began to increase his holdings in land, probably investing the proceeds of sales in Stafford and perhaps borrowing for additional purchases. In 1771 he acquired in Frederick County no fewer than eight pieces of real estate, as the deed books show. Two tracts were secured from Samuel Pearson, one of them 240 acres, a part of the Worthington land, the other 350 acres near Greenway Court, the country seat of Lord Fairfax. Two other tracts were obtained from Samuel Worthington, these two aggregating 431 acres. Three tracts, totaling 1457 acres, were bought from Isaiah and George Pemberton, adjoining the lands of Robert Worthington. And 212 acres near the North Mountain were purchased from Zachariah Connell. Altogether the eight tracts made a total of 2690 acres. The same year (1771) the 350-acre tract near Greenway Court was sold to Thomas Bryan Martin.

Not only was Samuel Washington an active dealer in land after his location in Frederick County, he also at once became prominent in the political, religious, and military life of the county. Already it has been pointed out that he was listed as one of the magistrates of Frederick in May and October 1769. The order books of the county show that he was sworn in as a justice on February 5, 1771, and that he on the same day also took the required oaths as a vestryman of Norborne Parish, which lay in that part of Frederick County now composing the counties of Berkeley and Jefferson, West Virginia. (See Frederick County Order Book No. 15, page 102.)

On May 7 of the same year (1771) Samuel Washington was sworn in as colonel of the militia of Frederick County. (See Order Book No. 15, page 183.) Among the militia captains under him were Robert Stephen, Daniel Morgan, Morgan Alexander, William Ashby, and Hugh Stephenson. Daniel Morgan at that time probably was living at Soldier's Rest, his old homestead near the locality now occupied by the town of Berryville. Four years later he led a company of riflemen from the "right bank of the Potomac," in a record march to Boston, thereby cheering mightily the heart of George Washington, the new commander-in-chief of the American forces. Soon Morgan won distinction at Quebec and Saratoga; later he achieved lasting renown at Cowpens and other places in the South, being fittingly celebrated in later years and unto the present as the "Thunderbolt of the Revolution." Hugh Stephenson also led a company of riflemen from the lower Shenandoah Valley to Boston in a "bee-line" march that rivaled Morgan's. William Ashby was doubtless one of the Ashby's Gap clan, from whom Turner Ashby and Dick Ashby of Civil War fame were descended.

In the spring of 1772 the northeastern part of Frederick County was cut off and erected into the new county of Berkeley. Thenceforth Samuel Washington, by virtue of his place of residence, was a citizen of Berkeley County. At once he was put forward in positions of responsibility and honor in the new civic organization.

The first court of Berkeley County was held on May 19, 1772, at the house of Friend (Quaker) Edward Beeson, which still stands a short distance northeast of the city of Martinsburg, county-seat of Berkeley. Samuel Washington was one of the nineteen men who had been appointed by Lord Dunmore, the royal governor of Virginia, to act as magistrates, and he was one of the eleven who were present at the first meeting of the court, as aforesaid. The eleven were Van Swearengen, Thomas Swearengen, Samuel Washington, James Nourse, William Morgan, William Little, James Strode, Robert Stephen, Robert Stogdon, Robert C. Willis, and James Seaton.

Samuel Washington was present also at the meeting of the court, as one of the county justices, on June 16, 1772, and at various other times later. In April, 1773, among the justices of Berkeley County who served with Samuel Washington were Adam Stephen and Horatio Gates, both of whom became general officers in the Revolution.

Colonel Samuel Washington was also active in local development and industry. On September 15, 1772, "On the motion of Samuel Washington, Gentleman, praying leave to Erect a Water Grist Mill on Bullskin Run on the land he purchased of Philip Pendleton, Ordered that a jury be Summoned for that purpose."

Bullskin is a small stream that heads, in its north fork, about three miles south of Harewood, flows southeastward between Charles Town and the village of Rippon, entering the Shenandoah River near Kable Town.

At the same court Samuel Washington also made petition that the road leading from Snicker's to Jacob Hite's, from the place commonly known by the name of Elk Spring, to the road leading from McCormack's to Harper's Ferry, be turned. A commission was appointed to view and make report.

"Snicker's" was probably in or near Snicker's Gap in the Blue Ridge, opposite Berryville. On the west side, as on the east side, roads radiate from the gap. One of these roads leading northwest to Hite's and the fords of the Potomac passed near Harewood, hence Samuel Washington's special interest in it. Jacob Hite, a son of Joist, lived at a place that has long been known as Leetown, about four miles north of Harewood. Soon after 1772 Jacob Hite, bitterly disappointed because Martinsburg and not his settlement (Leetown) was made the county-seat of Berkeley, sold out and moved to South Carolina, where he and most of his family were cruelly murdered (in 1776) by the Indians. (See Kercheval's History of the Valley of Virginia, Strasburg edition of 1925, pages 179, 180.) Jacob Hite's settlement took its name of Leetown after General Charles Lee, a prominent officer of the Revolution, who lived there in a house that still remains.

In April, 1773, Samuel Washington was sheriff of Berkeley County. He served in the same office also in 1776. On November 20, 1776, as the court record shows, he produced a commission from the governor and was sworn in, with John Coke and Robert Throckmorton his sureties. (See Berkeley County Order Book No. 2, page 504.)

In the years immediately preceding the Revolution Samuel Washington's name frequently appears in the court records of Berkeley, as a viewer of roads, a taker of tithables, etc., as well as in the capacity of magistrate and sheriff. At several meetings of the court, to wit, August 20 and November 19, 1776, and perhaps at other times, he signed the record of the court orders. This indicates that he was the presiding justice on these occasions.

On November 20, 1776, gentlemen justices present Samuel Washington, John Coke, Godwin Swift, Robert Worthington, and Morgan Morgan, Negro Nace, a slave belonging to General Horatio Gates, in gaol accused of breaking open the cellar of the said General Gates and feloniously taking from thence a "Chest Money and Cloaths," was brought before the bar. When he was asked whether he was guilty or not guilty, "he says he is guilty." It was therefore the judgment of the court that he be remanded back to gaol and that he continue therein till the 3d Friday in December next, and then be hanged by the neck "till he is dead." He was valued at 70 pounds, which sum was to be paid to his master, General Gates.

As a rule, when a prisoner was adjudged guilty of a serious criminal offense in the county court he was sent on to the superior court at Williamsburg, or in later times to some other place where a superior court was held; but in this case the execution was to follow the verdict of the county court. Perhaps this was due to the fact that Nace confessed his guilt; or it may be that inasmuch as Negro slaves were legal property, they could be disposed of by the local court without reference to a superior court. In 1814 a capital case involving a slave was similarly disposed of in Shenandoah County, by the county court. Hercules, a Negro man slave of Thomas Fox, was convicted of housebreaking and sentenced to be hanged therefor. (See "A History of Shenandoah County, Virginia," by John W. Wayland, 1927, page 252.) A subsequent act of the Virginia Assembly recites that Hercules broke jail and escaped "for good." Whether Nace escaped or was hanged is not known to the present writer.

Colonel Samuel Washington for some time, probably for only a short period, served Berkeley County as county lieutenant, that is, as commander of militia and chief military officer of the county. This appears from an entry in the court records of April 3, 1777:

On petition of Samuel Washington Gent setting forth his low state of health which renders him, unfit for publick business, and therefore prays that he may have leave to resign his Commission as County Lieutenant, which is granted.

Van Swearengen, Gent., was appointed county lieutenant in the room of Samuel Washington, Esq., "who hath resigned."

Here we perceive the reason, or one of the reasons, why Colonel Samuel Washington did not perform active military duty in the field in the war of the Revolution—he did not, so far as is known. Evidently his health was breaking down, and he therefore was not able to undergo the strenuous exertions and damaging exposures of camp and field. Obviously, however, he rendered such services at home as he was able to perform, and until his failing health made retirement necessary. Whether he was ever as vigorous physically as his older brother, General Washington, seems doubtful, though the portrait of him that hangs over the mantel at Harewood shows a well-favored young man, who, in the picture, might easily be mistaken for George Washington.

From items already presented and others that will appear farther on, it must be plain that Colonel Samuel Washington was a large landholder and a progressive man of affairs, though he was not as wealthy in lands and other resources as his brothers, especially General Washington. From the records of the courts it appears that he was an occasional party in a suit, though not very often. In this respect he seems to have fallen below the popular average for men of those times, which was rather high. Having cases in court was in that period of our history a favorite pastime. On the tablet which was erected in 1933 near Harewood by the Bee Line Chapter, D. A. R., it is stated that he was senior warden of St. George's Chapel.

On September 26, 1777, Samuel Washington and his wife Anne made a deed for land to James Kelso and James Wilson. This fact is of special interest as showing that his fourth wife, Anne Steptoe, was still living at that date. Exact information as to the dates of his several marriages has been difficult to obtain. Anne Steptoe Washington had at least four children, namely, Ferdinand, George Steptoe, Lawrence Augustine, and Harriet. Ferdinand, probably the oldest, was born in 1767; Harriet was the youngest of the four named. Prior to September 9, 1781, when Samuel Washington made his will, his fifth wife, Susannah, had borne him a son, John Perrin Washington. Following are the few facts that seem to be known about his several wives:

1. Jane Champe, daughter of Colonel John Champe of King George County, Va. If she had any children they died in infancy.

2. Mildred Thornton, daughter of Colonel John Thornton and his wife Mildred Gregory. Mildred had two sons: Thornton, born probably in 1760, who grew up and married; and Tristram, born in or about 1763, who did not grow up.

3. Lucy Chapman, daughter of Nathaniel Chapman. If she had any children they did not grow up.

4. Anne Steptoe, daughter of Colonel William Steptoe. She is said to have been the widow of Willoughby Allerton when she married Samuel Washington, probably in the autumn of 1766. She had at least four Washington children: Ferdinand, born July 16, 1767; George Steptoe, Lawrence Augustine, and Harriet, who married Parks. Evidently it is the opinion of John C. Fitzpatrick that Anne had other Washington children who did not grow up. (See his Diaries of George Washington, 1925 edition, Vol. I, page 285, note.) All of Anne's children must have been born prior to December 1780, since Samuel Washington married his fifth wife not later than that date.

5. The Widow Holding, who seems to have been born Susannah Perrin. She had a son, John Perrin Washington, who was born prior to September 9, 1781, when Samuel Washington made his will.

The provisions of Colonel Washington's will were as follows:

(1) The payment of his debts as soon as possible after his death;

(2) his wife to have the home place, 230 acres, with all its appurtenances, also a tract of 570 acres called Rutherfords, and 50 acres acres bought of Isaiah Pemberton, contiguous to the home place; also a fourth of all his Negroes, excepting those devised to his son Thornton and his daughter Harriet; the wife to have her choice of Aaron (a joiner) or Phil (a weaver); his phaeton and a fourth of the horses, sheep, and hogs; during her widowhood; upon her marriage to go to his son John Perrin Washington and his heirs;

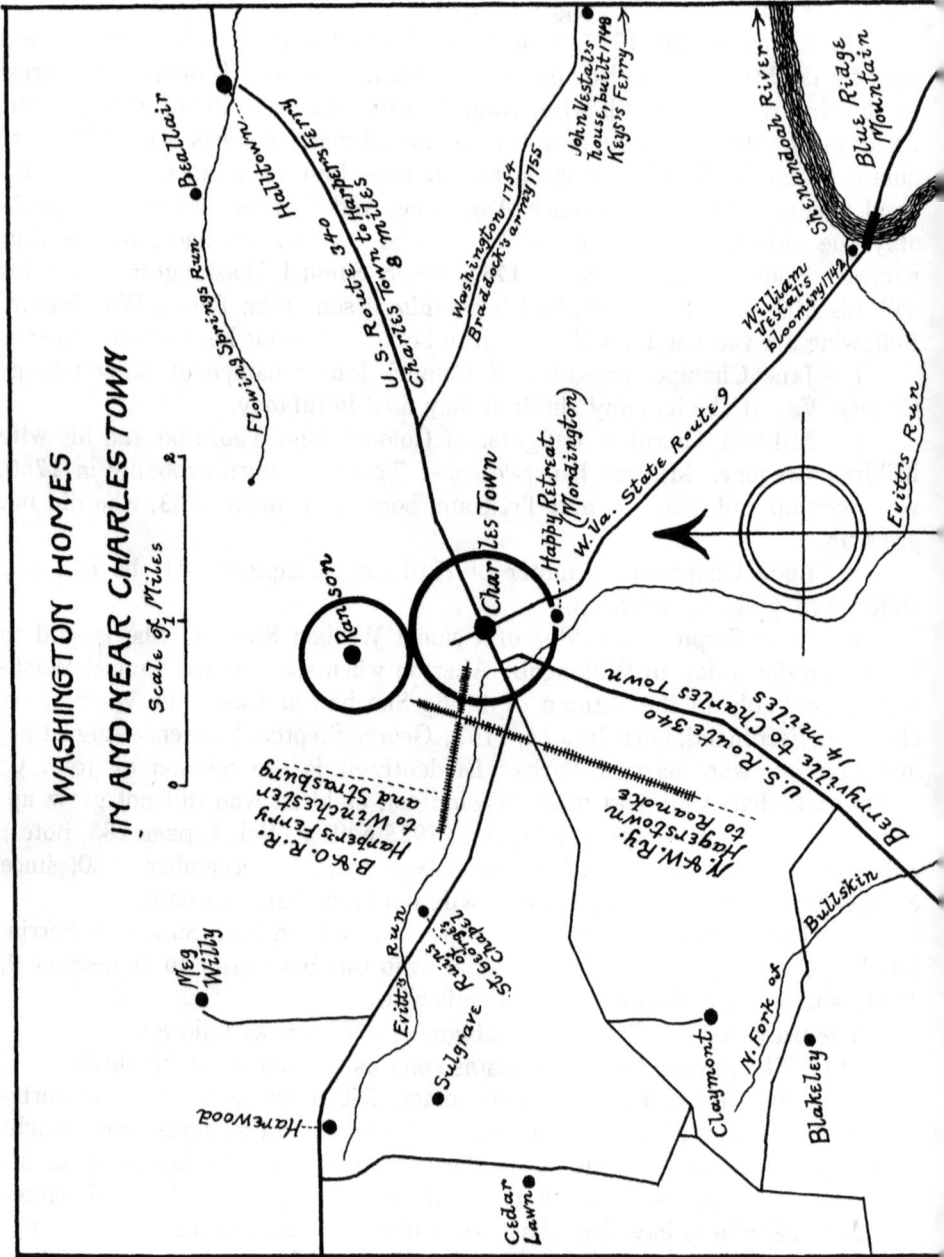

WASHINGTON HOMES IN AND NEAR CHARLES TOWN

Scale of Miles

(3)   his son Thornton to have a Negro man David (a cooper), a wench called Great Sall and her chidren, and two boys, Glasscow and Nelson; the 7,000 pounds which Thornton owed for his home place; also the privilege of getting on any part of the estate as much board timber as he might want for the use of his plantation for seven years to come;

(4)   his son Ferdinand to have the tracts of land bought of Samuel Pearson and Samuel Worthington; a fourth of all the Negroes, excepting those devised to Thornton and Harriet; also a fourth of all the horses, cattle, sheep, and hogs;

(5)   his son George Steptoe to have the land bought of George Pemberton; also that bought of Isaiah Pemberton, excepting the 50 acres devised to the widow, her 50 acres to include the orchard; George Steptoe to have also a fourth of all the Negroes, excepting those devised to Thornton and Harriet; and a fourth of all the horses, cattle, sheep, and hogs;

(6)   his son Lawrence Augustine to have the tract of land "known by the name of the Rushwoods or surplus," 700 acres; also the land bought of Wm. McCormick; together with a fourth of the Negroes, excepting those devised to Thornton and Harriet, and a fourth of all the stock;

(7)   his daughter Harriet to have 350 pounds of hard money, "to be raised out of my estate as soon as my debts are paid and to be put to interest for her use"; also a mulatto woman called Cecelia and her increase;

Item, it is my will and desire that if either of my said sons Ferdinand, George Steptoe, Lawrence Augustine or John Perrin die before they come of age the estate hereby devised to them or either of them be equally divided among my surviving sons, Thornton not excepted.

Item, It is my will & desire that my estate be kept together for the common use of my wife & children untill they my children respectively come of age when it is my will & desire that their estate be given them for their own absolute use & disposal.

Item, it is my further will & desire that my plate (except a large Salver a Tankard & a pint can which I leave to be equally divided among my other Children) go and be delivered unto my son Ferdinand when he comes of age.

Item, I give and devise unto my son Ferdinand a lot in the town of Mecklinburg [Shepherdstown] in the said county of Berkeley & its appurtenances to him & his heirs forever the said lot bought of David Shepherd.

Item, I give & devise unto my brother John Washington & his heirs an equal part of two Lots in Bath town [now Berkeley Springs] purchased of the commissioners, together with their appurtenances.

Lastly I do hereby appoint my worthy brothers George, John Augustine, and Charles Washington together with my esteemed friend James Nourse Senr. Executors of this my last will & Testament revoking all former and other wills. In witness whereof I have hereunto set my hand & seal this Ninth day of September, one Thousand Seven Hundred & eighty one.

SAMUEL WASHINGTON (LS)

(See Berkeley County Will Book No. 1, page 237.)

On December 18, 1781, the above will of Samuel Washington, deceased, was proved in court by the oaths of Charles Washington and James Nourse two of the witnesses thereto, and Charles Washington and James Nourse entered into bond as executors, with John Cooke and James Crane as their sureties, in the penalty of 10,000 pounds specie.

Although Samuel Washington had appointed his three brothers, George, John A., and Charles, executors of his will, only one of them, namely Charles, appeared to qualify for that service. The time, December 1781, and the impending condition of public affairs provide ample reason why General George Washington, commander-in-chief of the Revolutionary armies, could not take upon him the work of administering his brother's estate. John Augustine Washington lived at a considerable distance in the county of Westmoreland. Charles, as it appears, had already moved up from Fredericksburg and established himself at Happy Retreat, his home four miles southeast of Harewood, just south of the town-site which he laid out on his land five years later and named Charles Town.

Samuel Washington's fifth wife, the one so carefully provided for in his will, survived him less than two years. On December 5, 1782, she, Susannah Washington of Berkeley County, made her will. Therein she mentions her son, John Perrin Washington; her first husband, George Holding; her sister Willis of Gloster; her friend Dr. James Armstrong; her friend Mr. Dolphin Drew; her friend Mr. James Nourse Sr.; her friend Francis Willis of Gloster; and her sister Lewis of Gloster. Francis Willis and William Reynolds of York were appointed executors. The will was witnessed by Warner Washington Jr., who lived at or near Fairfield, now in the edge of Clarke County. The document was proved before the court of Berkeley County on May 20, 1783.

Thornton Washington, son of Colonel Samuel Washington and his second wife, Mildred Thornton, died in 1787 at the early age of 27 or thereabouts, having been twice married. His first wife was Mildred Berry of Stafford County, Va.; his second wife, married April 2, 1786, was Frances Townshend Washington. He lived at Cedar Lawn, called Berry's Hill prior to 1780, a fine old estate near Harewood. On July 26, 1787, he made his will. Therein he describes himself as of Berkeley County, Va. He names individuals: "My wife Frances Townshend Washington"; "My son by her, Samuel Washington"; "My other two sons which I had by my former wife, Mildred Washington"; "My three half-brothers and sister." He appoints his wife and his friends Lawrence Washington Jr. of Chotank and Warner Washington Jr. of Frederick executors. The will was probated October 16, 1787. From other records of Berkeley County, at Martinsburg, it appears that his "other two sons" by his first wife Mildred were named Thornton and Thomas. The former's full name was John Thornton Augustine Washington.

Ferdinand Washington, born 1767, the son of Colonel Samuel Washington and his fourth wife, Anne Steptoe, the Widow Allerton, died in Lancaster

County, Va., in 1788. An appraisement of his estate was made on June 4, 1789. (See Berkeley County Will Book No. 2, page 36.) His brothers, George Steptoe and Lawrence Augustine, in 1785 were going to school in Georgetown and Alexandria, under the supervision of their uncle, General George Washington. The latter, following the successful close of the Revolution, was now at home, in charge again of his personal business, improving the buildings and grounds at Mount Vernon, and at the same time giving generous attention to the orphan children of his bother Samuel, whose financial affairs had evidently been left in a condition far from satisfactory. Under date of November 20, 1785, he wrote in his diary: "My Nephew Lawe. Washington came here with a letter to day from Mr. Bayley respecting their Board, etca." He evidently refers to the board of Lawrence Augustine and George Steptoe. Mr. Bayley was a merchant of Georgetown. On Wednesday, November 23, the General made this entry:

> Sent Mr. Shaw through Alexandria, to agree for the Schooling and Board of My Nephews George Steptoe and Lawrence Washington now at the Academy of George Town, and thence to the latter place to conduct them to the former for the purpose of going to School at the Alexandria Academy.

Washington was one of the trustees of the Alexandria Academy. His nephew, George Steptoe, was now (1785) about fifteen years old, and Lawrence Augustine a year or two younger. Various passages in General Washington's will, made July 9, 1799, have reference to Alexandria Academy, certain business relations with his deceased brother Samuel, and the education of Samuel's sons, George Steptoe and Lawrence Augustine. Following are pertinent excerpts from his will:

> To the Trustees (Governors, or by whatever other name they may be designated) of the Academy in the Town of Alexandria, I give and bequeath, in Trust, Four thousand dollars, or in other words twenty of the shares which I hold in the Bank of Alexandria, towards the support of a Free School established at, and annexed to, the said Academy; for the purpose of educating such orphan children, or the children of such other poor and indigent persons as are unable to accomplish it with their own means; and who, in the judgment of the trustees of the said Seminary, are best entitled to the benefit of this donation. . . . The aforesaid twenty shares I give and bequeath in perpetuity; . . . the dividends only of which are to be drawn for and applied by the said Trustees for the time being, for the uses above mentioned; . . .
> I release exonerate and discharge, the estate of my deceased brother, Samuel Washington, from the payment of the money which is due to me for the land I sold to Philip Pendleton (lying in the County of Berkeley) who assigned the same to him the said Samuel; who, by agreement was to pay me therefor. . . . And whereas by some contract (the purport of which was never communicated to me) between the said Samuel and his son Thornton Washington, the latter became possessed of the aforesaid land, without any conveyance having passed from me, either to the said Pendleton, the said Samuel, or the said Thornton, and without

any consideration having been made, by which neglect neither the legal or equitable title has been alienated; . . . it rests therefore with me to declare my intention
concerning the premises. . . . And these are to give and bequeath the said land to,
whomsoever the said Thornton Washington (who is also dead) devised the same;
or to his heirs forever if he died intestate; . . . Exonerating the estate of the said
Thornton, equally with that of the said Samuel from payment of the purchase
money; which, with Interest, agreeably to the original contract with the said
Pendleton, would amount to more than a thousand pounds. . . . And whereas two
other sons of my said deceased brother Samuel . . . namely, George Steptoe
Washington and Lawrence Augustine Washington, were by the decease of those
to whose care they were committed, brought under my protection, and in conseqe
have occasioned advances on my part for their education at college, and other
schools, for their board . . . clothing . . . and other incidental expenses, to the
amount of near five thousand dollars over and above the sums furnished by their
estate wch sum may be inconvenient for them, or their father's Estate to refund
. . . I do for these reasons acquit them, and the said estate, from the payment
thereof. . . . My intention being that all accounts between them and me, and their
father's estate and me shall stand balanced.

To the same two nephews General Washington showed his generosity
otherwise in his will. To Lawrence Augustine he left one twenty-third part of
his residuary estate. To George Steptoe he left a sword and one twenty-third
part of his residuary estate. To their sister, Harriet Washington, who married
Andrew Parks of Baltimore in 1796, he left one twenty-third part of his
residuary estate. A like bequest was made to the heirs of Thornton Washington, deceased. He also appointed his nephew, George Steptoe Washington,
one of his executors.

George Steptoe Washington (1770?-1809) lived at Harewood, the home
of his father, Colonel Samuel Washington. His wife was Lucy Payne, a sister
to Dolly Payne Todd; and thus it came about that the marriage of James
Madison and Dolly Payne Todd, in September 1794, took place at Harewood.
The spacious northeast parlor on the main floor of the mansion, with its
exquisite paneling of fine wood work and its ample fireplace, is pointed out as
the room in which the "great little Madison" and the vivacious young widow
were joined in matrimony. The officiating clergyman was Rev. Alexander
Balmain, a chaplain of the Revolution and for many years thereafter a well-
known minister of Winchester and the surrounding region.

The porphyry mantel-piece in the parlor at Harewood is said to have been
sent over from France, a gift from Lafayette. Lafayette was a visitor here, as
were also many other distinguished men of the Revolutionary period. Here
three princes of France, Louis Philippe, afterwards king of France, and his
two brothers, lived for some time while exiles in America. The portrait of
Colonel Samuel Washington, in military uniform, hangs over the mantel.

Harewood is historic in itself, and it is surrounded by many other old
homesteads that have notable claims to distinction. Within a radius of twenty-
five miles or less lived for longer or shorter periods no fewer than nine generals

of the Revolution and years immediately following: Daniel Morgan, James Wood, Adam Stephen, Horatio Gates, Charles Lee, William Darke, John Smith of Hackwood, Daniel Roberdeau of Winchester, and Otho Williams of Williamsport, Md. Among other historic places in the neighborhood are a number of Washington homes that are presented in succeeding chapters. One of which little is known, but which should not be forgotten, is (or was) Meg Willie. It occupied a fine elevation a mile and a half northeast of Harewood and was the home of William Temple Washington, a son of George Steptoe Washington and his wife Lucy Payne. William Temple Washington married Margaret Calhoun Fletcher, and the name of their home was fabricated from the familiar forms of their first names.

The old house at Meg Willie was removed years ago but the cellar hole and the cistern indicate where it stood. The surface of the ground hereabout is broken by outcropping limestone ledges, as at Harewood. Numerous locusts and other old trees remain to give evidence of former beauty and culture. Many old farm buildings are still in use. The place is now owned by a Mr. Ambler of Charles Town.

CHAPTER IX

CHARLES WASHINGTON AND CHARLES TOWN

Charles Washington, youngest full brother of George, received by his father's will a number of Negro slaves and several tracts of land, among the latter 700 acres in the county of Prince William, purchased of Gabriel Adams. Augustine Washington's will was probated May 6, 1743, Charles, his youngest son, being then just five years old. Ten years later, by the will of Lawrence Washington of Mount Vernon, Charles's half-brother, Charles received an equal share, with his brothers Samuel and John Augustine, of certain valuable lands in Frederick County. These lands lie in what is now Jefferson County, West Virginia. By 1759 he was of legal age and entitled to assume the management of his various properties in Frederick, Prince Williiam, etc. He probably married about this time. His wife was Mildred Thornton, daughter of Colonel Francis Thornton and his wife Frances Gregory, of Spotsylvania County.

On August 3, 1761, by a conveyance from Warner Lewis and his wife Eleanor, Charles Washington for the sum of 80 pounds acquired two lots, No. 87 and No. 88, in a new addition to the town of Fredericksburg, lying in Spotsylvania County. This new addition had been authorized by an act of the General Assembly of the colony of Virginia in 1759, and a plan thereof had been made by Joseph Brock, surveyor of Spotsylvania County, in 1760. By means of maps to be seen in the clerk's office of the city of Fredericksburg the lots named above can easily be located. Four half-acre lots made up a block. Lots 87 and 88 formed the southeast half of a block and abutted on Fauquier Street. Lot 87 also abutted on Caroline or Main Street on the northeast. and Lot 88 on Princess Anne Street, on the southwest.

These particulars are recited because of their bearing on the locations of two old houses, the Rising Sun Tavern being one, which are said to have belonged to Charles Washington. According to some statements, this historic old tavern, which was celebrated before the Revolution, was built by Charles Washington. Whether he built it or not, it certainly stood (and still stands) on his land, this Lot No. 87. fronting on Caroline Street between Hawke and Fauquier, nearer the latter. It was a favorite meeting-place for the men of colonial and Revolutionary times. It has recently been repaired and is now used as a museum in which are kept many objects that are of interest to persons who are disposed to study the past.

The other house referred to is a quaint old brick structure which origi nally stood at the corner of Fauquier and Princess Anne. Some years ago it was moved a short distance along Fauquier towards Caroline Street, but it is still on Lot No. 88. It may have been the residence of Charles Washington, and perhaps both it and the Rising Sun Tavern were built by him.

Like his brothers and other young men with whom he was associated,

Charles Washington, youngest brother of General George Washington.

Charles Washington entered upon responsible duties of public service early in life. Published records show that he was a magistrate of Spotsylvania County in July 1765, April 1769, June 1769, and May 1773. No doubt he discharged the duties of the same office for the intervening periods and for several years thereafter. In February 1766 he was one of the signers of the celebrated Articles (resolutions) of the Association of Westmoreland, along with his brothers Samuel and John Augustine, and 112 other men of the Rappahannock and Potomac region, protesting against the British Stamp Act of 1765. Charles Mortimer, who later resided in a commodious brick house farther down on Caroline Street, was the first mayor of Fredericksburg (1782, 1783), and one of Mary Washington's physicians, also rode down to Leedstown in 1766, perhaps in company with Samuel and Charles Washington, and signed the Westmoreland Articles.

George Washington records in his diary that he dined at his brother Charles's on August 3, 1770; supped with him the evening of April 28, 1771; and dined with him again on September 16, 1772. Evidently Charles was living in Fredericksburg and was a man of standing in the town as well as in the county. He made occasional purchases of real estate, as already indicated. On August 1, 1771, Richard Lewis, saddler, of Fredericksburg, conveyed to him the upper part of Lot No. 76, "as it now stands divided," according to the plan of the town made by Joseph Brock in 1760. The grantee is written down as "Charles Washington, Esquire," of Fredericksburg. On March 11, 1773, he purchased from Mary Steward, widow, and her sons Benjamin and William, for 200 pounds, 200 acres in Spotsylvania County.

Entries in the diary of his distinguished brother show that Charles Washington was a rather frequent visitor at Mount Vernon. For instance, he was there in September 1770 for several days, with Colonel Fielding Lewis and his wife and Samuel Washington and his family, while the latter were sojourning there on their way to their new home (Harewood) in Frederick County, now in Jefferson County, West Virginia. In February 1771 he spent nearly a week at Mount Vernon shooting ducks with a Mr. Thompson, who may have been a son of Governor Spotswood's widow by her second husband, Rev. John Thompson of St. Mark's Parish, Culpeper County. In October 1773 he and a Mr. Willis were guests at Mount Vernon for six days, going at intervals "up to Church" and "up to Court" in Alexandria. After he moved to Berkeley County he still made occasional visits to Mount Vernon.

It was no little task while he lived in Fredericksburg to keep in touch with his lands in the Shenandoah Valley, distant by the most direct course no less than 70 miles, and farther by way of Mount Vernon. By good hard riding it was a journey of two or three days, with rivers and mountains to cross. Developments were in progress in the Valley. On March 14, 1771, Charles Washington was awarded damages for a mill race on his land in Frederick County. This land the next year fell into the new county of

Rising Sun Tavern on Lot 87 in Fredericksburg; once owned by Charles Washington. Photo October 18, 1938.

Berkeley, and later into what is now the county of Jefferson, in West Virginia. The records of Berkeley County, at Martinsburg, show that Charles Washington of the town of Fredericksburg on June 9, 1773, gave bond in the sum of 500 pounds to Robert Worthington to guarantee to the said Worthington the use and upkeep of a race (a tailrace) from the said Worthington's water grist mill on Worthington's Marsh, 58 poles through the land of the said Charles Washington. The witnesses to this bond were John Augustine Washington, Thomas Rutherford, Ben Tutt, and Edward Violett. Another record, dated two days later, shows an agreement that probably related to the same mill race; and twenty years later, October 12, 1793, the agreement was renewed.

On May 27, 1779, Edward Voss and others, for 1,000 pounds (probably paper money), conveyed to Charles Washington of Fredericksburg, Gentleman, two lots or half-acres of land in Fredericksburg, No. 79 and No. 80, bounded by the streets Caroline, Hawke, and Sophia. (See Spotsylvania County Deed Book J, page 482.) The high figure in this purchase was probably due mainly to the depreciated currency of the Revolution; but the lots conveyed may have had upon them valuable improvements. The same year, on July 15, Charles Washington gave bond for 200 pounds, with Mann Page and John Lewis his sureties, to execute faithfully the duties of the office of escheator for Spotsylvania County. In that period when sovereignty was being transferred and a number of titles were being questioned or invalidated, the office of escheator necessarily assumed considerable importance.

In the year 1780 appear two records, one at Spotsylvania Court House, the other in the city clerk's office in Fredericksburg, that are of special interest in showing the approximate time when Charles Washington removed from Fredericksburg to his new home in Berkeley County. On April 20, 1780, he and his wife Mildred for 8,000 pounds (Revolutionary curency, we assume) conveyed to Thomas Strachan 759 acres of land in Spotsylvania County. In this instrument the grantors are designated as of Spotsylvania County. The same year, evidently later in the year, though the month and day do not appear, Charles Washington and Mildred his wife, "late of the town of Fredericksburg," of the first part, Burgess Ball and Fanny his wife of the second part, and Robert Forsyth of the third part . . . Charles Washington, Esquire, being seized in Fee of two certain Lotts of Land known and described in the plan of the town of Fredericksburg by the Numbers of 79 and 80, and being so seized did for a valuable consideration and divers good causes him thereunto moving give, transfer, alien, and make over the two Lotts aforesaid to the aforesaid Burgess Ball . . . the said Charles and Mildred joined in the deed to Robert Forsyth. The deed was witnessed by John Augustine Washington, George A. Washington, Will. Drew, Rob. Rutherford, Jas. Craine, and Thornton Washington. (See Fredericksburg City Deed Book A, pages 9-11.) The witnesses to this deed were all "next-door" neighbors to Charles Washington in the Valley.

Old Charles Washington House on Lot 88 in Fredericksburg, near the Rising Sun Tavern, which was also owned by Charles Washington. Photo October 18. 1938.

Mordington ("Happy Retreat"), home of Charles Washington, at Charles Town. Photo by Morrison, 1929.

Evidently Charles Washington removed from Fredericksburg to the Valley at some time within the year 1780, after the date of April 20, when he was still of Spotsylvania County. At a subsequent date in the same year, when he joined in a deed with his son-in-law, Colonel Burgess Ball, he was "late of the town of Fredericksburg." The names of the witnesses to this deed, or most of them, indicate that he was in Berkeley County when he made it. William Drew, Robert Rutherford, James Crane, and Thornton Washington all lived in Berkeley County, near the new home of Charles Washington. William Drew was the first clerk of the court of Berkeley County. Robert Rutherford, with General Adam Stephen, represented Berkeley County in one of the early Revolutionary conventions at Williamsburg; he was later (1793-1797) a member of Congress. Thornton Washington was the eldest son of Colonel Samuel Washington, brother to Charles, who had located at Harewood in 1770.

Burgess Ball (1749-1800) had a distinguished Revolutionary record, having in 1776 at his own expense recruited, clothed, and equipped a regiment for the Continental Line. He was subsequently reimbursed, but impoverished himself by unrestrained generosity and hospitality. He married first Mary Chichester, who died in 1775. His second wife was Frances Washington, daughter of Charles and Mildred.

On December 18, 1781, the will of Colonel Samuel Washington was proved in the Berkeley court by the oaths of Charles Washington and John Cooke, two of the witnesses thereto. Samuel had appointed his brothers George, John Augustine, and Charles, and his friend James Nourse Sr. his executors. Charles Washington and James Nourse qualified, with John Cooke and James Crane as their sureties. General Washington was fully occupied with public affairs; John Augustine lived in Westmoreland County, distant 150 miles. Charles, living within four miles of Harewood, his brother Samuel's home, undertook the task of settling the estate, which was much involved.

Although Charles Washington's chief interests were in Berkeley County after 1780, he still held properties for some years thereafter in and near Fredericksburg. On October 17, 1785, Charles Washington of Berkeley County, Esquire, and Mildred his wife, Burgess Ball of Culpeper County, Esquire, and Fanny his wife, and Robert Forsyth joined in a deed to convey lots 79 and 80, with their appurtenances, in Fredericksburg, to John Legg of Fredericksburg, merchant; and on October 6, 1786, Charles and Mildred, with George Augustine Washington and Frances his wife, of Berkeley, conveyed a lot in Fredericksburg to Zachariah Lucas of Spotsylvania County. On the same date (October 6, 1786) the same parties as grantors, for 200 pounds and five shillings, conveyed 145 acres on Hazel Run (just outside of Fredericksburg) to George French.

The deed books of Berkeley County amply justify the statement that Charles Washington's chief interests during the last twenty years of his life were in that region. Between and including the years 1777-1799 he and his

Old shop at Mordington, "Happy Retreat," home of Charles Washington, at Charles Town. Photo 1929.

wife appear as grantors in no fewer than 87 conveyances of real estate. On March 13, 1783, they, for 295 pounds, conveyed to Ephraim Worthington 118 acres of land adjoining the lands of the said Charles Washington, Robert Worthington's heirs, James Nourse, and James Crane, being part of a larger tract belonging to Charles Washington. Four days later, on St. Patrick's day, the same grantors for 450 pounds made a deed to Robert Rutherford for 150 acres in Berkeley County and the Parish of Norborne, part of two separate tracts granted to Major Lawrence Washington, late of Fairfax County, on October 17, 1751.

Most of the 87 deeds referred to above were dated after 1786 and were for lots in Charles Town, which was established on Charles Washington's land and named for him. In regard to this town the following transcription from Hening's Statutes of Virginia is apropos:

LAWS OF VIRGINIA, OCTOBER 1786—11TH OF COMMONWEALTH
CHAPTER LXXX

An act to establish a town on the lands of Charles Washington,
in the county of Berkeley

BE *it enacted by the General Assembly,* That eighty acres of land, the property of Charles Washington, lying in the county of Berkeley, be laid out in such manner as he may judge best, into lots of half an acre each, with convenient streets, which shall be, and is hereby established a town, by the name of Charlestown. That John Augustine Washington, Robert Rutherford, William Darke, James Crane, Cato Moore, Benjamin Rankin, Magnus Tate, Thornton Washington, William Little, Alexander White, and Richard Ransone, gentlemen, are hereby appointed trustees of the said town, and that they, or a majority of them shall have full power from time to time, to settle and determine all disputes concerning the bounds of the lots, and to establish such rules and orders for the regular building of houses thereon, as to them shall seem best; and in case of the death, removal out of the county, or other legal disability, of any one or more of the said trustees, it shall be lawful for the remaining trustees to elect and choose others in the room of those dead or disabled, and the person or persons so elected, shall be vested with the same powers and authority as any one in this act particularly appointed. So soon as the purchasers or owners of lots within the said town shall have built thereon a dwelling house, sixteen feet square, with a brick or stone chimney, such purchaser and owner shall be entitled to, and have and enjoy, all the rights, privileges, and immunities, which the freeholders and inhabitants of other towns in this state, not incorporated, hold and enjoy.

As will be observed, the original trustees of Charles Town were a distinguished body of men. John Augustine Washington was the proprietor's brother, Thornton Washington was his nephew. Robert Rutherford, as already pointed out, was later a member of Congress. The same was true of Magnus Tate and Alexander White. William Little was one of the first magistrates of the County; Cato Moore and Magnus Tate were sheriffs. William Darke was a distinguished officer of the colonial and Revolutionary periods. In 1755 he had helped to save the remnant of Braddock's routed army, and in 1791 he

WASHINGTON STREETS AND GRAVES IN CHARLES TOWN

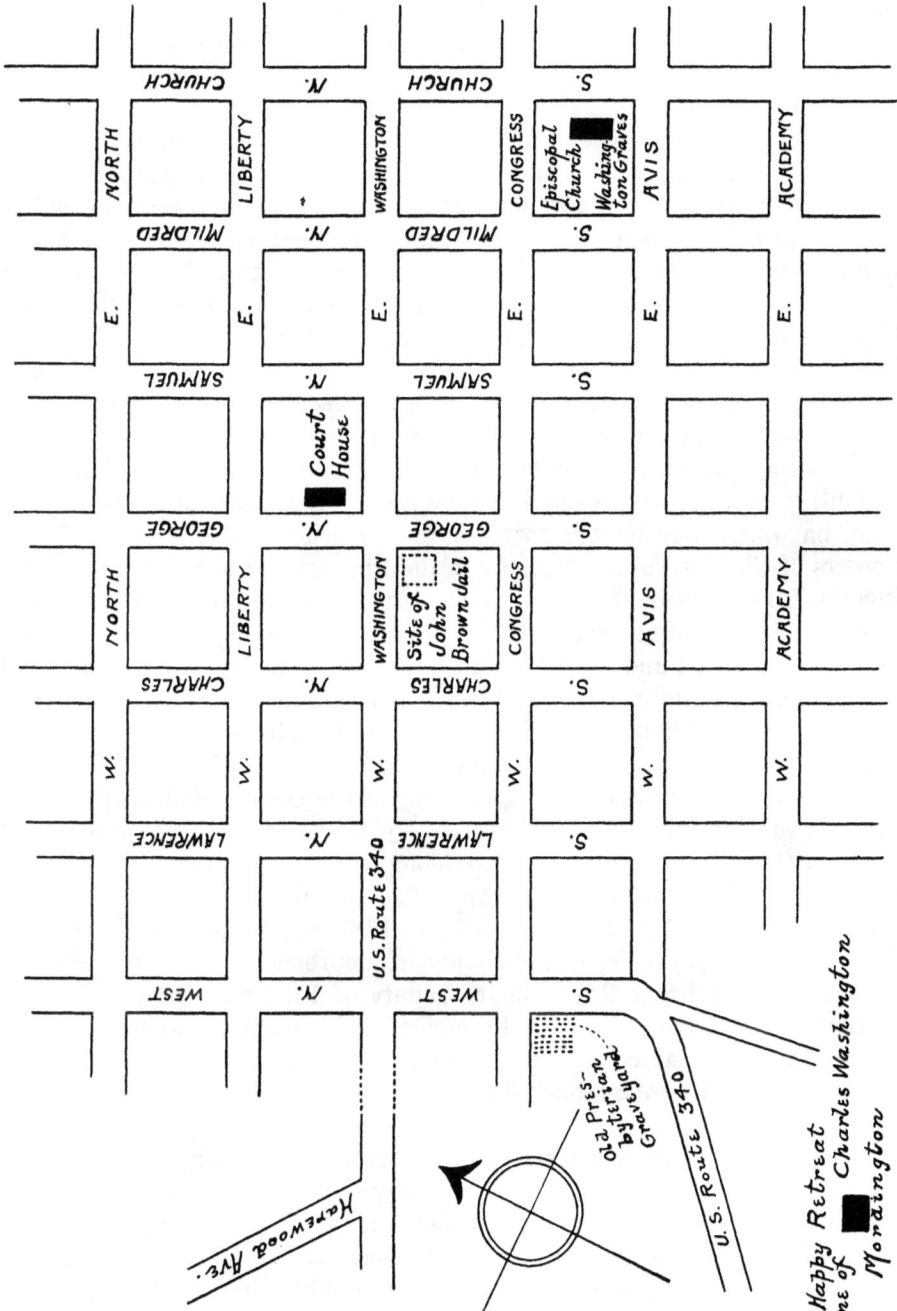

CHURCH   N.   CHURCH   S.

NORTH   LIBERTY   WASHINGTON   CONGRESS   AVIS   ACADEMY

Episcopal Church
Washington Graves

MILDRED   N.   MILDRED   S.

E.   E.   E.   E.   E.   E.

SAMUEL   N.   SAMUEL   S.

Court House

GEORGE   N.   GEORGE   S.

NORTH   LIBERTY   WASHINGTON   CONGRESS   AVIS   ACADEMY

Site of John Brown Jail

CHARLES   N.   CHARLES   S.

W.   W.   W.   W.   W.   W.

LAWRENCE   N.   LAWRENCE   S.

U.S. Route 340

WEST   N.   WEST   S.

Old Presbyterian Graveyard

Hapewood Ave.

U.S. Route 340

Happy Retreat
Home of Charles Washington
Mordington

covered St. Clair's retreat from the disaster it had suffered on the Miami. With General Adam Stephen he represented Berkeley County in the state convention of 1788 and cast his vote for ratifying the Federal Constitution. Richard Ranson was a member of a family that has been influential in the locality for generations. A considerable town on the northwest border of Charles Town now bears the name of Ranson.

The eighty acres of land originally constituting the territory of Charles Town were to be divided into half-acre lots and laid out with convenient streets in such manner as the proprietor might deem best. They were so laid out and the principal streets were given names of members of the Washington family, which names they still bear. The main street of the town, coursing generally east and west, is Washington Street. Parallel with it on the south is Congress Street, and on the north side is Liberty Street. Patriotism hedges in family pride. In the center of the town Washington Street is intersected at right angles by George Street. Parallel with George on the east are Samuel and Mildred, and on the west Charles and Lawrence.

Charles Town is a worthy and growing monument to Charles Washington and his near relatives. Around it they owned thousands of acres of fertile land, on which they built a dozen or more splendid homes; and within the borders of Charles Town, especially in the Episcopal churchyard, more Washingtons, it is believed, are buried than in any other town or city of the United States. The distant scenery, with the Blue Ridge forming an imposing background on the east and the Alleghanies marshaled against the horizon on the west, is pleasing and impressive. Beauty enhances history.

The period following the Revolution was signalized by the movement of population westward and the building up of new towns. In 1785 Clarksburg, in the county of Harrison, Morganstown, in the county of Monongalia, and Harrodsburg, in the county of Lincoln (Ky.), were authorized by acts of the Virginia General Assembly. In 1786, along with Charles Town, in the county of Berkeley, Frankfort, in the county of Fayette (Ky.), and Lynchburg, in the county of Campbell, were established. In 1787 Middleburg, in the county of Loudoun, and Maysville, in the county of Bourbon (Ky.), were given legal status. In 1788 Front Royal, in the county of Frederick (now in Warren), Pattonsburg, in the county of Botetourt, and Columbia, in the county of Fluvanna, were granted charter privileges. And these were by no means all of the towns that were established by acts of the General Assembly of Virginia in those four years.

As already indicated, Charles Washington found ready sale for the lots in his new town, Charles Town. To catalogue all the sales that are recorded in the county deed books would tax the reader's patience. On February 17, 1787, for 81 pounds and 10 shillings he conveyed lots No. 1 and No. 2 to William Cherry, tavern-keeper. Each of these, like others in the regular plan of the town, contained a half-acre. The same year other sales were made to

Allen Pollock, James Stewart, George A. Washington, and others. The last named was the proprietor's older son, now about 27 years of age. Two years before, October 15, 1785, at Mount Vernon, he had married Martha Washington's niece, Frances Bassett, daughter of Colonel and Mrs. Burwell Bassett of Eltham. Following his marriage he continued at Mount Vernon as superintendent for his uncle, under whom he had served in the Revolution. The General in his will paid him a glowing tribute and made substantial gifts to his sons, George Fayette and Charles Augustine Washington.

Among the purchasers in 1788 were Nicholas Roper, James Duke, David Cowan, and Abraham Branson. Branson was an eminent Friend (Quaker) of the colony that had settled in the Opequon country of the lower Shenandoah Valley at an early date under the leadership of Alexander Ross and Morgan Bryan. He was not one of the original colony, but he was active in the second or third generation and his name appears frequently in "Hopewell Friends History," a large and valuable work that was published by the Friends of Winchester and vicinity in 1936. Philip Welsh bought a lot in 1789; Jacob Stone and John Locke were purchasers in 1791; and Thomas Hammond was among those who invested in the new town in 1792. Hammond later married Mildred G. Washington, the proprietor's younger daughter. In 1793 Thomas Gibson was a purchaser, and in 1794 William Nourse. The latter may have been a brother or other near kinsman of James Nourse, who was one of the first magistrates of Berkeley County, and who appears in various connections in this narrative.

During the year 1795 conveyances were made to George Hite, Samuel Washington (the proprietor's younger son), Mahlon Anderson, and Edward Tiffin, among others. Tiffin, on September 15, purchased four half-acre lots in Charles Town, Nos. 99, 100, 109, and 110. He was a native of Carlisle, England, born June 19, 1766. He came to America with his family at the age of eighteen; studied medicine at the University of Pennsylvania; came to Charles Town, where his father had settled, and began practice in 1786. Ten years later he went to Chillicothe, Ohio. In 1799 he was one of the delegates to the territorial legislature, which met in Cincinnati, serving as speaker. In 1802 he was president of the constitutional convention and the next year was elected first governor of the new state. Later he was a U. S. Senator. His first wife was Mary Worthington, daughter of Robert, of Berkeley County. He married second Mary Porter of Delaware. The city of Tiffin, Ohio, was named in his honor.

Among the purchasers of lots in Charles Town in 1796 were Magnus Tate and General William Darke; in 1797, Abraham Davenport and Samuel Howell.

General George Washington paid an occasional visit to Charles Town in the early years of its history, notably in 1788. He at that time was much interested in the building of a canal up the Potomac River. On June 1 (1788) he inspected the construction work that was going on at the Great Falls and

A corner of the Episcopal churchyard, Charles Town, where many Washingtons are buried. There are other Washington graves in other parts of the churchyard. Photo 1935.

the Seneca Falls; dined at Leesburg. The next day he proceeded up country and, piloted by John Hough, crossed the Short Hill and spurs of the Blue Ridge to the mouth of the Shenandoah (Harper's Ferry), where he was met by several Maryland officials. On the 3d, having accomplished all the business that came before the canal board by 10 o'clock, he came up to the home of his brother Charles in time for dinner. In the afternoon he continued on to Fairfield, where he spent the evening and night with his cousin, Colonel Warner Washington.

On Wednesday, January 28, 1789, General Washington made in his diary the following entry: "Major Washington [George Augustine] set out for Berkley to see his Father who had informed him of the low state of health in which he was."

The father, Colonel Charles Washington, outlived his son by several years, but we may believe that his low state of health continued. By 1799 he evidently saw the end approaching. On April 14 of that year he conveyed four lots in Fredericksburg to his son-in-law, Colonel Burgess Ball, who then was a resident of Loudoun County. On July 5, for 4,000 pounds, he deeded the remaining moiety of his land adjoining Charles Town, about 800 acres, to his surviving son Samuel—having conveyed the other moiety to him on August 26, 1796. These transactions are of record in Martinsburg. On July 25 (1799) he transferred to Samuel a number of Negro slaves, with his farming utensils and live stock of all kinds, the consideration being natural love and affection and 1,000 pounds. The same day he made his will. He was then "sick and weak in body but of perfect sound mind and memory." By that time he had little else to dispose of. To his wife, Mildred Washington, he gave the Negroes Will and Nancy, unconditionally, and for her natural life Fortune, Manuel, and Winney, with his household and kitchen furniture, these to go after her death to their son Samuel. The will was witnessed by Abraham Davenport, John Briscoe, and Alex. Sanderson. It was proved before the court of Berkeley County on September 23, the same year. Charles's son, Samuel Washington, qualified as administrator; his son George Augustine had died in 1793. His illustrious brother died at Mount Vernon on December 14, 1799; only three or four months after his own demise.

Jefferson County, of which Charles Town is the county-seat, was not cut off from Berkeley and established by law until early in 1801; but in anticipation of such an event four choice lots in the heart of the town were reserved for a court house and other public buildings. The court house today, historic from the arraignment of John Brown in 1859 and other famous trials, stands in the northeast angle of George Street and Washington Street; and the jail in which Brown was confined stood in the southwest angle opposite. On the front of the court house is a large bronze tablet with the following inscription:

EXITUS ACTA PROBAT

1738   IN MEMORY OF   1799

COLONEL CHARLES WASHINGTON

BROTHER OF GENERAL GEORGE WASHINGTON

AND FOUNDER OF CHARLES TOWN, VIRGINIA

(NOW WEST VIRGINIA) IN 1786

THE FOUR CORNER LOTS

AT WASHINGTON AND GEORGE STREETS

WERE DONATED BY HIM

FOR THE PUBLIC BUILDINGS

FOR USE OF THE COUNTY AND TOWN

———————o———————

Erected by Bee Line Chapter
D.A.R. of Charles Town, 1925

Charles Washington's will was, of course, recorded originally in Martins-burg, the county-seat of Berkeley County; but after that part of Berkeley in which Charles Town lay was made the county of Jefferson, with Charles Town the county-seat, it was recorded also in the proprietor's own town.

The home of Charles Washington and his family was located a short distance due south of the town and was known as Happy Retreat. By subsequent owners it was named Mordington. The handsome brick house now standing there is perhaps a hundred years old, but is not the one in which the Washingtons lived. In the rear of the dwelling, however, are one or two old structures that may date from the time of the first residents. The graves of Colonel Washington and his wife are believed to be on the farm, near the dwelling place, but are not marked and cannot at this time be certainly located. In the meantime the town has grown out practically to the homestead.

CHAPTER X

FAIRFIELD AND WARNER WASHINGTON I

Warner Washington I was a first-cousin to George Washington, and although seventeen years his senior the two evidently were fond of each other's society. Many times Warner is mentioned in George's diaries. He was frequently at Mount Vernon, for instance, in February 1769, when he, Colonel George William Fairfax, and the host went fox-hunting. The diary entry reads:

Fox hunting with Colo. G. Fairfax and Mr. Warnr. Washington. Started and killed a Dog fox, after havg. him on foot three hours and hard runng. an hour and a Qr. Dined at Colo. Fairfax's.

Colonel Fairfax was Warner's brother-in-law and lived at Belvoir, on the Potomac, not far below Mount Vernon, where his father William, who had died in 1757, had lived. The next day, February 28, Washington wrote:

At home all day. Mr. Warnr. Washington and Lady and Miss Betcy Washington came here and staid all Night.

"Betcy" was probably the daughter of Augustine Washington, George's half-brother. The same company remained at Mount Vernon, in good old Virginia style, for four or five days longer. George Washington, in subsequent years, visited Warner a number of times at Fairfield.

Warner Washington I, born in 1715 at Bridges Creek, Westmoreland County, was the eldest son of John Washington (uncle to George) and his wife Catherine Whiting. His paternal grandparents were Lawrence Washington and Mildred Warner. He had a brother Henry Washington who lived in Middlesex County. Warner married (1) Elizabeth Macon, daughter of Colonel William Macon of New Kent County, by whom he had one child, Warner Washington II, named for the boy's father and his great-grandmother's family. In or about 1765 Warner I married (2) Hannah Fairfax, daughter of William Fairfax of Belvoir, and sister to Colonel George William Fairfax, who as a young man had been an associate of young George Washington as an explorer and surveyor for Thomas Lord Fairfax.

About the time of his second marriage Warner Washington I, by deeds of lease and release, acquired from his brother-in-law, George William Fairfax, 1600 acres of land on and near Long Marsh, then in Frederick County, whereon he built Fairfield and lived for the remainder of his life. Fairfield is now in Clarke County, about three and a half miles northeast of Berryville. The records of Warner's purchase on Long Marsh were made in the high court of chancery at Williamsburg and were destroyed in the burning of

Richmond in 1865, but references to the conveyances are to be found in the deed books of Frederick County in Winchester.

It has not been ascertained exactly when Warner Washington moved to Fairfield, but the approximate date is indicated by a number of incidents. In May 1769 he was listed as a magistrate of Frederick County. On the first of August of that year he was living at or near Fairfield, for on that date George Washington, his wife, and Patsy Custis stopped there with him, remaining several days. On September 10 (1769) they were at Warner's home again and were entertained over night. The next month (October 1769) Warner was listed again as a justice of the peace in Frederick County.

It is said that the third child of Hannah and Warner Washington was born in 1769 at Belvoir. This may have been early in the year before they moved to Fairfield or vicinity, or Hannah may have been at Belvoir temporarily even after settling in Frederick.

The visits of the Washingtons of Mount Vernon with Warner Washington in 1769 are of special interest. On the first occasion, August 1-4, they were enroute to Bath, a health resort 18 miles northwest of the present city of Martinsburg, near the Potomac River, now familiar as Berkeley Springs. Patsy Custis, the daughter of Mrs. Washington by her first marriage, was in poor health, and it was hoped that a sojourn at the medicinal springs would prove of benefit to her. The three, Washington, his wife, and Patsy Custis, traveled in the family chariot. They left Mount Vernon early on the morning of July 31, reaching West's ordinary near Bull Run Mountain in the evening, lodging there. The next day they dined at Snicker's and arrived at Warner Washington's about five o'clock in the afternoon.

Warner Washington was not at home—he was in Winchester on business —but he returned in the afternoon of August 2. On the 4th Rev. Charles Mynn Thruston, later one of the fighting parsons of the Revolution, and his wife were also guests of Warner Washington, dining with the Washingtons from Mount Vernon. Mr. Thruston had come up from Gloucester County just the year before to be rector of Frederick Parish. He and his wife were probably on their way to the springs at this time—he dined at the springs with George Washington and several other gentlemen on the 19th of the month.

The Mount Vernon group, on their way to the springs, did not get away from Warner Washington's until the morning of the 5th, being detained two days by the breakdown of the wagon in which goods and supplies for the sojourn at the springs were being carried. This evidently was a four-horse wagon, and heavily loaded, for two of the horses died on the way. It was the season of hot weather, and the long, rough road up from tidewater, culminating in the heartbreaking steeps of the Blue Ridge, had proved too much for the faithful beasts. The journey after leaving Warner's led by Jacob Hite's, now Leetown, and Joshua Hedges's, where the party lodged. They arrived at the springs on the 6th about one o'clock and dined with Colonel Fairfax.

When, in 1776, Lord Fairfax laid out the town of Bath and secured a

A view of the garden at Fairfield, old home of Warner Washington I.
Photo by Morrison, 1935.

charter for it, Warner Washington, Samuel Washington, and Rev. Charles M. Thruston were among the 14 trustees appointed. The 50 acres platted for the town were on the "Warm Springs Tract," which was a part of the "Swan Pond Tract."

At Berkeley Springs today is a magnificent tree known as the Washington Elm. It stands near the cottage which was frequently occupied by General Washington and other members of his family.

After 34 days at the springs in 1769, Washington, Mrs. Washington, and Patsy Custis set out for home, where they arrived in the afternoon of the 12th of September. Enroute they lodged at Warner's the night of the 10th.

In March 1771 George Washington again visited his cousin Warner at or near Fairfield. He was in the Valley this time for a period of ten days in conference at Winchester with officers who were to share with him extensive bounty lands in the Ohio Valley, and writing out instructions for the surveyors. Five days he spent with his brother Samuel at Harewood and other gentlemen in the vicinity, then on March 11 rode from Harewood to Warner's where he remained until the next day. The next year, in May, he spent several days with Warner Washington and at other places in the neighborhood.

In September 1784, when General Washington was starting on a tour westward, he held an important conference at the home of his brother Charles, at Happy Retreat, where the town was laid off two years later on Charles's land and given his name. By appointment, Warner Washington, whose home was about ten miles distant, came to this conference. Others were Ralph Wormeley, Thomas(?) Trickett, and General Daniel Morgan. General Washington made in his diary this note:

Colo. Warner Washington, Mr. Wormeley, Genl. Morgan, Mr. Trickett, and many other Gentlemen came here to see me—and one object of my journey being to obtain information of the nearest and best communication between the Eastern and Western Waters; and to facilitate as much as in me lay the Inland Navigation of the Potomack; I conversed a good deal with Genl. Morgan on this subject, who said, a plan was in contemplation to extend a Road from Winchester to the Western Waters, to avoid if possible an interference with any other State. but I could not discover that Either himself, or others, were able to point it out with precision. He seemed to have no doubt but that the Counties of Frederk., Berkeley and Hampshire would contribute freely towards the extension of the Navigation of Potomack; as well as towards opening a Road from East to West.

A month later General Washington returned from his western tour, coming down through Brock's Gap and across the county of Rockingham to Lynnwood, the home of surveyor Thomas Lewis, where he conferred with Mr. Lewis and Gabriel Jones, "The Lawyer," about a water-way from east to west, and particularly about the improvement of navigation on the Shenandoah River. Four years later, after inspecting the work in progress on the Potomac canal at Great Falls and Harper's Ferry, General Washington came up to Charles

Old barn at Fairfield, dating from the time of the Washingtons. Photo by

Town, dined there with his brother Charles, and then continued to Colonel Warner Washington's, at Fairfield, where he spent the evening and the night.

This was in June 1788. By this time Warner Washington was feeling the weight of years, being then seventy-three years old. The next year he declined serving any longer on the county court, as Cartmell tells us, being one of the "old members." We may assume that he had been on the court (one of the county justices) all or most of the time since May 1769. On November 20, 1789, he made his will, terming himself Warner Washington Senior and declaring himself to be in health and of sound mind and memory. To his daughters Elizabeth and Louisa he left five working slaves and four children each, to be given them as soon as they, Elizabeth and Louisa, were 21 years of age; the slaves thus given to be equal in value with those already given to his daughters Mildred, Hannah, and Catherine. To his wife Hannah he left his Negro woman Cynthia, and for her natural life all his estate and possessions, not otherwise devised, consisting of lands, Negroes, horses, stock of all kinds, plate, furniture, carriages, etc. After her death all this was to go to his sons Fairfax and Whiting, Fairfax to have first choice in the division.

To his son Warner Washington he gave his silver cross and silver salt cellars. Evidently Warner II had already received the bulk of his inheritance in lands, etc. To his grandson Warner Washington (Warner III) he left his silver watch. His wife Hannah was to be executrix and his son Warner executor of the will; they were also to be the guardians of Fairfax and Whiting until they were of legal age.

At a court for the judicial district composed of the counties of Frederick, Berkeley, Hampshire, Hardy, and Shenandoah, held at Winchester, the will of Warner Washington I was proved on September 1, 1791, by the oaths of William Herbert, Richard Willis, and Ephraim Garrison. Warner Washington II refused to qualify as executor. The widow, Hannah Washington, qualified as executrix, with Warner Washington II and Albion Throckmorton securities on her bond of 10,000 pounds. Albion Throckmorton was probably Hannah Washington's son-in-law, her daughter Mildred having married a Throckmorton in Frederick County on December 13, 1785.

On May 14, 1802, about eleven years after the death of Warner Washington I of Fairfield, his widow, Hannah Fairfax Washington, made her will. It is of special interest for two reasons: first because of the intimate family history it reveals; second, because of the large number of Negro slaves it names individually. While these names in a few cases, perhaps, were peculiar to this group, the majority of them, we may believe, were typical slave names of that time.

The testatrix makes bequests to her daughters: Mildred Thockmorton, Hannah Whiting (Mrs. Peter Beverly Whiting), and Catharine Nelson (Mrs. John Nelson); to her granddaughters: Lucinda and Hannah Nelson; Hannah and Catharine Throckmorton; Louisa and Hannah Whiting; to her sons

Old stone mill on Long Marsh at Fairfield, now used as a barn. View from the northeast. Photo September 8, 1938.

Fairfax and Whiting Washington; and to her nephew, "Mr. Tom. Fairfax."

The Negro slaves were named and disposed of as follows:

To her daughter Mildred Thockmorton, a woman named Mary and her children; also a boy Billy (son of Black Milly);

To her daughter Hannah Whiting, a woman named Nanny (daughter of Milly); also a boy named Ben (son of Edy);

To her daughter Catharine Nelson, a woman named Alice (daughter of Milly); also a boy named Billy (son of Sally);

To her granddaughter Lucinda Nelson, a girl named Milly (daughter of Jenny);

To her granddaughter Hannah Throckmorton, a woman named Aggy;

To her granddaughter Catharine Throckmorton, a girl named Fanny; (Fanny "I bought at a sale of Negroes belonging to the Estate of Mr. Albion Throckmorton");

To her granddaughter Louisa Whiting, a girl named Judy (daughter of Amey);

To her granddaughter Hannah Nelson, a girl named Kitty (daughter of Jenny);

To her granddaughter Hannah Whiting, a girl named Becky (daughter of Amey);

To her sons Fairfax and Whiting Washington, "the residue of my Negroes, to be equally divided between them," to wit, Old Charles, Dick, Tom, Bristol, Carpenter Bill, Carpenter Charles, Scipio, Ben, Kitt, Lewis, Stepney, Greenwich, Charles, Dick, James, Harry, Bob, Dick, Godfrey, Miles, Phill; the Blacksmith Billy "to work equally for both Plantations belonging to my two sons Fairfax and Whiting Washington"; the following women to Fairfax and Whiting: Old Nanny, Amey, Jenny, Sally, Sarah, Maria, Polly (a girl).

"I will and Devise that the Negro Woman Cynthia have her freedom directly after my decease. She was given to me by my husband to Dispose of as I pleased."

On September 3, 1804, the will of Hannah Fairfax Washington was presented in the Frederick County court and proved to be in her own handwriting. (See Frederick County Will Book No. 7, pages 238-240.)

Elizabeth and Louisa, the younger daughters of Warner Washington I and his second wife, Hannah Fairfax, both married, as Frederick County records show, Elizabeth on June 11, 1795, with George Booth; Louisa on January 18, 1798, with Thomas Fairfax; but evidently both had died before May 14, 1802, when their mother made her will. That document recognizes neither, nor any child of either. "Mr. Tom Fairfax" was doubtless the surviving husband of Louisa.

Fairfield has been among the celebrated farm homes of the Shenandoah Valley for more than a century. Samuel Kercheval, the Herodotus of the Valley, writes of it along with Claymont, Clifton, Tulyries, Greenway Court, Carter Hall, Belle Grove, and others. Of Fairfield he says:

Quaint old house near Fairfield, view from the west. By some it is believed that this house was occupied by the overseer of Warner Washington I; possibly Washington himself may have lived here while building at Fairfield.

Mr. John Richardson is now the owner of the fine tract of land formerly owned by, and the residence of the late Col. Warner Washington, called "Fairfield," on which he has established an extensive distillery. The stillhouse is built of brick, attached to which a large yard is enclosed and nicely floored with the same material, for the purpose of raising and fattening pork. About every two months he sends off to the Baltimore market from eighty to one hundred head of finely fattened hogs. Mr. Richardson is a man of great industry and enterprise, farms extensively, and raises a fine stock of improved cattle. He, like many of our citizens, is the builder of his own fortune, having commenced on a very small capital.

The first edition of Kercheval's book, "A History of the Valley of Virginia," a classic in its field, was published at Winchester in 1833. Three subsequent editions have been issued, two at Woodstock, one at Strasburg. Fairfield is still in the hands of the Richardsons, and has been constantly improved. At the same time, original features have been preserved as much as possible. The stone mansion has been enlarged from time to time, but parts of it date from the time of Warner Washington. The same is true of the large brick barn and several other old buildings that stand here and there. The gardens on the east, south, and southeast of the mansion house are extensive and beautiful.

A quarter of a mile north of Fairfield proper is an old stone building, formerly a grist mill run by the waters of Long Marsh. For many years now it has been used as a barn for storing hay and grain in the upper stories, with stables on the ground floor. The race that carried the impounded water for running the old mill can still be traced along some parts of its course, but it has been filled up by silt at many places and others leveled with the surrounding fields by repeated farming operations.

A short distance northwest of Fairfield is a very old dwelling house, a quaint rambling structure of stone, logs and brick, which attracts the notice of every antiquarian who passes along the highway (U. S. Route 340) between Berryville and Charles Town. No one seems to know the full history of this old building, but some believe that it was originaly the domicile of Colonel Warner Washington's overseer. For a considerable period years ago a school for boys was conducted by the gentleman who occupied it.

CHAPTER XI

WARNER WASHINGTON II

Warner Washington II, the eldest child of Warner Washington I and the only child of the latter's first wife, Elizabeth Macon, was born about the year 1750. The exact date of his birth has not been ascertained, but on August 16, 1769, he and his second-cousin, John Lewis of Fredericksburg, dined with Colonel George Washington at Bath (Berkeley Springs), and Colonel Washington wrote them down in his diary as "Mr. Jno. Lewis and Mr. Wr Washington Junr." Warner Junior evidently came to the Valley when his father settled at Fairfield, or soon thereafter. In 1774 his father conveyed to him 939 acres of land near Fairfield, and in 1783 made over to him another tract of 250 acres adjoining the first. On this land he resided until 1795 or 1796.

Warner Washington II is said to have been most unfortunate in business, but he owned at successive periods three splendid and historic homes in the neighborhood of Fairfield and Berryville, namely Clifton, Audley, and Llewellyn, and lived at each of them for a considerable number of years. His first wife, married on October 18, 1770, was Mary Whiting, daughter of Francis and Frances Perrin Whiting of Gloucester County. She had nine children, most or all of whom were born at Clifton, which is located three-quarters of a mile north of Fairfield, on the land conveyed to Warner Washington II by his father.

On June 13, 1795, Warner Washington II married his second wife, Sarah Warner Rootes, of Gloucester County, by whom he had seven children, all born at Audley, the first on May 18, 1796. Colonel Forrest W. Brown, in a letter written October 28, 1933, states that Mary Whiting Washington, Warner II's first wife, died at Clifton in 1794. From these facts it is evident that the removal from Clifton to Audley took place at some time between 1794 and the early part of 1796.

The Clifton estate was divided and sold at different times to several purchasers. The residence and 683 acres were acquired by Bushrod and Griffin Taylor. The daughter of Griffin Taylor married David Hume Allen, and Clifton is now owned by Mr. Allen's grandson, Dr. L. M. Allen, of Winchester. The elegant brick house now standing at Clifton was erected by the Allens. It is one of the homes featured by Kercheval, who describes it in the following paragraphs:

In the county of Clarke, David H. Allen, Esq., has lately erected a brick dwelling on a beautiful eminence, from which there is a most enchanting view of the Blue Ridge and adjacent country. It is sixty-six feet by fifty, with a splendid portico, supported by a beautiful colonnade twenty-five feet high of solid pine pillars.

In front of the house [southeast] is an extended lawn, partly covered with a sheet of transparent water, which adds greatly to the novelty and beauty of the

—From Historic Homes

Clifton, east front. Photo by Morrison, October, 1935.

scenery. Mr. Allen informed the writer that some years ago the watercourse contained much dark alluvial mud, on each side, very miry and difficult to cross. He hauled out six thousand wagon loads of the mud upon the adjoining high lands, which so increased the fertility that, for several years, it was too rich for the production of wheat.

Mr. Allen is pretty extensively engaged in the stock way. A few years ago, he at one time owned one hundred and twenty head of horses, and a large stock of improved black cattle, sheep and hogs. Mr. Allen was bred to the law, but having married the daughter of the late Col. Griffin Taylor, he got this fine estate by her; and his father being also wealthy, he soon abandoned the practice, and lived a retired and private life ever since.

The lake that formerly added its reflections to the landscape on the southeast side of Clifton has not been maintained, but the place is still celebrated for its horses and the beautiful prospect towards the Blue Ridge. The doorway on the portico is one of the finest in the country.

The records of Frederick County, of which Clarke was a part until 1836, do not show how Audley came into the possession of Warner Washington II, but it is probable that the land of Audley was at one time a part of the extensive holdings of Warner Washington I. Audley and Fairfield are about two and a half miles apart, in a direct line, northeast and southwest. The fact that the first child of Warner Washington II and his second wife, Sarah Warner Rootes, was born at Audley has been ascertained from family records.

The Washingtons resided at Audley for more than twenty years, in a period notable and celebrated in American history. The close of the year 1799 was made memorable by the death of General Washington. A year later the Federal City, named in his honor, became the capital of the nation. Almost immediately followed the political revolution in which the party of Washington and Adams was ousted from federal control and the party of Jefferson and Madison placed at the helm. In 1803 Jefferson purchased the vast Louisiana Territory, not because he thought the Constitution authorized it, but because he believed it was necessary for the public welfare. Anon came the second war with Great Britain, the re-chartering of the United States Bank, and the rising tumult over protective tariffs.

Red-letter years within the same period marked Virginia history. In 1801 the eastern part of Berkeley County was cut off and erected into the new county of Jefferson. This section, above all others west of the Blue Ridge, is the region of the Washingtons. Clifton, the first home of Warner Washington II, is within a stone's throw, almost, of the Jefferson County line, and Fairfield is not far away. In 1807 and 1811 came drama and tragedy—the trial in Richmond of Aaron Burr, which really was an episode in the national story, and the burning of the Richmond Theater, the first great theater disaster in the United States. Between 1810 and 1816 the Virginia Literary Fund, to provide free schools for indigent white children, was launched by James Barbour, Joseph C. Cabell, Thomas Jefferson, and others.

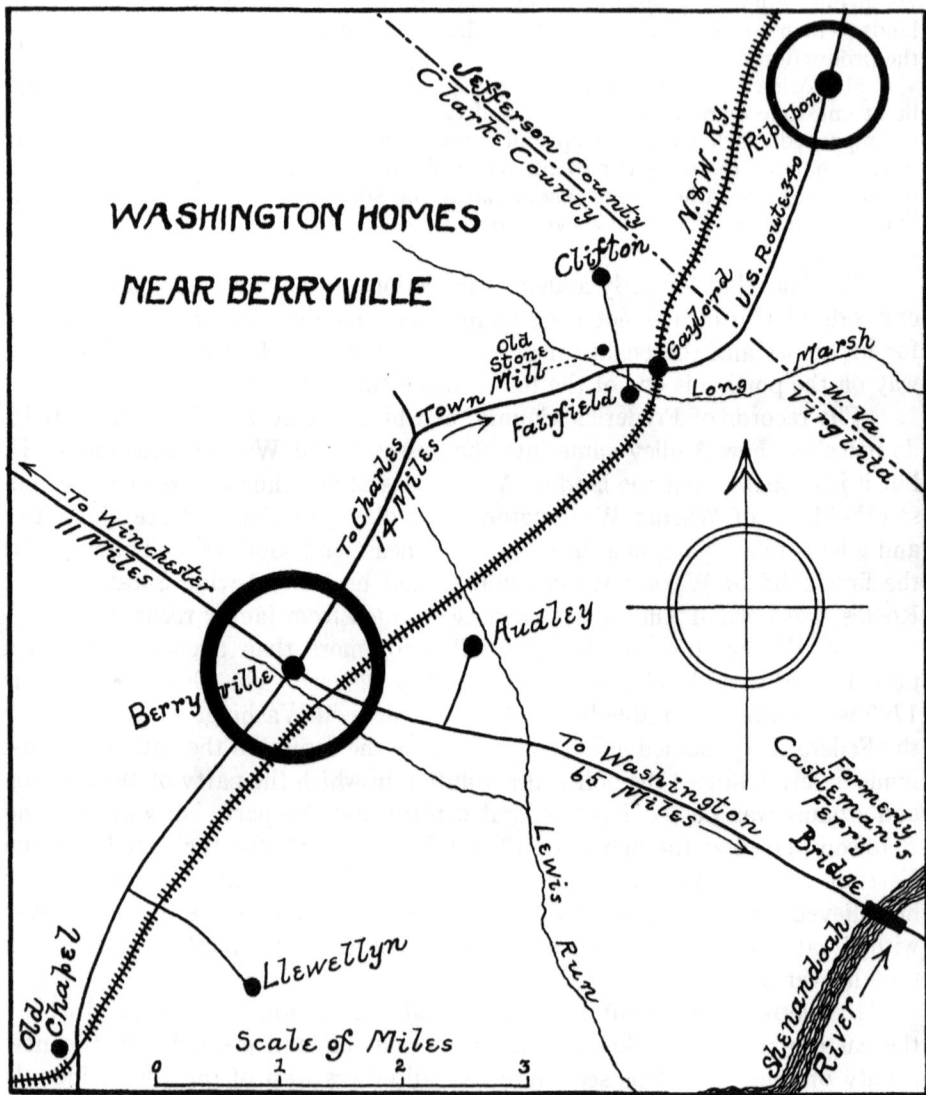

WASHINGTON HOMES

NEAR BERRYVILLE

Jefferson County
Clarke County

Clifton

N.&W. Ry.

Ripton

Gaylord

U.S. Route 350

Old
Stone
Mill

Town   Marsh

To Charles
14 Miles

Fairfield   Long   W. Va.
                            Virginia

To Winchester
11 Miles

W

Audley

Berryville

To Washington
65 Miles

Formerly
Castleman's
Ferry

Bridge

Lewis Run

Old
Chapel

Llewellyn

Shenandoah River

Scale of Miles

0   1   2   3

This period, moreover, was signalized by the births of many notable men in America and Europe: Matthew Fontaine Maury, Robert E. Lee, Henry W. Longfellow, Edgar Allan Poe, Abraham Lincoln, Tennyson, Darwin, Gladstone, Chopin: to mention only a few. But it was still the time of laborious travel and long delayed communication, when rutted and rocky wagon roads were the ways to market across the hills and mountains; and the rivers, obstructed by boulders and choked by mill dams, the seasonal and precarious arteries of commerce down the valleys. Only a few canals had been constructed; the building of good roads had hardly begun, and railroads were still in the unknown future.

But in spite of the isolation and material handicaps, the life of well-to-do families in the Shenandoah Valley was rich in many respects and not devoid of refinements. The hastily constructed log houses of the pioneers had been replaced in many instances with commodious dwellings of stone and brick, some of which approached a palatial size and elegance. This was true especially in the lower Valley, a point of converging immigration from Pennsylvania, New Jersey, Delaware, Maryland, and eastern Viriginia. Carter Hall at Millwood, home of the Burwells, Hackwood, near Winchester, the seat of General John Smith, Springdale, near Stephensburg (now Stephens City), the residence of Colonel John Hite, Belle Grove, near Middletown, built by Major Isaac Hite from plans suggested by Thomas Jefferson, are among the stately monuments that still remain to elicit admiration. Matin Hill and Mt. Pleasant, near Strasburg, Saratoga, near Millwood, Mt. Zion and Long Branch, near Greenway Court, Harewood, near Charles Town, Annefield, near Berryville, with other places in and near Winchester, should not be overlooked. Libraries were not large, but in them many choice volumes were collected and treasured. General Isaac Zane at Marlboro, his home and chief iron-working establishment on Cedar Creek, had a rather extensive library and had enriched his shelves with a number of books purchased from the unusual collection of Colonel William Byrd of Westover. Francis Orrery Ticknor, in his beautiful tribute to "The Virginians of the Valley," no doubt sacrificed truth to poetry in some of his lines. but the gentry of the Valley were a "kindly band that rarely hated ease"; and

"They climbed the blue embattled hills
Against uncounted foes,
And planted there, in valleys fair,
The lily and the rose."

Audley, we may believe, was in the days of Warner Washington II and his family, if not a place of financial prosperity, at least a home of culture and social hospitality. How much of the present mansion these Washingtons found there, or how much they added, cannot at this time be determined, but most of the quaint and rambling structure gives evidence of an age sufficient to date from the time of their occupancy. A brief history of Clarke County, published in 1936, states that Audley house was built by Warner Washington

Opposite is reproduced a photograph (by Barr of Winchester) of Audley, the old mansion in Clarke County, Va., a mile and a half east of Berryville. For 20 years or more Audley was the home of Warner Washington II. It then passed into the hands of Lawrence Lewis and was occupied by his son, Lorenzo. The latter's mother, Nelly Custis, Eleanor Parke Custis Lewis, lived here from 1839 until her death in 1852.

(presumably Warner I) in 1777. This date, if Kercheval may be relied upon, is seven years too early for brick houses in the Valley, but Warner I may have built this brick house before his death in 1791.

In the year 1818 or soon thereafter Warner Washington II moved away from Audley and located on a tract of land, about 1555 acres, not far away, which he had acquired from his second-cousin, Lawrence Lewis, and the latter's wife, Nelly Custis Lewis. An exchange was made—a trade, with money "to boot." Warner Washington gave Audley, house and lands, and received the 1555 acres, mentioned above, with $30,000 in money. Washington, we are told, needed money, to meet his obligations to certain Baltimore money-lenders. Evidently Audley was a valuable piece of property, as it still is. The present owner is Mr. B. B. Jones.

On his newly acquired land Warner Washington II erected a commodious stone dwelling and other stone buildings which still remain. This new home was named Llewellyn, and thus it is known today. It is located three miles south of Berryville. A public road formerly passed on the south and east of the house, but this has been closed. The present highway, leading from Berryville to Old Chapel, and thence to Boyce and Millwood, passes on the north west at a distance of about half a mile. The remains of an extensive flower garden may be traced among the knolls and ledges west of the dwelling, and many fine old trees shade the lawns and adjacent fields, among them a number of locusts that have weathered the storms of successive decades with a persistent vitality. Locusts were favorite trees at many of the old homes besides Llewellyn, notably at Greenway Court, Harewood, and Meg Willy. A locust tree in full bloom is a thing of beauty and fragrance, and if a storm breaks it down, or lightning shatters it, the stump will send up new shoots to face other storms.

By the year 1826 Warner Washington had reached an advanced age, and on July 7 of that year he made his will. To his son Reade he left his silver cross and four silver salt cellars, the same, no doubt, that he had received by his father's will, thirty-five years before. To the same son were bequeathed the testator's silver coat buttons. To his wife he left the household and kitchen furniture, the dwelling house and ten acres of land around it, for her natural life, thereafter to his daughters Elizabeth and Mary Washington, or the survivor of them. To the said Elizabeth he gave three Negroes "of equal value with those of hers I sold"; to Mary one Negro girl. "All the rest and residue of my estate, real and personal, to my sons Fairfax and Herbert Washington." Fairfax and Herbert were to supply the stoves and fireplaces with fuel and the table with food for the widow and daughters and furnish them with domestic servants; also to pay to each yearly for life the sum of $100.

The involved condition of the testator's affairs was implied in the following provisions: "If my sons shall save from my estate after payment of debts more than 400 acres of land, for each 100 acres so saved they shall pay my

Llewellyn, from the west. A recent photo by Morrison.

The spacious hall, Llewellyn, from the east entrance. At the left, at the foot of the stairway, is the door to the parlor; opposite, on the right, is the entrance to the dining room. The door at the distant end of the hall admits to the porch that extends along the west of the house.

wife and daughters each in addition the sum of $25 yearly"; and "I charge Fairfax and Herbert with the sum of $1,000 to be paid to my son Hamilton Washington in yearly payments of $200."

There were certain other provisions. The will was presented in the Frederick County court in Winchester on June 2, 1829. On March 3, 1830, Fairfax Washington qualified as executor, giving bond for $15,000, with Warner W. Throckmorton, Herbert Washington, and Reade Washington as sureties.

The other ten children of Warner Washington II, among whom was Warner III, do not appear in this will. Some probably had died, and others, we may assume, had received years before what their father was able to give them. Warner Washington II and other members of his family lie buried in a quiet spot, now unmarked, about a quarter of a mile west of the homestead at Llewellyn.

Another Warner Washington lived in Frederick County for some years within the period of Warner II's residence at Audley and Llewellyn. He was a son of Thacker Washington of King George County and his wife Harriet. Court records show that this Warner and his wife Ariana, who was probably Ariana Stith, in 1818 were living in Winchester. They rented a building that stood on South Braddock Street, west side, between Wolfe and Cork, and therein kept a tavern. Not long after 1818 they removed to Floyd County, Ga.; from thence to Rome, Ga.; and in June 1828 they were living in Alexandria, Va. The site of their old tavern in Winchester is now occupied by a Methodist church.

In 1833 Llewellyn, the mansion house and 415 acres of land, was conveyed to John Kerfoot, and the estate has been in the hands of himself and his descendants ever since. The present owners are Mr. and Mrs. Alfred M. Kerfoot, who reside there, having recently made extensive repairs and restorations in the house, grounds, and outbuildings. A number of ancient locusts remain at the southeast front of the house, and a short distance to the south, on a knoll, is a giant oak which no doubt was already a large tree when the first white men came.

For many of the items herein presented concerning Clifton, Audley, and Llewellyn the author is under obligation to Mr. Richard E. Griffith Sr., of Winchester, whose extensive researches in the records of Frederick and other Virginia counties over a long period of years have put him in possession of an unusual fund of information in regard to many old homes and families.

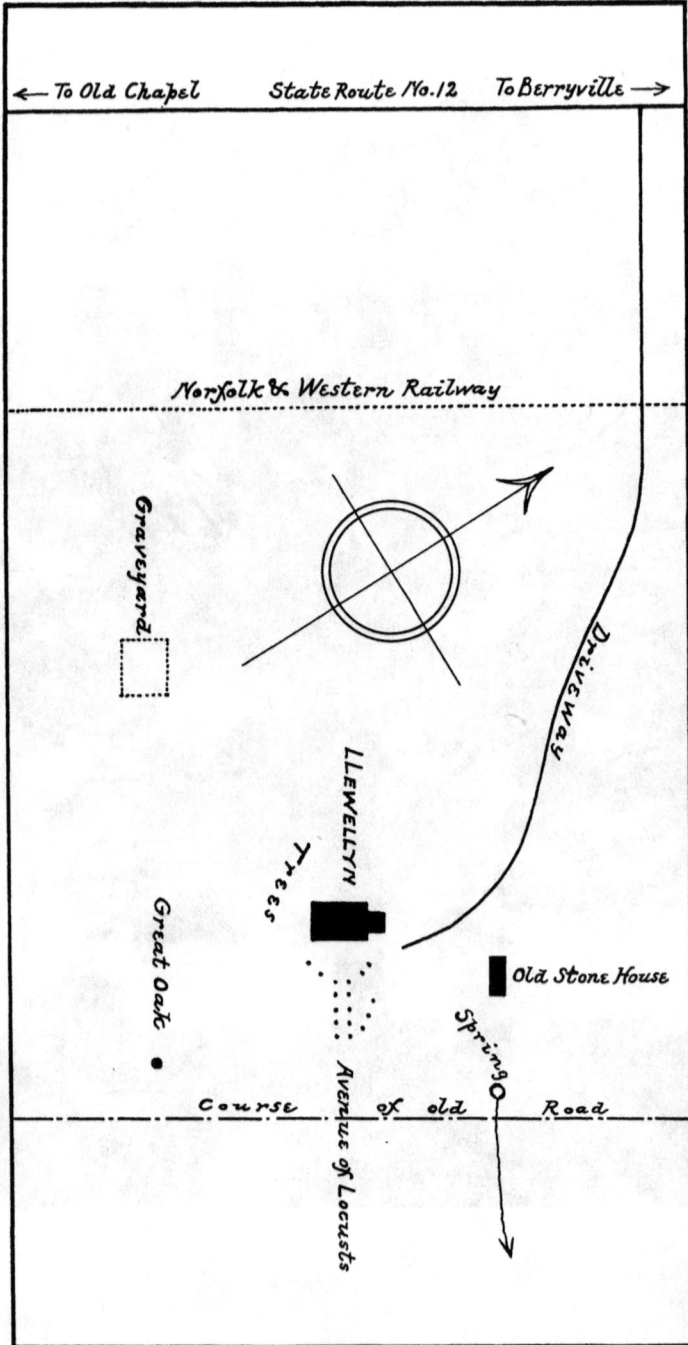

CHAPTER XII

NELLY CUSTIS LEWIS AT AUDLEY

Eleanor Parke Custis, familiarly known as Nelly Custis, daughter of John Parke Custis, had from first to last several homes, all historic. She was born at Abingdon, her father's residence on the Potomac about midway between Alexandria and the Federal City, on land acquired from the Alexanders, for whom Alexandria was named. She grew up with her grandmother, Martha Washington, at Mount Vernon and was married there. Most of her married life was spent at Woodlawn, about three miles northwest of Mount Vernon. After the death of her husband, Lawrence Lewis, in 1839, she lived at Audley, near Berryville, in Clarke County, Va., with her son, Lorenzo Lewis, and his family, where she died in 1852. She was buried at Mount Vernon.

John Parke Custis, one of the three children of Martha Dandridge and her first husband, Daniel Parke Custis, was born in New Kent County, Va., in 1755. After less than a year in King's College, New York City, in 1773, he on February 3, 1774, married Eleanor Calvert of Maryland. While serving as an aide to Washington in the Yorktown campaign he contracted camp fever and died at Eltham, New Kent County, on November 5, 1781. He left four children: Elizabeth Parke, who married Thos. Law; Martha Parke, who married Thomas Peter; Eleanor Parke (Nelly); and George Washington Parke Custis. Eleanor, born March 21, 1779, and George, born April 30, 1781, were adopted by General and Mrs. Washington. On February 22, 1799, Washington's birthday, Eleanor married Lawrence Lewis, the General's nephew, son of Betty Washington Lewis, late of Fredericksburg. In or about 1802 Lawrence Lewis and his wife built their handsome brick house at Woodlawn, on a choice site near Dogue Run and the Washington Mill, on the tract of 2,000 acres devised to them by General Washington in his will.

Nelly Custis Lewis's first child, Frances, was born at Mount Vernon on November 27, 1799. At the same place were born also another daughter, Martha, and a son, both of whom died in infancy. Lorenzo, Angela, and Agnes were born at Woodlawn. Agnes died at the age of eighteen, while attending school in Philadelphia. Frances married Edward George Washington Butler, of the United States army. Angela married Charles M. Conrad, of New Orleans; and Lorenzo married Esther Maria Coxe of Philadelphia, daughter of Dr. John Redman Coxe.

Major Lawrence Lewis, Nelly's husband, owned extensive tracts of land in the Shenandoah Valley, south and southeast of Battletown, now Berryville, in what is now Clarke County, Va. In 1818 he acquired from Warner Washington II the quaint and celebrated homestead Audley, with its surrounding tracts of fertile limestone land. The house is located a mile and a half east of Berryville, on ground which was at an early date a part of the extensive holdings of Warner Washington I, of Fairfield. The distance between Fairfield

Nelly Custis, Mrs. Lawrence Lewis, in early life.

and Audley, in a direct course, is less than three miles. It is probable that Major Lawrence Lewis and his wife, with their children, following the practice of other tidewater families of means, frequently spent their summers in the Valley. Their son, Lorenzo Lewis, after his marriage, lived at Audley and operated the farm. In view of all these facts we may be certain that Nelly Custis Lewis was a frequent sojourner at Audley prior to 1839; and after the death of her husband, on November 30 of that year, she moved to Audley. Woodlawn, the cherished mansion on Dogue Run, designed by William Thornton, architect of the Capitol in Washington City, was abandoned and neglected. "Woodlawn," says Charles Moore, "passed through many vicissitudes before it was restored to more than its pristine elegance by Miss Sharpe, of Wilkes-Barre, Pennsylvania. Now it has gone into the ownership of Senator Underwood, of Alabama, and will doubtless be maintained as the home of a statesman worthy of that title." (See "The Family Life of George Washington," by Charles Moore, 1926, pages 5, 6, 175, 176.) If well authenticated reports may be trusted, Nelly was rather extravagant—her improvident habits did much to impair the family fortune.

The old mansion at Audley, in which the chamber of Nelly Custis Lewis is still pointed out, is rambling, quaint, and fascinating. Like many other old Virginia houses, notably Tuckahoe, Castle Hill, and Plain Dealing, it is a double structure, and consequently has two fronts, one towards the northeast, the other towards the southwest. Both parts of the building are rectangular, the one on the southwest side being 24 by 60 feet in size, the other 24 by 108 feet. The two are centrally connected by a wide transverse hall. The height is a story and a half; the walls are built of brick, now painted white on the outside.

The large fields around Audley are mostly a champaign, excellent grazing land, interrupted here and there with cultivated areas devoted to wheat and maize in their seasons. Gentle undulations billow the level expanse and off in the east about six miles, beyond the Shenandoah River, the massive range of the Blue Ridge forms the horizon line. At intervals in the long crest of the mountain Ashby's Gap, Snicker's Gap, and Keys's Gap lead the eye down towards Harper's Ferry, where the great water gap of the Potomac and the Shenandoah presents a marvel of beauty and grandeur.

In the vicinity of Audley are other historic homes where congenial spirits, with the traditional hospitality and conviviality of the early Virginians, were always ready to keep the Widow Lewis from being homesick for Woodlawn and its waning glories. On the northeast were Claymont, Blakeley Fairfield, and Clifton; on the southwest were others: Annefield, home of "Sweet Ann Page" and her husband, Thomas Carter; quaint and idyllic New Market, where lived the Randolphs; Saratoga, mirrored in its wide-spreading crystal spring, built by General Daniel Morgan, but later held by the Burwells and the Pages; Carter Hall, palatial seat of the Burwells; Long Branch, with its

Ruins of the house at Abingdon, midway between Washington and Alexandria, the birthplace of Nelly Custis. Photo by the author, 1936.

classic columns and spiral stairway, beautiful home of the Nelsons; Greenway Court, alive still with traditions of old Lord Fairfax and young George Washingtgon; Pagebrook and Mt. Zion. Most of the large landholders of Clarke County and a considerable portion of Jefferson were English from east of the Ridge, and no doubt their fox-hunting, horse-racing, long visits, and lavish entertaining, with occasional ruinous gambling, severely shocked the frugal Germans, the circumspect Quakers, and the canny Scots who occupied most of the Valley to the north, west, and southwest, but their gallantry, elegance, and tone of culture must have given a pleasing welcome to the aging lady of Audley. The austere Bishop Meade lived at Mountain View, not far from Greenway Court, but he could not be everywhere at all times; besides, he had a sense of humor, and was more inclined to commend the good qualities in his neighbors than to expose and censure their weaknesses.

The death of her daughter Angela (Mrs. Charles M. Conrad) in September 1839, followed within two months by the demise of her husband, Major Lawrence Lewis, must have saddened Nelly Custis Lewis, but the children of her son Lorenzo at Audley no doubt kept up her spirits and diverted her thoughts from too much gloomy reflection. She rounded out her three-score years and ten, and made a hopeful start towards four-score, but not unmindful of life's uncertainties, and careful for those she loved, she sat down on August 19, 1850, and wrote—she did not call it a will, but it was so accepted and so recorded. Whatever it was from a legal standpoint, it certainly is a most interesting and revealing document, and is presented herewith in full for the reader's perusal and enlightenment:

Having arrived at my 71st year & my life very uncertain, I think it best to leave a memorandum of my Wishes in regard to articles in my care, the property of my Darling grandsons Charles and Lewis Conrad especially.—Their two cedar chests of Books &c The large hair trunk of Books, the table cloth in which they are wrapped. All the Books in my room marked with their names—in trunks tops of Trunks, drawers or closets.—all relics of their Beloved Mother wherever they may be—Jewelry, coins, curiosities, all in their Mothers trunks or in my trunks (except a table cover FP.B & two pieces of work the property of Isabella & Caroline Butler in my largest square trunk) 2 drawing Books in my Portfolio which belonged to their Dear Mother—2 paint boxes & the Houfleur box—Book marks &c the Parrot in tufler work is my Charleys, The Hungarian on Horseback in my Trunk The property of my Lewis.—The frame is in a box under Norah's Bed another box there contains some china, The drawers in my Bureau the closets in my room, all contain property belonging to them.—A Tin case of valuable engravings.—in one of the closets or in one of them.—2 sets in worsted work. —Silver articles & every thing in the long black Trunk except the patterns for work, floss Silk. & worsteds,—all such articles pertaining to work for my darling child F. P. Butler & her daughters, canvas worsted, floss silk, Silk canvas, all patterns for work except the blue vase & any other Esther may select.—The gold thimble is my Parkes, Grandmama's carpet Seat, the chair she gave Parke— Guitar, large Mahogany embroidery Frame, her profile, St. Elizabeth (Drawing) The green trunk is Lewis's, the largest high chair is Charley's, the Small one Lewis's—my darling Angelas flowers in worsted for her darlings C & L Conrad.—

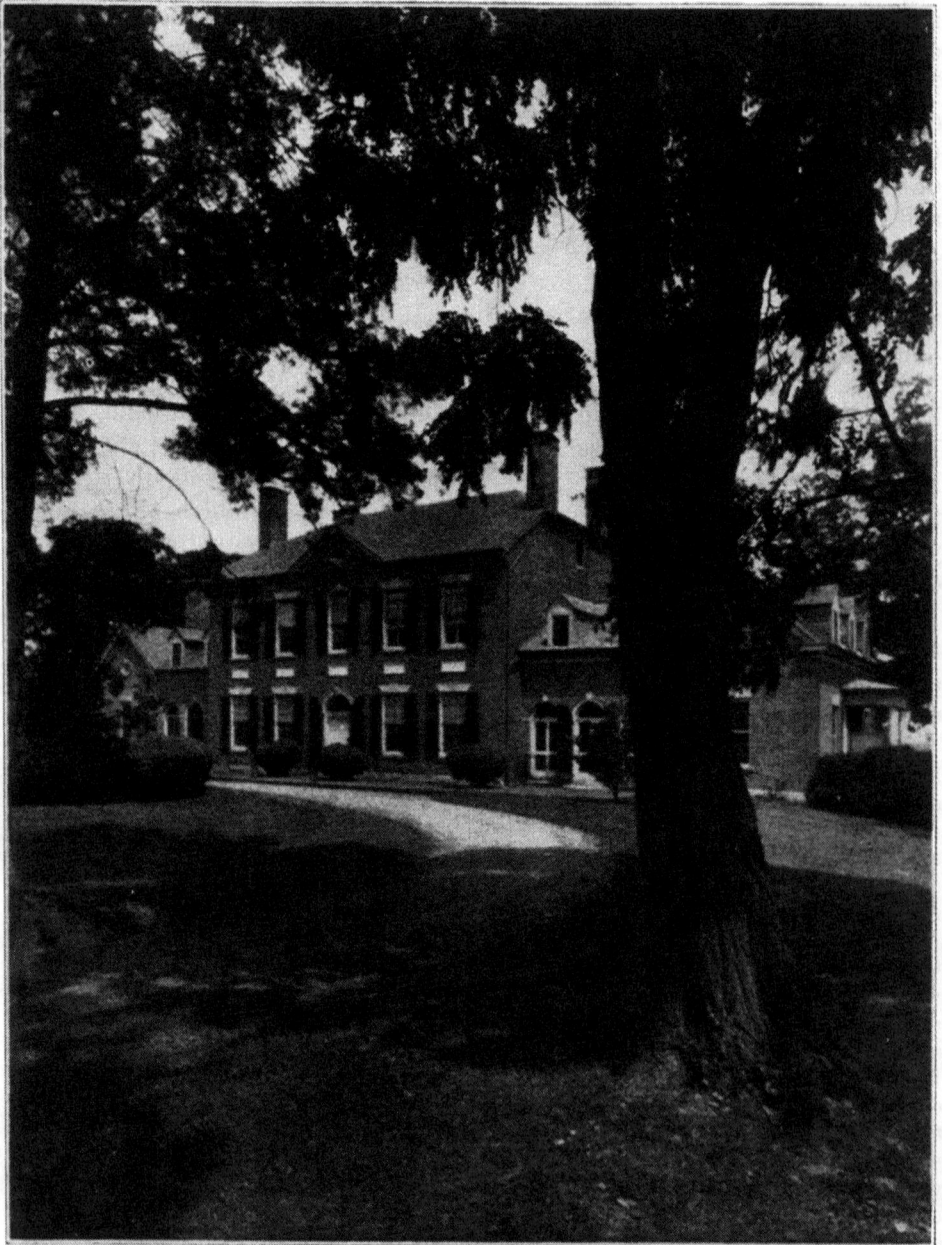

Woodlawn, three miles west of Mount Vernon, built by Lawrence Lewis and his wife Nelly Custis soon after 1800.

the old relicts of my Beloved Grand mother, silk dress or parts of dresses &c. my Parke will divide & give a piece as keep sakes to her children, to my precious C&L Conrad & to the six sons of my darling Lorenzo.—All Books not marked for my C & L Conrad for my Parke & her children.—The Bead work for Parke if she wishes to have it, if not, for my Charley and Lewis—miniatures of Genl W & Daguerreotype of Grand mama for my Lewis & the bust of Genl. Taylor, the Buckels topaz, equally divided (if they wish, between Charles A. & L. L. Conrad. —Charley will have Powers bust of Genl W., & Paintings of Genl & Mrs W from his Father. Genl T's cup & saucer for my Parke,—the miniature Genl T. Mr. Kimbal gave me is for H. L. D. Lewis. Grandmamas looking glass for C & L Conrad. the shell box, basket of Porcupine quills, china, Profile in flowers of B Franklin for C & L Conrad—every article that was their dear mothers is for them —my china purse from Mrs. Grant & my crochet box from Mrs. Oliver for my Parke—all my verses & the Book to Copy them in any she thinks worth having to be copied for my darlings—My large paint box for my Parke—I wish her to arrange all my articles & those belonging to my Charley & Lewis,—I will that my faithfull Sam shall be free at my death, & if $50 remain after my debts are paid —give them to him as a remembrance from his old Mistress whom he has served so faithfully, my devoted love & blessing to all my Darling children, may they ever be blessed by the Almighty Father of mercies.

August 19th, 1850   E. P. LEWIS.

My silk dress to A. C. N. Stuart—& if I leave a warm dress worth giving, to Miss Betty Roots,—my old clothes to the servants,

All colored & gilt paper for my Charles & L. Conrad embossed cards for my Parke & Sissy & Cass.

Last wishes of Eleanor Parke Lewis written at Audley, August 19th, 1850

Lorenzo Lewis had died at the age of 43 almost exactly three years before his mother prepared the foregoing memoranda. Esther was his widow. Parke was Mrs. Nelly Lewis's daughter, Frances Parke Butler. Charles and Lewis Conrad were the sons of Angela Lewis Conrad, Mrs. Lewis's daughter, who had died at Pass Christian, Miss., in 1839. "Sissy & Cass" were probably Isabella and Caroline, daughters of Mrs. Butler. H. L. D. Lewis was one of the six sons of Lorenzo. The number of books referred to and the importance attached to them is significant. The various portraits of General and Mrs. Washington, Benjamin Franklin, and others comprised a collection of great value, and the catalogue of them herein should prove of special interest to any person who is engaged in locating and identifying such articles. The terms of endearment used in referring to the several members of her family indicate the unbounded affection that Mrs. Lewis had for them, and her provision for the freedom and welfare of her faithful servant Sam is gratifying.

One might suppose from certain features of this writing, will or what not, that Mrs. Lewis at the time she penned it was rather feeble in body and mind, but the handwriting does not indicate anything of the kind. On the contrary, the manuscript, which is as clear and unfaded as the day it was written, shows a bold and vigorous driving of the pen, in a hand that would be guessed as

Another view of Audley. The room in which Nelly Custis died is on the right, near the entrance.

masculine. Mrs. Lewis lived two years after the date of this paper, which was admitted to record as her will at Berryville on Monday, August 23, 1852. Her hand was rather difficult to read, and the recording clerk evidently was inexperienced, careless, or had poor eyesight, for a number of blanks (of a word or two each) were left in the record; but fortunately the original has been preserved.

The body of Nelly Custis Lewis was carried to Mount Vernon for interment. Her son, Lorenzo Lewis, and other members of his family are buried in the Episcopal churchyard in Berryville. The names of the six sons of Lorenzo and his wife Esther were George Washington, John Redman Coxe, Lawrence Fielding, Edward Parke Custis, Charles Conrad, and H. L. Daingerfield. John Redman and Lawrence Fielding were twins. Three of these six sons are buried near their parents in Berryville: Lawrence Fielding, who died at Audley in 1857, in his 23rd year; Charles Conrad, who died at the University of Virginia in 1859, aged 19; and H. L. Daingerfield, born April 25, 1841, who died December 17, 1893.

Washington Irving in 1853 came to Audley and other places in the neighborhood in his search for materials to compose his life of Washington. He was a year too late to find Nelly Custis Lewis, the General's adopted daughter, but he was fortunate in finding another lady at Audley who was a zealous custodian of the literary treasures belonging to the family. The master of the house at that time, as Irving revealed in a letter to his nephew, was George Washington Lewis, one of the six sons, who hospitably entertained Irving and John Pendleton Kennedy, author of "Swallow Barn" and "Horse-Shoe Robinson," who accompanied Irving. His mother, Mrs. Esther Coxe Lewis, however, was in charge of the Washington relics and papers. These, said Irving, "she laid before me with great satisfaction." Among them, no doubt, were some of the heirlooms that Nelly Custis had enumerated in her will. Mrs. Lewis (Esther Coxe Lewis) lived to be four-score, dying at Audley on June 23, 1885.

In 1921 Mr. B. B. Jones bought Audley and 530 acres from Archibald Cummins, who had purchased from the heirs of Daingerfield Lewis in 1902. Lorenzo Lewis had left a will, but his estate was settled and his property divided through a chancery suit. The original Audley tract was divided into four farms of approximately 400 acres each. George Washington Lewis received the one called Monterey; to Edward Parke Custis Lewis was assigned another known by the appropriate name of Fielding; John Redman Coke Lewis received Buena Vista; and to H. L. Daingerfield Lewis was given Audley proper. The purchase by Mr. Jones in 1921 was made up of portions of several tracts, as enumerated above.

There is a very well preserved tradition at Audley that Nelly Custis Lewis's ghost appears now and then to strangers who sleep in the room in which she died. The author hereof slept in that room the night of December 8,

1923, and was very much disappointed—no ghost appeared to him. It was probably an off night for spiritual visitations. But even if Nelly's ghost does not always walk or speak,

"Voices linger at old Audley,
  Sounding low from out the past,
Like soft music in the twilight,
  With a sweetness that shall last."

The avenue leading in to Audley from the highway east of Berryville.

A tracing of Nelly Custis's handwriting.

CHAPTER XIII

CLAYMONT AND ITS GARDEN

About 1812 two young Washingtons, Bushrod Corbin and John Augustine, sons of Corbin, married Blackburn sisters, Thomasina and Jane Charlotte. A few years later they established neighboring homes. Claymont and Blakely, in Jefferson County, now West Virginia, on lands that had come down to them from their grandfather, John Augustine Washington, of Bushfield. This chapter relates to Claymont, its beautiful old garden, and its distinguished owners.

Claymont, or Claymont Court, is located three miles southwest of Charles Town. To reach it, one leaves Charles Town by the Summit Point Road, drives out two miles and turns to the left on a winding trail through native forest, mainly of oaks. After nearly a mile through the forest one stands at the northeastern entrance of the mansion. Around it are oaks, black walnuts, cedars, mahoganies, and cucumber trees. The main front is on the southwest, but the portico and doorway on the northeast are of surpassing beauty. On the southwest are cleared fields that decline gently to the north fork of the Bullskin, permitting an open view to Blakely and the higher lands around the village of Rippon.

Bushrod Corbin Washington, the builder of Claymont, was born in Westmoreland County, Va., December 25, 1790, the son of Corbin Washington and his wife, Hannah Lee, daughter of the celebrated orator and statesman, Richard Henry Lee. Bushrod Corbin's first wife, Ann Maria Thomasina Blackburn, was his senior by 56 days, her birthday having fallen on October 30, 1790. She lived only until September 21, 1833, a date 51 days before the stars fell. Of the remarkable meteoric shower that made that autumn memorable, a chronicler of the neighborhood of Claymont wrote as follows:

On Wednesday Morning (Novr. 13th) about 5 O'Clock, Commenced the Shower of Meteors, & which continued without any Sensible diminition untill day light, a Phenomena quite alarming, & Such as had never before appeared, in this country—Nor, it is believed, in no other part of this Globe to the Same extent.

The dates of the births and deaths of Bushrod Corbin Washington and his wives have been definitely ascertained from the inscriptions on their tombstones in the Episcopal churchyard in Charles Town.

John Augustine Washington, brother to George, died at Bushfield in 1787, having made his will three years earlier. He left to his son Corbin, his heirs and assigns, all his lands in Berkeley County not otherwise disposed of. Corbin died in Fairfax County in 1800, having in his will, made a few months before, devised to his "dear wife & Friend Hannah Washington" all his estate. Hannah, on June 17, 1800, wrote her will. To three of her sons, Richard Henry Lee, John Augustine, and Bushrod Corbin Washington, she left lands

The northeast entrance of Claymont.

in Berkeley County. These lands were in the southeastern part of Berkeley, the portion which was the next year (1801) cut off and erected into the new County of Jefferson. On these lands in Berkeley, later in Jefferson, John Augustine and Bushrod Corbin Washington built their homes, Blakeley and Claymont, in or about the year 1820.

It is very probable that Bushrod Corbin Washington and his family lived at Claymount for several years preceding 1820, in an older house, but it seems well agreed that the large brick mansion was erected at that time.

Maria P. Harrison, the second wife of Bushrod Corbin Washington, was his junior by almost exactly seven months, her birthday having been July 27, 1791. She lived until November 4, 1847. Bushrod's son, Thomas Blackburn Washington, born August 19, 1812, was by his first wife, Ann Maria Thomasina Blackburn. His daughter Hannah Lee, who was married in or before 1849, was also, we may assume, a child of the first marriage.

Bushrod C. Washington, like most of his near kinsmen, was a man of prominence in his community. He was a justice of the peace in 1836 and thereabouts, and for at least two sessions, 1829-30 and 1838-39, represented Jefferson County in the Virginia House of Delegates. In the election held in in the autumn of 1838 he and George Reynolds were the successful candidates for the General Assembly, running ahead of William Lucas and Henry Bedinger, the opposing candidates. For Washington, however, the political victory was soon overshadowed by a dire personal misfortune—the burning of his splendid residence. A graphic account of this disaster has been preserved in a letter which Mr. Bedinger thereafter wrote to his daughter, Mrs. Nancy Swearingen. The mild reflections in this letter, which is quoted below, may possibly have been inspired to some extent by the rivalries of politics.

About a week after the Election at Charles Town, the Elegant & Costly house of Mr. Bushrod Washington was reduced to Ashes by Accidental fire, there were large wings to the building, with basement Stories and fire places. Mr. Ransome said in one end of those wings Some of the blacks were Shelling Some Corn, of Course threw the Cobs into the fire, the day was quite windy and dry, that probably the Chimney Caught on fire and Sparks fell on the dry roof, that there the fire Commenced & no immediate means to extinguish, it had made Some progress in that wing before discovery, the fire was Soon seen by the Neighbors, and from Town, but too late to Save the building. Much of the furniture was Saved, though in all Such Cases, Some of the rescued a good deal injured, thus at one dash has been destroyed the Mansion house which but a few years Since Cost More than thirty thousand dollars, besides Some of the furniture. I am Sincerely Sorry for this loss, he is an innocent good man, And I deplore his weakness and folly in erecting Such an expensive building, because a house half or one quarter of the Cost would have Created as much if not greater real Comfort—but Pride & Ambition too often leads to great follies.

Kercheval, the Shenandoah Valley Herodotus, also tells us about the fire at Claymont, though he does not name the place nor chide the builder for his

Claymont from the southwest. Photo by Morrison in 1929.

—*From Historic Homes*

folly. At the very beginning of his chapter on "Splendid Improved Farms" are the following paragraphs:

Bushrod C. Washington, Esq., a few years ago erected a very large brick dwelling house, in the neighborhood of Charlestown, Jefferson County, with all the necessary offices. This building with other improvements cost upwards of thirty thousand dollars.

The building was finished in the most tasteful style of modern architecture; but unfortunately, some two or three years ago, it accidentally took fire; and all the interior works were consumed. But the writer is informed Mr. Washington has lately rebuilt it. The author obtained a sketch of its dimensions, but has unfortunately mislaid the memorandum. Suffice it to say, it is one of the largest and most elegant edifices in our country.

Evidently the original walls of the mansion were largely preserved and the reconstruction no doubt followed the general style and dimensions of the first edifice. Accordingly, a visitor to Claymont today may see with only slight modifications the same splendid structure that delighted the eye and depleted the purse of Bushrod C. Washington. The words of a recent writer are no exaggeration: "With the wings at each side of the house it is 250 feet long, and is one of the finest colonial homes in America."

But the mansion at Claymont cannot hold the visitor's undivided attention. The extensive and beautiful old garden has a rare charm, and invites one to linger among its quiet retreats, forgetful of the passing hours.

On February 1, 1849, Bushrod C. Washington made his will. His debts, of course, were to be paid. He refers to his "late dear wife Maria P. Washington." Her Negroes were to go to her relatives, "except Thompson & Henry, two boys she sold me in 1836." Her brothers, Henry T. Harrison, Burr W. Harrison, and John M. Harrison, and her sisters, Mrs. Margaret L. Cooke and Mrs. Sarah E. Powell (wife of Dr. Llewellyn Powell) are named. The testator's son, Thomas B. Washington, who was then living on Rich Woods Farm, was to have the Claymont estate; the testator's daughter, Hannah Lee Alexander, his late brother John A. Washington, and his nephew, John A. Washington, are mentioned. Disposition is made of "my Jackson County land, my Bank, Canal, and road stocks, my interest in the Dismal Swamp Land Company, my interest in the Shannondale Springs Company, and all my mountain land."

The will was proved before the court of Jefferson County on August 18, 1851, and the executors gave bond in the sum of $60,000.00. The testator had died on July 27, 1851. July 27 was his second wife's birthday.

In March 1877 a Bushrod C. Washington was appointed clerk of the circuit court in Charles Town. He was a son of Thomas B. Washington and a grandson of the builder of Claymont.

In 1899 Claymont came into the hands of its most famous owner. On June 24 of that year Miss Pauline Dawson deeds to Frank R. Stockton

A corner of Claymont garden.

of New Jersey for Claymont Farm and improvements, 149 acres, 2 roods, and 20 perches. The estate as thus conveyed was composed of three several tracts, which belonged, or had belonged, to Clement March. Frank R. Stockton paid $8,000 in cash and executed two bonds: one for $10,000, to be paid on or before June 15, 1902; the other for $12,000, to be paid on or before June 15, 1906. (See Jefferson County Deed Book 87, page 239.)

It is said that Mr. Stockton's last writings were done at Claymont. He must have found the place suitable to his tastes—a quiet retreat of beauty and serenity. And the rich literary traditions of the neighborhood were no doubt congenial to his spirit. Less than three miles away, near Charles Town, was Cassilis, the Kennedy home, where John Pendleton Kennedy, the author of "Swallow Barn," "Horse-Shoe Robinson," and "Rob of the Bowl," had been a familiar figure. At Cassilis Thackeray had been entertained. And Washington Irving. Driving out thence the Kennedys, John and Andrew, had taken Irving to Audley, Greenway Court, and Winchester, when the Sage of Sunnyside was collecting materials for his Life of Washington. At Shepherdstown lived Danske Dandridge, of no mean skill in poetry and prose. A short distance beyond Charles Town was Rion Hall, home of Daniel Bedinger Lucas, jurist, orator, and poet, whose throbbing voice woke echoes in "The Land Where We Were Dreaming."

And not far away were The Briars, where dwelt the author of "Surry of Eagle's Nest" and many other stirring romances, and The Vineyard, where the romancer's brother, Philip Pendleton Cooke, had written "Florence Vane."

In several interesting features Claymont reminds the author of Oak Hill, the home of President Monroe, in Loudoun County, Va. The main front of each is towards the southwest, and each has an entrance on the northeast of unusual beauty. Both are on commanding elevations, yet the approaches to both are so gradual and easy that neither can be said to stand on a hill. On the southwest of both are open fields that decline sufficiently to afford extended vistas—each can be seen at a distance of two miles: Oak Hill from the Little River Turnpike just east of Aldie; Claymont from U. S. Route 340 northeast of Rippon.

Oak Hill does not have a fine old garden, but at Oatlands House, near Oak Hill, is a garden that resembles in many of its charming features the one at Claymont.

Claymont was recently purchased from the heirs of Col. S. J. Murphy by Mr. Raymond J. Funkhouser.

Covered walkway in Claymont garden.

CHAPTER XIV

BLAKELEY AND ITS BOWERS

Blakeley, the home of John Augustine Washington II, is near Claymont, the home of John's brother, Bushrod Corbin Washington. The two houses are only about three-quarters of a mile apart, and are in plain sight of each other. Claymont House, the more pretentious structure, has an entrance on either side, but its main front is southwest, towards Blakeley. The latter fronts northeast, towards Claymont, but has an entrance also at the southeast end. About midway between the two homesteads is a hollow, down which flows, southeastwardly, the north fork of the Bullskin, a small stream, sometimes called a creek, sometimes a run, which heads only a short distance above. Three miles below it joins the south fork; then, three miles farther southeast, beyond Kabletown, it enters the Shenandoah River.

The name of this little creek is ancient if not quite honorable, dating from 1740 or earlier. "The tradition is," says Dr. James R. Graham, "that this singular name had its origin in the fact that when the first settlers arrived there they found on the bank of the stream the hide of a buffalo bull of enormous size, stretched out to dry, the bull having been killed by a party of hunters, or possibly of Indians." George Washington, who owned large tracts of land on the south fork of the Bullskin, mentions the stream a number of times in his diaries. The springs that feed the watercourse are never-failing and the bordering lands are generally fertile.

John Augustine Washington II, born in Westmoreland County, Va., in 1789, was a son of Corbin and his wife Hannah Lee, and thus a grandson of John Augustine Washington I, the General's second full brother. John Augustine II married Jane Charlotte Blackburn, a sister to his brother Bushrod Corbin's first wife, Ann Maria Thomasina. Bushrod and Thomasina were married prior to New Year's, 1812, for their son Thomas Blackburn Washington was born on August 19, 1812. John, who was his brother's senior by a year or so, married Jane Charlotte in 1814, according to Charles H. Callahan in "Washington, The Man and the Mason." The Blackburn sisters were the daughters of Captain Richard Scott Blackburn and his wife, Judith Ball. The Washington brothers, we are told, built their mansion houses, Blakely and Claymont, in 1820. Very probably both resided at the sites for several years preceding. John Augustine II's son, John Augustine III, the last Washington owner of Mount Vernon, was born, says Dr. Lyon G. Tyler, at Blakely. The date of his birth was May 3, 1820. Richard Blackburn Washington, another son of John Augustine II, was born at Blakeley on November 12, 1822, according to the inscription on his tombstone in Charles Town.

The lands whereon Blakely and Claymont were built came down from John Augustine Washington I, as shown in Chapter XIII. But Hannah Lee

Blakeley from the northeast. Photo 1938.

Washington, widow of Corbin, by will in 1800 left the Berkeley (soon to be Jefferson) County lands to three of her sons, John Augustine, Bushrod Corbin, and Richard Henry Lee. Evidently Richard Henry Lee Washington died early in life and unmarried, or at any rate without children living, for his lands, or part of them, descended by will or otherwise to his brother, John Augustine II, of Blakeley, as will appear. Evidently, therefore, John Augustine II was well-to-do in lands, but he did not build as lavishly as did his brother Bushrod Corbin, at Claymont. Or possibly he did. There was a fire at Blakeley too. The house now standing is extensive and substantial, but does not give evidence of excessive cost.

John Augustine Washington II, like his brother Richard Henry Lee, was short-lived even for a Washington. He died at the age of 43. We may be pretty certain that his health was poor for ten years before his death, for he made his will on August 6, 1822, when he was only 33, and just a year or two after he had finished his mansion house at Blakeley. His wife, Jane Charlotte Washington, was named as executrix. She was a woman of rather unusual executive ability, and we may assume that he depended upon her judgment and aid increasingly in his declining years. Two codicils were added to the will, one soon after it was made, the other after an interval of eight years. The first, dated September 10, 1822, had reference to the testator's daughter, Anne Mariah T. B. Washington, who evidently bore the name of her aunt, Mrs. Bushrod C. Washington. The other was dated July 8, 1830, and recited in its preamble that "my late uncle Bushrod Washington did by will give me Mount Vernon house & a certain parcel of land." The will was presented to the court of Jefferson County on July 16, 1832, and proved by Bushrod C. Washington and Edmund J. Lee Jr. (See Jefferson County Will Book 7, page 26.)

Mrs. Jane Charlotte Washington of Blakeley outlived her husband by twenty-three years. Even so she did not live to any great age. Her will, written October 3, 1854, is a long one, but it is so interesting and so valuable historically that it is given herewith in full.

I Jane C. Washington of Blakeley Jefferson County State of Virginia, knowing the uncertainty of life. and humbly resigned to the directing providence of God, thro faith. in the all prevailing merits and atonement of my Lord and Saviour Jesus Christ. Being yet blessed with a sound disposing mind and memory; do make and ordain this my last Will and Testament. Feeling very deeply the responsibility of the trust and confidence, reposed in me, by my honored and beloved Husband, John Augustine Washington, to make distribution of his Estate among our Children: I shall now proceed to execute the Same to the best of my Judgment, And as regards the Mount Vernon and Jefferson Lands, as agreed upon between us a Short time before his death.

First: Having hereto conveyed Blackburn Washington, certain Slaves, in Trust, for my daughter Anne Maria Thomasina Blackburn Alexander, the terms of the Trust being expressed in a Deed now of record in Alexandria County Virginia, I now give to my said Daughter's Son (without the intervention of a

Blakeley from the northwest. Photo 1938.

Trustee) John Augustine Washington Alexander, a negro boy named Jasper, and I also give to said Daughter's Daughter, Mary Fontaine Alexander a negro Girl named Sarah, also a boy named Charles, to Cary S. Alexander as it was the intention of my late Husband John A. Washington to have invested ten thousand dollars in the purchase of a farm for our Daughter, the said Anne M. B. Alexander, and have it secured to her and her family—I have heretofore advanced to her Husband Doctor William Fontaine Alexander, Ten Thousand dollars, with the understanding that he was to convey to my Nephew Thomas B. Washington In Trust, for my Said Daughter, Such a portion of the Farm he purchased from Mr. John Humphreys, including in that portion, the Houses Wood and Water, as at the price he paid for the Land would be equivalent to the Ten thousand dollars —this has been done, And the Deed recorded, And I hereby ratify and confirm the Same, Considering the said ten thousand dollars as part of my Daughter's distributive share of her father's Estate, and safely invested in real Estate for her & her heirs—

Under the authority Vested in me by my Husband's Will, to sell undivided land left to him by Judge Washington; I sold a parcel or Lot of Land in Jackson County, State of Virginia and received from the purchaser Six hundred dollars, which money was put out at interest & secured to my Daughter. The purchaser of the land failing to make the after payments, gave up the Land, which is therefore again at my disposal—I hereby give and bequeath this tract of Land to my said Daughter Anne Maria T. B. Alexander, and Dr. W. F. Alexander forever, to retain or dispose of as my said Daughter and her husband may think best for the interest of their Children. I have heretofore given my said Daughter and her husband Dr. W. F. Alexander, Eleven Shares of stock in the Bank of Potomac, Alexandria, divided to my Husband from Judge Washington's Estate, at one hundred dollars a share, I also at the same time gave them stock in the Union Bank of George Town divided from Judge Washington's Estate to my Husband valued at Eight hundred and sixty five dollars. I also gave my Daughter's Husband a chk. for eight hundred dollars to purchase Furniture, and gave my Daughter plate & House hold equipment of Various kinds, which I estimate at one thousand dollars. I also gave Dr. W. F. Alexander six hundred dollars to Assist in paying for Howard, as he sold the above mentioned Bank Stock for only twelve hundred dollars, And I also gave him four hundred dollars to purchase a negro boy. These advances I have always meant & considered as on account of my daughter's portion of her Father's Estate and I hereby ratify and confirm the same.

Secondly: I will and bequeath to my son, John Augustine Washington, the Mount Vernon Estate, as devised to his Father by Judge Washington, which includes not only the land, fisheries, but the Books—plate Household and kitchen of every kind, except the Chamber furniture Books Book Case, which Judge Washington devised to me, and which I now leave to my Son's second Daughter, Jane Charlotte Washington, and in Case of her dying in infancy, then to my Son's Elder Daughter Louisa Fontaine Washington. I also give and bequeath to my Said Son John A. Washington, the Land in Jefferson County, Virginia, Inherited by my Husband from his Brother Richard Henry Lee Washington. Also the Land purchased by my Husband from Mr. Mathew Ranson—Also the second purchase of mountain Land from Mr. William Herbert. I also give and bequeath to my Sd. Son the one fifth of a Share of Dismal Swamp stock divided to my Husband from Judge Washington's Estate; also one third of the Chesapeake Ohio Canal & Old Potomac stock whether subscribed for by my Husband, or inherited from Mr. Corbin Washington, or Judge Washington's Estate—I also give and bequeath to

View from Blakeley towards Claymont.
Photo 1938.

my Son John A. Washington, a Negro Boy Called John Lyons, the Son of my faithful servant Harry, with the request that my sd. Son will have him Carefully trained in sound moral & religious principals, and industrious habits, and when he attains the age of twenty five, manumit him, and send him to Liberia in Africa, where his Uncle Charles Starks now is, I give and bequeath to my son John A. Washington the slaves hereintofore in his possession, under the lease from me to him, bearing date 15th September 1842 together with the descendants of the females, that may have been born since they came to my sons possession, or which may hereafter be born—I also give to my said son, one half of the other Slaves belonging to his Father's Estate, not specially devised or otherwise disposed of to his Brother or Sister or my Grand Children during my life.

Thirdly: I will and bequeath to my son Richard Blackburn Washington, all the land in Jefferson County Virginia belonging to my late Husband or which may belong to me, and which has not been bequeathed to my son John A. Washington in the second part of this will, Viz. Blakeley farm where I now live. the whole of it, as originally divided to my Husband, as his proportion of his Father's Estate; also the land my Husband purchased from Nathan Haines—the land I also purchased from Adam Grubb & the land purchased from Thomas West, and deeded to me. I also give and bequeath to my said Son Richard B. Washington, my Husband's first purchase of Mountain land from Mr. William Herbert —I also give my Sd. Son the Household & kitchen furniture of every kind; Farming Implements, Wagon Carts Horses—Cattle, stock of every kind belonging to me on the Blakely Farm—I also give and devise to said Son nineteen shares of [stock] in the Bank of the Valley in Virginia—also Devise to my Said Son Richard one third of the Chesapeake and Ohio Canal and Old Potomac stock whether subscribed for by my Husband, or inherited from Mr. Corbin Washington, or Judge Washington—I also give to my said son Richard the slaves heretofore in his possession under a lease from me to him, and the increase of females born while in his possession, or at any time afterwards—also one half the other belonging to his Father's Estate, not specifically devised or otherwise given to my other children or grand children.

Fourthly: I give and bequeath to my Grand daughter Jean Charlotte Alexander, Ten shares of stock in the Bank of the Valley in Virginia, and in case of her death under age, or without a Will, The Said Ten Shares of Valley Bank Stock shall go to her sisters Mary Fontaine Alexander, & Anna Burnett Alexander, or the Survivor. Under this fourth section of my Will, I give and bequeath to my daughter Anne Maria T. B. Alexander the remaining third of the Chesapeake and Ohio Canal stock and Old Potomac stock, both that subscribed for by my Husband and inherited by him from his father Mr. Corbin Washington, also Judge Washington. I gave and transferred to Dr. W. F. Alexander three shares of Alexander Canal stock which I hereby ratify and confirm.

Fifthly: I desire my executors out of my portion of Crops raised on the Blakeley Estate, and rents from other property, also Hires due for servants—and other money due me at the time of my death—to pay any Debt or Debts I may owe—which must be small if any—and the balance remaining in their hands, give toward making an Iron railing Enclosure round our Burying place in the Church yard in Charlestown. I hereby will and bequeath to my sons John A. and Richard B. Washington every thing in possession, Revertion, or Remainder, belonging or in any way coming to the Estate of my Husband or myself. And do earnestly commit to their respectful and tender care my sister Christian Blackburn, to whom and my dear Sister Judith I bequeath my wearing apparel, my Watch also to my Sister Judith; with my Writing Desk and Traveling Trunk.

Lastly, I hereby appoint my sons John A. Washington and Richard B. Washington, Executors of this my last Will and Testament, written altogether in my own hand Writing, and desire no security may be required of them. In Testimony whereof I do hereto set my hand & seal this third Day of October—one thousand Eight hundred and fifty four.

                              JANE CHARLOTTE WASHINGTON
                              Blakeley, Jefferson County, Virginia

The foregoing instrument was written solidly from beginning to end, or was so recorded. It has been separated into paragraphs for the convenience of present readers, but the spelling, punctuation, and use or non-use of capitals have been preserved literally. On September 17, 1855, it was proved before the court of Jefferson County by the oaths of Edward E. Cooke, Edmund J. Lee, and Richard T. (?) Blackburn. A bond of only $3,000 was required of the executors. (See Jefferson County Will Book 14, page 341.)

In this document Mrs. Washington wrote what was certainly and thoroughly a woman's will, yet at the same time she gave evidence of remarkable business acumen and put on record a fine piece of family history. In it the reader will observe the repetition of family Christian names from generation to generation, a feature that is typical of many Washington wills, and one which has entailed endless difficulties to genealogists.

Evidently John Augustine Washington II and his wife Jane Charlotte Blackburn Washington had three children, or three who grew to maturity and married: Anne Maria Thomasina Blackburn Washington, who married Dr. William Fontaine Alexander; John Augustine Washington III, who married Eleanor Love Selden (in 1842); and Richard Blackburn Washington (1822-1910), who married Christian Maria, who was also probably a Washington. The inscription on her tombstone in Charles Town states that she was born at Harewood on December 16, 1826, and died at the same place June 10, 1895.

Many more particulars about John Augustine Washington III will be presented in subsequent chapters. His second daughter, Jane Charlotte, who bore her grandmother's name and by her will received the chamber furniture, books and bookcase at Mount Vernon, was born at Mount Vernon on May 26, 1846. She married Nathaniel Hite Willis. Her older sister, Louisa Fontaine, married Colonel R. P. Chew.

The Blackburn Washington, who had held certain slaves in trust for Mrs. Alexander, was doubtless the Thomas B. Washington, son of Bushrod C., who is mentioned farther on in the will of his aunt, Mrs. Jane Charlotte Washington. By this will Blakeley, with the farming implements, livestock, etc., went into the hands and possession of the testatrix's younger son, Richard Blackburn Washington. Blakeley was his birthplace and he lived there for a number of years. His daughter, Christine Maria Washington, born at Blakeley on June 13, 1858, lived to an advanced age, dying in Charles Town on May 15, 1937. But evidently Blakeley passed out of the hands of

Richard Blackburn Washington, "Colonel Dick," as he was called, prior to 1895. His wife died at Harewood, her birthplace, and he died in Charles Town. Colonel Dick Washington, like his distant cousin, Colonel Lewis W. Washington of Beallair, figured prominently in suppressing the John Brown raid at Harper's Ferry in October 1859, as will appear in Chapter XVI.

"Blakeley and Its Bowers!" So far as evidence is now apparent, Blakeley has had no such splendid garden of shrubs and flowers as may be seen at Claymont, yet there are abundant proofs to show that the successive residents at Blakeley loved flowers, shrubs, and trees. Numerous old trees shade the grounds and the stumps of others that formerly added a stately grace may be found. At several places are dense clumps of shrubs and vines that are veritable bowers.

The present (1938) owner of Blakely is Dr. A. O. Albin of Charles Town, who acquired the property in 1937 and is making extensive improvements. The preceding owner was Mrs. Thomas C. Frazier, who lived here for many years.

CHAPTER XV

SONS AND DAUGHTERS OF CEDAR LAWN

For many years one of the chief authorities on the Washingtons in Virginia was Colonel Forrest Washington Brown (1855-1934) of Charles Town, Jefferson County, W. Va., the historic town that was laid out by Charles Washington in 1786 and given his name. As the bi-centennial of George Washington's birth approached, Colonel Brown, responding to many appeals from various quarters for information, devoted much time and labor to special research, accumulating a large collection of interesting records concerning the Washington families in and around Charles Town and in other parts of the country. With these materials and his first-hand knowledge he was very generous, graciously receiving those persons who came to him and taking many valuable hours from his own business to answer inquiries in person or by correspondence through the mails. The author of this work makes grateful acknowledgment to him for the courtesy of repeated interviews and for numerous letters in answer to various requests in reference to particular incidents and individuals. On April 12, 1933, and at other times he gave me extended recitals of facts about Cedar Lawn, one of the old Washington homes in the neighborhood of Charles Town. On one occasion he drove with me out to Cedar Lawn, of which he was then the owner, and provided in every possible way to make the trip profitable and enjoyable.

Colonel Brown was the son of Thomas A. Brown and his wife, Annie S. C. Washington (1831-1911), who was born at Harewood, a daughter of Dr. Samuel Walter Washington (1797-1831), the eldest son of George Steptoe Washington and his wife Lucy Payne. George Steptoe was a son of Colonel Samuel Washington of Harewood and his fourth wife, Anne Steptoe. George Steptoe's wife, Lucy Payne, was a sister to Dolly Payne Todd, whose marriage to James Madison took place at Harewood in 1794. The wife of Dr. Samuel Walter Washington was Louisa Clemson, of Pennsylvania. Her eldest brother, Thomas G. Clemson, married a daughter of John C. Calhoun and was the founder of Clemson College.

Thornton Washington, the eldest son of Colonel Samuel Washington, or the eldest to grow up, lived at Cedar Lawn, which was at first called Berry's Hill, in honor of Thornton's first wife, Mildred Berry. At Cedar Lawn (Berry's Hill), on May 20, 1783, was born Thornton Washington's son, John Thornton Augustine Washington, whose daughter Mary was the poetess of Cedar Lawn; and John Thornton's son, Benjamin Franklin, wrote a prose epic in deeds, if not in words.

Cedar Lawn is located a mile and a half southwest (almost south) of Harewood. The massive brick house now standing there, erected by John Thornton Augustine Washington in 1825, occupies a commanding position on

Cedar Lawn from the highway. Photo 1933.

the slope of a gentle hill and faces southeast. A number of beautiful old trees adorn the grounds, survivors of a larger number, among which were the ancient cedars that formerly stood at intervals in stately grace and gave the place its name. All of these, or nearly all, have been cut down—only their stumps remain. Two miles southeast of Cedar Lawn are Claymont and Blakeley; less than a mile northeast is Sulgrave, the home of Annie Washington Brown and her husband, Thomas Augustus Brown (1822-1909).

Cedar Lawn was doubtless the "home place" on which Thornton Washington was living in September 1781 when his father, Colonel Samuel Washington, made his will; for which place Thornton still owed 7,000 pounds, a debt that was given to him as his main portion in his father's estate; the title to which was made free and clear, so far as original claims were concerned, eighteen years later in the will of General George Washington. The General wrote:

I release exonerate and discharge, the estate of my deceased Brother, Samuel Washington, from the payment, of the money which is due to me for the land I sold to Philip Pendleton (lying in the County of Berkeley) who assigned the same to him the said Samuel; who, by agreement was to pay me therefor.—And whereas by some contract (the purport of which was never communicated to me) between the said Samuel and his son Thornton Washington, the latter became possessed of the aforesaid land, without any conveyance having passed from me, either to the said Pendleton, the said Samuel, or the said Thornton, and without any consideration having been made, by which neglect neither the legal or equitable title has been alienated;—it rests therefore with me to declare my intention concerning the premises—and these are to give and bequeath the said land to, whomsoever the said Thornton Washington (who is also dead) devised the same; or to his heirs forever if he died intestate:— Exonerating the estate of the said Thornton, equally with that of the said Samuel from payment of the purchase money; which, with Interest, agreeably to the original contract with the said Pendleton, would amount to more than a thousand pounds.

The discrepancies in figures may be accounted for by the different kinds of money (specie and depreciated paper currency) that were in use at different times, or, more probably, by the fact that the value of the property had been enhanced by buildings and other improvements by the time Colonel Samuel Washington made his will in 1781. Possibly both factors entered into the case.

John Thornton Augustine Washington had a large family, as appears from his will, which was made on July 16, 1840, and was proved at Charles Town on October 18, 1841, nine days after his death. He named his sons: Daniel B., Thornton Augustine, Lawrence B., Benjamin Franklin, and George; and his daughters: Sally E., Georgiana A., Mary, Mildred B., and Susan E. He owned lands on the Bullskin, a small stream near Cedar Lawn, and also on the Great Kanawha, in Mason County, now West Virginia. His sons Daniel

A close-up view of the house at Cedar Lawn. Photo 1933.

B., Thornton Augustine, and Lawrence B. were given portions of land on the Great Kanawha. His son Benjamin Franklin Washington was made executor of his will and guardian for those of his children who were still under legal age. The witnesses to the instrument were Alexander Jones, William T. Washington, and E. I. Lee, Jr.

John Thornton Augustine Washington and his wife, Elizabeth C. (1793-1837), are both buried at Harewood. Elizabeth was a Bedinger of the well-known Shepherdstown family, and the B's that appear as initials in the names of several of her children are no doubt thus explained. It is probable, indeed, that she was a daughter of Daniel Bedinger (1764-1818), an officer of the Revolution, who later purchased the masts of the old frigate *Constitution* and used them as pillars for the portico of the house he built in Shepherdstown, a house that was burned in the Civil War by order of General David Hunter.

Some of the Bedingers had considerable literary talent. The late Judge Daniel Bedinger Lucas of near Charles Town was widely known as an orator and man of letters. Danske Dandridge, a daughter of Hon. Henry Bedinger (1810-1858), was recognized in an anthology of Virginia poets. She was the author, too, of several prose works of merit. Perhaps Mary Washington of Cedar Lawn inherited qualities that distinguished others of her kinsfolk, and she may have inherited also a literary tradition. She at any rate had some skill in versification, as her stanzas on Cedar Lawn indicate. A copy of this composition was preserved by Colonel Forrest W. Brown.

CEDAR LAWN
TO MY BROTHERS AND SISTERS

O Cedar Lawn, I love thee well,
    With all thy trees and flowers;
For never can my heart forget
    The home of childhood's hours.

With spirit sad we left thy walls,
    Another home to seek;
And even now remembrance calls
    The warm tear to my cheek.

Ah, once again, "in fancy free"
    I wander o'er the place,
And in each bush and flower and tree
    Sweet recollections trace.

Or underneath the gay green woods,
    Where oft we roved in spring,
A merry and a blithesome throng,
    To hear the wild birds sing.

Methinks I see the green boughs bend,
    Our youthful hands to meet;
The violets and the daisies spring
    In beauty round our feet.

Again we pluck the gay wild flowers
    From out their mossy beds,
And twine them into garlands fair
    Around our sunny heads.

Once more upon the grassy lawn
    I bound with footsteps free,
Or seated with my parents dear,
    Beneath the cedar tree.

Those guardians of our infant days
    Have long since gone to rest;
O Mother, would thy child might sleep
    In peace, upon thy breast!

For thy dear ones are scattered now,
    And some are far away,
And some I see around me still,
    But they are not so gay.

And when in happy childhood we
    Were gathered in our home,
While thou wert here, our Mother dear,
    We never wished to roam.

Oh, those indeed were joyous hours;
    Though never to return,
They still must live, the brightest flowers
    In Memory's sacred urn.

And when our hearts are sad to think
    They ne'er can come again,
To muse upon their joyousness
    Will rob them of their pain.

Oft when in pleasure's throng so gay,
    I seem the gladdest there,
My heart—my heart is far away,
    With scenes more sweet and fair.

I think of thee, dear Cedar Lawn,
    With all thy trees and flowers,
For never can my heart forget
    The home of childhood's hours.
                            (Signed) MARY.
    March, 1842.

Evidently Mary and other members of her family moved away from Cedar Lawn soon after the death of her father, John Thornton Augustine Washington, in 1841. Her mother had died four years earlier.

Colonel Brown told me that Benjamin Franklin Washington was a Forty-Niner—that he led a company of adventurers to California in the early days of the gold rush; then came back to Jefferson County and got his wife (who was a Miss Ranson) and his children. From another source more details of the first trip to the West have been gathered. In the party with Benjamin Franklin Washington was one Benjamin Hoffman, who kept a diary. This was published in 1901, and contains a graphic account of high hopes, hardship, and adventure. According to Hoffman's narrative, 80 young men, mostly of Jefferson County, in the spring of 1849 formed an organization styled the Charles Town Mining Company, each contributing $300 to the joint capital. The president of the organization was Benjamin Franklin Washington. Robert H. Keeling was first commander; William H. Mackaran, second commander. The treasurer was E. M. Asquith; the secretary, J. Harrison Kelly. Dr. Bryarly Balts was surgeon.

In the party were two other Washingtons, T. F. and Lawrence. The latter was probably Benjamin Franklin Washington's brother.

The company purchased horses, mules, wagons, and supplies and left Charles Town late in March. They went to Pittsburgh and there took boat down the Ohio River to Cairo, Illinois. Thence they proceeded up the Mississippi to the mouth of the Missouri, and up that stream to St. Joseph. This point was reached within a month after the start from Charles Town. The next four months were spent trekking across the plains and climbing over the mountains—the Rockies and the Sierras. The dangers encountered and the hardships endured were similar to those that fell to the average lot of the overland argonauts of those years: the uncertain temper of the Indians; hazardous crossings of strange rivers; exposure to violent storms; lack of pasturage for the horses and mules and of food for the men; long stages without water; and occasional disease and painful mishap.

On August 17 "the long-dreaded Sierra Mountains" were seen in the distance. On the 24th Hoffman wrote: "Pursued our regular course, winding and twisting about through the mountains and over great cliffs all day long. Night caught us on top of a great precipice. Only five miles and busy all day." The next day, Saturday: "We managed to get our mules down, one at a time, after which we attached ropes to the wagons and by using trees as snubbing posts we got all down in safety. Made some eight miles today." On Sunday the labor continued. The hollows or canyons seemed almost bottomless. "We are all out of heart and almost ready to give up. By taking out the mules and using ropes as before, going from one tree to another until we reached the bottom, the whole day was spent in getting down." But at the bottom was found a valley in which water and grass were abundant.

To lighten the burdens of the draught animals, half of the wagons were abandoned. From first to last, five members of the party died en route.

Finally, with empty stomachs, the toilers of the trail reached Johnson's Settlement, where they were well fed. After resting there a few days they pushed on to Sacramento.

An interesting sidelight is shed on Benjamin Franklin Washington, president of the Charles Town Company, by a passage in the diary of another argonaut of '49. Alonzo Delano of Ottowa, Ill., and his party were detained for several days early in July at Green River, in southwest Wyoming, awaiting their turn at the ferry. A trial was held in the camp—a number of parties were halting at the ferry—to try a man who had overtaken and killed a murderer. The prevailing opinion was that the man on trial had been justified in his act, but inasmuch as his best witnesses were not at hand he was somewhat uneasy. Accordingly, in the words of Delano, "he employed B. F. Washington, Esq., a young lawyer from Virginia, to defend him."

Because certain statements made by Washington hurt the pride of the improvised court, and because "fire water" was circulating rather too freely— it was July 4—the trial was noisy and otherwise not in keeping with the traditional decorum of regular tribunals; however, Washington's client got off without any punishment, an outcome which was generally approved.

Hubert Howe Bancroft, in his voluminous history of the Pacific Coast, shows that B. F. Washington was a collector of customs in 1857. Colonel Brown said that he was elevated to the bench in California. In an official publication of the state of West Virginia it is stated that Benjamin Franklin Washington was a judge in California, and his brother George a judge in St. Louis. David M. Potter of Yale University says that in 1852-53, in Sacramento, Benjamin F. Washington and Vincent Geiger, from Augusta County, Va., collaborated in editing the *Democratic State Journal*.

In the Robert S. Franklin collection of manuscripts at Charleston (not Charles Town), W. Va., are a number of records from the pen of Major Henry Bedinger, covering the period from 1795 to 1840. Major Bedinger was a prominent member of the Shepherdstown family and a near relative of Elizabeth, the wife of John Thornton Augustine Washington of Cedar Lawn. Through the kindness of Dr. Roy Bird Cook of Charleston and Mr. Richard E. Griffith Sr. of Winchester, the author hereof has been provided with copies of a number of the items in Major Bedinger's records. One is of special though tragic interest in connection with Cedar Lawn. It reads:

> Edwin G. Bedinger was thrown off his horse at Mr. Jn. Thornton Washington's Gate in the Morning of the 4th December, 1835, and died in about four hours—Aged 21 years, and about 3 months.

This unfortunate young man, Edwin G. Bedinger, was probably a nephew or other near relative of Mrs. John Thornton Augustine Washington.

CHAPTER XVI

BEALLAIR AND LEWIS WILLIAM WASHINGTON

Beallair, formerly the home of Colonel Lewis William Washington, is located three-quarters of a mile west of Halltown, Jefferson County, West Virginia, and is thus almost equidistant from Harper's Ferry and Charles Town: four miles from the former and about three and a half from the latter. The rambling old house is double or triple, the front part of brick and shaped much like an orange crate. It stands on a gentle hillside and faces south over a wide meadow that is well watered by several vigorous springs which unite two miles above in Flowing Springs Run. This stream traverses Beallair farm, where, a short distance below the dwelling, it is diverted from its natural course into a race or canal which skirts the hillside and thus delivers the stream at Halltown with elevation sufficient to enhance its utility. Below the village the waters revert to their natural channel; then after two miles towards the southeast they fall into the Shenandoah River at Millville.

The ravine which was cut through the bluffs between Halltown and the river by Flowing Springs Run was found very convenient by the railroad builders of 1835, when a track was graded from Harper's Ferry to Winchester. The railroad, after coming up the river to Millville, follows up the course of the run for several miles, passing through Halltown, in front of the mansion house at Bellair at a distance of 200 yards, and so on to and through Charles Town.

A few willows and other trees stand in the meadow at Beallair alongside the run, between the house and the railroad. In ante-bellum days the number of outhouses was greater than at present. Among those that remain are two built of limestone, one a barn, the other a dwelling that was originally, no doubt, occupied by servants and used in part as a kitchen. Both these stone buildings, judging from appearances, were erected more than a century ago, but both are so staunch and unshaken that they bid fair to endure easily enough for another hundred years. Beallair is reached only by farm lanes and through gateways. The nearest public highway is U. S. Route 340 at Halltown.

Lewis William Washington, for a number of years the master of Beallair, was born in Georgetown, D. C., November 30, 1812, the son of George Corbin Washington and his first wife, Eliza Beall, daughter of Thomas Beall of Georgetown. George Corbin Washington inherited Wakefield ("Burnt House Plantation") from his father, William Augustine Washington, who died in 1810. George Corbin Washington in 1813, when his son Lewis William was one year old, sold Wakefield to John Gray, reserving the family graveyard and the spot of ground (a square of 60 feet) on which had stood the house in which George Washington was born.

George Corbin Washington was a member of Congress from Maryland in 1827-1833 and in 1835-1837. After the death of his first wife (Eliza Beall)

A view of Beallair from near the railroad. Photo 1933.

he married Ann Thomas Beall Peter. Accordingly, both the mother and the stepmother of Lewis William Washington bore the name Beall, and evidently his home, "Beallair," was named for them. It appears in various spellings as it passes through different hands, but "Beallair" is the logical form as derived from the family name, and thus it is engraved on a map of Jefferson County that was published in 1883.

Colonel Lewis W. Washington, like his father, was married twice. His first wife, married November 17, 1836, was Mary Ann Barroll, daughter of James Barroll and his wife, Mary Ann Crockett, of Baltimore. She was the mother of three children, a son named James Barroll, and two daughters. His second wife was Ella M. Bassett, daughter of George Washington Bassett and his wife Betty Lewis; born at Eltham, in New Kent County, Va. The Bassett home was later at Clover Lea, in Hanover County. Ella Bassett Washington had a son, William De Hertburn, born at Clover Lea, June 29, 1863; who died in New York, August 30, 1914.

Colonel Washington and his cousin, Richard Blackburn Washington, "Colonel Dick Washington," whose home was at Blakeley, both figured prominently in the John Brown raid at Harper's Ferry in October, 1859, the former as a captive in the hands of Brown, the latter as a member of one of the local posses that attempted to quell or capture the raiders. Richard B. Washington, then a man of thirty-seven, was in the party of John Avis, deputy sheriff and jailer, who later held Brown and several of his men in custody in the jail at Charles Town. George Turner, one of Avis's posse, or at least a neighbor and friend, was shot and killed by one of Brown's party, a mulatto, who was sheltered between two houses across the street from the building in which Avis and his men were stationed. Dick Washington, a celebrated squirrel hunter and a crack shot, was delegated by Avis to shoot the mulatto who had killed Turner. This Washington did, firing from an upstairs window while Avis and others diverted attention by making a demonstration on the ground floor. The details of this incident were related to the author in 1916 by Dr. James L. Avis, the deputy sheriff's son, who as a well grown boy in 1859 was with his father at Harper's Ferry at the time of the raid.

Rather early Sunday night, October 16, Brown and his men came over from the Maryland side of the Potomac and succeeded in getting control of the U. S. armory on the Potomac, the engine house near it, Hall's rifle works on the Shenandoah, half a mile above the town, and other strategic points before 11 o'clock, without creating much disturbance. Brown took his station in the engine house and sent Stevens, Cook, Tidd, Leary, Shields Green, and O. P. Anderson to bring in Colonel Lewis Washington and others as hostages. According to Richard J. Hinton, an intimate and supporter of Brown, in his "John Brown and His Men," first published in 1894, Colonel Washington delivered the sword of Frederick the Great and the pistols of Lafayette to O. P. Anderson. "Stevens, who was dramatic in manner as well as command-

A close-up view of the house at Beallair from the south. Photo 1933.

ing in appearance, briefly told him that they would take his slaves, not his life, and that he must go to the Ferry with them as a prisoner." The slaves in the meanwhile had harnessed up horses and hitched them to the family carriage and a four-horse wagon. Amid the lamentations of his family, Colonel Washington, under guard in his carriage, and his slaves in the wagon with several of Brown's men, were taken to the scene of the raid.

The particulars of Colonel Washington's experiences at the Ferry, in the hands of Brown and his associates, have been preserved in the following account which was printed in a local newspaper, date of November 4, 1859.

Brown was put upon his trial on Wednesday evening [October 26, 1859] when the evidence proved the following facts:

The first active movement in the insurrection was made about half past ten o'clock on Sunday night [October 16]. William Williamson, the watchman at Harper's Ferry bridge, whilst walking across toward the Maryland side, was seized by a number of men, who said he was their prisoner and must come with them. He recognized Brown and Cook among the men, and knowing them, treated the matter as a joke; but, enforcing silence, they conducted him to the armory, which he found already in their possession. He was detained till after daylight and then discharged.

The watchman who was to relieve Williamson at midnight found the bridge lights all out, and was immediately seized. Supposing it was an attempt at robbery, he broke away, and his pursuers stumbling over him, he escaped. The next appearance of the insurrectionists was at the house of Col. Lewis Washington, a large farmer and slave owner, living about four miles from the ferry. A party, headed by Cook, proceeded there, and arousing Col. Washington, told him he was their prisoner. They also seized all the slaves near the house, took a carriage, horse, and a large wagon with two horses.

Whn Col. Washington saw Cook he immediately recognized him as the man who had called upon him some months previous, to whom he had exhibited some valuable arms in his possession, including an antique sword presented by Frederick the Great to George Washington, and a pair of pistols presented by Lafayette to Washington, both being heirlooms in the family. Before leaving, Cook wanted Col. W. to engage in a trial of skill at shooting, and exhibited considerable skill as a marksman. When he made the visit on Sunday night [October 16] he alluded to his previous visit and the courtesy with which he had been treated, and regretted the necessity which made it his duty to arrest Col. Washington. He, however, took advantage of the knowledge he had obtained by his former visit, to carry off all the valuable collection of arms, which the Colonel did not re-obtain till after the final defeat of the insurrection.

From Col. Washington's he proceeded with him as a prisoner in the carriage, and twelve of his negroes in the wagon to the house of Mr. Oldstadt and [he and] his son, a lad of sixteen, were taken prisoners, and all their negroes within reach forced to join the movement.—He then returned to the armory at the Ferry.

The townspeople of Harper's Ferry slept in blissful ignorance—the situation was not understood by them until the forenoon of the next day, Monday. At daylight Cook with two white men and 30 Negroes took Colonel Washington's wagon and team, crossed the bridge over the Potomac, and "struck up the mountain road toward Pennsylvania." It was believed by some that the

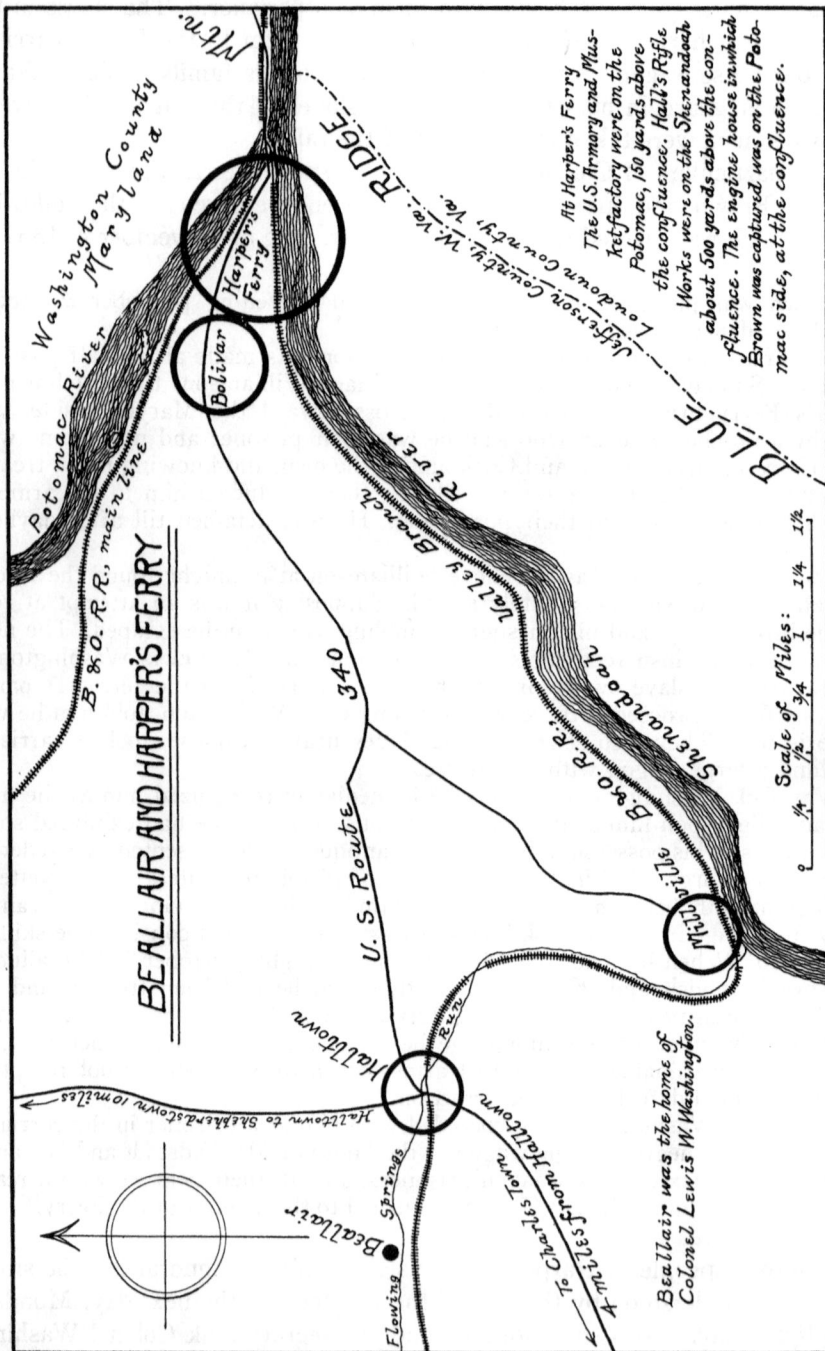

BE ALLAIR AND HARPER'S FERRY

At Harper's Ferry
The U.S. Armory and Mus-
ketfactory were on the
Potomac, 150 yards above
the confluence. Hall's Rifle
Works were on the Shenandoah
about 500 yards above the confluence. The engine house in which
Brown was captured was on the Potomac side, at the confluence.

Washington County
Maryland

Potomac River

B. & O. R.R., main line

Harper's Ferry

Bolivar

BLUE   RIDGE

Jefferson County, W. Va.
Loudoun County, Va.

Valley Branch River

B. & O. R. R.

Shenandoah

340

U. S. Route

Millville

Halltown

Halltown to Shepherdstown 10 miles

To Charles Town

4 miles from Halltown

Run

Flowing Springs

Beallair

BeAllair was the home of
Colonel Lewis W. Washington.

Scale of Miles:
0   1/4   1/2   3/4   1   1 1/4   1 1/2

large wagon was used the carry away the paymaster's safe from the armory, containing $17,000 in government funds, and a lot of Minie rifles to supply other bands in the mountains, who were to come down upon Harper's Ferry in overwhelming force. These suppositions were both proved untrue, as neither money nor arms were disturbed.

In addition to Colonel Washington and the Oldstadts, the insurgents held other hostages, among them Armistead Ball, draftsman of the armory, Benjamin Mills, master armorer, and John P. Dangerfield, pay clerk. It was the presence of these men in the engine house and at other places with Brown and his comrades that kept the attackers from firing with cannon, several of which were at hand. In the engine house Phil, one of Colonel Washington's slaves, was ordered by Brown to cut a porthole in the brick wall. The man went at it and continued until the work attracted a brisk fire from without, whereupon he exclaimed, "It's gettin' too hot for Phil," and ducked down, dropping the tools. Brown himself then took up the tools and finished cutting the hole.

On Tuesday morning, October 18, U. S. marines under command of Colonel Robert E. Lee battered down the door of the engine house and captured Brown and those of his followers who were not already killed. Colonel Washington and the other hostages were thus released. Fortunately none of them had been seriously injured, though their escape was rather remarkable in view of the perilous situation in which they had been placed. These men, of course, were among the witnesses who were called to testify against Brown and his associates in the trials which were held at Charles Town soon thereafter. Brown on at least one occasion remarked that the testimony of Colonel Washington and Conductor Phelps was strictly truthful.

An interesting though brief description of Colonel Washington's personal appearance in 1859 is given by Richard J. Hinton on page 346 of his book, "John Brown and His Men," revised edition, as follows:

Col. Lewis W. Washington was naturally also a conspicuous figure. A handsome man, of medium height, with slow, grave speech and walk, he looked like Trumbull's portrait of his great-uncle.

Hinton certainly was not prejudiced in favor of Colonel Washington or any of the other slave-holders.

Concerning Col. Lewis W. Washington at the time of the Harper's Ferry raid, Major Henry Kyd Douglas relates interesting particulars in his book, "I Rode with Stonewall," pages 1-4. Douglas's home was in Washington County, Md., not far from Harper's Ferry and the Kennedy Farm where Brown and his men rendezvoused, and on the morning of October 18, 1859, when the U. S. Marines took Brown and his associates and hostages from the engine house ("John Brown's Fort"), Douglas, then a youngster of 19, was present. He says that at the time he paid more attention to Colonel Washington than he did to Brown, being attracted by Colonel Washington's "coolness and nonchalance"—walking quietly away from the "fort" with some excited acquaintances and pulling on a pair of dark-green kid gloves which he took from his pocket. One of his friends, as they approached the Wager House, invited him to go in and "take something." "Thank you," he smilingly replied, "I will. It seems a month since I've had one."

The graves of Colonel Washington, his second wife, Ella M. Bassett, and their two children, Betty Lewis and William De Hertburn, are to be found at Charles Town in the Episcopal church yard, near those of numerous relatives, Washingtons, Alexanders, and others. The daughter, Betty Lewis Washington, died at Clover Lea, Hanover County, Va., on July 25, 1862, aged 11 months and 4 days. William De Hertburn Washington, the son, was born at Clover Lea on June 29, 1863; he died in New York, August 30, 1914. It seems probable that Mrs. Washington refugeed at the Bassett home in Hanover because of the active military operations that were carried on around Beallair from the very beginning of the war in 1861.

Colonel Washington died early, according to the Washington tradition. A week after his death the following obituary appeared in the *Virginia Free Press*, the Charles Town newspaper:

DEATH OF COL LEWIS W. WASHINGTON

Col. Lewis W. Washington died at "Beall-Air," his residence in this County, on Sunday last, Oct. 1st, 1871, aged 58 years, 10 months, and 1 day. He was the son of Hon. George Corbin Washington of Maryland, the great-grandson of two Brothers of General George Washington, being descended from them both by his Father and his Mother. He was first commissioned as Colonel by President Jackson, again by the Governor of Maryland, and a third time by Gov. Wise of Virginia, for efficient civil service during the "Brown Raid." He was among the citizens captured as hostages by John Brown. His death is to be regretted, as Jefferson has lost one of her most public-spirited citizens, his family an affectionate head, and his friends a genial and pleasant companion.

Colonel Lewis William Washington's father, George Corbin Washington, was descended from two of General Washington's brothers. His father was William Augustine, son of Augustine II, the General's half-brother; his mother was Jane Washington, daughter of John Augustine, the General's full brother.

Mrs. Ella M. Bassett Washington, the second wife of Colonel Lewis W. Washington, made her will, writing it with her own hand, on November 20, 1880, leaving everything to her son (then her only child), William De Hertburn Washington. She probably spent her last years with him in New York. She died in New York, January 17, 1898. Her will was proved at Charles Town on February 7, 1898, by the oaths of Laura L. Mitchell and L. Nevelle Mitchell.

Inasmuch as the name De Hertburn seems unusual in the Washington family, one may be pardoned for some curiosity concerning it. Just recently a statement has appeared in the newspapers to the effect that the first ancestor of George Washington known to history was a knight in the army of William, Duke of Normandy, by the name of William De Herthburn.

CHAPTER XVII

THE WASHINGTONS OF WAVERLY AND WINCHESTER

Waverly is a well-known homestead seven miles northeast of Winchester. For many years it was occupied by successive generations of Washingtons, and it has other claims to distinction. It was originally the dwelling place of Alexander Ross, an eminent Friend (Quaker), who, with Morgan Bryan, arranged for the settlement of a colony of Friends in the lower Shenandoah Valley, the Opequon country, in 1730 and 1731. On October 28, 1730, Ross and Bryan at Williamsburg obtained a grant of 100,000 acres "lying on the west and north side of the River Opeckan & extending thence to a mountain called North Mountain & along the River Cohongaruton [Potomac] & on any part of the River Sherundo not already granted to any other Person."

Among the families who settled on this grant and near it were Hollingsworths, Thomases, Parkinses, Hiatts, Cochrans, Ballingers, Hoggs, Bordens, Littlers, Bransons, Morgans, Davises, Millses, and Hoods. Alexander Ross had a tract of 2373 acres, and selected for his home site a spot about 100 yards west of a great spring which gushes forth from the rugged ledges of limestone which give character to the soil and landscape. This spring is the head of Clearbrook, which is the more northerly branch of Littler's Run. Near his dwelling, on the hill above the great spring, Alexander Ross laid off a plat of ten acres for the meeting house of the colony. Thereon a log building was soon erected; a meeting for worship was set up in 1734, and the next year a monthly meeting for business and discipline was authorized, both receiving sanction from the East Nottingham Monthly Meeting of Cecil County, Maryland, and the Chester Quarterly Meeting, held at Concord, Chester County, Pennsylvania. In 1759 the log meeting house was replaced with a substantial structure of limestone. This in 1788-89 was enlarged to its present size, and in it meetings are still regularly held each First Day—teaching classes conducted first for the children and young people, then the usual meeting for worship. Special meetings are frequent and notable. The Quarterly Meeting which is held at Hopewell each May has been a feature of the community life for generations.

Hopewell Friends Meeting is the oldest continuous religious body or organization in Northern Virginia, west of the Blue Ridge, and in 1934 the congregation took steps for an appropriate celebration of their bi-centennial. A monument bearing a handsome bronze memorial tablet was erected on the highway at the entrance to Hopewell; on a set day, June 20, 1936, historical addresses were delivered at the monument, in the meeting house at Hopewell, and in Winchester. The exercises were attended by representatives of old Hopewell families from eleven different states and the District of Columbia. Not the least important feature of the Hopewell bi-centennial was the publication of a splendid historical volume of 671 pages: "Hopewell Friends History:

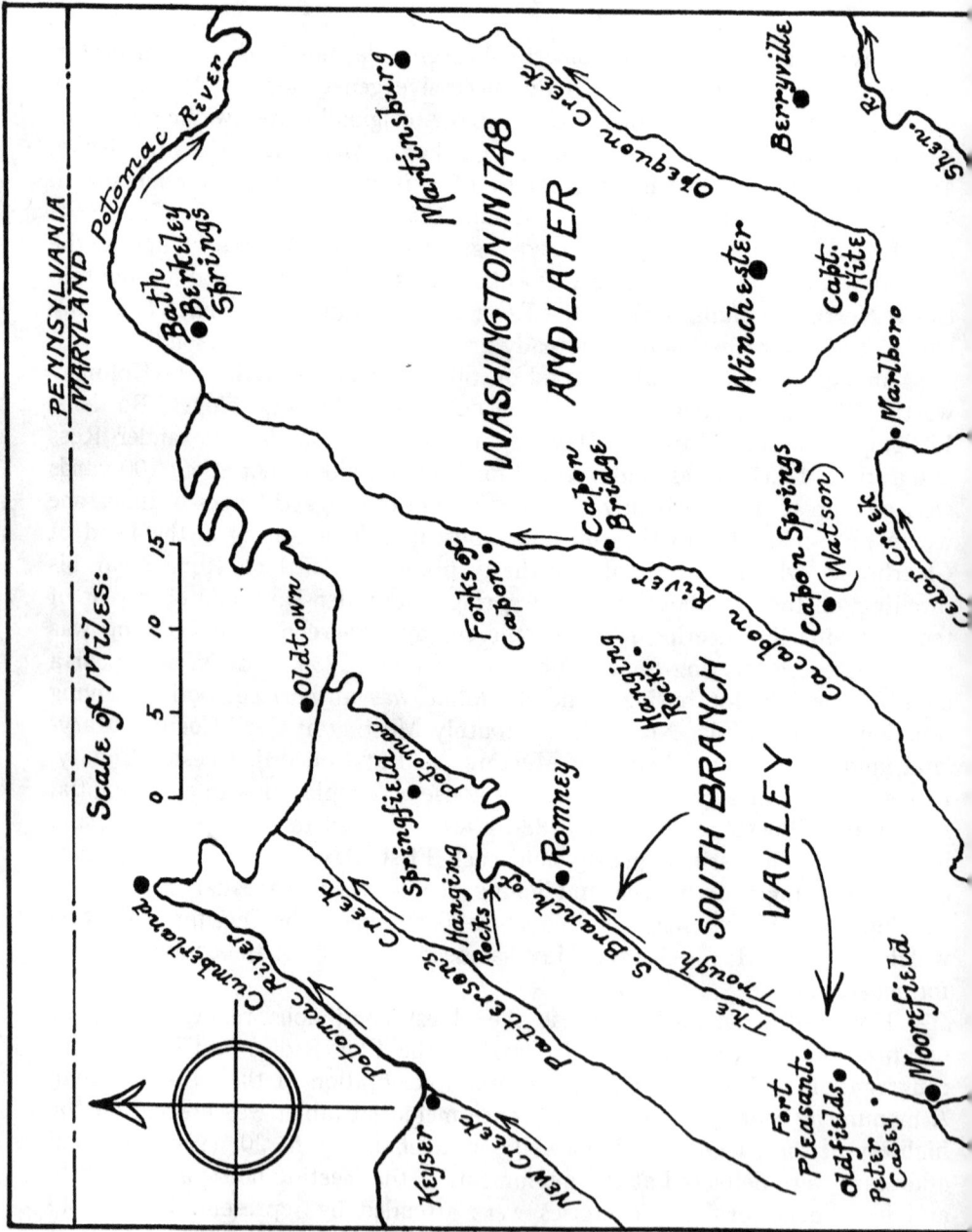

WASHINGTON IN 1748 AND LATER

1734-1934: Frederick County, Virginia: Two Hundred Years of History and Genealogy."

Alexander Ross and his neighbors could not have chosen a more beautiful and commanding site for their religious shrine. The foothills of the Alleghanies are not far away in the background (towards the northwest), while the broad valley of the Opequon and the Shenandoah spreads out eastward to the Blue Ridge, and on the northeast to the Maryland mountains just beyond the Potomac. On a clear day one may stand at the eastern end of the meeting house at Hopewell and see the deep water gap at Harper's Ferry; thence running his eye along the crest of the Blue Ridge southward he may recognize Vestal's Gap, Snicker's Gap, Ashby Gap, and other passes in the historic mountain on up to Manassa's Gap and Chester Gap at Front Royal.

Waverly and Hopewell, the cherished places of homelife and worship for the peace-loving Friends, have been disturbed more than once by the rude sounds of war. Alongside their northern borders is the old Braddock Road, the toilsome way by which the proud Britisher's Red Coats and young George Washington's "Buckskin" colonials passed westward in 1755, headed for tragedy on the Monongahela. Early in the Revolution from this vicinity Morgan's riflemen marched to Boston; not far away were kept prisoners from Trenton, Saratoga, and Yorktown. Late in 1791 fugitives from St. Clair's defeat on the Miami came limping by; and during the hectic years from 1861 to 1865 the days were rare when the Stars and Bars or the Stars and Stripes could not be seen, or the sounds of battle heard. Staunch against all winds that blow, the gray walls of Hopewell and Waverly have been landmarks through the years. The dreamer wishes they could speak to him, but they answer only in echoes. Yet for responsive hearts, if not for listening ears, they do have a voice:

> "They tell of those who bore the stress,
> Whose faith and works were blended,
> Who caused to bloom the wilderness
> Ere tasks of peace were ended."

After the death of Alexander Ross in 1748 Waverly passed to the heirs of his daughter, Mary Littler, and from them by a marriage to the Stribling family. Then came the Washingtons. The first owner of that name was George Fayette Washington, who acquired possession in the year 1826. He was the son of Major George Augustine Washington, who was a son of General George Washington's youngest brother, Colonel Charles Washington, founder of Charles Town. George Augustine (1763-1793) was an officer of the Virginia Line in the Revolution. On October 15, 1785, at Mount Vernon, "after the candles were lighted," he married Frances Bassett, daughter of Burwell Bassett. From 1789 till his death he was manager at Mt. Vernon for his uncle

Waverly, the Washington home near Hopewell Photo 1936

George, who was then President. The latter in his will made handsome provision for his nephew's sons, George Fayette and Charles (or Lawrence) Augustine:

In consideration of the consanguinity between them and my wife, being as nearly related to her as to myself, as on account of the affection I had for, and the obligation I was under to, their father when living, who from his youth had attached himself to my person, and followed my fortunes through the vicissitudes of the late Revolution—afterward devoting his time to the superintendence of my private concerns for many years, whilst my public employments rendered it impracticable for me to do it myself, thereby affording me essential services, and always performing them in a manner the most filial and respectful: for these reasons I say, I give and bequeath to George Fayette Washington and Lawrence Augustine Washington & their heirs, my estate East of little hunting creek, lying on the River Potomac;—including the farm of 360 acres leased to Tobias Lear as noticed before and containing in the whole, by deeds Two thousand & twenty seven acres—be it more or less,—which said Estate it is my will and desire should be equitably and advantageously divided between them, according to quantity, quality and other circumstances when the youngest shall have arrived at the age of twenty-one years, by three Judicious and disinterested men;—one to be chosen by each of the brothers, and the third by these two.

General Washington in his will left one twenty-third part of his residuary estate to the three children, two sons and a daughter, of his deceased nephew, George Augustine Washington. The daughter was Anna Maria, and the sons in this connection are called George Fayette and Charles Augustine.

George Fayette Washington, who was born January 17, 1790, married at Charles Town, November 18, 1813, Maria Frame, who died in February 1860. He made his will on October 19, a notable anniversary, in the year 1865. He ordered the payment of his debts and expressed the desire to be buried in Winchester. "To my nephews John Bell & Fayette Washington Roe" a note of Joseph O. Coyle for $500, "executed by him to my son Charles but which now belongs to me."

Charles Augustine Washington, eldest son of George Fayette and Maria F. Washington, born August 9, 1814, was evidently named after his father's brother. He died in February 1861, and his grave, with the graves of his parents, is in Mount Hebron Cemetery, Winchester, near the northwest side.

After the bequest of the $500 note to John Bell and Fayette W. Roe, George Fayette Washington continues: "The rest & residue of my estate to Philip Williams in trust for the joint use & benefit of my son Matthew Burwell Bassett Washington & his wife Anna for their lives, but not subject to the debts of my said son." He made his said son, M. B. B. Washington, and his friend, Thomas Buchannon, executors. On June 12, 1866, by codicil, another note, this one of $250, was left to John Bell and Fayette W. Roe, nephews of the testator's deceased wife. The will was proved at the January 1868 term of court

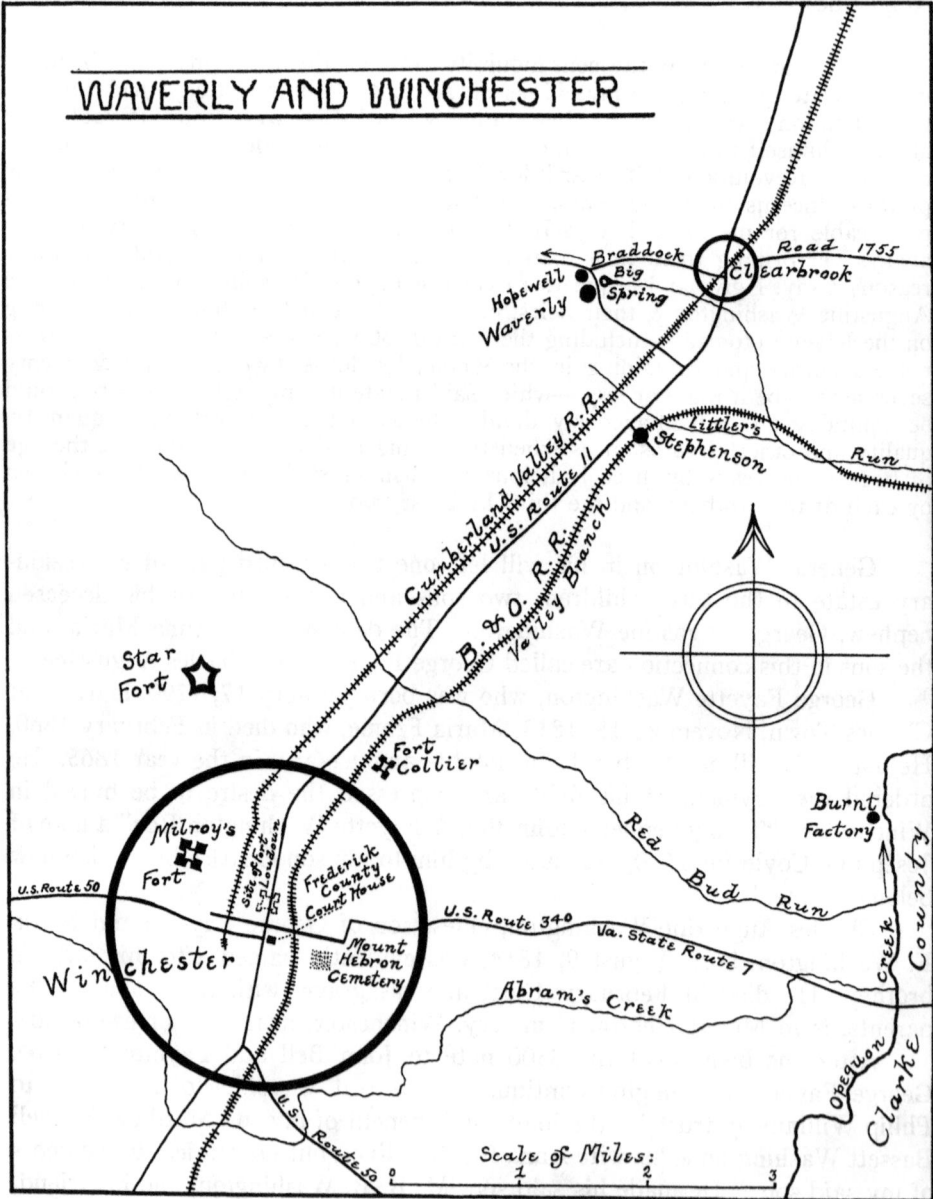

WAVERLY AND WINCHESTER

for Frederick County, the testator having died on September 6, 1867, as shown by his tombstone.

With the will of George Fayette Washington, the original of which is preserved at Winchester, is folded a letter which gives additional information concerning the testator's nephews and his son Charles.

A small stone in the family plat in Mount Hebron Cemetery is inscribed, without dates, to "Our beloved son Geo. F. Washington," who probably was a child of George Fayette Washington and his wife Maria Frame. Dr. A. D. Henkel, of Winchester, states that they did have a son named George Fayette, born February 21, 1823, who died at Waverly, unmarried, about 1853. Their youngest son, Matthew Burwell Bassett Washington, named for his great-grandfather, Burwell Bassett, was born August 15, 1830. On March 20, 1862, he married Nannie (Anne) Bird Dandridge Buchannon, daughter of Thomas Ely and Ann Spotswood (Dandridge) Buchannon. He was a Confederate soldier, though but little information concerning his services in the army has been preserved. An interesting sidelight is afforded by a record recently discovered by Mr. Richard E. Griffith Sr. of Winchester. At a court held for Frederick County on July 1, 1861, the will of Sarah Carey was probated. Was this Sarah Carey related to the vivacious young women who figured with some romance in George Washington's early life?—she had the same name. The witnesses to Sarah Carey's will in 1861 were G. F. Washington and B. B. Washington. These evidently were George Fayette Washington and his son Matthew Burwell Bassett Washington of Waverly. In the probate order it was noted that B. B. Washington, "the other subscribing witness," was absent in the military service of the state.

Matthew Burwell Bassett Washington, known as "Major Washington," did not outlive his father by quite a year. He died on August 1, 1868, at the age of 38, as shown by his tombstone in Mount Hebron Cemetery. Near by was buried his wife, "A. D. B. W." (1833-1920): Anne Dandridge Buchannon Washington. Nannie Bird (Byrd) Washington, who died December 31, 1919, was his daughter. The repetition of given names in successive generations of the Washington family, as in many other families, has been a source of grief to genealogists.

Descendants of Major Burwell B. Washington occupied the old stone mansion at Waverly until a few years ago, when the property was sold to Mr. William Robinson, a member of Hopewell Friends Meeting. It is now (1939) owned by his heirs.

In this chapter on the Washingtons of Waverly it is deemed appropriate to point out certain places in Winchester with which various members of the Washington family were associated, and others to which their names are attached. George Washington, probably, was the first of the name to visit Winchester, though it is not impossible that his older half-brother Lawrence may have been here ahead of him. Courts for Frederick County were set up

Washington's Headquarters at Winchester.

in 1743, the year that Lawrence married and established himself at Mount Vernon, and he acquired lands in Frederick County as early as 1747. In September of that year he purchased 100 acres on the west side of Shennandore River of Samuel Walker, the said tract being part of 668 acres granted to Jost Hite on October 3, 1735. In this record of 1747 is the first apearance of the Washington name in the Frederick County archives.

George's first visit to this locality was in March 1748, when he, with James Genn, the surveyor, and George William Fairfax, came over the Blue Ridge on his first tour for Lord Fairfax. On Wednesday the 16th he wrote in his diary:

> We . . . then Travell'd up to Frederick Town where our Baggage came to us we cleaned ourselves (to get Rid of y. Game we had catched y. Night before) and took a Review of y. Town and thence return'd to our Lodgings where we had a good Dinner prepar'd for us Wine and Rum Punch in Plenty and a good Feather Bed with clean Sheets which was a very agreeable regale.

The next month (on Monday, April 11, 1748) young Washington and his companions, returning from their strenuous work on the South Branch of the Potomac, reached Winchester at noon; dined there; and then went out to Captain Hite's at Springdale, six miles, where they lodged. In whose house or tavern in Winchester they had good dinners, the plentiful supply of punch, and the feather beds with clean sheets, cannot be determined at this time, but more definite information is available for later associations. From 1755 to 1758 Winchester was practically home for George Washington, and from 1758 to 1761 he served in the House of Burgesses at Williamsburg as the delegate from Frederick County, though he was not at that time resident in the county.

In 1756 and 1757 he was building Fort Loudoun, which was the main unit in the chain of forts with which he was endeavoring to protect the Virginia frontier against the Indians and the French. At this time he had his headquarters in a small building of logs which still remains at the corner of Cork Street and Braddock. This, after the Revolution, was enlarged by Adam Kurtz with a stone addition. At the same time Washington lodged and took his meals with Captain William Cocke, whose house stood on the west side of Loudoun Street, between Cork and Boscawen. About this time he acquired a lot in the town, located in the southeast angle of Braddock Street and Fairfax Lane. On this, it is said, he had a blacksmith shop, to which he brought his own blacksmith from Mount Vernon to fabricate the iron work for Fort Loudoun, which stood on the hill just a block to the northeast. The site of the old blacksmith shop is near the Sarah Zane fire station. It is just south, across Fairfax Lane, from the United Brethren Church, which fronts on Braddock Street. In July 1799, when General Washington made his will, he owned a

West's Ordinary, near Aldie, where George Washington and other members of the family frequently stopped on their journeys between Mount Vernon and the Shenandoah Valley. The old building was torn down some years ago. See "Historic Homes," pages 446-453.

half-acre lot, No. 77, in Winchester and an "out-lot," No. 16, of about six acres in the commons.

Hon. W. W. Glass has recently found old papers at Winchester which show that an early fort, long lost sight of, was located here, one, at least, within a short distance of the center of the town, as originally laid out by James Wood. It stood on the rocky ridge just west of Braddock Street, opposite Washington's headquarters and the parade ground adjacent. It was named Fort George, in honor of the king, no doubt, and was in use in 1754 and 1755. There seems to have been another, named Fort Washington, the location of which has not been determined; but circumstances indicate that it was in the vicinity. A Captain Bell was in command at Fort Washington in 1756, as shown by a list of supplies lately discovered by Mr. R. E. Griffith Sr. These two forts were probably stockades hastily constructed at the outbreak of the French and Indian War, used ahead of Fort Loudoun and also during the time in which the latter was being erected. A short distance south of Fort Loudoun was the residence of Dr. James Craik, a physician with Washington on the Braddock expedition and one of those in attendance upon General Braddock at the time of his death. Dr. Craik was also present at General Washington's death.

In March 1771 Washington spent three days in Winchester according to appointment with various officers who claimed parts of the 200,000 acres of land which had been allotted them by the colonial government of Virginia for miliary services in the French and Indian War. He states in his diary that his lodging on this occasion was at Mr. Philip Bush's. Fitzpatrick, in his 1925 edition of Washington's diaries, asserts in a footnote that Philip Bush's inn was called "The Golden Buck." It stood on the west side of Cameron Street, between Boscawen and Cork. The house now occupied by Dr. A. D. Henkel stood adjacent, on the same lot, and was Mr. Bush's residence. In later life Mr. Bush had as his guests in the "Golden Buck" Louis Philippe of France and his brother, the Duke of Montpensier. When dinner was announced by the banging of a triangle the two aristocratic guests did not appear. A servant who was sent upstairs to call them brought back word that the Frenchmen wanted their dinner served in their room. Mr. Bush at once lost his temper and declared that if the gentlemen were too good for the common table they might move out and get lodgings elsewhere. They did so.

Lawrence Augustine Washington, a nephew of General Washington, resided for some years at Federal Hill (later Hawthorn), now within the corporate limits of Winchester. He was one of the sons of Colonel Samuel Washington and his fourth wife, Anne Steptoe. His education and that of his brother, George Steptoe Washington, had been directed and mainly paid for by his uncle, General Washington. On November 6, 1797, Lawrence Augustine Washington married Dorcas Wood, daughter of Robert Wood and his wife Comfort Welsh. Robert was the youngest son of Colonel James Wood, founder

THE WASHINGTONS IN WINCHESTER

[Map showing streets and sites in Winchester including:
Clark St., Baker St., Lane, Street, George Washington Hotel, Street, County Court House, Rouss Ave., Cameron, Site of Golden Buck, House of Philip Bush now Dr. A.D. Henkel, London, Site of Fort Loudoun, Loudoun St., Site of Washington's Blacksmith Shop, Site of Dr. Craik's House, Alley, Street, Braddock, Site of Capt. Wm. Cocke Home, Indian, Washington's Hqrs., Street, Peyton, Fairfax, Piccadilly, Street, Christ Church, Boscawen, Street, Site of Warner Washington Tavern, Cork St., Clifford, Fairmont Avenue, Washington St., Amherst Street, Tomb of Lord Fairfax, Wolfe Street, Site of Fort George, Stewart St., Washington Inn, U.S. Route 50, N.W. Turnpike, Romney Road, Town Spring, Spring, Federal Hill A. Washington Home of Lawrence later called Hawthorn, Glen Burnie Home of Col. James Wood, founder of Winchester]

of Winchester, and brother to General James Wood, who was governor of Virginia, 1796-1799. Lawrence A. Washington and his wife lived on a portion of Glen Burnie, the Wood ancestral estate, until 1811 when they moved to Kanawha County, now West Virginia. Their home here, Federal Hill, was later the home of Colonel Angus McDonald, who renamed the place Hawthorn. It was in the line of the Confederate advance upon Milroy's Fort on June 14 and 15, 1863, and suffered severely. Many interesting details of those tragic days may be found in "A Diary with Reminiscences of the War and Refugee Life in the Shenandoah Valley, 1860-1865," by Mrs. Cornelia McDonald, published by Hunter McDonald in 1934.

Hawthorn (Federal Hill) has had five or six different owners since the McDonalds. It is now the residence of Dr. Emmart C. Stuart.

In the spring of 1817 Lawrence A. Washington, his wife Dorcas Wood, and their children, moved from the Kanawha country up to Waddell's Run, near Wheeling, where they died (Lawrence, February 15, 1824; Dorcas, November 9, 1835) and are buried. Ther son, Dr. Lawrence A. Washington, figured prominently on the Kanawha and elsewhere. By an act of the Virginia General Assembly, passed March 16, 1849, he was made one of the trustees of Buffalo Academy in Putnam County. He, it is said, spent much time in Winchester.. His wife, married November 29, 1839, was Martha Dickenson Shrewsbury (?). In 1850, with his family, he moved to Dennison, Texas, going down the Ohio and the Mississippi in flatboats, piloted by an old sea captain named Buckle. (For an interesting account of these Washingtons, see an illustrated article in the *West Virginia Review* of August, 1936, by Peter Campbell Boyd.)

Already in Chapter XI mention has been made of the fact that a Warner Washington, not of the Fairfield line, whose wife was Ariana (Stith), kept a tavern in Winchester in the early years of the 19th century. The house in which they operated their tavern is not now standing. It occupied a site on the west side of Braddock Street, between Cork and Wolfe, almost or exactly on the spot where Fort George stood in 1755, and opposite the old building on the east side of Braddock Street in which Washington had his headquarters while building Fort Loudoun.

In 1924 a handsome hotel was erected on the southwest corner of Cameron Street and Piccadilly and fittingly named in honor of George Washington, the town's most illustrious inhabitant. On the west side of Stewart Street, between Cork Street and Stonewall Avenue, is the "Washington Inn." It is a recent construction and is operated as a tourist home by the Misses Jones, who are descendants of Gabriel Jones, a famous lawyer who was a contemporary and personal acquaintance of General Washington.

CHAPTER XVIII

THE HAMPSHIRE COUNTY WASHINGTONS

For nearly 200 years the Washingtons have been connected with the history of the South Branch Valley, especially the part now in Hampshire County, West Virginia. George Washington's first tour for Lord Fairfax in 1748 was carried on mainly in this region. At that time it was still a part of Frederick County, Virginia. Hampshire was the northwestern portion of Frederick, cut off by act of Assembly in the year 1753.

On Saturday, March 12, 1748, George Washington, then just a month over 16, George William Fairfax, aged 23, and "Mr. James Genn ye surveyor," with chain-bearers and other helpers, came over the Blue Ridge at Ashby's Gap. On Monday they sent their baggage to Captain Hite's, to be forwarded thence to Winchester. This Captain Hite was Joist Hite or his son John, both of whom lived at Springdale, between Stephens City and Winchester. The latter was then called Frederick Town. After two or three days spent in surveying along the Shenandoah River, the party went up to Winchester, where their baggage was brought to them. On the 17th and 18th they proceeded northward to the Potomac, and tarried a day or two at Bath (Warm Springs, Berkeley Springs) waiting for the river to go down. On the 20th their horses were made to swim over, so as to get pasturage at Charles Polk's, in Maryland; and on the next day the surveyors went over in a canoe and then traveled upstream on the Maryland side, reaching Thomas Cresap's, at Oldtown. There they tarried several days and were entertained by a party of 30-odd Indians, returning from war against another tribe, with one scalp.

Until 1754 the Indians did not attack the white settlers in this part of the country. Their tolerance was doubtless due in large measure to the presence here of the Friends (Quakers), who made earnest efforts to determine which tribe had best title to the lands in order that payment might be made for the lands.

On the 25th the surveyors went on up the river on the Maryland side and swam their horses across into Virginia at the mouth of Patterson's Creek. Following up the course of this stream they turned back towards the southeast and crossed over the mountains to the South Branch of the Potomac above the site of Romney and there spent two weeks surveying, subsisting on wild turkeys and such scant provisions as they could obtain from the scattered settlers; sleeping (or trying to sleep) in the open when their tent blew down, and narrowly escaping death one night when the straw on which they were lying caught fire.

Among the settlers named in Washington's journal were Solomon Hedges, a magistrate, Henry Van Metre, James Rutledge, a horse jockey, Michael Stump, and Peter Casey.

By reference to the map it will be observed that Washington and his

Ridgedale, Washington home five miles north of Romney. Photo October 27, 1938.

companions made a wide circuit to the north in going to the South Branch. Returning, they came directly across the mountains by Coddy's (Caudy's), now Capon Bridge, on Cacapon River, and so on to Winchester. A short distance below Capon Bridge was later built Fort Edward, which was one of the chain of frontier forts under command of Washington in the French and Indian War.

Several times in later years George Washington was on the South Branch. In the fall of 1770, for instance, on his way to the Ohio Valley, he came up from Cresap's at Oldtown to Romney, where Dr. Craik and his servant with the baggage met him. Again, in the autumn of 1784, returning from the Ohio Valley, he came across from the head waters of Patterson's Creek to Colonel Abraham Hite's, at Fort Pleasant. Hite evidently lived in or near the Old Fields, above the Trough, where, as Kercheval tells us, eighteen men in the time of the French and Indian War had been enticed out from Fort Pleasant and ambushed by the Indians.

In 1799 Washington owned 240 acres of land in Hampshire County, as shown in the schedule which he prepared to supplement his will.

The records at Romney show that three other Washingtons were early landowners in Hampshire County. On June 12, 1797, John Kincheloe and his wife Milly of Prince William County, Virginia, for 246 pounds, 11 shillings, and 1 penny, Virginia currency, specie, conveyed to Lund Washington of the City of Washington a messuage and tenement of land, 788 acres, on the waters of Counard's Run, a branch of Great Cacapehon, between Sideland (Sidelong) Hill and Cacapehon Mountain. Cacapehon is another writing of Cacapon, river and mountain.

On October 4, 1808, Andrew Woodrow and Henry Beattie, trustees of the town of Watson, in Hants (Hampshire County), Virginia, for 7 pounds and 4 shillings, conveyed to Laurence A. Washington of Frederick County, one certain lot in the said town of Watson, one-half acre, No. 2 in the plan of the town; adjoining the Watson heirs. Watson was for some time the name of Capon Springs, in the Cacapon Valley, about twenty miles southwest of Winchester. After rowdies at Bath (Berkeley Springs) made a sojourn there precarious, Watson (Capon Springs) was developed and for many years was a popular watering place.

On December 28, 1809, Henry Lee of Westmoreland County, Virginia, and Anna his wife, for $17.000, sold to William A. Washington of the District of Columbia a share in 8508 acres in Hampshire County, consisting of one undivided fourth part of the following tracts:

300 acres on Potomac River, on which was a valuable coal mine;

4630 acres purchased of George Gilpin and others, about two miles from the mouth of New Creek;

1950 acres purchased of George Gilpin and others, about one mile from New Creek;

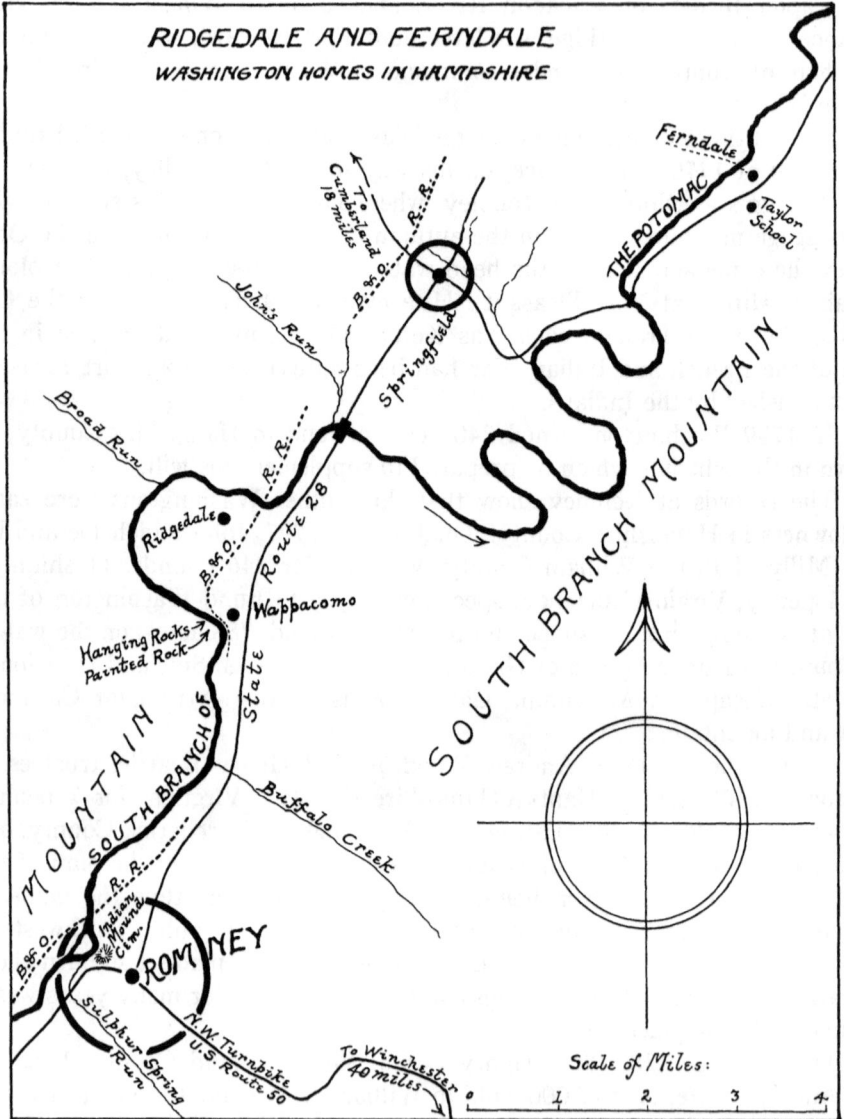

RIDGEDALE AND FERNDALE
WASHINGTON HOMES IN HAMPSHIRE

770 acres purchased from Gilpin and others, near the above tract;

500 acres granted to James Machir and by him conveyed to Henry Lee, December 5, 1795;

358 acres from James Machir.

The witnesses to the conveyance to William A. Washington were Therit Towles, Paul Jones, Lewis Minor, Henry Gerard Letuz, and George Washington. The grantor, Henry Lee, was "Light-Horse Harry," and Anna was his second wife, the mother of Robert E. Lee, who was at the time of this transaction not quite two years old. The grantee, William A. Washington, was probably William Augustine Washington I (1757-1810), who died in Georgetown, D. C., and was buried at Mount Vernon. He was a son of Augustine Washington, George's half-brother. The George Washington who signed as a witness was probably the grantee's brother. Most of the land conveyed was on or near New Creek, at or near the present town of Keyser. Keyser is the county-seat of Mineral County, which was formerly a part of Hampshire.

In 1834 or earlier a George Washington became a permanent resident of Hampshire. This was George William Washington (1809-1876), a son of Edward Washington of Fairfax County, Virginia, who died in 1813; and he was a grandson of another Edward Washington who died in Fairfax County in 1792. George William Washington's wife was Sarah (Sally) A. Wright (1811-1886), of Loudoun County, Virginia, a daughter of John Wright and his wife Rebecca Lockhart. Rebecca was a sister to General Josiah Lockhart of Frederick County. Their father was Major Robert Lockhart, a native of Lancaster County, Pennsylvania, where he served on the committee of public safety in the Revolution and was also a major in the county militia. Later he came to Frederick County, Virginia. The records at Winchester show that John Wright and Rebecca Lockhart were married in Frederick County, June 14, 1810, the officiating minister being the noted Lutheran divine, Christian Streit, who had been a chaplain in the Revolution.

George William Washington and Sally Wright, as stated by their descendants, were married in 1830 and shortly thereafter settled in Hampshire County, where the court records show that he was a grantee in 1834 from Henry Leslie, in 1837 from John Wright and wife, in 1838 from George Hern and wife, in 1846 (trustee) from James Taylor, and in 1850 from John Kern Jr. Mr. Washington and his wife made their home five miles north of Romney, on a productive farm that lies in a horseshoe bend of the South Branch River, first in a log house, later in a spacious brick dwelling which they built in 1850, and which still remains in good condition. The place has long been familiar as Ridgedale. A branch of the Baltimore & Ohio Railroad passes through the farm, a short distance east of the residence. Ridgedale was a part of 700 acres devised in 1817 to Sarah A. Wright (later Washington), her brother and sister, by their grandfather, Major Robert Lockhart.

George William Washington and his wife Sally Wright had a number of

Ferndale, Washington home eleven miles northeast of Romney. Photo 1938.

children, among whom were two sons by the name of John. The elder, John W., died August 14, 1838, aged a year and a half, as shown by his gravestone in Indian Mound Cemetery at Romney. The other John was a soldier in the Civil War and lost his life in that conflict. This information has been supplied by Miss Isabella Miller of Romney, a great-granddaughter of George William Washington. The latter made his will on May 29, 1871, naming therein his wife, Sally A., and "all his children": Edward, Rebecca, Ettie, Bettie, George, Robert, and Sallie. He died February 6, 1876, and his will was proved four days later.

In January 1879 Robert M. Washington, one of the sons named above, purchased Ridgedale from the other heirs and devisees of his father. Those signing the conveyance were the following: Sarah A. Washington, the widow; Edward Washington and wife Susan; James B. Rees and wife Rebecca (Washington); Ettie Washington; George W. Washington and wife Ann E.; John J. Inskeep and wife Bettie (Washington); and Sallie G. Washington.

Edward Washington (1834-1901), son of George William and Sally A., married Susan Ann Taylor (1836-1924), daughter of William, and lived at Ferndale in a stone house built by William Taylor in 1834, and still standing. Ferndale is located on the east side of the river, four miles northeast of the village of Springfield and about 12 miles northeast of Romney. It is at present the home of Mr. Henry Campbell, whose mother was Mary Washington, a daughter of Edward and Susan. The author is indebted for information to Mr. Campbell, Miss Isabella Miller, and Mrs. P. Tulane Atkinson of Hampden-Sydney, Va.; also to Mr. Richard E. Griffith Sr. of Winchester, who has long been familiar with the South Branch Valley and who accompanied me on a recent tour of investigation.

Edward Washington and his brother John, who was killed, were the only sons of George William Washington who were soldiers in the Civil War. George W. and Robert M. were too young for service. George W. many years ago moved to Kansas. Robert M. (1852-1930) married a lady from Texas and lived at the home place, Ridgedale. Their sons, Lawrence and Robert, died unmarried. Two daughters, Miss Kitty Washington of Washington City and Mrs. Betty Copeland of Rockville, Maryland, survive.

Rebecca Washington, daughter of George William and Sally A., married James B. Rees; Bettie (1847-1921) married John J. Inskeep (1844-1918); Sallie married Joseph S. Pancake (1856-1931). Ettie, unmarried, died March 20, 1940, at the advanced age of 99 years. She was buried at Romney.

The graves of George William Washington and his wife, their son Edward and his wife, and a number of their descendants are in the beautiful Indian Mound Cemetery at Romney. Near them is the grave of Nicholas Casey (1744-1833), a son of the Peter Casey who was a host to young George Washington and George William Fairfax, when they and James Genn were surveying in the Old Fields in 1748.

View downstream of the South Branch of the Potomac from the bridge on the highway between Ridgedale and Ferndale.

On June 19, 1861, Captain John Q. Winfield, writing from Hanging Rock, near Romney, said: "I am much pleased with our present location, which is in the midst of wealthy and hospitable people. The Inskips, Washingtons, and Parsons live around here in this valley. I am at present writing from the home of Mrs. Inskip."

There are two "Hanging Rocks" in Hampshire County—one on the Northwestern Turnpike, fifteen miles east of Romney, the other on the South Branch, four miles below Romney. The latter, near an old settlement known as Wappacomo, is the one at which Captain Winfield had his camp in the summer of 1861. It is within a mile of Ridgedale, the old home of George William Washington; later the home of his son Robert M. Washington. Here the river breaks through the mountain, exposing on the northeast side a towering precipice of rock. Of this Kercheval, writing about 1830, gives the following description:

"These [the Hanging Rocks], or as they are sometimes called, 'Blue's Rocks,' are another wonderful work of nature. They are situated on the Wappatomaka [South Branch], about four miles north of Romney, the seat of justice for the county of Hampshire. The author has several times viewed this place with excited feelings and admiration. The river has cut its way through a mountain probably not less than five hundred feet high. By what extraordinary agency it has been able to do this, it is impossible to conceive, unless we look to that Almighty Power whose arm effects all his great objects at pleasure. On the east [northeast] of the river is a huge mass of rocks which forms a perpendicular wall several hundred yards in length, and not less than three hundred feet high. The opposite point of the mountain is more sloping, and may be ascended by a man on foot. . . .

"The public road, leading from Romney into the great western highway, passes between the margin of the river and the great natural wall formed by the rocks. The center of the rocks for about eighty or one hundred yards is composed of fine gray limestone, while on each side are the common granite mountain stone.

"The reader will recollect that this is the place where a most bloody battle was fought between contending parties of the Catawba and Delaware Indians, noticed in a preceding chapter of this volume."

These cliffs are often spoken of in the community as the painted rocks, because of certain colored figures or formations on them. Near the mouth of the South Branch, and also at the mouth of Seneca Creek in Pendleton County, West Virginia, are painted rocks, so called. None of the figures of colorings on any of these rocks are believed to be the work of man, but they are evidently produced by the chemical action of certain minerals in the ledges of rocks, the seepage of water probably being a factor in the process.

The Baltimore & Ohio Railroad passes through the gap at the Hanging Rocks, which are just above the Ridgedale farm, but the wagon road has been rerouted in recent years, passing down the valley just east of the gorge, but in plain sight of it.

Clarence Thomas in his book, "General Turner Ashby, the Centaur of the South," states that Ashby and his command, in the early summer of 1861, occupied a position several miles below Romney on the river, "upon the estate of Col. George Washington." Winfield, quoted above, was under Ashby and Colonel Angus McDonald. There is a tradition in the Washington family that Ashby had his headqquarters at or near Ridgedale. Thomas also says that Captain Dick Ashby, Turner's brother, after he was mortally wounded, was carried on a litter to the Washington home at Ridgedale, dying there after about a week. This statement is at variance with the assertion of Maxwell and Swisher in their history of Hampshire County, who say that Dick Ashby, after being wounded by bayonet thrusts on the B. & O. Railroad, near the mouth of Dan's Run, on June 26, 1861, died on July 4, at the house of a Mr. Cheshire, half a mile from Springfield. All agree that he was buried in the Indian Mound Cemetery at Romney, until his body was later moved to Winchester, where the tomb of the two brothers may now be seen.

Until recently there has been some uncertainty as to the forebears of George William Washington of Hampshire, though it was well known by his descendants that he came from Fairfax County. Mr. Henry Campbell had the tradition that George William was a son of Edward, and that there were two Edwards. He and Miss Isabella Miller, a granddaughter of George William's son Edward, both had heard of a Lawrence far back in the line. Mrs. Tulane Atkinson tabulated the descent as follows:

VI.   George William Washington, born September 15, 1809, at Belmont; died February 6, 1876; married Sallie Ann Wright, February 19, 1832;

V.   Edward Lawrence Washington, born 1770 at Belmont; died 1813; married Elizabeth Sanford, 1792;

IV.   Edward Lawrence Washington, born 1745; died 1791; married Catherine Whiting (?);

III.   John Washington, born 1707;

II.   John Washington, born 1667;

I.   Lawrence Washington, immigrant to Virginia in 1658.

Mrs. Atkinson states that it is the opinion of some that a Bailey Washington was the father of Edward Lawrence (IV above).

The public records of Fairfax County confirm parts of the foregoing. On April 8, 1813, Edward Washington of Fairfax County made his will. Therein he named his sons: John, Edward Sandford, George William, and Joseph Hough; his daughters: Margaret Sandford, Mary Ann, Elizabeth Catharine; a niece, Peggy Sandford; a nephew, John H. Manley; and an aunt, Sarah Washington. He did not name his wife, who probably was dead at the time, but she evidently was a Sandford (Sanford). His will was proved June 21, 1813.

This Edward who died in 1813 was the son, heir, and executor of his father, Edward Washington, who made his will in Fairfax County on June 30, 1791; witnesses, Joshua Coffer, James Hereford, and Joseph Reed. His will was probated on September 18, 1792.

An Edward Washington, probably of the foregoing line, acquired Belmont, the home of Catesby Cocke, on Occoquan Creek, in 1746 or at some time thereafter. See Fitzpatrick's 1925 edition of Washington's diaries, Vol. I, page 112, note. An Edward Washington obtained a patent for 614 acres of land on Pignut Ridge, supposed to be in what is now Fauquier County, on December 12, 1739. Fauquier was formed from a part of Prince William County in 1759.

Belmont is situated on the north side of Occoquan Creek, two miles below Woodbridge and about midway between Woodbridge and Gunston Hall, the homestead of George Mason. Belmont is now in Fairfax County, which was until 1742 a part of Prince William. Near Belmont was the home of Rev. Lee Massey (1732-1814), who succeeded Rev. Charles Green as minister of Truro Parish. Mr. Massey's third wife was Elizabeth Bronaugh, a cousin to George Mason. Mr. Massey was occasionally a guest at Mount Vernon. On June 20, 1773, he read the funeral service for Patsy Custis, daughter of Martha Washington.

CHAPTER XIX

LATER YEARS AT MOUNT VERNON

General Washington in his will, written with his own hand and dated July 9, 1799, bequeathed the use, profit, and benefit of his whole estate, real and personal, except such parts as were specifically disposed of otherwise, to his wife, Martha Washington, for the term of her natural life.

She did not long survive him. He died Saturday night, December 14, 1799. On September 22 following she made her will, and her death occurred on Saturday, May 22, 1802. Thereupon the Mount Vernon estate, in accordance with the terms of the General's will, descended to his nephew, Judge Bushrod Washington, the older son of the General's second full brother, John Augustine Washington, and his wife Hannah Bushrod.

For his second brother, "dear Jack," as he called him in early life, Washington had a special affection. This appears in the General's will:

And now, Having gone through these specific devises, with the explanations for the more correct understanding of the meaning and design of them; I proceed to the distribution of the more important parts of my Estate, in manner following:

First—To my nephew Bushrod Washington and his heirs (partly in consideration of an intimation to his deceased father, while we were bachelors, and he had kindly undertaken to superintend my Estate during my military services in the former war between Great Britain and France, that if I should fall therein, Mt. Vernon, then less extensive in domain than at present, should become his property) I give and bequeath all that part thereof which is comprehended within the following limits——

The testator then proceeds to indicate boundaries which comprehended a tract containing upwards of 4,000 acres. This tract, together with the mansion house and all other buildings and improvements thereon, became the property of Bushrod and his heirs.

"Dear Jack" had died twelve years before. Bushrod, when he came into this inheritance, was forty years of age. He was master of Mount Vernon for twenty-seven years, though absent from it on his official duties much of the time. If affection for and a promise to his father had incited his uncle's generosity, his own abilities, worth, and achievements proved that the choice which placed him in an illustrious line of succession was also an act of good judgment. By 1799 he had already given evidence of merit and had been elevated to high station.

After graduating at the College of William and Mary in 1778, he became a student of law under James Wilson of Philadelphia, recommended to Mr. Wilson by his uncle, who was then commander-in-chief of the Revolutionary armies. In 1780 and 1781 he served in Colonel J. F. Mercer's troop, which was disbanded after the capture of Yorktown. His preceptor Wilson, who had

Judge Bushrod Washington
Photo by Cook of Richmond of a portrait.

signed the Declaration of Independence and served in the Continental Congress, was appointed a brigadier-general of Pennsylvania militia in 1782, but won his chief honors later as statesman and jurist.

The young lawyer, Bushrod Washington, began practice in his native county of Westmoreland, in Virginia, but soon located in the town of Alexandria. Here he was only seven miles from Mount Vernon. In 1785 he married Anne Blackburn, daughter of Colonel Thomas Blackburn of Rippon Lodge. Because the early marriage records of Fairfax County have been destroyed, the day and month of the wedding at Rippon Lodge have not been ascertained, but the date was prior to October 19, 1785; for on that day, when General Washington reached home a little after noon, as he notes in his diary, he found Bushrod and his wife there.

With them were Bushrod's father and mother, his brother Corbin and sister Milly, and Anne's father, Colonel Blackburn; also William Augustine Washington, his wife, and four children. Women had husbands and husbands had wives in quick succession in those days, and William Augustine Washington had three. His first wife was his cousin, Jane Washington, Bushrod's sister. She it probably was, with her four children, who was found in the house party at Mount Vernon in October of 1785. This was obviously a family party, and we may guess that it was also a wedding party, shortly following the marriage of Bushrod Washington and Anne Blackburn. To be sure, George Augustine Washington and Frances Bassett had been married at Mount Vernon only four days before; accordingly, this gathering may have been an infair for them.

Soon Bushrod Washington began to take part in public civil life. In 1787 he was a member of the Virginia House of Delegates, and shortly thereafter he sat in the state convention in Richmond and cast his vote to ratify the new Federal Constitution which his uncle, General Washington, and his former teacher, James Wilson, had helped to frame. In 1790 he settled in Richmond. Eight years later President John Adams appointed him an associate justice of the U. S. Supreme Court to succeed his old teacher, James Wilson, who had died.

James Bryce has declared that James Wilson's expositions of the United States Constitution place him in the front rank of the political thinkers of his age, and by general consent Bushrod Washington is given high rank as a jurist. His colleagues regarded him as one of the greatest *nisi prius* judges in English history, not excepting Chief Justice Holt or Lord Mansfield. In personal appearance he was not commanding. One writer described him as of "small and emaciated frame, and countenance like marble," but he was eminent for learning and ability. If not commanding in stature, his presence was impressive, and when on the bench he was always treated with respect. He was fond of music, enjoyed the society of women, was kind and genial in social intercourse. He spent much of his time when off the bench reading novels to

Part of flower garden at Mount Vernon.

his ailing wife. He would stop an advocate in the middle of a sentence, to get home on the minute, so his wife would not worry about his tardiness.

Like General Washington, Judge Washington had no children of his own. Like him, again, he did well by his nephews. Three of them, we are told, John Augustine, Richard Henry Lee, and Bushrod Corbin, sons of the judge's brother, Corbin Washington, made their home for some years at Mount Vernon, under the guardianship of their uncle. Richard Henry Lee Washington died unmarried in 1819; his brothers were remembered handsomely in their uncle's will, which was opened ten years later.

Judge Washington had much trouble with his Negro slaves. They were insubordinate, refused to work, and at different times were actually a menace. On one occasion, at least, some of them were implicated in an attempt to set fire to the mansion at Mount Vernon. Instead of realizing a profit from their labor, Judge Washington lost annually from $500 to $1,000 in supporting them. This loss he had to make up from other sources of income. The fact that General Washington had provided generously for his slaves, and that Judge Washington was known to be favorable to a plan by which the slaves of the country might be emancipated with a fair chance of self-support, engendered a spirit of unrest and hasty ambition among his Negroes. Besides, agitators were at work among them. For years Judge Washington was president of the Colonization Society. He liberated and sent to Liberia some of his slaves, whom he deemed qualified, and contributed to their support, but he at the same time recognized the difficulties and dangers that would attend indiscriminate emancipation by individual slaveowners here and there.

On July 10, 1826, Judge Bushrod Washington wrote his will—a long one. To his wife and her heirs he left ten or a dozen Negroes; for her natural life he devised her all of the Mount Vernon lands, except such part thereof as he put in trust for his nephew, Bushrod Washington. To her also were bequeathed household goods, the organ and pianos, books of music, her library of books, "also interest on debts due me & dividends upon bank & road stock."

After the death of Anne, the major part of the Mount Vernon estate, as bounded by lines specified in the will, together with all the greenhouse and hothouse plants, tools and instruments belonging to the gardens, the furniture in the mansion house, kitchen, and other houses were to go to the testator's nephew, John A. Washington, and his heirs. After the death of Anne the liquors were to be equally divided among "my nephews: Bushrod Washington of Mt. Zephire, George C. Washington, John A. Washington, & Bushrod C. Washington." Also, after the death of Anne, a part of the Mount Vernon tract of land was to go to the testator's niece, Mary Lee Herbert, and her heirs. His nephew, George C. Washington, and his heirs were to have a tract near Gum Spring. His tract of land in Ohio was to be divided equally among George C. Washington, Mary Lee Herbert, George Washington. John A. Washington, Bushrod C. Washington, and their heirs.

An unusual view of Mount Vernon.

Bushrod and George C. Washington were sons of the judge's sister Jane, and had married her cousin, William A. Washington. George C. Washington lived many years in Georgetown; was a member of Congress from Maryland between 1827 and 1837. Bushrod married Henrietta Bryan Spotswood, had eight children, and lived at Mt. Zephyr, provided for him from the Mount Vernon estate by the will of his uncle, Judge Bushrod Washington.

Judge Bushrod continued his lengthy testament: "All my law books in Philadelphia & a few others left with Mr. Berkham in Trenton are to be moved to Mt. Vernon & with those now there remain in the study under the care of John A. Washington till Bushrod Washington Herbert, son of my niece aforesaid, is twenty-one—& if he should be educated to practice law the books are to go to him: otherwise they are to be sold & the proceeds to sink into the residuum of my estate."

The papers and letter books of General Washington and the other books not law books in the study at Mt. Vernon were to go to the testator's nephew, George C. Washington; "the books in the cases in the dining room to my nephew John A. Washington; the sword left to me by General Washington I give to the said George C. Washington, under the same injunction with which I received it; my gold watch to my friend Robert Adams of Philadelphia."

This watch had been worn by General Washington. After the death of Robert Adams it was to go to his son, Bushrod Adams. Busts of General Washington and Jacques Necker, the French statesman and financier, were to go to John A. Washington; the bust of Paul Jones to Mr. Mumford, for his museum; "my double-barrel gun to my nephew Bushrod Washington Jr. & the pistols which belonged to and were used by General Washington to George C. Washington."

Debts due the testator from the estates of his deceased friends, Major Richard Blackburn and Thomas Blackburn were to be forgiven. His nephews John A. Washington and Bushrod C. Washington were appointed executors.

Under the same date, July 10, 1826, Judge Washington added a codicil to his will. In this codicil bequests were made to Jane C. Washington, wife of John A., and the following disposition was made of certain literary properties.

Whereas Chief Justice Marshall and myself contemplate publishing some volumes of Letters from General Washington, all or the most of which are already Copied, and also publishing a second edition of the life of Washington, it is my will that whatever sum of money may accrue from these sources be invested by my Executor in some productive fund, the interest or dividends whereof are to be paid to my wife during her life and after her death to be divided and to rest in the persons to whom the residue of my estate is given.

Marshall's Life of Washington, written by the Chief Justice at the request of Judge Washington, had appeared from 1804 to 1807. A reprint of portions of this work was issued in two volumes in 1824, but the revised and condensed edition was not published until 1832, three years after Judge Washington's

View of Mount Vernon from an airplane over the river.

death. The contemplated publication of the writings of Washington was still more delayed, appearing finally from 1834 to 1837, in twelve volumes, edited by Jared Sparks, whose biography of Washington made up the first volume of the twelve. Judge Washington himself, the same year in which he was elevated to the bench, published two volumes of reports of the Virginia courts of appeals, and within the last years of his life got out four volumes of Federal reports, of the Third Circuit.

In this connection it may be fitting to note that Henry Augustine Washington, professor of history, political economy, and international law in the College of William and Mary, and a distant relative of Judge Washington, edited the writings of Thomas Jefferson, which were published in eight volumes from 1853 to 1855. Professor Washington also prepared for the press "A Digest of the Laws, Customs, Manners, and Institutions of the Ancient and Modern Nations," by Thomas R. Dew, late president of the college.

On January 9, 1828, Judge Washington added to his will a second codicil —his beloved niece, Mary L. Herbert, having died, "her property which I gave her to be equally divided between her two sons, Bushrod W. Herbert and Noblet Herbert and their heirs"; and on July 19, 1828, he wrote a third codicil concerning a line between the lands of the testator and those of Major Lewis, and several other items.

Judge Washington died in Philadelphia, November 26, 1829, and his wife died two days later, before she reached Mount Vernon with his body. Six years later Chief Justice Marshall died in Philadelphia, and his son Thomas, traveling to his bedside, was struck and killed by a falling brick in Baltimore.

Judge Washington's will, with its three codicils, was proved before the Fairfax County court on December 21, 1829, by the oaths of George Mason, George Millan, Dennis Johnson, and William Moss to be wholly in the handwriting of the testator, Bushrod Washington, and was admitted to record. Inasmuch as the death of his wife was practically coincident with his own, his nephew, John A. Washington II, entered at once into possession of the Mount Vernon estate.

John A. Washington and his brother, Bushrod C. Washington, for some years previous to this date (1829) had been living in Jefferson County, Virginia, now West Virginia, upon lands inherited from their father, Corbin Washington, and their brother, Richard Henry Lee Washington, John at Blakeley, Bushrod at Claymont Court. They had married Blackburn girls, sisters, Jane Charlotte and Thomasina. John did not long enjoy his new inheritance, for he died at Mount Vernon on June 16, 1832, at the age of forty-three.

Jane Charlotte Washington, the widow, appears to have spent most of her time at Blakely, carrying on at Mount Vernon through the agency of an overseer. It was not long until her son, John Augustine III, born in 1820 or 1821, was of an age to be of assistance to her. His brother, Richard Blackburn, was a year or two younger.

About the time that John A. Washington II came into possession of Mount Vernon an attempt was made to steal General Washington's body from the old vault. Not long afterwards the new vault was constructed at the place which the General himself had designated· Several years later the lead coffins which contained the bodies of General Washington and his wife were enclosed in coffins of marble. Says Charles Moore:

> The features of Washington were seen for the last time October 7, 1837, when the remains of George and Martha Washington were placed in two solid marble coffins, given by John Struthers, a Philadelphia stone-cutter, whose generosity Lawrence Lewis rewarded by allowing him to place thereon the record of his gift. The vault had been enlarged by building a chamber large enough to permit the coffins to be placed in dry air, the dampness of the inner tomb having thrice destroyed the wooden cases enclosing the lead coffins.

(See "The Family Life of George Washington," by Charles Moore, edition of 1926, pages 198, 199.)

Lawrence Lewis, Washington's nephew, and George Washington Parke Custis, Mrs. Washington's grandson, were two of the executors of Washington's will, appointed by him. They directed the work of improving the vault and were present when the lead coffins were finally enclosed in the marble sarcophagi. Present also at the same time were Lawrence Lewis's son Lorenzo, Mrs. Jane Charlotte Washington, and her son John Augustine Washington III. In 1839 Lawrence Lewis and his daughter, Mrs. Charles M. Conrad, were given resting-places near by; and in 1852 Nelly Custis, Mrs. Lawrence Lewis, her body brought from Audley.

In December 1835 the greenhouse (conservatory) at Mount Vernon burned, the fire originating in a defective flue. The servants' quarters adjoining were also consumed. The ruins from this fire still remained when Benson J. Lossing wrote of Mount Vernon about 1870.

John A. Washington III, after the death of his mother at Blakely in 1855, entered upon full title to Mount Vernon. For a number of years preceding that date he had been established there. In 1842 he had married Eleanor Love Selden, daughter of Wilson Cary Selden, and between 1844 and 1858 their seven children, five daughters and two sons, were born at Mount Vernon. The daughters were Louisa Fontaine, Jane Charlotte, Eliza Selden, Anna Maria, and Eleanor Selden; the sons were Lawrence, born in 1854, and George, born in 1858.

Thousands of visitors were coming to Mount Vernon every year. Efforts were made to have the Federal Government or the State of Virginia purchase the estate and make it a public shrine, but without success. In the meantime the owner, John A. Washington III, was confronted with impossible tasks in maintaining his family, keeping the property in repair, and entertaining the crowds of visitors. As a matter of fact, his own time and business were seriously interrupted, while the buildings, fences, and grounds were neglected.

Temporary props were placed here and there on the east portico to keep the ceiling from falling. One of the eight pillars along the front was gone altogether.

One night as a steamer on the river was passing Mount Vernon, the tolling of the ship's bell, as was the custom in tribute to the Father of His Country, stirred sympathy and patriotic aspirations in the heart of one of the passengers, a Mrs. Cunningham of South Carolina. To her daughter, Miss Ann Pamela Cunningham, she wrote: "Let the women of America own and preserve Mount Vernon."

After years of effort, beset with countless discouragements, it was done. Miss Cunningham, an invalid unable to walk, writing under the pen-name "The Southern Matron," organized the Mount Vernon Ladies Association. Edward Everett contributed his oratory and money was raised. Mr. Washington felt that his honor would suffer if he surrendered the traditional hospitality of his family and sold the property. "The Southern Matron" undertook the long journey to confer with him in person. Unable to travel so far by rail, she went by water to Baltimore and thence returned to Mount Vernon, being carried up to the decaying mansion in a chair. Even so, her visit seemed to fail, and she was preparing to depart. By a lucky accident she missed the evening boat and was compelled to remain over night. In the renewed conference she persuaded Mr. Washington to agree to her plan, and Mount Vernon, on February 22, 1859, passed into the hands of the Association. In the autumn of the same year Mr. Washington and his family moved to Waveland, their new home in Fauquier County, Va., which had been purchased in the late summer of 1858.

On November 8, 1937, at the George Mason Hotel in Alexandria, died Mrs. Eleanor Selden Howard, the last of the children of John A. Washington III, the last Washington owner of Mount Vernon. In the *Washington Post* of the next day, in connection with an obituary notice, appeared the following:

Just a year ago, when she was dean of the Washington clan, Mrs. Howard ruefully explained why her father sold Mount Vernon to the Mount Vernon Ladies Association when she was but 4 years old.

"My father," she said, "was actually eaten out of house and home. People came every day to look at the estate, ate our food, accepted our hospitality—and then went off without so much as a 'thank you.' The estate was never self-supporting, and with our family large as it was, the expenses just couldn't be met."

Mrs. Howard was born in 1856, sixth of the seven children and youngest daughter of the five. She was orphaned when her father was killed on a reconnaisance in the West Virginia hills; her mother had died the year before.

Though Mount Vernon was sold by her father for $200,000, he actually realized nothing from it, Mrs. Howard once said. She explained that he turned his fortune as well as his life over to the Confederacy at the outbreak of the Civil War.

Mrs. Howard was the widow of Julian Smith Howard, of Warsaw, Va., and is survived by a daughter, Mrs. Howard Caldwell, of Seattle, Wash., four grandchildren, and two great-grandchildren.

CHAPTER XX

THE WASHINGTONS AT WAVELAND

Waveland, the country estate to which John A. Washington III and his family moved from Mount Vernon, lies in Fauquier County, Virginia, three miles south of the town of Marshall (formerly Salem) and ten miles northwest of Warrenton, the county-seat, in a region of fertile grass lands, with small wooded mountains near by and with the Blue Ridge in sight at a distance of twenty miles along the horizon to the northwest. One needs only to visit the place and look around over the rolling fields to see the fitness of the name, Waveland. In an air line it lies distant from Mount Vernon about 42 miles, northwest—almost due west. The best way of approach from Mount Vernon is along the roads leading past Fairfax Court House, Centerville, and Gainesville; thence through Thoroughfare Gap in Bull Run Mountain and so on by way of The Plains (formerly White Plains). One going out from Marshall should go down on the road towards Warrenton a mile or so and then turn to the right on the dirt road that leads past Waveland.

The Waveland fields drain into the headwaters of Carter's Run, an affluent of the Rappahannock River. Other historic homes in the vicinity are Gordonsdale, three miles to the northeast, in the direction of The Plains; Belvoir, in recent years the home of Fairfax Harrison, a short distance from Gordonsdale, in the direction of Marshall; and Oak Hill, the home of Thomas Marshall, his son John (later Chief Justice), and other members of the Marshall family. Oak Hill is three miles northwest of the town of Marshall, and distant from Waveland about five miles in a straight line.

On August 25 and 26, 1862, Stonewall Jackson and his "foot cavalry" circled around Waveland on the west, north, and northeast, through Marshall (then Salem) and The Plains, to go down through Thoroughfare Gap in Bull Run Mountain and get in the rear of Pope's army at Warrenton; and a day or two later Lee and Longstreet, with the remainder of the Confederate army, passed over the same route. (For maps showing these movements and pictures of Thoroughfare Gap, see Wayland's "Stonewall Jackson's Way," 1940, pages 172, 173.)

The deed by which the title to Waveland was conveyed to John A. Washington III is on record in the Fauquier County clerk's office in Warrenton, and reads as follows:

Whereas by indenture made and entered into between Bedford Brown and wife of the one part and James Rogers of the other part. bearing date the 13th day of Aug: 1855 and duly admitted to record in the clerks office of the County Court of Fauquier County, the said parties of the first part bargained and sold unto the said party of the second part a certain tract or parcel of land lying and being in the upper part of said County, called "Waveland": and whereas the said Rogers and Martha his wife in order to secure the deferred payments upon the said tract or parcel of land unto the said Brown, by indenture of even date with

Colonel John A. Washington of Mount Vernon and Waveland.

the indenture aforesaid conveyed the said tract or parcel of land to Richard
Payne, in trust for the uses and purposes therein set forth: and whereas
the said Rogers and Martha his wife by indenture made and entered into
the 24th day of Sept: 1857 and admitted to record, amongst other things,
conveyed unto Robert E. Scott and John A. Spilman the aforesaid tract or
parcel of land subject to the trusts and limitations in said indenture contained:
and whereas the said Robert E. Scott and John A. Spilman trustees under and
by virtue of said indenture were authorised and empowered by the terms and provisions thereof "to act separately or together in all matters": And whereas by
memorandum of agreement made the 17th day of Aug. 1858 between the said
John A. Spilman of the County of Fauquier and State of Virginia and John A.
Washington then of the County of Fairfax and same State, the said Spilman, as
one of the trustees of said Rogers and wife sold unto the said Washington the
aforesaid tract or parcel of land, called "Waveland" for the sum of thirty five
thousand dollars, to be paid in manner as provided and set forth in said memorandum: and whereas the said Bedford Brown and Richards Payne have executed
and delivered unto the said Rogers an indenture of release bearing date the 7th
day of Dec: 1858 for the aforesaid parcel or tract of land, *This Indenture* made
and entered into between Robert E. Scott and John A. Spilman trustees of James
Rogers and wife, both of the County of Fauquier and State of Virginia, And John
A. Washington of the County of Fauquier and same State, witnesseth, that the
said Robert E. Scott and John A. Spilman trustees as aforesaid and parties of the
first part, for and in consideration of the sum of thirty five thousand dollars, to
them in hand paid at or before the ensealing and delivery of these presents, by
the said John A. Washington, receipt whereof is hereby acknowledged, have
given, granted, bargained and sold and by these presents do give, grant, bargain
and sell unto the said Washington a certain lot or parcel of land, called "Waveland," situate lying and being in the upper part of the County of Fauquier and
bounded as follows viz Beginning at two chestnut stumps, a tree or sprout from
the eastern stump, marked as a pointed corner to Dr. Wright and running with his
line No 48¾ W 33 poles to a stone; thence No 44 W 85 poles, 11 links to two
apple trees; thence N 35½ E 184 8/10 poles to three small gums and a fence;
thence N 48½ W 103 poles to a black oak, Dr. Wright's corner, same course continued 111 9/10 poles to a stone in Dr. Newman's line (now Adams), three black
oaks, a chestnut oak and white-oak pointers; thence with the line of said Newman
(now Adams) S 34 W 108 9/10 poles to a white-oak; thence S 25¾ W 15 6/10
poles to a stone; thence S 30 W 37 poles to a stone in the center of the road leading from Dr. Newman's (now Adams) to Waveland; thence with the road N 41 W
22 poles; N 22 W 17 poles; N 78 W 28 poles; N 60 W 11 poles; N 40¼ W 13
7/10 poles to a sycamore, corner to Dr. Newman (now Adams); thence leaving the
land of said Newman (now Adams), N 36¾ W 7 poles to northern gate-post;
thence N 85 W 23 4/10 poles to a white-oak; thence N 60½ W 10¾ poles to a
white oak; thence N 79 W 26 2/10 poles to a stone; thence S 76 W 21 8/10 poles
to a stone at the end of a stone fence; thence S 26 W 36 8/10 poles to a stone;
thence S 35 W 40 poles to a gatepost; thence N 71 W 217 poles to a stone in John
Strother's line, 8 links N.E. from said Strother's corner; thence with the line of said
Strother and Marshall S 12 degrees 21 minutes W 107 4/10 poles to a pine stump,
stones piled around it, to Loughborough; thence with his line S 51 E 234 poles to
a stone; thence S 52 E 21 1/10 poles to a red-oak; thence S 85 E 265 2/10 poles
to a stone; thence S 67½ E 128 5/10 poles to a stone, corner to Smith; thence N
55¾ E 211 4/10 poles to a stone in the forks of a branch; thence N 3 degrees
25 minutes E 63 poles to a stone on the west side of a branch, corner to the afore-

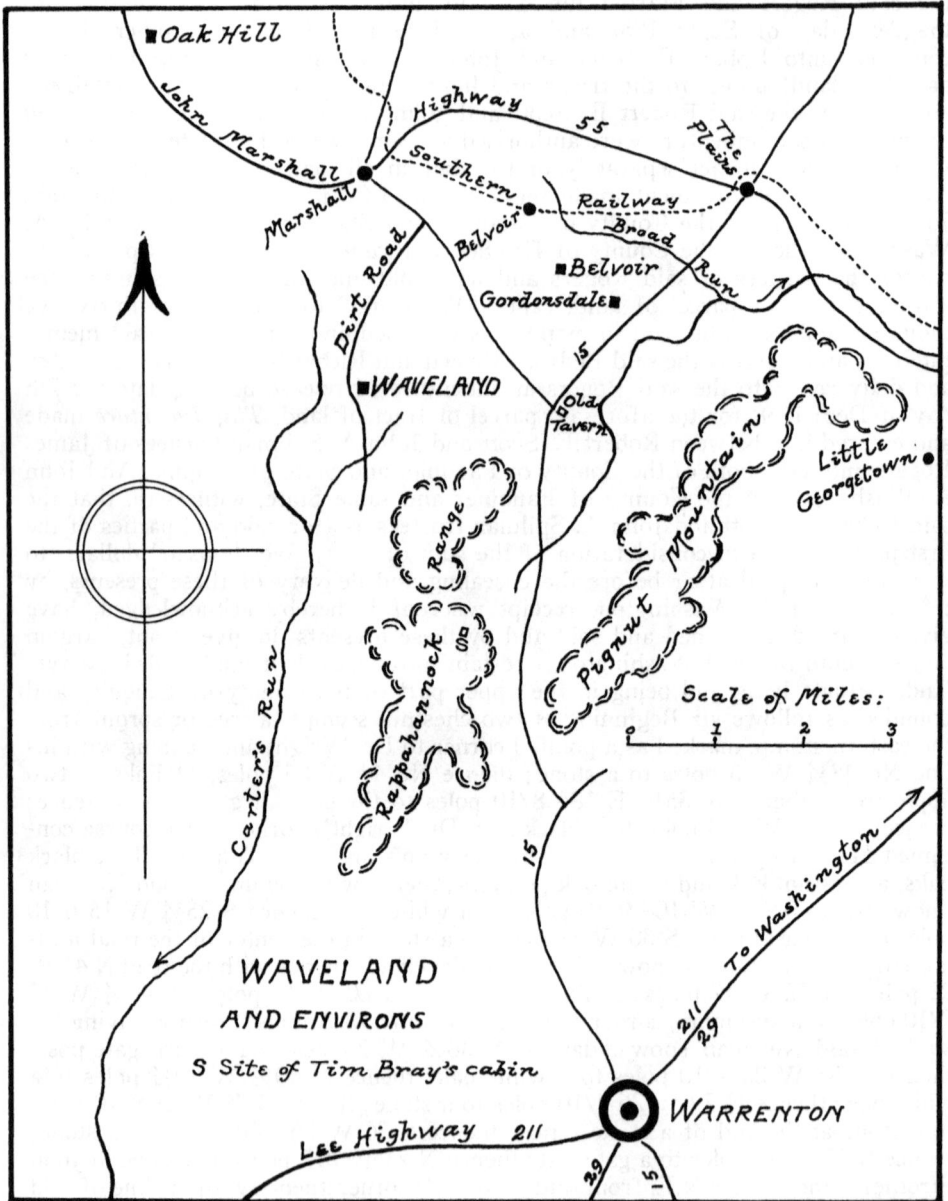

Oak Hill

John Marshall Highway 55

The Plains

Marshall

Southern Railway

Dirt Road

Belvoir Broad Run

Belvoir

Gordonsdale

15

WAVELAND

Old Tavern

Pignut Mountain

Little Georgetown

Range

Rappahannock

Scale of Miles:
0   1   2   3

Carter's Run

15

To Washington

211
29

WAVELAND

AND ENVIRONS

S Site of Tim Bray's cabin

Lee Highway   211

WARRENTON

29
15

said Dr. Wright; thence with his line S 67 W 216 poles to the beginning, containing eight hundred and sixty six acres, be the same more or less, together with all the rights, privileges and appurtenances thereunto appertaining or belonging: to have and to hold, &c.

R. E. Scott   (Seal)
Jno. A. Spilman   (Seal)

Admitted to record Feb. 2, 1860.
Teste Wm. A. Jennings C. C. pro-tem.

As stated in the preceding chapter, the Washingtons moved from Mount Vernon to Waveland in the autumn of 1859. This was the autumn that was so greatly disturbed by the John Brown raid at Harper's Ferry. The distance from Harper's Ferry to Waveland, by way of Key's Gap or Snicker's Gap in the Blue Ridge, is about 40 miles, and news of the raid quickly spread to much greater distances. John A. Washington's brother, Richard B. Washington, of near Charles Town, and his cousin, Lewis W. Washington, of Halltown, as already noted, both figured prominently in connection with the Harper's Ferry outbreak and in the trial of Brown and several of his associates at Charles Town shortly afterward. A year later came the first ordinances of secession, and in the spring of 1861 the outbreak of civil war.

John A. Washington III enlisted in the Confederate cause and served as an aid to General Robert E. Lee in the campaigns against the Federals in what is now the state of West Virginia. He was killed at the Elkwater, in Randolph County, September 13, 1861. The spot where he fell is now marked by a massive granite boulder, appropriately inscribed:

'61   '65

LT. COL. JOHN AUGUSTINE WASHINGTON, C. S. A.
OF MOUNT VERNON
AIDE-DE-CAMP TO GENERAL ROBERT E. LEE
KILLED, ELKWATER, SEPTEMBER 13, 1861
BURIED IN ZION CHURCHYARD
CHARLES TOWN, WEST VIRGINIA

At Warrenton on Monday, October 28, 1861, the following entry was made in the minute book of the county court: "A Certificate of the qualification of Jno A Washington to his Commission as Lieut Colonel was returned to the Court and ordered to be recorded." Two days later Colonel Washington's will was produced in court. To it there were no subscribing witnesses, but William P. Quesenberry and Turner Dixon took oath that they were familiar with Colonel Washington's handwriting and believed the will and the signature thereto to be wholly written by the said testator, and the writing was ordered to be recorded as the true last will and testament of the said John A. Washington. The will was written on campaign and dated August 5, less than a month and a half before the testator's death. It is brief but explicit:

A view of Waveland while still occupied by the Washingtons.

In the name of God: Amen. I John A Washington of Waveland in Fauquier County, Virginia do make and ordain this to be my last will and testament hereby revoking every other will and testament by me heretofore made

1st I desire that my Executors, hereafter to be named will pay all of my Just debts as soon after my decease as practicable.

2nd I give and bequeath to my son Lawrence Washington all of the Books, Manuscripts, papers, engravings, pictures, Medals and Arms of which I may die possessed, also my watch chain & Seal—Should my son Lawrence die before attaining the age of twenty one years—I then give and bequeath the above property to my son George Washington, and should neither of them arrive at the age of twenty one years I then give & bequeath the above property to the oldest of my daughters, who may be living at the time of the death of the last surviving of my sons.

3rd I give all the property of which I may die possessed other than that just mentioned to be equally divided among my children as they respectively become twenty one years old, and until then to be maintained and educated out of the proceeds arising from it

4th I constitute and appoint my Brother, Richard B Washington, and my friends William Fontaine Alexander and Edward C Turner Executors of this my last will and testament, and I hereby *empower* them or the survivors or survivor of them to sell any property of which I may die possessed, and which is beyond the limits of Virginia, in such manner and on such terms and for such price as to them or him may seem best for the interest of my children—and to reinvest the proceeds arising from such sale in such other property as they may *think best for my children,* and I *hereby request the Court before which* they may qualify not to require from them any security on their Executorial bond.

Witness my hand & Seal this 5th day of August 1861 at Huntersville, Pocahontas County—Virginia

JOHN A. WASHINGTON (Seal)

Proved October 30, 1861. See Will Book of Fauquier County, Va., No. 29, page 228.

In the minute book of the court for the years 1859-65, page 350, it is recorded that on November 25, 1861, Richard B. Washington qualified as an executor, and on the same date William I. Morgan, John Baker, John Walden, and John Shumate (or any three of them) were appointed to appraise the estate. On December 23, 1861, Edward C. Turner, one of the executors named in the will, by his note in writing renounced the "burthen of the Execution thereof."

On August 27, 1866 (minute book for 1865-67, page 230) Richard B. Washington was appointed guardian of Lawrence Washington, Eleanor S. Washington, and George Washington, infants under 14, orphans of John A. Washington, deceased, giving bond and security in the sum of $10,000. On the same date Jane C. Washington, Eliza S. Washington, and Anne Maria Washington, infants over 14, chose Richard B. Washington as guardian, he giving bond and security in the sum of $10,000. Frcm 1874 to 1879 John W. Burke was administrator of the estate of John A. Washington, deceased, and guardian of the children. On July 22, 1879, George, the youngest, was of age.

Monument at Elkwater, where Col. John A. Washington was killed.

Richard B. Washington, brother of Colonel John A. Washington, was still living. He died in Charles Town on October 15, 1910.

The seven children of John A. Washington III and his wife, Eleanor Love Selden, married in 1842, were all born at Mount Vernon. Their names, birth-dates, and other pertinent items follow.

Louisa Fontaine was born February 19, 1844; on August 15, 1871, in Jefferson County, W. Va., married Col. R. P. Chew. She died on July 1, 1927.

Jane Charlotte was born May 26, 1846; on January 13, 1869, in Jefferson County, W. Va., married Nathaniel H. Willis. She died August 7, 1924.

Eliza Selden was born July 17, 1848; married Major Robert W. Hunter. She died in Charles Town, August 28, 1909.

Anna Maria was born November 17, 1851; on July 22, 1873, in Jefferson County, married Rev. Beverley D. Tucker of Norfolk. She died January 7, 1927, in Norfolk.

Lawrence was born January 4, 1854; on June 14, 1876, married Fannie Lackland, daughter of Thomas, of Jefferson County. He died on January 28, 1920, leaving 12 children.

Eleanor Selden was born in 1856; on May 5, 1880, married Julian Howard of Richmond County, Va. In later life she lived in the District of Columbia. She died in Alexandria on November 8, 1937.

George was born July 22, 1858; married Emily Serena Porterfield. He died in Charles Town on December 31, 1905.

All or nearly all of these and many other Washingtons are buried in the cemetery around the Episcopal Church in Charles Town.

Lawrence Washington, the older son of Col. John A. Washington, by inheritance and purchase came into the possession of the home place, Wave-land, and lived there with his family for many years.

By the courtesy of Lawrence Washington's daughter, Miss Anne Madison Washington, writing from Washington City on December 7, 1938, I am enabled to give the names of the twelve children of Lawrence Washington and his wife Fannie Lackland: John Augustine, Lawrence, Patty Willis, Anne Madison, Louisa Fontaine, Willis Lackland, Wilson Selden, Preston Chew, Frances Jacqueline, Richard Blackburn, Julian Howard, and Francis Ryland. They were all born at Waveland.

By deed of May 27, 1895, Lawrence Washington and wife, Fannie Lackland Washington, sold Waveland, with 866 acres of land, to Bedford Glascock and moved to Alexandria. Of this land, 437½ acres, the home tract, had been allotted to Lawrence from his father's estate; 428½ acres had been allotted to his brother George. The latter had sold to Charles R. Lake, and Lake had sold to Fannie, wife of Lawrence.

Before me is a letter written from Mount Vernon on January 16, 1939, by Lawrence's son, Julian Howard Washington, in which he gives interesting facts about his father, mother, brothers and sisters, and Waveland:

A recent view of Waveland.

Lawrence Washington married Fannie Lackland of Jefferson County, West Virginia. At the time of the marriage she was living with her parents at River Side on the Shenandoah River, about 4 miles from Charles Town. There were twelve children born, all living to date, four girls and eight boys, five of whom were in the service during the World War.

My father was such a young boy when he left Mount Vernon that very little of his life here was remembered by him, but he was always extremely interested in the work of the Association and assisted this group of Ladies by gift and sale of Washingtoniana in the restoring of the home.

After completing private elementary schooling, he entered V.M.I. where he studied civil engineering for over three years, but did not complete the course on account of financial difficulties. Before coming into possession of Waveland, he was employed in Texas and later in Virginia on surveying parties for different railways. His farming activities meeting with reverses, he sold Waveland and moved to Alexandria and then to Washington, D. C. He was employed by the government for, I think, over 25 years at the Library of Congress. He became head of the Representative Reading Room and served there until his death.

I can recall that he was a very conscientious student of the life of General Washington and assisted several authors in preparing histories on the subject of the General's life, namely, Charles H. Callahan, Eugene Prussing, the late Woodrow Wilson, and Paul Wilstach. He was a very constant attendant and confirmed member of the Protestant Episcopal Church.

The chapters outlined in your book lead me to believe that you giving the public information not now compiled, so far as I know, and I should think it will be an extremely interesting history of the Washington family—certainly to me. I would particularly like to know more about Blakeley, as my father's family lived there for some time and also at Harewood. My grandfather's brother owned Harewood, and my father's immediate family spent considerable time there until reaching maturity.

On May 3, 1910, in presenting the portrait of Judge Bushrod Washington to the court of Westmoreland County, at Montross, Lawrence Washington delivered an informing historical address which was printed in 1912 in Wright's History of Westmoreland.

George Washington, the younger son of Col. John A. Washington, died in Charles Town in 1905, aged between 47 and 48 years. His wife, Emily Serena, was a daughter of Col. George Porterfield. His son, Rev. Richard Blackburn Washington, is a Catholic priest, who for a number of years has been stationed at Hot Springs, Va.

George Baylor of Charles Town, captain of Co. B, 12th Va. Cavalry, C.S.A., in 1900 published his valuable book, "Bull Run to Bull Run," in which, page 322, he speaks of Waveland, "the hospitable mansion where pleasure and enjoyment could always be found with the hosts of young company usually found there."

On page 157 of the same volume Captain Baylor relates an interesting story of Lieut. Bushrod C. Washington (1831-1919) of Company B. In an engagement in Madison County, Va., Lieutenant Washington in a hand-to-hand saber contest with Major McIrwin of the 2d N. Y. Cavalry, took the latter prisoner. Baylor's account follows:

Washington being left-handed, held his saber in his left hand, while the Major, a West Pointer, versed in military art, held his in the right. Washington made the first pass, and the skillful Major attempted to parry his blow, but his saber being constructed to guard against a right-handed antagonist, Washington's saber struck the Major's, passed down the blade, and there being no guard on that side, the blow fell on the Major's hand, causing him to drop his weapon, and Washington, taking advantage of the situation, forced his surrender. In speaking of this contest, while a prisoner, the Major said he had never been taught to fight with a left-handed man. When Washington brought the Major to General Stuart, he recognized him, and said, "Hello, McIrwin, what are you doing here? I paroled you in Pennsylvania." "Yes," said the Major, "but our people would not recognize your parole and ordered me to duty." The Major's horse and trappings were given to Washington, and the Major sent to the rear. For gallant conduct on this and other occasions, Washington was made second lieutenant in Company B.

A COMPENDIUM OF WASHINGTON BIOGRAPHY

(Biographical Sketches of Over 400 Washingtons)

The items in this compendium have been compiled from county and city records, tombstone inscriptions, family Bibles, and documents in the Archives Division of the Virginia State Library. Colonel Forrest W. Brown (1855-1934) of Charles Town, West Virginia, whose mother was a Washington, was a very generous helper. For supplementary facts the following books and periodicals have been freely consulted: "The Authentic Guide Book of Historic Northern Neck of Virginia" (1934), by H. Ragland Eubank; "Wills of Westmoreland County, Virginia" (1925), by Augusta B. Fothergill; "Westmoreland County, Virginia" (1912), by T. R. B. Wright; "Old Churches, Ministers, and Families of Virginia" (1857 and 1900), by Bishop William Meade; The Diaries of George Washington (1925), edited by John C. Fitzpatrick; "Washington, the Man and the Mason" (1913), by Charles H. Callahan; "The Family Life of George Washington" (1926), by Charles Moore; "A Portrait of Old Georgetown" (1933), by Grace Dunlop Ecker; *Tyler's Quarterly Historical and Genealogical Magazine; William and Mary College Quarterly Magazine;* and the *Virginia Magazine of History and Biography.* Among the various individuals who have answered inquiries, special acknowledgment is made to Mr. Richard E. Griffith Sr. and Dr. A. D. Henkel of Winchester, Miss Anne Madison Washington of Washington City, and Mr. Julian H. Washington of Mount Vernon.

ADDIE C., wife of Dewitt N. Washington of Rockingham County, Va.; daughter of Isaac and Susan Rhinehart; died in 1933.

AGNES, wife of George Washington of Caroline County, Va.; daughter of Dr. William Wirt and Betty Selena Payne; living in 1934 at Oak Grove, Westmoreland County, Va.

ALICE, wife of Robert Washington of King George County, Va. She had children: Thomas, born September 5, 1758; William Strother, born April 20, 1760; Anne, born November 10, 1761; Townshend, born February 20, 1764; Lund, born September 25, 1767. Evidently Robert was a son of Townshend and Elizabeth Lund Washington, and a brother to Susanna, born 1727, and to Lund, born 1737.

AMELIA STITH, daughter of Henry Thacker Washington (I) and his wife Amelia Stith; born 1810; married Dr. Mann P. Nelson in Frederick County, Va., September 7, 1826; died 1831.

ANN, wife of John Washington (1632-1676); mother of Lawrence Washington (1659-1698); grandmother of Augustine (1694-1743); great-grandmother of George (1732-1799). She was born Ann Pope, in Maryland; died 1668 or 1669; had five children, of whom three, Lawrence, John, and Ann survived childhood.

ANN, wife of Capt. John Washington (1663-1697?). She was born Ann Wickliffe. After the death of Capt. John Washington she married Col. Charles Ashton. She died 1704.

ANN, daughter of Colonel John Washington (1632-1676) and his first wife, Ann Pope. She married Maj. Francis Wright; had a son, John Wright; lived at King Copsico, Westmoreland County, Va.; died 1698.

ANN, wife of Lawrence Washington (1718?-1752) of Mount Vernon; eldest daughter of William Fairfax of Belvoir; married Lawrence Washington 1743. After his death she married George Lee of Westmoreland County, Va. She died in 1761. Her daughter, Sarah Washington, did not survive childhood.

ANN, wife of Augustine Washington Jr. (1720?-1762); daughter of Capt. William Aylett and wife Ann Ashton. She was a widow in 1771 and died in 1774 at Wakefield. Her husband, Augustine Washington, was an older half-brother to George Washington.

ANN, daughter of Augustine Washington Jr.; sister to William Augustine Washington, Elizabeth W. Spotswood, and Jane W. Thornton. She was born 1752; married Burdett Ashton, December 19, 1768; died 1777. Her father in his will called her Nancy. Her heirs (the heirs of Ann Ashton) were named in George Washington's will, made July 9, 1799.

ANN, daughter of Henry Washington. Henry, a brother to Warner, made his will in Middlesex County, Va., December 29, 1763. At that time Ann was under 21.

ANN, wife of Henry Washington of King George County, Va. She was born Quarles and married Henry Washington in Albemarle County, Va., in April 1785.

ANN, a granddaughter of Mrs. Washington of Bushfield. Both were at Mount Vernon, August 2, 1798, as recorded in Washington's diary.

ANN MARIA T. B., daughter of John A. Washington (II) and his wife Jane Charlotte Blackburn. She was born about 1815; married Dr. William Fontaine Alexander.

ANN MARIA THOMASINA, first wife of Bushrod C. Washington of Claymont; born Blackburn, October 30, 1790; died September 21, 1833; buried in Charles Town.

ANN THOMAS BEALL, born Peter in Georgetown, Md.; was the second wife of George Corbin Washington (1789-1854).

ANNA, wife of George Fayette Washington; living when he made his will in Frederick County, Va., October 19, 1865.

ANNA LOUISE, daughter of Dr. Bailey Washington of the U. S. Navy. She on January 9, 1862, married Walter Dorsey Davidge of Maryland.

ANNA MARIA, spoken of in Martha Washington's will (1802) as "the daughter of my niece." She was probably the same as Maria, spoken of in the same will as "the daughter of my deceased nephew," and is supposed to have been the daughter of George Augustine Washington (1763-1793), son of Col. Charles Washington, brother to George. Reference may be had to the will of George

Washington, also to the will of George Augustine Washington in Fairfax County (Va.) Will Book F, pages 243-248.

ANNA MARIA, daughter of John A. Washington (III) of Mount Vernon and his wife Eleanor Love Selden; born at Mount Vernon November 17, 1851; married Beverley Dandridge Tucker July 22, 1873; died in Norfolk January 7, 1927; buried in Charles Town.

ANNA MARIA T. B., daughter of Richard B. and Christian M. W. Washington. She was born November 1, 1849, and died September 14, 1852; buried in Charles Town.

ANNE, daughter of John and Mary Washington; born in King George County, Va., in 1723.

ANNE, daughter of John Washington (1730-1782) and wife Catherine Washington, daughter of John Washington (II) of Chotank and his wife Mary Massey; born 1761, married Thomas Hungerford, June 22, 1780, in King George County, Va.

ANNE, daughter of Lawrence Washington of Chotank; married John Stith in King George County, Va., December 11, 1783.

ANNE, who married William Thompson in King George County, Va., August 3, 1785.

ANNE, 4th wife of Col. Samuel Washington; daughter of William or James Steptoe. She was the Widow Allerton when she married Samuel Washington, brother to George.

ANN BLACKBURN, daughter of Col. Thomas Blackburn; married Bushrod Washington in 1785; died, widow of Judge Washington, November 27 or 28, 1829. Her full maiden name was Julia Anne Blackburn.

ANNE MADISON, daughter of Lawrence Washington (1854-1920); lives in Washington City.

ANNIE S. C., daughter of Dr. Samuel W. Washington; born at Harewood September 8, 1831; married Thomas A. Brown; died July 19, 1911; buried in Charles Town. Mother of Forrest Washington Brown.

ARIANA, granddaughter of John Stith. She in 1805 married Warner Washington, son of Thacker, who was a son of Henry Washington of Middlesex County, Va. She had sons Francis Whiting, John Stith, Henry Thacker, and a daughter Harriet Ann who married William Garrett Jr. and lived in Alabama.

AUGUSTINE I (1694-1743), son of Lawrence (1659-1698) and Mildred Warner; married (1) Jane Butler; (2) Mary Ball, in 1731; father of George Washington and others.

AUGUSTINE II (1718?-1762), often called Austin; son of Augustine I and his first wife Jane Butler. He married (1) Ann Aylett, 1743, who had children, William Augustine and others; (2) Jane, granddaughter of Col. Ashton. He lived at Wakefield. Some give his birth year as 1718 or later.

AUGUSTINE, DR., eldest son of William Augustine Washington, born at Wakefield 1778; was professor of philosophy in the College of William and Mary.

BAILEY, born September 10, 1731, in King George County, Va., son of Henry (1694-1748) and Mary Bailey Washington; married Catherine Storke January 12, 1749. Col. William Washington, distinguished at Cowpens, was a son. Bailey was a justice in Stafford County 1766-1768 and 1773.

BAILEY, of Stafford County, Va., who married Euphan Mason, daughter of John Thompson Mason and Elizabeth (Westwood) (Wallace) Mason. See Meade, Vol. II, page 230.

BAILEY, DR., surgeon in the U. S. Navy. His daughter Anna Louise married, January 9, 1862, Walter Dorsey Davidge, lawyer, of Maryland.

BENJAMIN FRANKLIN, son of John T. A. Washington; a 49-er; was collector of customs and a judge in California.

BESSIE PAYNE, born Wirt, wife of Col. Robert James Washington of Campbelton, Westmoreland County, Va.

BETSY, probably a daughter of Augustine Washington II. In February 1769 a Betcy Washington was at Mount Vernon with Warner Washington and his wife. Augustine II mentions in his will (1758) a daughter Betsey.

BETSY WASHINGTON; married Nathan Smith, April 4, 1790, in King George County, Va.

BUSHROD (1762-1829), son of John Augustine and Hannah Bushrod Washington; married 1785 Julia Anne Blackburn; in 1798 was made associate justice of the U. S. Supreme Court. He inherited Mount Vernon under the will of his uncle, George Washington.

BUSHROD (1785-1830), son of William Augustine Washington and wife Jane Washington of Westmoreland County, Va.; married Henrietta Bryan Spotswood; had eight children; lived at Mt. Zephyr, near Mount Vernon, until his death in 1830.

BUSHROD CORBIN, born December 25, 1790, son of Corbin and Hannah Lee Washington; lived at Claymont, Jefferson County, Va., now W. Va.; died July 27, 1851; buried in Charles Town.

BUSHROD C., lieutenant in C.S.A. in 1864; said to have been living in Charles Town in 1889. In Charles Town is a tombstone inscribed "Bushrod Corbin Washington: 1831-19—: Interred Elmira, Washington." He was probably a son of Thomas B. Washington and a grandson of Bushrod C. Washington (1790-1851). Near his grave are tombstones to Catherine T. Blackburn (1840-1876) and Emma Allen (1864-1934), both wives of Bushrod C. Washington. Jefferson County records show a marriage of a B. C. Washington and Emma E. Willis, November 20, 1878. A picture of Lt. B. C. Washington may be found on page 359 of George Baylor's "Bull Run to Bull Run."

BUTLER, son of Augustine Washington I and his first wife, Jane Butler; born in 1716 or 1724; died in infancy.

BUTLER (W. Butler) was mentioned in Martha Washington's will (1802). A Butler Washington was quartermaster 2 months and 21 days in the 25th regiment, Va. militia, commanded by Lt.-Col. Austin Smith, in the service of the United States from July 14 to 27, 1813, and July 20 to October 8, 1814.

B. C. Washington, formerly of Charles Town, W. Va., on October 20, 1934, married Mrs. Ruby McDonald Stringer, formerly of Shepherdstown, W. Va., in North Carolina. Was living, November 1934, in Walnut Cove, N. C.

Catherine, wife of John Washington, uncle of George. She was born Whiting and was the mother of Warner Washington (1715-1791), of Fairfield, who had a son named Whiting.

Catherine, daughter of John Washington and wife Catherine Whiting; was the first wife of Col. Fielding Lewis of Fredericksburg.

Catherine—See Katherine Washington, born January 13, 1740/41.

Catherine, born Storke; married Bailey Washington in King George County, Va., January 12, 1749.

Catherine, daughter of Henry Washington of Middlesex County, Va. Henry, who had a brother Warner, made his will December 29, 1763, and therein named Catherine, who was under 21.

Catherine, wife of Lawrence Washington; married in King George County, Va., October 5, 1774. She was born Foote. Her Lawrence was probably Lawrence Jr. of Chotank.

Catherine, daughter of Warner Washington of Fairfield; married John Nelson in Frederick County, Va., November 3, 1789; was living in May 1802 when her mother made her will.

Catherine T. Blackburn (1840-1876), wife of Bushrod Corbin Washington; buried in Charles Town.

Catherine Campbell, daughter of Thomas B. and Rebecca J. Washington; died August 20, 1817, aged 1 year, 10 months, and 22 days.

Cecelia P., daughter of Henry Thacker Washington I; married Edwin B. Burwell, March 15, 1822, in Jefferson County, Va. She was probably Cecelia Peyton Washington who later married John W. Owen and died at Woodland, Clarke County, Va., October 16, 1841; buried at Old Chapel, Clarke County, Va.

Cecil Wood, born 1858, son of Dr. Lawrence A. and Martha D. Shrewsbury Washington.

Charles, born May 2, 1738, son of Augustine I and Mary Ball Washington; married Mildred Thornton, daugher of Col. Francis Thornton, of Spotsylvania County, Va. Charles in 1765, 1769, 1773, etc., was a magistrate in Spotsylvania County, Va. In 1784 (and earlier) he was living in Berkeley County, the part now Jefferson County, W. Va. He laid out Charles Town on his land. His will was probated September 23, 1799.

Charles, son of George Fayette Washington and wife Anna; mentioned in his father's will, which was made October 19, 1865, and proved in Winchester January 1868. June 8, 1867, a Charles Washington married Mary Ross in Jefferson County, W. Va.

Charles Augustine, son of George Augustine and wife Frances Bassett, who were married at Mount Vernon in 1785; he died, it is said, at Cadiz, unmarried.

CHRISTIAN MARIA, born at Harewood December 16, 1826, daughter of Dr. Samuel Washington; married Richard B. Washington; died at Harewood June 10, 1895; buried in Charles Town.

CHRISTINE MARIA, born June 13, 1858, at Blakely, daughter of Richard B. Washington and wife Christian M.; died May 15, 1937; buried in Charles Town.

CORBIN, born 1765, son of John Augustine Washington I and wife Hannah Bushrod; married Hannah Lee, daughter of Richard Henry Lee; lived at Walnut Farm, Westmoreland County, Va.; had four sons; made his will October 19, 1799, in Fairfax County, Va.; will probated April 21, 1800.

CORBIN THOMAS, son of Corbin (1765-1800) and wife Hannah Lee Washington; had brothers Richard Henry Lee, John Augustine (II), and Bushrod Corbin, and sisters Jane Mildred and Mary Lee Washington. By his mother's will, made June 17, 1800, he inherited her home, Selby, in Fairfax County, Va.

DEWITT N., son of Thomas and Julia Washington of Augusta County, Va.; born Sept. 12, 1852; married December 9, 1874, Addie C. Rhinehart, daughter of Isaac and Susan, in Rockingham County, Va., where he lived and died April 8, 1918.

EDWARD, December 12, 1739, obtained a patent for 614 acres on Pignut Ridge, supposed to be in Fauquier County, Va. In 1746 or soon thereafter an Edward Washington acquired Belmont, home of Catesby Cocke, on Occoquan Creek. Belmont, since 1742, has been in Fairfax County. On June 30, 1791, an Edward Washington of Fairfax County made his will, which was probated September 18, 1792.

EDWARD, son of Edward Washington who made his will in Fairfax County in 1791. This Edward, also of Fairfax County, on April 8, 1813, made his will, in which he names his sons: John, Edward Sandford, George William, and Joseph Hough, and daughters: Margaret Sandford, Mary Ann, and Elizabeth Catherine; a niece Peggy Sandford, a nephew John H. Manley, and an aunt Sarah Washington; will probated June 21, 1813.

EDWARD, perhaps EDWARD CARTER, born November 9, 1834, in Hampshire County, now W. Va., son of George William Washington and wife Sally A Wright; married Susan Ann Taylor, daughter of William; died June 2, 1901; buried in Romney.

EDWARD SANDFORD, son of Edward Washington of Fairfax County, Va., who died in 1813. He had a sister Margaret Sandford (Sanford), and their mother was doubtless a Sandford, though apparently she was not living in April 1813, when Edward Washington made his will.

ELEANOR, wife of John Washington, married in King George County, Va., December 24, 1787. She was born Massey.

ELEANOR ANN, daughter of George Corbin Washington (1789-1854) and his first wife, Eliza Beall, of Georgetown, Md.

ELEANOR BLACKBURN, daughter of Bushrod C. Washington Jr., born December 15, 1896; married Stuart Kean Joice; died August 13, 1920; buried in Charles Town.

ELEANOR LOVE SELDEN, wife of Col. John A. Washington (1821-1861) of Mount Vernon, was born April 12, 1824; married 1842; died October 9, 1860, at Waveland. Buried in Charles Town. Her husband, John A. Washington III, was the last Washington owner of Mount Vernon.

ELEANOR SELDEN, daughter of John A. Washington III; born at Mount Vernon in 1856, one of seven children—the youngest of five daughters. She married Julian Smith Howard of Warsaw, Va., May 5, 1880; died in Alexandria November 8, 1937; buried in Charles Town.

ELEANOR THOMAS, born Blackburn October 22, 1844; married Thomas B. Washington (1851-1923); died September 1, 1921; buried in Charles Town.

ELIZA, daughter of William Augustine Washington and wife Jane Washington, daughter of John Augustine I; married Gen. Alexander Spotswood, grandson of Gov. Alexander Spotswood and a soldier of the Revolution. Probably the same as Elizabeth, wife of Alexander Spotswood.

ELIZA, daughter of Thomas Beall of Georgetown; the first wife of George Corbin Washington (1789-1854).

ELIZA SELDEN, daughter of John A. Washington III and wife Eleanor Love Selden of Mount Vernon, born July 17, 1848. She was the second wife of Maj. R. W. Hunter; died August 28, 1909; buried in Charles Town.

ELIZABETH, born Lund; wife of Townshend Washington, married December 22, 1726, in King George County, Va. She had a number of children, among them Lund Washington, born October 21, 1737.

ELIZABETH, daughter of John Washington and wife Catherine Whiting; sister to Henry Washington of Middlesex County, Va.; died unmarried at the age of 20.

ELIZABETH, daughter of Henry Washington of Middlesex, who made his will December 29, 1763, and therein named Elizabeth, then under 21.

ELIZABETH, wife of Henry Washington Jr.; married May 18, 1743, in King George County, Va. She was born Storke.

ELIZABETH, daughter of Col. William Macon of New Kent County, Va.; first wife of Warner Washington (1715-1791) of Fairfield.

ELIZABETH, wife of Lawrence Washington, who died in Westmoreland County, Va., in 1740. This Lawrence named in his will (probated June 24, 1740) his wife Elizabeth and sons John, James, and Thomas.

ELIZABETH, daughter of Augustine Washington II; wife of Alexander Spotswood, son of John, who was a son of Gov. Alexander Spotswood. She had seven children. Her father in his will, probated May 25, 1762, in Westmoreland County, Va., calls her Betsey. She was probably the same as Eliza, wife of Gen. Alexander Spotswood.

ELIZABETH, born Dade, married Lawrence Washington in King George County, Va., July 31, 1751. On January 4, 1758, George, a son of Lawrence and Elizabeth Washington, was born in King George County, Va.

ELIZABETH, second child and first daughter of Augustine Washington I and his second wife, Mary Ball, was born at Wakefield, June 20, 1733. In 1750 or 1751 she married Col. Fielding Lewis of Fredericksburg (his second wife). She lived at Kenmore, in Fredericksburg; had a number of children; died March 31, 1797; buried at Western View, Culpeper County, Va. She was known as Betty.

ELIZABETH, daughter of Capt. John Washington, born in King George County, Va., December 21, 1737, was probably the Elizabeth Washington who married Thomas Berry in the same county, November 18, 1758.

ELIZABETH, born Foote, was the wife and widow of Lund Washington (1737-1796). She lived at Hayfield, near Alexandria. George Washington in his will (1799) left her a ring; Martha Washington in her will (1802) left her five guineas. Elizabeth made her will December 16, 1810; probated June 18, 1812. She apparently had no children, but recognized nephews and nieces.

ELIZABETH, born Washington, married John Buckner in King George County, Va., December 11, 1760.

ELIZABETH, daughter of Lawrence Washington, who died in Westmoreland County, Va., in 1774. In December 1773, when Lawrence made his will, his daughter was Elizabeth Storke. She had a sister Katy and a brother Henry. Was her husband William Storke? See *William and Mary Quarterly*, April, 1939, page 189.

ELIZABETH, daughter of Warner Washington of Fairfield, was named in his will, November 1789, when she was still under 21. On June 11, 1795, Elizabeth Washington, presumably the foregoing, married George Booth in Frederick County, Va. She and her sister Louisa both probably died prior to 1802, since they are not mentioned in the will of their mother, Hannah Fairfax Washington, made in 1802.

ELIZABETH, daughter of Warner Washington II, who made his will in Frederick County, Va., July 7, 1826. Therein he mentions Elizabeth.

ELIZABETH, born Coates, wife of George Washington (1775-1815); probably of Westmoreland County, Va.

ELIZABETH, granddaughter of William Augustine Washington of Westmoreland County, Va., who married John E. Wilson in 1856.

ELIZABETH C., wife of John Thornton Augustine Washington; born September 27, 1793; died October 21, 1837; buried at Harewood.

ELIZABETH C., daughter of R. B. and C. M. Washington; born August 21, 1845; married George H Flagg; outlived him 11 years and died October 3, 1911; buried in Charles Town.

ELIZABETH CATHARINE, daughter of Edward Washington of Fairfax County, Va., who made his will April 8, 1813. She had two sisters and four brothers. Her mother was probably a Sandford (Sanford).

ELIZABETH FISHER, artist; born in Lehigh Valley, Pa., daughter of George Lafayette Washington and wife Ann Bull Clemson; established her studio in Philadelphia in 1913.

ELIZABETH W., evidently a daughter of Warner Washington II. She had brothers Fairfax, Reade, Herbert, and Hamilton. On November 17, 1837, Hamilton deeded to Elizabeth W. 1 acre and 17 poles of land at or near Berryville. On September 2, 1882, Elizabeth made her will, which was proved in Clarke County court in February, 1883.

ELLA M., daughter of George Washington Bassett and his wife Betty Lewis; born at Eltham, New Kent County, Va.; was the second wife of Col. Lewis William Washington of Jefferson County, W. Va. She died in New York January 17, 1898; buried in Charles Town.

EMMA ALLEN (1864-1934); apparently the 2d wife of Lt. Bushrod Corbin Washington (1831-19—); buried in Charles Town.

EMMA TELL, daughter of Lawrence A. Washington and wife Dorcas Wood; died November 9, 1838, aged 26; buried near Wheeling.

EMMA TELL, born in 1849; daughter of Dr. Lawrence A. Washington and wife Martha D. Shrewsbury.

EUGENIA, daughter of William Temple and Margaret C. Washington; born in Jefferson County, W. Va.; went to D. C. in 1867; died unmarried in D. C. November 30, 1899; buried in Fredericksburg.

EUPHAN, born February 1, 1790, daughter of Bailey Washington and wife Euphan Wallace of Stafford County, Va.; married (1) John Macrae of Prince William County, Va.; (2) William Storke Jr. of Fredericksburg; died February 1, 1847. See *William and Mary College Quarterly*, April, 1939, page 189.

FAIRFAX, son of Warner Washington I, of Fairfield; was under 21 in November 1789 when Warner made his will; was living May 14, 1802, when his mother, Hannah Fairfax Washington, made her will at Fairfield, Frederick County, Va. On October 15, 1798, Fairfax Washington and Alexander Balmain gave bond in Frederick County for Fairfax to marry Sarah Armistead.

FAIRFAX, son of Warner Washington II. The latter made his will in Frederick County, Va., July 7, 1826, and therein mentioned his son Fairfax with others, Reade, Herbert, and Hamilton

FERDINAND, son of Col. Samuel Washington and his 4th wife, Anne Steptoe (widow of Willoughby Allerton when she married Washington); born in King George County, Va., July 16, 1767; died in Lancaster or New Kent County, Va. in 1788.

FRANCES Washington; married Charles Stuart in Stafford (now King George) County, Va., February 23, 1751-52. On October 20, 1731, was born Frances, daughter of John and Mary Washington, in King George County.

FRANCES (1763-1815), daughter of Col. Charles Washington (1738-1799) and his wife, Mildred Thornton; married Col. Burgess Ball in 1781—his second wife. She is called Frances Ball in the will of her brother, George Augustine Washington, January 24, 1793.

FRANCES, born Frances Townshend Washington, August 18, 1767; daughter of Lawrence and Elizabeth Washington of King George County, Va.; married Thornton Washington April 2, 1786, his second wife. He died about September 1787. She had a son Samuel when Thornton made his will, July 26, 1787; probated October 16, 1787. On June 14, 1788, Frances Townshend Washington married Griffin Stith in King George County, Va.

FRANCES, daughter of Col. Burwell Bassett; married George Augustine Washington at Mount Vernon, October 15, 1785; had children George Fayette, Charles Augustine, and Maria; was living January 24, 1793, when her husband made his will in Fairfax County, Va.

FRANCES Washington, married William Tapscott, February 1, 1789; record in Winchester. Could this have been Frances Townshend Washington, widow of Thornton Washington? See above.

FRANCES Washington, married William Snickers, June 4, 1793; record in Winchester. Written consent was given by Warner Washington (probably Warner II), father of Frances.

FRANCES GERARD, daughter of Dr. Thomas Gerard and wife Susanna Snow; married five times. She, as the Widow Appleton, became the 3d wife of Col. John Washington (1632-1676); he was her 4th husband.

FRANCES TOWNSHEND, born Washington; married Griffin Stith in King George County, Va., June 14, 1788. She may have been the widow of Thornton Washington of Berkeley County, Va., who died in the autumn of 1787. See above.

FRANCIS WHITING, son of Warner and Ariana Washington; under 21 in 1819; died prior to September 25, 1833.

GEORGE, born 1700? On September 28, 1730, King George II, by his governor, William Gooch, granted to George Washington of Isle of Wight County, Va., 235 acres lying between Nottoway Swamp and the Flag Swamp, on the north side of Nottoway River, in Isle of Wight County; corner to said Washington's other land; adjoining Richard Drake. See Va. Patent Book 13, page 515, in Richmond.

GEORGE, born February 22, 1732, at Wakefield, Westmoreland County, Va., son of Augustine Washington I and his second wife, Mary Ball; married Mrs. Martha Dandridge Custis, probably at the White House, New Kent County, Va., January 6, 1759; died at Mount Vernon, December 14, 1799.

GEORGE Washington appears as a justice in King George County, Va., between 1760 and 1770. On November 22, 1762, and November 24, 1766, he is named with the notation "removed." This was probably George Washington of Mount Vernon. In 1782 "General Washington" was listed as head of a family of two white souls, besides himself, and 188 blacks in Fairfax County; in 1785 "Genl. Geo. Washington" was listed as head of a family of 30 white souls besides himself, and as owning 39 dwellings and 21 other buildings, in the same (Fairfax) county; and the same year (1785) "Genl. George Washington" was listed as head of a family of 6 white souls besides himself, and as owning one dwelling and 10 others buildings in Stafford County. See "Heads of Families," first census of the United States, 1790, state enumerations of Virginia from 1782 to 1785, pages 17, 85, 108.

GEORGE, son of Lawrence Washington of Chotank and wife Elizabeth (Dade?); born in King George County, Va., January 4, 1758; died young.

GEORGE, born February 16, 1762, son of Augustine Washington II and wife Jane; named in the will of his father, probated in Westmoreland County, Va., May 25, 1762.

GEORGE (1775-1815), great-grandson of John Washington (1661-1698) ; married Elizabeth Coates. They had a daughter Selena Washington, born October 15, 1808.

GEORGE (1806-1831), youngest son of George Steptoe Washington; died October 13, 1831; buried in Charles Town.

GEORGE, son of Col. John Washington (1800-1850) of Caroline County, Va., and wife Ann Hawes; born January 23, 1821; married Mildred Chandler, daughter of Thomas Coleman Chandler, April 4, 1851; had children: John, superintendent of schools of Caroline County; George, who married Agnes Wirt; and others; died August 6, 1889.

GEORGE, son of George Washington (1821-1889) of Caroline County, Va.; married Agnes Wirt, daughter of Dr. William Wirt of Wirtland, Westmoreland County, Va.

GEORGE, born February 22, 1842, son of Thomas B. Washington, who was a son of Bushrod C. Washington; died June 30, 1863; buried in Charles Town.

GEORGE, born about 1845 at Ridgedale, Hampshire County, Va., now W. Va., son of George William Washington and wife Sally A Wright; had a wife Ann in January 1879; went to Kansas.

GEORGE, born July 22, 1858, son of Col. John A. Washington of Mount Vernon and wife Eleanor Love Selden; married Serena Porterfield, daughter of Col. George Porterfield; died in Charles Town December 31, 1905. Rev. Richard Blackburn Washington of Hot. Springs, Va., 1938, is a son.

GEORGE AUGUSTINE (1763-1793), son of Charles Washington (1738-1799) and wife Mildred Thornton; married Frances Bassett, daughter of Col Burwell Bassett, October 15, 1785; was an officer in the Virginia Line in the Revolution. He made his will in Fairfax County, Va., January 24, 1793; names therein his wife Frances; sons George Fayette and Charles Augustine; daughter Maria; his sister Frances Ball; sister Mildred Washington; brother Samuel; his father and mother (both then living, evidently) ; his aunt, Martha Washington; and his uncle, President of the United States. His will was proved July 15, 1793. He was manager at Mount Vernon, 1789-1793.

GEORGE CORBIN, son of William Augustine Washington, who was a son of Augustine II; inherited Wakefield and in 1813 sold it to John Gray. He then (1813) was residing in Georgetown. He was born August 20, 1789; married (1) Eliza Beall, daughter of Thomas Beall of Georgetown, in 1807; (2) Ann Thomas Beall Peter; was a member of Congress from Maryland, 1827-1833 and 1835-1837; died in Georgetown July 17, 1854. Was the father of Col. Lewis W. Washington of Beallair.

GEORGE FAYETTE (1790-1867), son of George Augustine Washington and wife Frances Bassett; lived at Waverly, 7 miles northeast of Winchester, Frederick County, Va.; made his will October 19, 1865, and therein named his wife Anna and sons Charles and Matthew Burwell Bassett Washington; will proved in January 1868. His wife was Maria (probably Anna Maria) Frame (1793-1860).

GEORGE ROBERT Washington died in Washington City May 15, 1939, aged 64 wife Edna Welty; sons John and George Robert Jr.; daughter Mrs. George M Miller of Baltimore.

GEORGE STEPTOE (1774?-1809), son of Col. Samuel and his 4th wife, Anne Steptoe (Widow Allerton); married Lucy Payne, sister to Dolly Payne Todd (later Madison) about 1793; lived at Harewood; died in Georgia—buried there. On August 27, 1793, his wife, Lucy Payne, was disowned by the Friends for marrying out of meeting. Her sister, Dolly Payne Todd, and James Madison were married at Harewood, September 15, 1794.

GEORGE S., born November 3, 1900; died September 15, 1901; buried in Charles Town.

GEORGE WILLIAM, born September 15, 1809, son of Edward of Fairfax County, Va., who made his will April 8, 1813; probated June 21, 1813. Edward's wife was probably a Sanford. George William married Sally A. Wright of Loudoun County about 1830 and soon thereafter settled in Hampshire County, now W. Va. His home is well known as Ridgedale, 5 miles north of Romney. He died February 6, 1876; buried in Indian Mound Cemetery, Romney.

GRAY Washington in December 1799 was living in Brunswick County, Va., when he signed a petition to the Virginia General Assembly with Thomas Washington, Benjamin Harrison, Willy Harrison, Robert Harrison, Burwell Willis, and Edward Branch. See the petition in the Archives Division, Virginia State Library, Richmond.

HAMILTON, son of Warner Washington II, who on July 7, 1826, made his will in Frederick County, Va., and therein named his sons Hamilton, Reade, Fairfax, and Herbert. See Elizabeth W. Washington.

HAMPTON H., son of Thomas and Julia Washington of Augusta County, Va., married Ann C. Baker, daughter of James and Anna, in Rockingham County, Va., October 21, 1873.

HANNAH, second wife of Warner Washington 1, of Fairfield. She was the daughter of William Fairfax; lived at Belvoir on the Potomac with her brother George William Fairfax till her marriage in 1765. She is named in her husband's will (1789) and in George's will (1799). She made her will May 14, 1802, and therein named her daughters Mildred Throckmorton, Hannah Whiting, and Catharine Nelson, and her sons Fairfax and Whiting. Her will was proved in Winchester, September 3, 1804.

HANNAH, wife of John Augustine Washington I (1736-1787); daughter of Col. John Bushrod of Bushfield. She was living July 9, 1799, when her brother-in-law, General Washington, made his will.

HANNAH, wife of Corbin Washington (1765-1800); daughter of Richard Henry Lee. She, on June 17, 1800, soon after Corbin's death, made her will, wherein she mentions her late husband, Corbin Washington, her sons, Richard Henry Lee, John Augustine (II), Bushrod Corbin, and Corbin Thomas Washington; her daughters, Jane Mildred and Molly Lee Washington; her brothers, Cissius Lee (deceased) and Thomas Lee Sr. of Prince William County, Va.; her sisters, Anne, Elizabeth, and Sarah Lee, and Harriet Turberville. Her home was Selby, Fairfax County, Va. She desired to be buried at Bushfield, with her husband.

HANNAH FAIRFAX, daughter of Warner Washington 1 and his 2d wife, Hannah Fairfax, of Fairfield; married in Frederick County, Va., June 10, 1788, Peter Beverly Whiting of Gloucester County, Va.; died in 1828; buried at Old Chapel, Clarke County, Va.

Hannah Fairfax, daughter of Perrin Washington of Washington, D. C.; died August 19, 1856; buried at Old Chapel.

Hannah M., "child of Dr. Henry Washington, of Berryville"; died in 1822; buried at Old Chapel.

Harriet, born 1776 at Harewood, daughter of Col. Samuel Washington and his 4th wife Anne Steptoe, Widow Allerton; married Andrew Parks of Baltimore, July 4, 1796; in 1816 moved to Kanawha Salines, now Malden, five miles above Charleston, W. Va. A letter from General Washington, October 10, 1790, states that she had just turned 14. Acknowledgment to Roy Bird Cook, Charleston, W. Va.

Harriet Ann, daughter of Warner and Ariana Washington; married William Garrett Jr. and was living in Montgomery County, Ala., in 1833.

Helen Ames Washington, of Overbrook, Pa., queen of the apple blossom festival at Winchester in 1932, is a granddaughter of Richard Blackburn Washington Jr., of Jefferson County, W. Va., who was a grandson of John Augustine Washington II, of Blakely and Mount Vernon. Helen is a daughter of George Lafayette Washington and wife Catherine Ames of Boston. Catherine's sister, Marie Ames, married Admiral R. E. Byrd.

Henrietta E. C., daughter of John Cobb Washington of Lenoir County, N. C., in 1855 married Col. John Lewis Peyton of Staunton, Va.

Henry, son of John Washington (died 1697) and wife Ann Wickliffe (died 1704), had brothers Lawrence, John, and Nathaniel, named in their father's will which was made in Westmoreland County, Va., January 22, 1697; probated February 22, 1697. Henry received personal property and land in Stafford County. He married Mary Bailey and had sons John, Henry (died 1745), Nathaniel (1726-1745), and Bailey. He made his will in 1747; died October 22, 1748. Was a justice in Stafford County, 1731-1745; was known as "Capt. Henry Washington."

Henry, brother to Warner I; born at Bridges Creek, Westmoreland County, Va., about 1718, son of John Washington and wife Katherine Whiting of Gloucester County, Va.; married Anne, daughter of Colonel Thacker of Middlesex County, Va. Henry made his will in Middlesex County, December 29, 1763; mentions therein his wife (not named); names his children: Elizabeth, Catherine, Ann, all under 21, and son Thacker; names his brother Warner as one of five executors.

Henry, son of Townshend and Elizabeth Washington, born in King George County, Va., August 29, 1742.

Henry, son of Bailey and Catherine Storke Washington, born December 5, 1749, in King George County, Va.

Henry, son of Lawrence Washington and wife Susannah (Jett?) of Westmoreland County, Va. Lawrence made his will in 1773; probated March 29, 1774. Henry had sisters Elizabeth Stork and Katy Washington.

Henry, son of John and Catherine Washington, born in King George County, Va., October 26, 1760. John and Catherine were married in King George County December 23, 1759. Henry married Mildred Pratt in King George County March 12, 1779. In April 1785 a Henry Washington of King George County married

Ann Quarles, spinster, of Albemarle County, Va. In 1788 a Henry Washington died in Albemarle. On February 12, 1799, a Henry Washington was at Mount Vernon.

HENRY: Dr. Henry Washington of Berryville, Clarke County, Va., had a daughter, Hannah M. Washington, who died in 1822 and was buried at Old Chapel, near Millwood. He also had a son, John Cary Washington, who died in 1825 and was buried at Old Chapel.

HENRY AUGUSTINE, son of Lawrence Washington and wife Sarah Tayloe, was born at Haywood, Westmoreland County, Va., August 24, 1820; graduated at Princeton in 1839; studied law in Fredericksburg; was professor of history, political economy, and international law at William and Mary. In 1853 he prepared for the press "A Digest of the Laws, Customs, Manners, and Institutions of the Ancient and Modern Nations," by Thomas R. Dew (1802-1846); also the writings of Thomas Jefferson, published in 8 volumes, 1853-1855. He married, at Williamsburg, July 8, 1852, Cynthia Beverley Tucker; had two children, who died young. He died in Washington, D. C., February 28, 1858. Acknowledgment to Miss Anne Madison Washington. Bishop John Johns wrote a memoir of him which was published in 1859.

HENRY JR., son of Henry Washington (died 1748) and wife Mary Bailey; married Elizabeth Storke, May 18, 1743, in King George County, Va.; died in 1745.

HENRY M. (Col.), born in Fauquier County, Va., was governor of New Mexico Territory; drowned in Delaware Bay. See Fauquier Historical Society Bulletin.

HENRY STEPHENS, geologist, was born January 15, 1867, at Newark, N. J., son of George and Eleanor P. Stephens Washington; graduated at Yale 1886; Ph.D. of Leipzig 1893; died January 7, 1934.

HENRY THACKER I, son of Thacker (son of Henry of Middlesex); married Amelia Stith, daughter of Robert Stith and Mary Townshend Washington. In 1826 Henry Thacker Washington I had four children: Henry Thacker II (1802-1855), Cecelia Washington Burwell, Amelia Stith Washington, and Putnam Stith Washington.

HENRY THACKER II, born January 18,1802; married Virginia Grymes (1812-1871) of Eagle's Nest, daughter of William Fitzhugh Grymes. He about 1830 acquired Windsor, in King George County, Va.; had several children, among them William Henry and John Peyton Washington.

HENRY THACKER III, son of Warner and Ariana Washington; was still under 21, September 25, 1833.

HERBERT, son of Warner Washington II; named in Warner's will, made in Frederick County, Va., July 7, 1826, with Reade, Fairfax, and Hamilton Washington.

HORACE LEE, foreign service officer; born in Washington City June 4, 1864, son of Richard and Kate Lee Washington; married Helen Stuart Williams, September 22, 1897.

JAMES of Surry County, Va., in 1732 received a patent for 225 acres on the south side of the main Clark Water Swamp, in Surry County, and another patent for 140 acres on the south side of the main Clark Water Swamp in Isle of Wight County, Va. See Virginia Patent Book 14, pages 502, 519. Lawrence Washington, who died in Westmoreland County, Va., in 1740 had a son James; also sons John and Thomas and wife Elizabeth

JAMES A., physician, in 1839; apparently in Philadelphia or New York.

JAMES BARROLL, major C.S.A.; son of Col. Lewis W. Washington of Beallair and his first wife, Mary Ann Barroll; married Jane Bretney Lanier; had a son William Lanier Washington. He was at Wakefield in 1882—was the last Washington owner of the Wakefield estate.

JAMES C., son of Thomas B. Washington (who was a son of Bushrod C. Washington); born September 14, 1847; died February 28, 1865; buried in Charles Town. Items regarding him on pages 301-303 of George Baylor's "Bull Run to Bull Run."

JAMES TURNER, born 1847, son of Dr. Lawrence A. Washington and wife Martha D. Shrewsbury.

JANE, daughter of Caleb Butler and wife Mary Foxhall; was the first wife of Augustine Washington I (1694-1743). On her tombstone at Wakefield (Bridges Creek) it is stated that she was born December 21, 1699, and died November 24, 1729.

JANE (1722-1735), daughter of Augustine Washington I and his first wife, Jane Butler; died January 17 (probably Old Style), 1735.

JANE, daughter of Col. John Champe of King George County, Va.; was the first wife of Col. Samuel Washington (1734-1781), brother to George.

JANE, a granddaughter of Colonel Ashton; second wife of Augustine Washington II (1720-1762), who made his will in Westmoreland County, Va., September 18, 1758. At that time he had a son William Augustine under 21, and daughters Betsey, Nancy, and Jane. On February 16, 1762, he added a codicil, speaking of his wife being delivered of a son named George; will probated May 25, 1762.

JANE, daughter of Augustine Washington II; named in her father's will, 1758. She married John Thornton, son of Francis.

JANE, oldest child of John Augustine I and wife Hannah Bushrod; married William Augustine Washington I, son of Augustine II and his first wife Ann Aylett; died 1791, leaving four children.

JANE, daughter of William Temple Washington and wife Margaret C. Fletcher of Meg-Willy; married Moncure.

JANE CHARLOTTE, daughter of Col. Richard S. Blackburn; married John Augustine Washington II in 1811. The latter inherited Mount Vernon from his uncle, Judge Bushrod Washington. Bishop Meade speaks of the widow, Jane Charlotte, living at Mount Vernon in 1839, but she also kept up an establishment at Blakeley, where she was living in 1854 when she made her will.

JANE CHARLOTTE, daughter of John Augustine Washington III and wife Eleanor Selden; born at Mount Vernon May 26, 1846; married Nathaniel Hite Willis; died August 7, 1924, in Charles Town; there buried.

JANE MILDRED, daughter of Corbin Washington (1765-1800) and wife Hannah Lee; named in her mother's will, made at Selby, Fairfax County, Va., June 17, 1800. Jane Mildred had a sister, Molly Lee Washington, and brothers R. Henry Lee, John A. (II), Bushrod C., and Corbin Thomas Washington.

JANE WRAY, daughter of Nedham Langhorne Washington, son of Lawrence (born 1728) of Chotank. She was named in her father's will, 1833.

JANET, wife in 1934 of Dr. Richard Washington of Claymount, Westmoreland County, Va. Born Latané?

JEANNIE K., daughter of Rev. C. E. and S. W. Ambler; born February 8, 1862; wife of John A. Washington (1847-1923); died July 4, 1891; buried in Charles Town.

JOHN, immigrant; born in England in 1632/33, son of Lawrence, who was born in 1602; great-grandfather of George; came to Virginia in 1656. In 1664 he purchased land in Westmoreland County, at Bridges Creek, where he lived thereafter. In 1674 he and Nicholas Spencer patented 5,000 acres on Hunting Creek— his half included the Mount Vernon tract. This land he devised to his son Lawrence, who left it to his daughter Mildred; she sold it to her brother Augustine I, George's father; from the latter it descended to Lawrence (1718-1752), who willed it to his half-brother George. John was a colonel of Virginia militia; was called by the Indians Conotocarious, "Destroyer of Villages," as George was in 1754. John's first wife was Ann Pope, who was the mother of all his children (5), two of whom died before him; the others were Lawrence, John, and Ann. He married (2) Widow Anne Brett; (3) Widow Frances Appleton. He made his will September 21, 1675; probated January 10, 1677.

JOHN (Jr.) (1663-1697/98), son of John Washington the immigrant; married Ann Wickliffe and had children: Lawrence, John, Nathaniel, Henry; Anne, who married Wright, and another daughter who married Lewis. He lived in his father's house, east of Bridges Creek, near the family cemetery; made his will January 22, 1697; probated February 22, 1697/98.

JOHN (I) (1668-1721), of Chotank, son of Lawrence Washington and his 2d wife, the Widow Fleming; married Mary Townshend, daughter of Robert, in Westmoreland County, Va., 1686; had sons John and Townshend. John (I) was guardian of his cousin Lawrence's children, John, Augustine, and Mildred. They grew up at Chotank, now Waterloo.

JOHN (II), Capt.; son of John Washington (I) and wife Mary Townshend; inherited Chotank; married Mary Massey, daughter of Dade, 1721; had a number of children, among them, Anne, born 1723; Mary, born February 28, 1726; Lawrence, born March 31, 1728; Frances, born October 20, 1731; John (1734-1736); Elizabeth, born December 21, 1737; Katherine, born January 13, 1740/41; Sarah, born October 28, 1742. Capt. John Washington died in King George County, Va., February 27, 1742.

JOHN, born 1692 at Bridges Creek, son of Lawrence Washington (1659-1698) and wife Mildred Warner; married Catherine Whiting; had children: Warner

(1715-1791); Catherine, first wife of Fielding Lewis of Fredericksburg; Elizabeth, who died unmarried; Henry, who married Anne Thacker; and others.

JOHN, son of John Washington (1663-1698) and wife Anne Wickliffe; named in his father's will made in Westmoreland County, Va., January 22, 1697; to have the home plantation after his mother, Anne.

JOHN, of Dismal Swamp; was with George Washington in that region in October 1768. See Washington's Diaries, 1925 edition, Vol. I, page 296.

JOHN; at Mount Vernon, with a Miss Terrett, June 17, 1773. George Washington in his diary calls him "Lame Jno. Washington."

JOHN, November 23, 1738, married Margaret Storke in Stafford or King George County, Va. On December 9, 1748, in King George County, was born William, son of John and Margaret Washington. See *William and Mary College Quarterly*, January 1933, pages 32, 33.

JOHN, November 17, 1749, married Betty Massey in Stafford, now King George County, Va. See *William and Mary College Quarterly*, January 1933, page 30. In Stafford County, perhaps the part now King George, a John Washington was a justice in 1766, 1767, 1768, 1772, and 1773, and sheriff in 1766.

JOHN (1730-1782), son of Henry Washington (1694-1748) and wife Mary Bailey, of Stafford County, Va., married Katherine Washington, December 23, 1759; lived at Hylton, King George County; had 12 children, among them Ann, born 1761, who married Thomas Hungerford. See the next item.

. JOHN, son of Townshend and Elizabeth Lund Washington, born March 14, 1740, in King George County, Va.; had a twin brother Lawrence. Possibly it was this John who married Katherine Washington, December 23, 1759. See item above. In King George County were born children of John and Catherine Washington: Henry, October 26, 1760; Nathaniel, October 1, 1762; Mary, June 17, 1764. See *William and Mary College Quarterly*, January 1933, page 33. This John Washington is said to have been a captain in the Revolution, and to have died in service. Under date of February 12, 1799, Washington at Mount Vernon wrote in his diary, "Mr. Hen. Wash. came to dinnr." Fitzpatrick notes: "Probably a son of John Washington, who married his cousin Catherine Washington."

JOHN, son of Robert Washington, whose will was probated in Westmoreland County, Va., September 24, 1765. This John had a sister Sukey and was probably the John Washington who made his will July 3, 1785; probated in Westmoreland County June 26, 1787. His wife was Constant (Constantia); had children: John Terrett, William Henry, Thomas Lund, Robert Pitt, George, Louisa Hassaker Washington, Nancy Constantia, Sarah Harper (married), and Robert Townshend, dec'd. He appointed William Fitzhugh of Chatham and his nephew Henry Washington executors.

JOHN of Washington Parish and Westmoreland County, Va., September 12, 1798, made his will, wherein he named his son, George, his granddaughter Caty Storke Washington, and his son John. The will was proved March 25, 1805. The testator's wife, Elizabeth Washington, was executrix.

JOHN (Jr.) of Westmoreland County, September 8, 1802, made his will, wherein he named his brother George, his niece Caty Storke Washington, and his father, John Washington. The will was proved April 25, 1803.

JOHN married Eleanor Massey in King George County, Va., December 24, 1787. He may have been a son of the John Washington who married Betty Massey in 1749.

JOHN married Frances Baylor, January 16, 1799; record in Winchester.

JOHN (Col.) was born September 13, 1800, son of George Washington (1775-1815) and wife Elizabeth Coates, daughter of Dr. John Coates of Maryland. Col. John Washington married Ann Hawes (1803-1863) in King William County, Va., March 7, 1820; had children: George (1821-1889), Dorothea (1822-1849), Walker H. (1824-1911), and John (1827-1887); died September 20, 1850. His home was Woodpecker, Caroline County, Va.

JOHN, son of Lawrence of Virginia, settled in Pittsford, N. C.

JOHN of Newbern, N. C., was a son of John of Pittsford; married Eliza Cobb; had a son John Cobb Washington. See "Memoir of William Madison Peyton," by John Lewis Peyton, 1873, pages 335, 380-383.

JOHN, born April 17, 1827, son of Col. John Washington (1800-1850), married Roberta Bird Boyd, daughter of Robert Bird Boyd and wife Mary Pryor of King and Queen County, Va.; had children: Thomas Boyd, Mary, Walker Hawes, Dollie Beverley, Fanny Pryor, Eugene, and Roberta: died September 25, 1887. His home was Spring Hill, Caroline County, Va.

JOHN, son of George (1821-1889) and wife Mildred Chandler, married Nannie Taylor of Blenheim. He was for many years superintendent of schools of Caroline County, Va.

JOHN (Dr.) son of Samuel Walter Washington (1853-1923) and wife ———— Willis; has an older brother, Samuel Walter Washington.

JOHN AUGUSTINE (I), son of Augustine (I) and his second wife, Mary Ball; born January 13, 1736; married Hannah Bushrod, daughter of Col. John Bushrod of Bushfield, Westmoreland County, Va., in 1756; lived at Mount Vernon and Bushfield; had children: Jane, born 1758, Mildred, born 1760, Bushrod, born June 5, 1762, and Corbin (1765-1800); died in 1787.

JOHN AUGUSTINE (II), son of Corbin Washington and wife Hannah Lee; born in 1789. In 1811 he married Jane Charlotte Blackburn, daughter of Col. Richard S. Blackburn. He inherited Mount Vernon from his uncle, Judge Bushrod Washington, in 1829; had brothers R. H. Lee, Bushrod C., and Corbin Thomas Washington; died June 26, 1832.

JOHN AUGUSTINE (III), son of John Augustine Washington II, was born May 3, 1821, at Blakeley; married Eleanor Love Selden in 1842; was the last private owner of Mount Vernon; killed near Elkwater, Randolph County, now W. Va., September 13, 1861. Buried in Charles Town.

JOHN AUGUSTINE (IV), born May 27, 1847, son of Richard Blackburn Washington (1822-1910); died August 14, 1923; buried in Charles Town.

JOHN AUGUSTINE (V), eldest son of Lawrence Washington; born at Waveland, Fauquier County, Va.

JOHN AUGUSTINE (VI), born March 19, 1891, son of Richard Blackburn Washington Jr. (1856-1922); died October 5, 1928; buried in Charles Town.

JOHN CARY, "child of Dr. Henry Washington of Berryville." Died in 1825; buried at Old Chapel, Clarke County, Va.

JOHN COBB, of Lenoir, N. C.; member of N. C. secession convention in 1861; son of John Washington of Newbern, N. C., and wife Eliza Cobb.

JOHN HOOE, mentioned in the will of his uncle, William Washington, Westmoreland County, Va., 1786. He owned land in Westmoreland in 1796, 1813, etc.

JOHN MARSHALL, born in Virginia in October 1797; graduated from U. S. Military Academy in 1814; participated in the Seminole War, 1836-39. In the Mexican War he won distinction in the battle of Buena Vista; was a major; brevetted lt.-col.; was lost with the *San Francisco* off the capes of Delaware, December 24, 1853, when he, others officers, and 180 soldiers were drowned.

JOHN PERRIN, son of Col. Samuel Washington and his 5th wife, Susannah Perrin Holding; born in 1780 or 1781. A Perrin Washington married Farinda Fairfax in Jefferson County, Va., now W. Va., February 5, 1822.

JOHN PEYTON, son of Henry Thacker Washington (II) (1802-1855) and wife Virginia Grymes (1812-1871) of King George County, Va.

JOHN SHREWSBURY, born in 1845, son of Dr. Lawrence A. Washington and wife Martha D. Shrewsbury.

JOHN STITH, son of Warner and Ariana Washington; living in Montgomery County, Ala., in 1833.

JOHN T. On December 19, 1796, William H. Washington and wife Elizabeth of Fairfax County, Va., conveyed to John T. Washington of Westmoreland County 221 acres of land in Spotsylvania County, Va.

JOHN T., prior to January 8, 1810, joined in a deed of partition of lands, probably in Jefferson County, Va., with Lawrence Augustine Washington and George Steptoe Washington. Was he John Thornton Augustine Washington?

JOHN THORNTON AUGUSTINE, son of Thornton Washington, who was a son of Col. Samuel of Harewood. He was born May 20, 1783; lived at Cedar Lawn, near Harewood; died October 9, 1841; buried at Harewood.

JOSEPH EDWIN, born in Robertson County, Tenn., November 10, 1851, son of George Augustine Washington and wife Jane Smith; graduated at Georgetown College, D. C., in 1873; member of Congress from Tennessee, 1887-97; married Mary Bolling Kemp of Gloucester County, Va., January 15, 1879; died August 28, 1915. He was a descendant of John Washington of Surry County, Va.

JOSEPH HOUGH, son of Edward Washington of Fairfax County, Va., who made his will April 8, 1813. Joseph's mother was probably a Sandford (Sanford).

JOYCE, wife and widow of Lawrence Washington (1635-1676). She is said to have been a daughter of William Jones. She married (1) Anthony Hoskins; (2) Alexander Fleming; (3) Lawrence Washington; (4) James Yates. See *Virginia Magazine of History and Biography*, April, 1941, pages 191-193.

JULIA AUGUSTA (1830-1888), daughter of William Augustine Washington II; married Dabney Carr Wirt (1817-1893); no children; buried at Haywood.

JULIA WOOD, born in 1850, daughter of Dr. Lawrence A. Washington and wife Martha D. Shrewsbury.

JULIAN HOWARD, son of Lawrence Washington (1854-1920) and wife Fanny Lackland. Writing from Mount Vernon in 1938 and 1939, he supplied much information for this work. Grateful acknowledgment is made also to his sister, Miss Anne Madison Washington, of Washington City.

J. K. was a vestryman of St. Paul's Church in King George County, Va., about 1820. See Bishop Meade's "Old Churches, Ministers, and Families of Virginia," 1900, Vol. II, page 192.

J. TAYLOE, of Westmoreland County, Va., on July 4, 1844, read the Declaration of Independence at the Leedstown celebration. See Wright's "Westmoreland County, Virginia," 1912, page 140.

KATHERINE, daughter of Capt. John and Mary Washington; born January 13, 1740/41 in King George County, Va.; married John Washington, son of Henry (1694-1747) December 23, 1759; had children: Henry, born October 26, 1760; Nathaniel, born October 1, 1762; Mary, born June 17, 1764; all in King George County.

KATHERINE Washington Ward, daughter of Bushrod Washington of Charles Town, died in Spokane, Wash., July 2, 1940.

KATY came to Mount Vernon May 1, 1770, with Mrs. Bushrod. Toner thinks that she (Katy) was a daughter of Warner Washington. In December 1773, when Lawrence Washington made his will, probated in Westmoreland County, Va., 1774, he had a daughter Katy Washington; also a daughter Elizabeth Stork and a son Henry.

KITTY. On October 14, 1785, "Miss Kitty Washington" came to Mount Vernon with Miss Sally Ramsay, to be bridesmaid the next day at the wedding of Frances Bassett and George Augustine Washington. Kitty was at Mount Vernon occasionally in later years.

LAWRENCE, born at Sulgrave, England, in 1602; father of John and Lawrence, who came to Virginia.

LAWRENCE (1635-1676), born in England, son of Lawrence (born 1602); came in 1658 or 1659 to Virginia where his brother John had been already two or three years; returned to England and about 1660 married (1) Mary Jones, who never came to Virginia; neither did her daughter, Mary Washington, who married Rev. Edward Gibson. Lawrence married (2) in Virginia, about 1670, Joyce Fleming, widow of Alexander Fleming; her only daughter, Anne, died early; her son, John Washington I, established himself at Chotank. Lawrence's will, made in 1675, is recorded in Essex County, Va.; he is buried at Bridges Creek, Westmoreland County.

LAWRENCE (Major), eldest son of Col. John Washington and wife Ann Pope, born at Mattox, Westmoreland County, Va., September 1659; married Mildred Warner; had children: John, 1692; Augustine, 1694; Mildred, 1686. He inherited from his father land on which Mount Vernon later was built; had a brother John; his son Augustine was the father of George. Lawrence made his will March 11, 1697; died in March 1698; will probated in Westmoreland County, March 30, 1698.

LAWRENCE, son of John Washington and wife Anne Wickliffe; named in his father's will January 22, 1697; will probated February 22, 1697, in Westmoreland County, Va. In the same county a Lawrence Washington made his will February 5, 1739; probated June 24, 1740; therein named his wife Elizabeth, sons John, James, and Thomas.

Lawrence (1716?-1752), son of Augustine Washington I and his first wife, Jane Butler; in 1743 married Ann, eldest daughter of William Fairfax of Belvoir on the Potomac; lived at Mount Vernon, which he named; made his will June 20, 1752. At that time his wife Ann and daughter Sarah were living. He was a large landowner; had stock in five iron works in Virginia and Maryland; was a member of the Ohio Company; died July 26, 1752; will probated September 26, following.

LAWRENCE made his will December 4, 1773; probated in Westmoreland County, Va., March 29, 1774; wife Susannah (Jett?); daughters Elizabeth Stork and Katy Washington; son Henry; sisters Elizabeth, Ann, and Mary Jett and Peggy Skinker; brother-in-law William Stork Jett. (Fothergill, page 171.)

LAWRENCE (Sr.?) of Chotank, born March 31, 1728, son of Capt. John Washington (John II) and wife Mary Massey; married Elizabeth Dade July 31, 1751; had children: Lawrence, died 1809; Geeorge, born 1758, died young. Nedham Langhorne; Mary Townshend, married Robert Stith; Ann, married John Stith; Frances Townshend, married Stith. Query: Did Frances T. Washington first marry a Thacker Washington? See Eubank, page 20. This Lawrence Washington of Chotank was visited by George Washington in 1768 and later. He was probably the Lawrence of Chotank mentioned by G. W. in his will, 1799.

LAWRENCE, born March 14, 1740, in King George County, Va., son of Townshend Washington (died 1743) and Elizabeth; had a twin brother John. His brothers and sisters were: Susanna, born 1727; Thomas, 1731; Townshend, 1733; Townshend, 1736; Lund, 1737; John, 1740; Henry, 1742; and Robert, born probably in 1729 or 1739.

LAWRENCE, born February 10, 1744, in King George County, Va., son of Henry Washington and Elizabeth. See *William and Mary Quarterly*, January 1933, page 33.

LAWRENCE (Jr.), of Chotank, born about 1752, son of Lawrence Washington (Sr.) of Chotank; married Catherine Foote in King George County, Va., October 5, 1774; in 1787, was one of the executors of the will of his brother-in-law, Thornton Washington. On July 27, 1785, "Mr. Lawe. Washington, son of Lawrence," dined at Mount Vernon. Lawrence Jr. died in 1809.

LAWRENCE of Fairfax County was at Mount Vernon in February 1786; and on March 20, 1798, "Mr. Lawe. Washington of Chotank and Mr. Lawe. Washington of Belmont came to Dinner" (at Mount Vernon). November 15, 1799, Lawrence Washington of Belmont, Fairfax County, Va., made his will; named therein his niece Ann Thompson, wife of William Thompson of Colchester; his nephew Hayward Foote, executor; witnesses, Lee Massey, Elizabeth Washington, Robert Washington, Alexander Wade; will probated December 16, 1799. See Fairfax County Will Book, H1, pages 53-55.

LAWRENCE Sr. of Westmoreland married his cousin Sarah Tayloe Washington (1800-1886), daughter of William Augustine I and his 3d wife Sally Tayloe; lived at Campbellton; father of Robert J. and Lloyd Washington. See Eubank, page 34, and Wright's Westmoreland, page 152.

LAWRENCE Jr. of Westmoreland; lived at New Blenheim. See Wright's Westmoreland, page 152.

LAWRENCE, elder son of Col. John A. Washington III and wife Eleanor Love Selden; born at Mount Vernon January 14, 1854; married Fanny Lackland of Jefferson County, W. Va., June 14, 1876; had 12 children, 8 sons and 4 daughters, all living in January 1939; inherited Waveland from his father; employed many years in the Library of Congress; died in Washington January 28, 1920; buried in Charles Town.

LAWRENCE AUGUSTINE, born 1768?, son of Col. Samuel Washington and his 4th wife Anne Steptoe; education directed by General Washington, his uncle—see the latter's will; married Mary Dorcas Wood in Frederick County, Va., November 6, 1797; lived for some time at Hawthorn, part of the Glen Burnie estate, at Winchester; removed in 1811 to the Ohio Valley. Died near Wheeling, Feb. 15, 1824, in the 56 year of his age; buried near Wheeling.

LAWRENCE AUGUSTINE (Dr.), born in 1813 in Putnam County, Va., son of Lawrence Augustine and Dorcas Wood Washington; married Martha Dickinson Shrewsbury November 29, 1839, in Kanawha County; seven children; moved to Dennison, Texas, in 1850.

LAWRENCE AUGUSTINE, born in 1841, son of Dr. Lawrence A. Washington and wife Martha D. Shrewsbury.

LAWRENCE E., born 1890 in Hampshire County, W. Va., son of Robert M. Washington Sr.; died in 1909; buried in Romney.

LEWIS WILLIAM (Col.), born in Georgetown, D. C., November 30, 1812, son of George Corbin Washington; married (1) Mary Ann Barroll of Baltimore, who had a son James Barroll and two daughters; married (2) a Miss Bassett, who had a son William De H. Washington; lived at Beallair, one mile west of Halltown, Jefferson County, W. Va. Taken and held prisoner by John Brown in the raid on Harper's Ferry, October 1859; died October 1, 1871; buried in Charles Town.

LILA; married Major R. W. Hunter. See Wright's Westmoreland, page 11.

LLOYD of Westmoreland County, Va.; brother to Robert J. Washington; of the period 1840-1900. See Wright's Westmoreland, page 115.

LOUISA; married Thomas Fairfax, January 18, 1798; record in Winchester. Was she a daughter of Warner Washington I (1715-1791)? Warner in his will, made in November 1789, names a daughter Louisa, then under 21. She is not named in her mother's will, 1802.

LOUISA, daughter of Thomas Greene Clemson; wife of Dr. Samuel W. Washington of Harewood. She died February 14, 1882, aged 76 years, 6 months; buried in Charles Town.

LOUISA C., daughter of Richard B. and Christian M. Washington; born November 17, 1851; died September 22, 1852; buried in Charles Town.

LOUISA FONTAINE, born February 19, 1844, oldest daughter of Col. John A. Washington and wife Eleanor Love Selden of Mount Vernon; married Col. Roger Preston Chew, August 15, 1871; died July 1, 1927; buried in Charles Town.

LOUISA FONTAINE, born January 15, 1889, daughter of George Washington and wife Serena Porterfield; died September 8, 1898; buried in Charles Town.

L. Quinton (Col.) was at or near Fredericksburg in 1900 or thereabout. He had to do with moving the body of R. M. T. Hunter from Essex County, Va., to Richmond. The Life of Hunter (by Neale) contains an address delivered at Fredericksburg by Col. L. Quinton Washington.

Lucinda W. Her grave is in the Episcopal church yard at White Post, Clarke County, Va. "Our Grandmother"; born May 18, 1793; died August 29, 1863.

Lucy, third wife of Col. Samuel Washington (1734-1781); daughter of Nathaniel Chapman.

Lucy, wife of George Steptoe Washington; sister to Dolly Payne Todd who married James Madison, 1794. After the death of George Steptoe Washington in 1809 Lucy married (2) Judge Thomas Todd; she outlived him also, spending her last years with her son, William Temple Washington, near Charles Town; died January 29, 1846, aged about 74; buried in Charles Town.

Lund (I), born October 21, 1737, son of Townshend and Elizabeth Lund Washington of Chotank. Lund's great-grandfather (Lawrence) and George's great-grandfather (John) were brothers. During the Revolution Lund lived at Mount Vernon and managed the estate in the absence of General Washington. Lund married Elizabeth Foote; he had brothers Lawrence and Robert of Chotank. February 13, 1793, Lund Washington of Fairfax County, Va., made his will— left all to his wife Elizabeth. Witnesses, David Stuart, Eliza P. Custis, Patty Custis; will probated September 19, 1796. See Fairfax County Will Book G, pages 213, 214. Eubank says that Lund lived at Hayfield, near Alexandria.

Lund (II), born September 25, 1767, in King William County, Va., son of Robert and Alice Washington. In 1797 a Lund Washington was a grantee for land in Hampshire County, now W. Va.

Margaret, wife of John Washington. November 23, 1738, Margaret Storke married John Washington in King George County, Va. December 9, 1748, was born in the same county William, son of John and Margaret Washington.

Margaret; married Andrew Monroe, December 21, 1761, in now King George County, Va.

Margaret Sandford, daughter of Edward Washington, who died in Fairfax County, Va., in 1813. She had brothers John, Edward Sandford, George William, Joseph Hough and sisters Mary Ann and Elizabeth Catherine. Her mother, probably a Sandford (Sanford), evidently was not living when her father made his will, April 8, 1813.

Maria, daughter of George Augustine Washington (1763-1793) and wife Frances Bassett; named in her father's will, January 24, 1793; also in George Washington's will, July 9, 1799.

Maria P., born Harrison, July 27, 1791; second wife of Bushrod C. Washington of Claymont; died November 4, 1847; buried in Charles Town.

Martha, wife of George Washington; daughter of Col. John Dandridge of New Kent County, Va., and wife Frances Jones, born June 2, 1731; married (1) Daniel Parke Custis, in 1749; (2) George Washington, probably at the White House, New Kent County, January 6, 1759; died at Mount Vernon May 22, 1802. Her two Custis children that grew up were John Parke and Martha. Martha died unmarried, June 19, 1773, aged 17; John Parke married Eleanor Calvert, February 3, 1774; died November 5, 1781, leaving a widow and four children: Elizabeth, Martha, Eleanor (Nelly), and George Washington Parke Custis.

MARTHA, born in Floyd County, Va., daughter of Reed Peppers Washington and his wife, Sarah Ann Prillaman; in July, 1896, married Allen S. Harris of Clay County, Mo.; lived in Idaho for years, home now in Kansas; children.

MARY, sister of John Washington I of Chotank (1668-1721); married Gibson and was living in England in 1699 when her brother John wrote her a letter. See Eubank, page 19.

MARY, daughter of Dade Massey; wife of John Washington II of Chotank. A John and Mary Washington had a daughter Anne born in King George County, Va., in 1723; a daughter Mary, February 28, 1726; a son Lawrence, March 31, 1728; other children later. "Mary Washington Jr." died May 11, 1746.

MARY, wife of Henry Washington, had a son Nathaniel born January 16, 1726, in King George County, Va.; a son Bailey, September 10, 1731. Mary, wife of Henry Washington, died January 19, 1735, in Stafford or King George County, Va.

MARY, widow of Nathaniel Washington, died in King George County, Va., October 23, 1747. Was she the widow of Nathaniel Washington who died September 15, 1718?

MARY, daughter of Joseph Ball and his 2d wife, Mary Montague, the widow Johnson, was born in Lancaster County, Va., in 1708. She grew up, after the age of 13, under her guardian, Col. George Eskridge, at Sandy Point, Westmoreland County, Va.; married Augustine Washington March 6, 1731; had children, George, Betty, and others; died in Fredericksburg August 25, 1789; buried in Fredericksburg, where a tall monument marks her grave. A tombstone is also inscribed to her in the family cemetery at Wakefield (Bridges Creek), where Augustine is buried.

MARY, daughter of John and Mary Washington, was born in King George County, Va., February 28, 1726. A "Mary Washington Jr." died May 11, 1746.

MARY, born Whiting, of Gloucester County, Va., married Warner Washington II in 1770; died at Clifton, near Fairfield, in 1794. Or did she die in Gloucester County?

MARY, daughter of Richard Henry Lee; second wife of William Augustine Washington I.

MARY, daughter of John and Catherine Washington; born June 17, 1764, in King George County, Va.

MARY, daughter of Warner Washington II. On July 7, 1826, Warner made his will in Frederick County, Va., and therein named his daughters Mary and Elizabeth and his sons Fairfax, Hamilton, Herbert, and Reade. The will was proved June 2, 1829.

MARY, daughter of John Thornton Augustine Washington of Jefferson County, now West Virginia. She in 1842 wrote a poem on her childhood home, Cedar Lawn. June 8, 1867, a Mary Washington married David Johnson in Jefferson County, W. Va.

MARY (?). A Mrs. M. Washington died in Stafford or King George County, Va., April 28, 1728. Was she Mary Townshend, wife of John Washington, who died in 1721? Mary Townshend Washington, widow, willed Chotank in 1727 to her son, John Washington II. John Washington I had lived at Chotank. Mary Townshend, daughter of Robert, married John Washington I of Chotank in 1686. See Eubank, page 27. The register of St. Paul's Parish shows that a Mary Washington died in Stafford County in 1721; another in 1729.

MARY ANN, daughter of Edward Washington of Fairfax County, Va., who died in 1813. She was a sister to George William Washington of Hampshire County, now W. Va.

MARY DORCAS, daughter of Robert Wood of Winchester, married Lawrence Augustine Washington in Frederick County, Va., November 6, 1797. See Morton's "Story of Winchester," 1925, page 83. In 1811 these Washingtons moved to the Kanawha country; later to the vicinity of Wheeling, where they are buried. She died November 9, 1835, aged 54.

MARY T. (Townshend?) Washington married Robert Smith (Stith?), July 29, 1773, in King George County, Va. Eubank (pages 20, 21) says that Mary Townshend Washington, daughter of Lawrence (born 1728), married Robert Stith.

MARY WEST, daughter of Lawrence Washington and wife Sarah Tayloe, married Dr. Walker Washington of Claymount, Westmoreland County, Va.

MATTHEW BURWELL BASSETT (1830-1868), known as Bird; son and 5th child of George Fayette Washington, who mentions him in his will made October 19, 1865, in Frederick County, Va.; proved in January 1868. See Will Book 28, page 396. George Fayette was a son of George Augustine Washington and wife Frances Bassett, daughter of Col. Burwell Bassett. M. B. B. Washington married a Miss Buchanan. See Cartmell, "Shenandoah Valley Pioneers," 1909, page 250.

MILDRED, wife of Maj. Lawrence Washington (1659-1698); born Warner. She was buried in England, 1701—so stated on a slab at Wakefield (Bridges Creek).

MILDRED, daughter of Maj. Lawrence Washington (1659-1698) and wife Mildred Warner; aunt and godmother to George Washington. She married (1) Roger Gregory by whom she had 3 daughters, who married 3 Thornton brothers. She was (2) the 3d and last wife of Col. Henry Willis, founder of Fredericksburg. By the will of her father she received a 4th of his estate and (or including) 2500 acres of land on Hunting Creek, Stafford County, Va., now in Fairfax. See Fothergill, page 19.

MILDRED; married Langhorne Dade, February 14, 1743, in King George County, Va.

MILDRED, 6th child and 2d daughter of Augustine Washington I and his second wife, Mary Ball; born at Ferry Farm June 21, 1739; died October 23, 1740.

MILDRED, daughter of Col. John Thornton and wife Mildred Gregory; second wife of Col. Samuel Washington.

MILDRED, wife of Col. Charles Washington. She was the daughter of Col. Francis Thornton of Spotsylvania County, Va., and his wife Frances Gregory. She was living in July 1799.

MILDRED, born Pratt; married Henry Washington in King George County, Va., March 12, 1779.

MILDRED (MILLY), daughter of John Augustine Washington I and wife Hannah Bushrod; married Thomas Lee, son of Richard Henry Lee, April 1791; lived near Dumfries.

MILDRED, daughter of Warner Washington I and his 2d wife, Hannah Fairfax. Warner in his will (1789) named his daughter Mildred who evidently was 21 or upward at that time. She had married Throckmorton in Frederick County, Va., December 13, 1785. Her mother, Hannah Fairfax Washington, made her will in May 1802. Mildred was then living. See Frederick County Will Book 7, page 238.

MILDRED, born Berry in Stafford County, Va., married Thornton Washington (1760-1787) about 1780; had two sons, John Thornton Augustine and Thomas Washington; died about 1784.

MILDRED ANN, born August 17, 1797, daughter of Samuel Washington and wife Dorothea; died November 15, 1799. Was this Samuel the son of Col. Charles Washington? See *William and Mary College Quarterly*, April, 1939, page 190.

MILDRED B., daughter of John T. A. Washington and his wife Elizabeth C. Bedinger; married Solomon T. Bedinger February 8, 1854.

MILDRED G., daughter of Col. Charles Washington of Charles Town and wife Mildred Thornton; born about 1777; was unmarried January 24, 1793, when her brother George Augustine made his will—he names her as "my sister Mildred Washington." She was the first wife of Thomas Hammond who married (2) Nancy Collins. Her will was made in Jefferson County, Va., in 1804; proved 1805. Gen. George Washington in his will (1799) calls her Mildred Hammond.

MOLLY (MARY) LEE, daughter of Corbin Washington (1765-1800) and wife Hannah Lee; named in her mother's will, 1800. Her mother then lived at Selby, Fairfax County. Molly had a sister Jane Mildred and 4 brothers: Richard Henry Lee, John Augustine (II), Bushrod Corbin, and Corbin Thomas Washington.

NANCY (ANNIE?) was at Mount Vernon in November 1777. See Washington's diaries, 1925, Vol. II, page 41. Augustine Washington II, half-brother to George, in his will, made September 18, 1758, proved in Westmoreland County, Va., May 25, 1762, speaks of his daughter Nancy, also of Betsey and Jane. See Ann Washington, who married Burdett Ashton.

NANNIE BIRD, daughter of Matthew Burwell Bassett Washington of Waverly, died December 31, 1919.

NATHANIEL, son of John Washington of Westmoreland County, Va., and his wife Anne Wickliffe. See Eubank, page 42. John made his will January 22. 1697; probated February 22, 1697; therein he names his sons Lawrence, John, Nathaniel, and Henry. Nathaniel received land at the head of Appomattox Creek. See

Fothergill, page 19. A Nathaniel Washington died in Stafford County, Va., September 15, 1718. Mary, widow of Nathaniel, died October 23, 1747.

NATHANIEL, son of Henry Washington (1694-1748) and wife Mary Bailey, was born January 16, 1726, in King George County, Va. Nathaniel, son of Capt. Henry Washington, died November 28, 1745.

NATHANIEL; married Sarah Hooe, December 17, 1767, in King George County, Va.

NATHANIEL, son of John and Catherine Washington, was born in King George County, Va., October 1, 1762.

NEDHAM LANGHORNE, son of Lawrence Washington (born 1728) of Chotank, married Sarah Ashton. He inherited Chotank (Waterloo); made his will October 15, 1833; left Chotank to his wife, Sarah Ashton Washington; named his daughter Jane Wray Washington and his son Nedham H. Washington. See Eubank, page 20, and King George records.

NEDHAM H., son of Nedham Langhorne Washington and wife Sarah Ashton. In 1809 a Nedham Washington had as wife Sarah, daughter of Gerard Alexander, dec'd. See Frederick County Deed Book 32, page 73.

PERRIN; married Farinda Fairfax in Jefferson County, Va., now W. Va., February 5, 1822. This may have been John Perrin, son of Col. Samuel Washington, born at Harewood about 1781.

POLLY. April 10, 1770, and January 20, 1772, "Miss Polly Washington" was at Mount Vernon. Toner thinks she was a daughter of Lawrence Washington of Chotank. Capt. John Washington and wife Mary had a daughter Mary, born 1726; John and Catherine Washington had a daughter Mary, born June 17, 1764.

PUTNAM STITH, son of Henry Thacker Washington I and his wife Amelia Stith. See Eubank, page 21. He was living in 1828 when he made a deed in King George County, Va.

READE, son of Warner Washington II of Audley and Llewellyn. July 7, 1826, in Frederick County, Va., Warner made his will, naming therein his sons Reade, Fairfax, Hamilton, and Herbert.

REBECCA, born Smith, married Whiting Washington in Frederick County, Va., February 23, 1804. Record in Winchester. Whiting was a son of Warner Washington I (1715-1791) of Fairfield.

REBECCA JANET, born Dec. 3, 1875, daughter of Thos. B. and Eleanor Thomas Washington; died March 8, 1939. Buried in Charles Town.

REED PEPPERS, lived in Floyd County, Va.; son of David who was a son of Solomon Washington. Solomon went from Virginia to Georgia and was not heard of afterwards.

RICHARD of London. To him in 1760 George Washington shipped 5846 pounds of tobacco. "Mr. Richard Washington" was at Mount Vernon December 24, 1774, and January 2, 1775, and probably the days intervening.

RICHARD (Dr.) in 1934 was living at Claymount, Westmoreland County, Va. He is a son of Dr. Walker Washington and wife Mary West Washington (daughter of Sarah Tayloe Washington-Washington). He married his cousin Janet (Latané) Washington. See Eubank, page 35.

RICHARD BLACKBURN, son of John A. Washington II and wife Jane Charlotte Blackburn; born at Blakeley, Jefferson County, Va., November 12, 1822; died in Charles Town October 15, 1910; buried in Charles Town.

RICHARD BLACKBURN, son of Richard Blackburn Washington (1822-1910); born March 21, 1856; died October 13, 1922; buried in Charles Town.

RICHARD BLACKBURN, son of George Washington (1858-1905) and wife Serena Porterfield; grandson of Col. John A. Washington (1821-1861); educated in this country and in Rome; ordained to the Catholic priesthood at Mount Saint Mary's College, Md., June 13, 1920; has been stationed in Richmond, Norfolk, Fort Monroe, Fredericksburg, and Hot Springs, Va. He is now (1939) in his second pastorate at the Shrine of the Sacred Heart, Hot Springs.

RICHARD BLACKBURN, son of Lawrence Washington (1854-1920) and wife Fanny Lackland; grandson of Col. John A. Washington (1821-1861); attorney-at-law, Alexandria, Va.

RICHARD BLACKBURN, born August 20, 1887; died April 15, 1898; buried in Charles Town.

RICHARD HENRY LEE, son of Corbin Washington and wife Hannah Lee; died 1819, unmarried. His mother's home in 1800 was Selby, Fairfax County, Va. In August and September 1814 his team was impressed to haul powder for the U. S. government between Washington City and Falls Church, upon approach of the British. See report of Mordecai Booth in *Americana*, January 1934.

ROBERT; made his will February 11, 1763; probated in Westmoreland County, Va., September 24, 1765; had a son John and a daughter Sukey; grandchildren Sarah and Robert Townshend Washington. See Fothergill, page 156.

ROBERT of Chotank; born about 1728? son of Townshend and Elizabeth Lund Washington; brother to Lund (born 1737) and Lawrence (born 1740); justice of the peace in Stafford County, Va., 1766, 1767, 1768, 1772, 1773. His wife was probably Alice. In July 1785 a Robert Washington's son Thomas dined at Mount Vernon. George Washington in his will (1799) mentioned Robert Washington of Chotank as an acquaintance and friend of "my juvenile years." On November 15, 1799, a Robert Washington (with Elizabeth Washington, Lee Massey, and Alexander Wade) witnessed the will of Lawrence Washington of Belmont, Fairfax County, Va.

ROBERT JAMES (Col.), son of Lawrence Washington Sr. and wife Sarah Tayloe Washington; married Bessie Payne Wirt, daughter of Dr. William Wirt and wife Betty Selma Payne; lived at Campbellton, Westmoreland County, Va.; at one time owned Cabin Point. Had a brother Lloyd. See Eubank, page 34; Wright's Westmoreland, pages 115, 150, 152.

ROBERT LUND, son of John Washington whose will was probated in Westmoreland June 26, 1787; had several brothers and sisters. See Fothergill, page 186.

ROBERT M., born 1852 in Hampshire County, now W. Va., son of George William Washington and wife Sally A. Wright; lived at Ridgedale; died 1930; buried in Romney.

ROBERT M., born 1893 in Hampshire County, son of Robert M. Washington (1852-1930); died 1918; buried in Romney.

ROBERT TOWNSHEND, grandson of Robert Washington whose will was probated in Westmoreland September 24, 1765; had a sister Sarah. See Fothergill, page 156. Apparently this Robert T. Washington was not living in 1785. See will of John Washington, Fothergill, page 186.

SALLY, born Tayloe, of Mt. Airy; third wife of William Augustine Washington I. See Eubank, page 43.

SAMUEL, born at Wakefield November 16, 1734, 3d child and 2d son of Augustine Washington I and his 2d wife, Mary Ball. He was a signer of the Leedstown Declaration in 1766, with Charles, Lawrence, and John Augustine Washington; was sheriff and county lieutenant of Berkeley County, Va., now W. Va.; had five wives: Jane, Mildred, Lucy, Anne, Susannah; died at Harewood in 1781.

SAMUEL, born about 1765, son of Col. Charles Washington and wife Mildred Thornton; unmarried in May 1792; named by his brother George Augustine in his will, January 24, 1793; at Mount Vernon August 12, 1797; was still living in 1804 when his sister, Mildred G. Hammond, made her will in Jefferson County, Va. Was his wife Dorothea in 1797? See *William and Mary College Quarterly*, April, 1939, page 190.

SAMUEL, born about 1786, son of Thornton Washington (1760-1787) and his 2d wife, Frances Townshend Washington.

SAMUEL WALTER (Dr.), eldest son of George Steptoe Washington; born 1797; married Louisa Clemson, daughter of Thomas Greene Clemson and wife Elizabeth Baker; died October 12, 1831; buried in Charles Town.

SAMUEL WALTER, born November 1, 1853, son of Richard Blackburn Washington; married a Miss Willis; had two sons, Samuel Walter and Dr. John. The former was in diplomatic service in 1933. Died August 16, 1923.

SAMUEL WALTER, son of Samuel Walter Washington (1853-1923) and wife, Miss Willis. The latter's mother was a Washington, sister to Mrs. Chew.

SARAH, daughter of Capt. John Washington and wife Mary, born October 28, 1742, in King George County, Va.

SARAH, daughter of Maj. Lawrence Washington of Mount Vernon and wife Anne Fairfax; named in her father's will, 1752. She evidently died soon thereafter.

SARAH, wife of Nathaniel Washington, married in King William County, Va., December 17, 1767. She was born Sarah Hooe.

SARAH, daughter of John Washington of Westmoreland County, Va.; married Robert Harper, son of John, of Alexandria.

SARAH, granddaughter of Robert Washington, whose will was probated in Westmoreland County, September 24, 1765. She had a brother Robert Townshend Washington. See Fothergill, page 156.

SARAH, wife of Warner Washington II. Born Rootes; married Warner in 1795; had 7 children.

SARAH, born Ashton; wife of Nedham Langhorne Washington of Chotank (Waterloo); named in Nedham's will, October 15, 1833. See Eubank, page 20.

SARAH, aunt of Edward Washington of Fairfax County, Va., who named her in his will, 1813. See Fairfax County Will Book K, pages 106-109.

SARAH TAYLOE (1800-1886), daughter of William Augustine Washington I and his 3d wife, Sally Tayloe; married her cousin Lawrence Washington; had a son Col. Robert James Washington, who lived at Campbellton, Westmoreland County, Va.; her 5th child was Mary West Washington. See Eubank, pages 34, 35.

SELENA, born in Westmoreland October 15, 1808, daughter of George Washinggton and wife Elizabeth Coates; married Daniel Payne of Baltimore, merchant, who owned Bleak Hall, Westmoreland County, Va. She had only one daughter, Betty Selena Payne, who married Dr. William Wirt, builder in 1852 of Wirtland, Westmoreland County. See Eubank, pages 34, 36.

SERENA, daughter of Col. George Porterfield and wife of George Washington (1858-1905), son of Col. John A. Washington III.

SUKEY, daughter of Robert Washington whose will was probated in Westmoreland September 24, 1765. She had a brother John. William Bernard was made her guardian. See Fothergill, page 156.

SUSAN, born Washington; a descendant of Augustine Washington II, halfbrother of George; wife and widow of Rev. William C. Latané who was for many years rector at Oak Grove, Westmoreland County, Va.; died March 2, 1936, in Alexandria, aged 78; left 5 sons and 2 daughters, one of the latter Mrs. Richard Washington of Oak Grove.

SUSANNA, born in King George County, Va., November 3, 1727, daughter of Townshend and Elizabeth Washington.

SUSANNAH, wife of Lawrence Washington. His will was probated in Westmoreland County, Va., March 29, 1774. She apparently was born Jett. Lawrence speaks of his brother-in-law William Stork Jett. She had daughters Elizabeth Stork and Katy Washington and a son Henry. See Fothergill, page 171.

SUSANNAH, 5th wife of Col. Samuel Washington. She had been the widow of George Holding; was probably born Susannah Perrin. She had a son John Perrin Washington, born prior to September 9, 1781, when Samuel made his will. She made her will December 5, 1782, in Berkeley County, Va. It was probated May 20, 1783.

THACKER, born about 1740, son of Henry Washington and wife Anne Thacker, of Middlesex County, Va.; married Harriet Peyton, daughter of Sir John, and had several children. His father (Henry) made his will December 29, 1763; names therein Thacker and 3 daughters under 21: Thacker's age is not indicated. Henry also names his brother Warner Washington and four other men executors. Thacker had sons Henry Thacker Washington I and Warner Washington; daughters: Cecelia, who married Burwell; Mrs. William P. Flood. He died in 1798. See records of Middlesex; also Eubank, page 21.

THOMAS, born March 24, 1731, in King George County, Va., son of Townshend and Elizabeth Washington. In 1765 a Thomas Washington was a justice in Brunswick County, Va. In December 1799 a Thomas Washington, living in Brunswick, signed a petition to the General Assembly of Virginia with Gray Washington, Benjamin Harrison, Willy Harrison, Burwell Willis, and Edward Branch. Petition in Richmond.

THOMAS, son of Lawrence Washington and wife Elizabeth. Lawrence made his will February 5, 1739; proved in Westmoreland County, Va., June 24, 1740. He had sons John, James, and Thomas; wife Elizabeth. See Fothergill, page 110. On February 3, 1791, a Thomas Washington made his will in Westmoreland County, Va.; proved June 24, 1794. This Thomas had a wife Anne, daughter of William Walker; sons Thomas Muse and William, and daughters Elizabeth and Ann Washington and Jemima Jenkins. See Fothergill, page 197.

THOMAS, born September 5, 1758, son of Robert Washington and wife Alice, in King George County, Va. On July 27, 1785, "Mr. Thos. Washington, son to Robert," dined at Mount Vernon.

THOMAS, born about 1784, son of Thornton Washington (1760-1787) and his first wife, Mildred Berry. Thornton married a second wife and by her had a son Samuel prior to July 26, 1787, when he made his will.

THOMAS: In 1825 Thomas Washington, a lawyer, was practicing at Franklin, Williamson County, Tenn. .

THOMAS; married Julia Ann Diller in Augusta County, Va., May 26, 1842; minister, Rev. Peter Shickel. This Thomas Washington had sons Dewitt and Hampton who married in Rockingham County, Va. Thomas, apparently, was the first Washington to purchase land in Augusta County (1850).

THOMAS (Admiral), born in Goldsboro, N. C., June 6, 1865, son of James A. and Virginia N. Washington; married Genevieve F. Clement of Morrow, Ohio, June 12, 1900; sons John Clement and Thomas.

THOMAS, naval officer, born in Goldsboro, N. C., December 2, 1889, son of Dr. George Foote Washington and wife Marion Guyon Foster; married Helvig Bigelow Chandler of Philadelphia September 15, 1912. Has children.

THOMAS BLACKBURN, born August 19, 1812, only son of Bushrod C. Washington and wife Ann M. T.; died August 3, 1854; buried in Charles Town.

THOMAS B. (BLACKBURN?), born January 11, 1851, son of Thomas Blackburn Washington (1812-1854); died August 9, 1923; buried in Charles Town.

THOMAS MUSE, son of Thomas Washington and wife Anne Walker of Westmoreland County, Va.; had a brother William and sisters Elizabeth, Ann, and Jemima Jenkins. See Fothergill, page 197.

THORNTON, born probably in 1760, son of Col. Samuel Washington and his 2d wife, Mildred Thornton; married (1) Mildred Berry of Stafford County, Va.; (2) Frances Townshend Washington in King George County, Va., April 2, 1786. Frances was living July 26, 1787, when Thornton made his will, and had a son Samuel. Thornton lived at Cedar Lawn (Berry's Hill prior to 1780), which descended by the wills of Lawrence of Mount Vernon, Col. Samuel of Harewood, and Gen. George of Mount Vernon.

THORNTON A. (Hon.) was at Wakefield in 1882. See *Tyler's Quarterly* of July 1933, page 20.

TONY: It is said that prior to 1930 a Tony Washington was a resident of Garden City, Missouri.

TOWNSHEND of Chotank married Elizabeth Lund, December 22, 1726, in King George County, Va.; had a number of children including Lund (1737-1796); died December 31, 1743.

TOWNSHEND, son of Townshend Washington and wife Elizabeth Lund; born in King George County, Va., September 21, 1733. See *William and Mary Quarterly*, January 1933, page 33. He probably died soon, for Townshend and Elizabeth had another son Townshend, born in King George February 25, 1736. Same reference.

TOWNSHEND, born February 20, 1764, in King George County, Va., son of Robert Washington and wife Alice. See *William and Mary Quarterly*, January 1933, page 33.

VIRGINIA (1812-1871), wife of Henry Thacker Washington II; born November 25, 1812, daughter of William Fitzhugh Grymes of Eagle's Nest, King George County, Va.; had several children, among them William Henry and John Peyton Washington. She made her will August 19, 1865. See Eubank, page 23.

VIRGINIA GRYMES of Windsor, King George County, Va., wife of Horace Ashton Fitzhugh of Bedford, King George County, in 1934. See Eubank, page 16.

VIRGINIA THORNTON, born March 2, 1816, daughter of John Thornton Augustine Washington and wife Elizabeth C.; died November 13, 1839; buried at Harewood.

WALKER (Dr.) of Claymount, Westmoreland County, Va.; married his cousin Mary West Washington, daughter of Lawrence and wife Sarah Tayloe Washington; had a son, Dr. Richard Washington, who was living at Claymount in 1934. See Eubank, page 33.

WALTER GOOD (WOOD?), born in 1843, son of Dr. Lawrence A. Washington and wife, Martha D. Shrewsbury.

WARNER I (1715-1791), eldest son of John Washington (uncle to George) and wife Catherine Whiting. His grandmother was Mildred Warner. He was a brother to Henry of Middlesex County, Va.; was a justice of Frederick County, Va., in 1769 and 1772; married (1) Elizabeth Macon, daughter of Col. William Macon of New Kent County, Va. From 1765 or thereabouts he lived at Fairfield, now Clarke County, Va.; married (2) in 1765 Hannah Fairfax, daughter of William and youngest sister to George William Fairfax of Belvoir on the Potomac. Hannah is named in his will, 1789. He then had two young sons, Fairfax and Whiting. General Washington frequently visited Warner at Fairfield. On November 11, 1799, Mrs. Warner Washington and son Whiting dined at Mount Vernon.

WARNER II, son of Warner I; named in the latter's will, 1789, as Warner Jr.; he then had a son Warner (III). See Superior Court Will Book 1, page 104, in Winchester. In July 1787 Warner Washington Jr. of Frederick County was appointed by Thornton Washington as one of his executors. Col. Forrest W. Brown of Charles Town, October 28, 1933, wrote:

"Warner Washington 2nd came with his father after his second marriage to Fairfield and thence to Clifton, and thence to Audley and thence to Llewellyn where he died. He married (1) Mary Whiting of Gloucester in 1770."

Mary had 9 children. She died at Clifton in 1794. Warner Jr. married (2) Sarah Warner Rootes, 1795. They had 7 children, born at Audley. On July 7, 1826, Warner II made his will; mentions therein his sons Reade, Fairfax, Herbert, and Hamilton, and daughters Elizabeth and Mary; refers to his wife but does not name her; will admitted to record (Frederick County Will Book 16, page 20) June 2, 1829. Warner II died at Llewellyn and is there buried.

WARNER III, son of Warner II. See will of Warner Washington I, Superior Court Will Book No. 1, page 104, at Winchester.

WARNER, son of Thacker Washington, who was a son of Henry of Middlesex. This Warner had a brother Henry Thacker Washington; his wife was Ariana. See Eubank, page 21. This evidently was the Warner Washington who kept a tavern in Winchester. His wife Ariana was still living in 1833. See Winchester Corporation Deed Book 7, page 324.

WHITING, son of Warner Washington I of Fairfield. In 1789 when Warner made his will Whiting was still under 21. Whiting is named also in his mother's will made in 1802 and proved in 1804. See Frederick County Will Book 7, page 238. On February 23, 1804, Whiting Washington and Rebecca Smith were married in Frederick County, Va.

WILLIAM, probably a son of Augustine Washington II, half-brother to George. On April 21, 1775, George's brother John and Billy Washington were at Mount Vernon. On April 26, following, Washington noted in his expense account gifts to his nephews, "Willm. Washington & George & Charles Lewis." Several days in October 1785 "Mr. Willm. Washington" was at Mount Vernon with his wife and 4 children. This, Fitzpatrick thinks, was William, son of Augustine II. This William married (1) Jane, daughter of John Augustine Washington I. See William Augustine Washington I.

WILLIAM, born December 9, 1748, in King George County, Va., son of John Washington and wife Margaret. Was she Margaret Storke, married November 23, 1738? See *William and Mary Quarterly*, January 1933, page 33.

WILLIAM; made his will March 2, 1786, probated in Westmoreland County, Va., March 25, 1788. Therein he mentions his niece Peggy Buckner, his nephew John Hooe Washington, his nephew Richard Henry Buckner, and his brother John Washington. See Fothergill, page 188. Was he the William who was born in 1748?

WILLIAM, lt.-colonel in the Revolution from Virginia; later of Charleston, S. C.; died March 6, 1810. Warrants 9964 and 9965 were issued to the administrators of Col. William Washington. He is said to have been a son of Bailey Washington of Hilton, on Chotank Creek. In 1824 William Washington and Jane Ancrum were assigned one-half of the land bounty allowed them as representatives of Col. William Washington.

Col. William Washington (1752-1810) of South Carolina was a relative of General Washington. He and his son were at Mount Vernon in August 1799. He was distinguished at Cowpens; wounded at Eutaw Springs. He was born February 28, 1752, in Stafford County, Va., son of Bailey Washington; was a captain in the early Revolution in the North; later was a lt-colonel in the South; was captured at Eutaw Springs. In 1782 he married a Miss Elliot of Sandy Hill, S. C.; settled in Charleston; died there March 6, 1810. He was known as the "Sword of the Army." See "Quaint Old Charleston," page 16. At his death he left his widow, a son, and a daughter. He served in the Revolution altogether 7 years and 5 months. Bailey Washington (his father?) and Catherine Storke were married January 12, 1749. See, among other references, Howe's History of Virginia, pages 484-486.

WILLIAM (Major), son of W. Warren (1878-1921) and Margaret B. Washington; grandson of D. N. Washington (1852-1918) of Rockingham County, Va.; married Margaret McCue of Greenwood, Albemarle County, Va., in December 1941; wounded in North Africa; in June 1944 was a major with the 1st Div. American Expeditionary Force in France; decorated with the Purple Heart and Silver Star, with oak-leaf cluster; home, Crozet, Albemarle County, Va.

WILLIAM AUGUSTINE I (1757-1810), son of Augustine Washington II (half-brother to George) and wife Ann Aylett; inherited Wakefield; after 1780 built at Blenheim; later at Haywood, 1783. See Eubank, pages 41, 43. He married (1) Jane Washington, daughter of John Augustine Washington I; (2) Mary Lee, daughter of Richard Henry Lee; (3) Sally Tayloe of Mt. Airy. He had in all 9 children, among them George Corbin Washington and (by his 3d wife) Sarah Tayloe and William Augustine II. He died in Georgetown; buried at Mount Vernon. General Washington in his will (1799) names William Augustine Washington, "son . . . of my deceased brother, Augustine Washington"; leaves him a sword; lot No. 265 in the town of Manchester (opposite Richmond); also one 23d part of his residuary estate. See the first William above.

WILLIAM AUGUSTINE II, son (9th child) of William Augustine Washington I and his 3d wife, Sally Tayloe—her only son. See Eubank, page 36. In 1809 a William A. Washington was grantee for land in Hampshire County, now W. Va.

WILLIAM COOPER Washington: On November 5, 1725, the governor and council of Virginia allowed John Parsons to take up 1500 acres in Surry County, lying between the lines of his own lands and those of Richard Wiggins, William Cooper Washington, Edward Scarborough, and William Proctor. See Executive Journals of the Council of Colonial Virginia, Vol. IV, page 93.

WILLIAM D., artist; painted the "Burial of Latané." See the Southern Historical Society Papers, April, 1914, page 89.

WILLIAM DE HERTBURN, son of Col. Lewis William Washington and his 2d wife, Ella M. Bassett; born at Clover Lea, Hanover County, Va., the old Bassett home, June 29, 1863; died in New York August 30, 1914; buried in Charles Town.

WILLIAM HENRY, son of John Washington who died in Westmoreland County, Va., in May or June 1787 (not John Augustine Washington); had several brothers and sisters. See will of John Washington, Fothergill, page 186.

WILLIAM H. (HENRY?) Washington and wife Elizabeth of Fairfax County, Va., on December 19, 1796, conveyed to John T. Washington of Westmoreland County, Va., 221 acres of land in Spotsylvania County, Va. Was this William H. Washington the William Henry Washington above?

WILLIAM HENRY, son of Henry Thacker Washington II (1802-1855) and wife Virginia Grymes (1812-1871) of King George County, Va.; married Rosalie Catlett; his daughters living at Windsor, King George County, in 1934. See Eubank, page 23.

WILLIAM HENRY, born in Wayne County, N. C., February 7, 1813; lawyer; member House of Representatives 1841-1843; later served in the state legislature; died at Newbern, N. C., August 12, 1860.

WILLIAM LANIER, descendant of Augustine II and John Augustine I; born at Montgomery, Ala., March 30, 1865, son of Maj. James Barroll Washington and his 2d wife, Jane Bretney Lanier; married (1) Mary Bruce Brennan of Louisville, Ky., June 6, 1906; married (2) and (3). See "Who's Who in America," Vol. 13. He died 1933.

WILLIAM STROTHER, born April 20, 1760, in King George County, Va., son of Robert Washington and wife Alice. See *William and Mary Quarterly*, January 1933, page 33.

WILLIAM TEMPLE, born 1800 (?), son of George Steptoe Washington and wife Lucy Payne; married Margaret Calhoun Fletcher; children: Eugenia and Jane; lived at Meg-Willie, adjoining Harewood.
————— Washington. She married (1) Dr. Nelson of Berryville; (2) Mr. Milton; died 1846; buried at Old Chapel, Clarke County, Va.

W. WARREN, son of Dewitt N. and Addie C. Washington; born February 15, 1878; died October 21, 1921; buried at Spader's Church, Rockingham County, Va.

A WASHINGTON CHRONOLOGY

244 Incidents in Washington History

1633, John Washington, great-grandfather of George, born in England.

1656, John Washington comes to Virginia.

1659, Lawrence, grandfather of George, born in Westmoreland County, Virginia.

1664, John Washington buys land in Westmoreland County.

1674, John Washington patents land on Hunting Creek, including the later Mount Vernon.

1694, Augustine Washington, father of George, born near Bridges Creek, Westmoreland County, son of Lawrence Washington and wife Mildred Warner.

1708, Mary Ball, later the wife of Augustine Washington, born at Epping Forest, Lancaster County, Virginia, daughter of Joseph Ball and wife Mary Montague, widow Johnson.

1711, Joseph Ball, father of Mary, dies.

1715, Augustine Washington marries his first wife, Jane Butler.

1715, Warner Washington, first-cousin to George, born at Bridges Creek, son of John Washington and wife Catherine Whiting.

1718, Lawrence Washington, half-brother to George, born in Westmoreland County; or 1716?

1720, Augustine Washington, half-brother to George, born in Westmoreland County; or 1718?

1721, Augustine Washington, later George's father, moves to his new house on Pope's Creek, near Bridges Creek.

1721, Mary Ball's mother, then widow of Richard Hewes, dies.

1726, Augustine Washington I, later George's father, purchases Hunting Creek land from his sister Mildred.

1728, Jane Butler, first wife of Augustine Washington I, dies at Pope's Creek.

1730, a George Washington granted land in Isle of Wight County, Va.

1731, March 17, Augustine Washington I and Mary Ball married; March 6, O. S.

1731, June 13, Martha Dandridge, later wife of George Washington, born in New Kent County, Va.; June 2, O. S.

1732, February 22, George Washington born at Wakefield, on Pope's Creek; February 11, O. S.

1732, April 16, George Washington baptized; April 5, O. S.

1733, July 1, Elizabeth (Betty) Washington, George's sister, born at Wakefield; June 20, O. S.

1734, November 27, Samuel Washington, George's oldest full-brother, born at Wakefield; November 16, O. S.

1735, January 28, Jane Washington, George's half-sister, dies at Wakefield; January 17, O. S.

1735, Augustine Washington I moves from Wakefield to Hunting Creek.

1736, January 24, John Augustine Washington, George's second full-brother, born at Hunting Creek; January 13, O. S.

1736, Hannah Bushrod, later wife of John Augustine Washington, born in Westmoreland County.

1736, Thomas Lord Fairfax visits his Virginia lands; surveys made of the Potomac and the Rappahannock.

1737, November 12, Lund Washington, a relative of George and later his manager at Mount Vernon, born at Chotank; November 1, O. S.

1738, May 13, Charles Washington, youngest full-brother to George, born at Hunting Creek; May 2, O. S.

1738, November 13, Augustine Washington I buys the Ferry Farm, opposite Fredericksburg; November 2, O. S.; later the same year moves from Hunting Creek to the Ferry Farm.

1738, December 12, Augustine Washington I buys more land at the Ferry Farm; December 1, O. S.

1739, July 2, Mildred Washington, George's younger full-sister, born at the Ferry Farm; June 21, O. S.

1740, Lawrence Washington, George's half-brother, appointed a captain in the expedition against the Spaniards at Cartagena; served under Admiral Vernon.

1740, November 3, Mildred Washington, George's younger sister, dies at the Ferry Farm; October 23, O. S.

1742, Augustine Washington I made a trustee of Fredericksburg.

1743, April 22, Augustine Washington I makes his will; April 11, O. S.

1743, April 23, Augustine Washington I dies at the Ferry Farm; April 12, O. S.; buried at Bridges Creek.

1743, May 17, will of Augustine Washington I proved in King George County, Va.; May 6, O. S.

1743, Augustine Washington II, George's half-brother, marries Ann Aylett, daughter of Colonel William.

1743, Lawrence Washington, George's half-brother, marries Ann Fairfax, daughter of William of Belvoir.

1747, September, Lawrence Washington, George's half-brother, purchases 100 acres of land of Samuel Walker in Frederick County, Va.

1748, George Washington employed by Lord Fairfax to explore and survey his lands.

1748, March 27, George Washington's first visit to Winchester (Frederick Town); March 16, O. S.

1748, March-April, Washington and George William Fairfax, with James Genn, surveyor, and others in the South Branch Valley.

1749, July 20, George Washington commissioned as surveyor of Culpeper County, Va.

1749, Martha Dandridge and Daniel Parke Custis married in New Kent County, Va.

1750, May 18, Betty Washington and Col. Fielding Lewis married; May 7, O. S.

1751, May 16, Lawrence Washington, George's half-brother, purchases more land in Frederick County, Va.

1751, October 4, George Washington and his half-brother Lawrence start for Barbadoes.

1751, November 17, Washington wrote in his diary: "Was strongly attacked with the small Pox."

1751, December 14, two women tried in Spotsylvania County for "robing the Cloaths of Mr. George Washington."

1752, February 28, William Washington, later colonel in the Revolution, born in Stafford County, Va.

1752, March 6, George Washington reaches Mount Vernon, returning from Barbadoes, with letters, etc., from Lawrence.

1752, June 20, Lawrence Washington makes his will at Mount Vernon.

1752, August 6, Lawrence Washington dies at Mount Vernon.

1752, October 7, will of Lawrence Washington proved at Fairfax Court House.
1752, Fielding Lewis and his wife Betty Washington build in Fredericksburg the brick house later known as Kenmore.
1753, October 31, George Washington commissioned by Governor Dinwiddie a messenger to the French on the Ohio.
1754, George Washington, by purchase of his sister-in-law's interest, becomes full owner of Mount Vernon.
1755, July 9, Washington in the Braddock disaster on the Monongahela.
1756, Washington building Fort Loudoun in Winchester.
1756, John Augustine Washington I and Hannah Bushrod married.
1759, January 6, George Washington and Martha (Dandridge) Custis married in New Kent County, Va.
1760, March, Washington and his blacksmith Peter make a plow of the former's invention.
1760, April 19, Washington's "chair" breaks down in Maryland, on his way to Williamsburg.
1760, The buildings and grounds at Mount Vernon improved.
1761, August 3, Charles Washington buys two lots in Fredericksburg.
1761, September 21, John Augustine Washington I sells cattle at or near Mount Vernon.
1762, June 5, Bushrod Washington, later celebrated jurist, born in Westmoreland County, Va.
1762, Augustine Washington II, half-brother to George, dies at Wakefield.
1765, Warner Washington, first-cousin to George, marries his second wife, Hannah Fairfax.
1765, Warner Washington acquires 1600 acres of land on Long Marsh, Frederick County, Va.
1765, Hannah Lee, daughter of Richard Henry, later the wife of Corbin Washington, born in Westmoreland County, Va.
1765, Lund Washington comes to Mount Vernon as foreman or manager.
1766, February 27, four young Washingtons sign the Leedstown Declaration.
1768, George Washington several times visits his brothers Samuel and Charles near and in Fredericksburg and his brother John in Westmoreland.
1769, February, Warner Washington and George William Fairfax fox-hunting at Mount Vernon.
1769, August, the Washingtons of Mount Vernon sojourn at Fairfield, Frederick County, home of Warner Washington, on their way to Bath (Berkeley Springs).
1770, February 22, Samuel and John Augustine Washington at Mount Vernon.
1770, September, Samuel Washington and family move to their new home, Harewood, in Frederick, later Berkeley, now Jefferson County.
1770, October 5, George Washington visits his brother Samuel at Harewood.
1770, October 18, Warner Washington II marries Mary Whiting of Gloucester County, Va.
1770, October and November, George Washington in the Ohio Valley, spying out the land.
1771, March 3, Washington revisits Greenway Court, the Valley home of Lord Fairfax.
1771, March 4, Washington dines in Winchester with other officers of the French and Indian War.
1771, March 14, Charles Washington awarded damages for a mill race on his land in Frederick County.

1771, May 7, Samuel Washington sworn in as colonel of militia in Frederick County.

1771, September 13, George Washington surveys the Ferry Farm.

1771, the Washingtons of Mount Vernon in Williamsburg.

1771, Samuel Washington buys 2690 acres of land in Frederick County.

1772, May 19, Col. Samuel Washington one of the first justices of Berkeley County, Va., now W. Va.

1772, May, Charles W. Peale makes a portrait of George Washington at Mount Vernon.

1772, September 18, Washington purchases a home for his mother in Fredericksburg.

1773, June 19, Martha (Patsy) Custis dies at Mount Vernon.

1774, February 3, John Parke Custis and Eleanor Calvert married at Mt. Airy, Md.

1774, March, Washington visits Fairfield and Harewood.

1774, John Augustine Washington I chairman of the relief committee in Westmoreland County.

1774, George Washington feasts the boys of Fredericksburg.

1776, November 20, Samuel Washington sworn in as sheriff of Berkeley County.

1777, April 3, Col. Samuel Washington resigns as county lieutenant of Berkeley County.

1778, Bushrod Washington graduates at the College of William and Mary.

1779, March 21, Eleanor (Nelly) Custis, daughter of John Parke Custis and wife Eleanor Calvert, born at Abingdon, near Alexandria.

1779, July 15, Charles Washington qualifies as escheator for Spotsylvania County, Va.

1780, Charles Washington moves from Fredericksburg to Berkeley County, Va.

1780, December 25, the Washington house at Wakefield, George Washington's birthplace, burns.

1781, Lund Washington saves Mount Vernon from depredations by the British and is reprimanded by General Washington.

1781, September 9, Col. Samuel Washington makes his will.

1781, November 5, John Parke Custis dies at Eltham.

1781, December 18, Col. Samuel Washington's will proved at Martinsburg.

1781, Col. Fielding Lewis dies in Fredericksburg.

1782, December 19, General Washington resigns his commission as commander-in-chief.

1783, May 20, John Thornton Augustine Washington born at Berry's Hill (Cedar Lawn).

1784, Washington invites Madame Lafayette to his "cottage."

1784, June 22, John Augustine Washington I makes his will.

1784, September, Washington holds a conference at his brother Charles's home in Berkeley County, Va.

1784, September 30, Washington, returning from the West, comes down through Brock's Gap in the Alleghanies.

1784, October 1, Washington dines with Gabriel Jones, "The Lawyer," at his home on the Shenandoah River.

1784, October 2, Washington rides homeward, accompanied by Thomas Lewis to Swift Run Gap, where he crosses the Blue Ridge.

1785, Washington lays off the grounds at Mount Vernon and makes extensive plantings of trees, shrubs, vines, and flowers.

1785, Bushrod Washington marries Julia Anne Blackburn.

1785, October, John Augustine Washington I and family at Mount Vernon.
1785, October 15, George Augustine Washington and Frances Bassett married at Mount Vernon.
1785, November, General Washington provides schooling in Georgetown and Alexandria for his nephews, George Steptoe and Lawrence Augustine Washington.
1786, Charles Washington establishes Charles Town on his lands in Berkeley County, W. Va.
1787, January 10, General Washington receives news of the death of his brother John.
1787, July 26, Thornton Washington, son of Colonel Samuel, makes his will.
1787, July 31, will of John Augustine Washington I admitted to record.
1787, General Washington at Mount Vernon continues making trial of plows, seeds, and composts.
1788, May 20, Mary Washington makes her will in Fredericksburg.
1788, June 3, General Washington visits Charles Town and Fairfield.
1788, June 11-16, General and Mrs. Washington in Fredericksburg; on Sunday, June 15, a panic in church.
1789, April 30, Washington inaugurated President in New York City.
1789, August 25, Mary (Ball) Washington dies in Fredericksburg.
1789, October 23, Mary Washington's will proved by the oath of James Mercer.
1789, November 20, Warner Washington I makes his will at Fairfield.
1789, John Augustine Washington II born in Westmoreland, son of Corbin Washington and wife Hannah Lee; grandson of John Augustine Washington I and wife Hannah Bushrod.
1790, December 25, Bushrod Corbin Washington, son of Corbin and wife Hannah Lee, born in Westmoreland; Bushrod Corbin Washington later built Claymont Court in Jefferson County.
1791, President and Mrs. Washington tour the country.
1791, Warner Washington I dies at Fairfield; his will proved in Winchester, September 1.
1792, General Washington still experimenting with plows, etc.
1793, George Augustine Washington, third Washington overseer at Mount Vernon, dies; the first was John Augustine I, the second, Lund.
1794, September 15, James Madison and Dolly Payne Todd married at Harewood.
1794, Betty (Washington) Lewis sells Kenmore in Fredericksburg and goes to live with her daughter, Betty Carter, at Western View, Culpeper County.
1795, June 13, Warner Washington II marries Sarah Warner Rootes of Gloucester County; moves from Clifton to Audley.
1797, March 31, Betty (Washington) Lewis dies at Western View.
1798, Bushrod Washington appointed an associate justice of the U. S. Supreme Court.
1799, February 22, Lawrence Lewis and Nelly Custis married at Mount Vernon.
1799, Gray Washington and Thomas Washington sign a petition in Brunswick County, Va., to the General Assembly of Virginia.
1799, July 9, George Washington makes his will.
1799, July 25, Charles Washington, George's brother, makes his will.
1799, September 23, the will of Charles Washington proved at Martinsburg.
1799, December 14, George Washington dies at Mount Vernon.
1800, June 17, Hannah (Lee) Washington, widow of Corbin, makes her will at Selby, Fairfax County.

1800, September 22, Martha Washington makes her will at Mount Vernon.
1800, Weems's Life of Washington first published.
1801, Jefferson County, home of many Washingtons, cut off from Berkeley.
1802, May 14, Hannah (Fairfax) Washington, widow of Warner I, makes her will at Fairfield.
1802, May 22, Martha Washington dies at Mount Vernon.
1802, George Washington Parke Curtis builds Arlington; Lawrence Lewis builds Woodlawn.
1804, September 3, the will of Hannah (Fairfax) Washington proved at Winchester.
1804, October 22, Mary Washington's will proved by the oath of Joseph Walker at Fredericksburg.
1804, the first volume of Marshall's Life of Washington published.
1809, September 15, George William Washington born in Fairfax County.
1809, December 28, Henry Lee sells land in Hampshire County to William A. Washington.
1810, March 6, Col. William Washington dies in Charleston, S. C.
1811, John Augustine Washington II and Jane Charlotte Blackburn married.
1811, Lawrence Augustine Washington moves from Winchester to the Ohio Valley.
1812, November 30, Lewis William Washington born in Georgetown.
1813, George Corbin Washington sells Wakefield to John Gray.
1814, the mansion house at Bushfield shelled and burned.
1815, George W. Parke Custis marks Washington's birthplace at Wakefield.
1818, Lawrence Lewis acquires Audley from Warner Washington II; Warner moves to Llewellyn.
1820, August 24, Henry Augustine Washington born at Haywood, Westmoreland County.
1821, May 3, John Augustine Washington III, son of John Augustine Washington II, born at Blakeley.
1825, John Thornton Augustine Washington builds the brick house at Berry's Hill (Cedar Lawn).
1826, March 4, George Fayette Washington purchases Waverly of Taliaferro Stribling.
1826, July 7, Warner Washington II makes his will at Llewellyn.
1826, July 10, Judge Bushrod Washington writes his will.
1829, June 2, the will of Warner Washington II proved at Winchester.
1829, November 26, Judge Bushrod Washington dies in Philadelphia.
1829, November 28, Julia Anne Blackburn, wife of Judge Bushrod Washington, dies enroute from Philadelphia to Mount Vernon.
1832, June 16, John Augustine Washington II dies at Mount Vernon.
1833, Kercheval wries of Claymont Court, Clifton, and Fairfield.
1833, May 7, President Jackson in Fredericksburg at the laying of the cornerstone of a monument to Mary Washington.
1835, the greenhouse at Mount Vernon burns.
1837, the burial vault at Mount Vernon improved.
1838, fire at Claymont Court.
1839, November 30, Lawrence Lewis dies at Arlington; his wife, Nelly Custis, soon thereafter moves to Audley.
1842, March, Mary Washington, daughter of John Thornton Augustine, writes a poem on Cedar Lawn.
1842, John Augustine Washington III and Eleanor Love Selden married.

1843, December 25, George Washington, lawyer, born in Campbell County, Ky., son of George and Martha D. Washington; died at Newport, Ky., August 23, 1905.
1846, January 29, Lucy (Payne) (Washington) Todd dies near Charles Town.
1848, the cornerstone of the Washington Monument in Washington City laid.
1849, March 16, Dr. Lawrence A. Washington an incorporator of Buffalo Academy in Putnam County, Va.
1850, August 19, Nelly (Custis) Lewis writes her will at Audley.
1851, November 10, Joseph Edwin Washington born in Tennessee.
1852, Nelly (Custis) Lewis dies at Audley; buried at Mount Vernon.
1852-1853, Benjamin F. Washington and Vincent Geiger edit the *Democratic State Journal* at Sacramento, Calif.
1853, Henry A. Washington's edition of Jefferson's writings appears.
1853, Washington Irving at Greenway Court and Audley collecting materials for his Life of Washington.
1853, December 24, John Marshall Washington lost at sea.
1854, January 14, Lawrence Washington, elder son of John Augustine III, born at Mount Vernon.
1854, October 3, Jane Charlotte Blackburn, widow of John Augustine Washington II, writes her will at Blakeley.
1855, September 17, Jane Charlotte (Blackburn) Washington's will proved at Charles Town.
1858, February 28, Henry Augustine Washington dies.
1858, July 22, George Washington, younger son of John Augustine III, born at Mount Vernon—the last Washington born there.
1858, Virginia purchases Wakefield from Lewis William Washington.
1859, February 22, John Augustine Washington III sells Mount Vernon to the Ladies Association.
1859, autumn, John Augustine Washington III moves to Waveland, in Fauquier County.
1859, October 16, Col. Lewis William Washington taken prisoner by John Brown.
1861, September 13, Col. John Augustine Washington III killed in Randolph County, now W. Va.
1865, June 6, Admiral Thomas Washington born in Goldsboro, N. C.
1867, January 15, Henry Stephens Washington born in New Jersey.
1867, September 6, George Fayette Washington dies at Waverly.
1868, August 1, Matthew Burwell Bassett Washington dies at Waverly.
1871, October 1, Col. Lewis William Washington dies at Beallair.
1876, February 6, George William Washington dies at Ridgedale.
1876, June 14, Lawrence Washington and Fanny Lackland married in Jefferson County, W. Va.
1878, Wakefield visited by William M. Evarts, Gen. William T. Sherman, and others.
1879, January, Robert M. Washington purchases Ridgedale.
1882, the state of Virginia transfers its holdings at Wakefield to the Federal Government.
1883, the U. S. Government purchases 11 acres at Wakefield.
1889, the movement for a monument to Mary Washington revived.
1894, May 10, President Cleveland at the dedication of a monument to Mary Washington in Fredericksburg.
1896, the foundations of the old house at Wakefield uncovered and mapped.

1896, a monument erected at Wakefield.

1899, June 24, Claymont Court purchased by Frank R. Stockton.

1901, Edward Washington dies at Ferndale, Hampshire County.

1915, August 28, Joseph Edwin Washington dies in Tennessee.

1917, the mansion at Bushfield reconstructed.

1920, January 28, Lawrence Washington, elder son of Lt. Col. John Augustine Washington, dies in Washington City.

1923, Wakefield National Memorial Association organized.

1924, Wakefield National Memorial Association purchases 70 acres at Wakefield.

1927, Daughters of the American Revolution mark the grave of Betty (Washington) Lewis at Western View.

1930, Wakefield monument moved to its present site.

1932, Wakefield Memorial Association conveys its holdings at Wakefield to the Federal Government.

1932, Helen Ames Washington queen of the Apple Blossom Festival at Winchester.

1932, the Wakefield mansion restored.

1932, the Washington mill at Dogue's Run restored.

1932, the Washington graveyard at Bridges Creek repaired.

1934, January 7, Henry Stephens Washington dies.

1940, March 20, Etta, daughter of George William and Sally Wright Washington, dies at Romney, aged 99.

1944, Major William Washington decorated for service in North Africa and France.

Cherry Point 19 22
Cherry tree story 5 35 40 131
Chesapeake & Ohio Canal 227 229
Cheshire, Mr. 280
Chester Gap 257
Chester Quarterly Meeting 255
Chew, R. P., Col. 230 307 334
Chichester, Mary 160
Children of John A. Washington III, 294
  305 307
Children of Lawrence Washington 307 309
Chillicothe, Ohio 165
Chilton, Charles 115
Chilton, Thomas 115 117
Chilton, Will. 115
Chinn's Lane 17
Chiswell, Charles 35
Chiswell, John 35
Chopin, F. F. 189
Chotank 40 42 43 119 131 315 322
Christian house 12
Christmas Day fire 1 3 8
Cincinnati 165
Civil War (1861-65) 277 295
Clarksburg 164
Clark Water Swamp 327
Claymont 213-220 293 316 335
Claymount 328 337 339 344
Clearbrook 255
Clement, Genevieve F. 343
Clemson, Ann Bull 320
Clemson, Louisa 235 334 341
Clemson, Thos. G. 235 334 341
Clemson College 235
Cleveland, President 83 355
Clifton 185-188 196 336 344
Clinton, George, Gov. 95
Clothes robbed 48 350
Clover Lea 247 252 346
Coates, Elizabeth 320 323 330 342
Coates, John, Dr. 330
Co. B, 12th Va. Cav. 309
Cobb, Eliza 330 331
Cochrans 255
Cocke, Catesby 281 318
Cocke, William 115
Cocke, William, Capt. 263
Coddy's 273
Codley's, Old 135 136
Coffer, Joshua 281

Coke, John 141
Colchester 63 83 333
Colchester arbitration 135
Colchester, near tragedy 108
Collins, Nancy 338
Colonial Beach 14 111
"Colonial Churches" 117
Colonization Society 289
Columbia 164
Committee of Safety 117
Concord, Pa. 255
Conference at Happy Retreat 175
Congress Street 164
Connell, Zachariah 139
Conrad, Angela (Lewis) 207 294
Conrad, Charles 201 205 207
Conrad, Mrs. Chas. M. 207 294
Conrad, Lewis 205 207
Constitution, The 239
Constitution ratified 164
"Contemplations," Hale's 30 40
Convention of 1788, 287
Cook, J. E. 247 249
Cook, Roy Bird, Dr. 242 325
Cooke, Edward E. 230
Cooke, John 146 160
Cooke, John Esten 219
Cooke, Mrs. Margaret L. 217
Cooke, Philip P. 219
Copeland, Mrs. Betty (Washington) 277
Cople Parish 28
Corbin, Mildred 111
Corbin, Richard, Hon. 111
Corbin home 23
Cork Street 263 267
Cornerstone laid in 1833, 354
Cornstalk 98
Costume of 1773, 50
"Cottage" at Mount Vernon 93 352
Counard's Run 273
Count d'Estaing 79
Counties formed 133 140 155 157 167
  187 215 271
County lieutenant 129 142 341 352
Court house at Fredericksburg 37 39
Cowan, David 165
Cowart's Point 19
Cowpens battle 140 316 345
Coxe, Esther M. 201
Coxe, John R., Dr. 201